Fast Guide to Cubase VST

Simon Millward

PC Publishing

PC Publishing
Export House
130 Vale Road
Kent TN9 1SP
UK

Tel 01732 770893
Fax 01732 770268
email info@pc-pubs.demon.co.uk
web site http://www.pc-pubs.demon.co.uk

First published 1998

ISBN 1 870775 57 0

British Library Cataloguing in Publication Data
A catalogue record for this book is available from the British Library

Printed in Great Britain by Bell and Bain, Glasgow

Contents

Acknowledgments

My thanks to:

Niels Larsen, Maria Hall and the Steinberg team – Arbiter Pro Audio
Paul Beecham
Cathy Tattersall and Mark Balogh – Et cetera Distribution
Lars Hakansson – SCV London

Introduction

Welcome to the *Fast Guide to Cubase VST*.

Musicians, sound engineers and producers have for some time dreamt of the idea of the affordable, personal desktop recording studio. Cubase VST, which is Steinberg's Cubase sequencer with the addition of 'Virtual Studio Technology', has brought this idea closer to reality. The advantages and convenience are undeniable.

This book aims to give users the skills to be able to operate the essential elements of the Cubase VST sequencer and audio recording package. It serves as a handy printed reference for those who need more than the electronic documentation and provides a painless method of getting into the details of the program. The features described here are relevant to all Cubase VST users and many topics are also relevant to those using non-VST versions of the program. This book concentrates on the PC version but most of the examples given are also accurate for the Macintosh.

It has been assumed that readers are already experienced with the general operation of their intended computer platform, so the text concentrates on the operational aspects of the software with particular emphasis on the practical uses of each part of the system. However, since the recording of digital audio is highly influenced by the actual hardware, details of hardware specifications and audio cards are also provided. This book explores the 'virtual studio' and audio aspects of Cubase VST and also provides details of the most important MIDI sequencer elements, which form a large part of the package.

Before looking at Cubase VST in detail it is worth considering some of the broader implications of this kind of technology. The software is extremely efficient. It incorporates the use of 'native audio processing', which means that no additional hardware is required in order to record and process audio material. In order to do all this smoothly the host computer must also be extremely efficient. The more facilities you require from Cubase VST the more processing power will be needed from the computer. For example, using one or more of the available Steinberg or third party 'plug-ins' puts more pressure on your system than simply running the basic core program, as will increasing the number of audio tracks used. It is worth noting, however, that the processing power of computer technology is likely to increase for some time so, as users upgrade their hardware, Cubase VST actually increases its capacity for recording and processing audio.

A common misconception with Cubase VST is that it will cater for absolutely *all* your recording studio needs. It's certainly not far off and it is, indeed, a virtual recording studio inside your computer, but it will not perform absolutely every function associated with the studio recording process. For example, it will not provide you with a microphone to record a vocalist and, if you already have a microphone, it will not set the correct record level automatically! Of course, even the most advanced recording studios also need to use microphones to record vocalists and sound engineers to set the correct record level so Cubase VST is not really missing anything. The concerns of which microphone to use and how to feed an audio signal into the computer are parts of the larger recording process.

In short, the tendency to assume that the software will do *everything* automatically by some weird and wonderful magic should be avoided. Cubase VST can do an awful lot but it is you the user who needs to know how to enhance its power and that is the point of this book.

The *Fast Guide to Cubase VST* supplies all the essential information to get you up and running in the shortest possible time. A book of this size cannot cover every aspect of the program but the most important details are provided. In addition, a host of tips and practical tutorials help to ensure that you get the most out of Cubase VST.

Chapters 1–10 cover Cubase VST essentials, where 1, 2 and 3 help you get started, 4 and 5 concentrate on MIDI sequencing and 6, 7, 8 and 9 concentrate on audio recording and editing. Chapter 10 outlines general control and editing functions and completes the coverage of the fundamental aspects of the program. Chapters 11–13 describe the more specialist features including audio processing, VST functions and plug-ins. Specialist MIDI editors and the Mastertrack are covered in chapters 14–16. Chapters 17 and 18 provide information on audio cards and PC hardware. A comprehensive glossary provides explanations of much of the terminology associated with MIDI and digital audio technology.

1 ❖

Description and overview

What is Cubase VST?

Steinberg Cubase VST is an integrated music software environment for the recording, editing and processing of MIDI and audio material. It belongs to a type of software commonly referred to as a 'MIDI+Audio' sequencer but, with Cubase VST, Steinberg have advanced the technology still further. VST is short for 'Virtual Studio Technology', the tag given to this particular kind of Cubase sequencer, and the central concept of VST is the creation of a virtual recording studio inside the computer.

Cubase VST is a complete rewrite of the Cubase package in 32 bit code (PC version) which means that the program is faster and more efficient. All audio processing is performed by the CPU (central processing unit) of the computer, known as 'native audio processing', and this means that audio recording and processing can be performed with less hardware. The program runs on PC and Macintosh computers.

Cubase VST provides up to 64 audio tracks (depending on the speed and efficiency of the host computer and the program version) each with 4 band parametric EQ; four real-time auxiliary effects slots, four real-time master insert effects slots, and four real-time insert effects slots per channel; plug-in architecture for third party effects and processors; mixer automation; audio mixdown facility; time stretch and 'formant' pitch shifting; audio bus system for patching signals to different locations including to external processing hardware; 'groove analysis' allowing the analysis of the rhythmic structure of an audio recording which can then be applied to the feel of MIDI parts; audio quantize; support for multiple I/O hardware and, of course, all the normal MIDI sequencing functionality as available in previous versions of the program.

The program normally runs at a sampling rate of 44.1kHz with 16 bit resolution. There is also a 24 bit version of the program known as Cubase VST24.

Who can use Cubase VST?

Newcomers to the software and also experienced sequencer users may have to learn new skills in order to have meaningful contact with the VST aspects of the program. The MIDI sequencer element of the package requires knowledge of the normal techniques associated with MIDI recording but the audio aspects require knowledge from a wider range of music technology disciplines.

Of course, anyone can use Cubase VST, but since the package involves the concept of a self-contained virtual recording studio then it follows that having some knowledge of the skills required to operate a real recording studio will be useful. This encompasses such things as sound engineering and music production. However, even users with limited sound recording skills will be able to quickly benefit from the advantages of VST, but the learning curve will obviously be a little slower.

Why use Cubase VST?

There are many reasons why Cubase VST is an excellent music software choice. The seamless combination of MIDI, audio recording and audio processing together with the possibility of recording up to 32 audio tracks each with 4 band parametric EQ are just some of the advantages encompassed by the program. The package is very cost effective since the audio processing takes place in the computer's main processor, so there is no need for additional DSP (digital signal processor) hardware. Cubase VST will produce excellent results using just one Pentium PC running at 166Mhz and a good quality audio card. The convenience of this compact arrangement is an obvious advantage.

How do I use Cubase VST?

This is the key question! Before you can use Cubase VST you must have some idea of how to record and manipulate MIDI data, how you are going to get an audio signal into the computer, how you are going to record, process and edit this signal once it arrives, and how you are going to feed it back out to the real world. These questions, and many other matters related to Cubase VST, form the subject matter of this book.

The big picture

In order to understand what is included in the Cubase VST package it is important to be able to visualise a graphic representation of the system (see Figure 1.1). The details of the system will vary according to exactly which version you have chosen but the overall picture remains the same.

Figure 1.1 Visualising Cubase VST

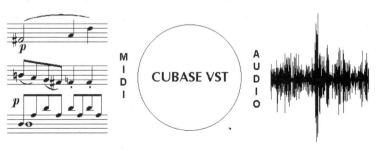

On the one hand, there is the normal MIDI sequencer functionality of the program. MIDI is a note-based interface i.e. music is represented in terms of individual note events. What we see in Cubase VST is a representation of these events in the form of notes on a score, or graphic blocks in a piano-roll style editor.

On the other hand, there is the audio recording capability of the program. This involves the recording of the actual audio signal itself. The audio is represented as waveforms of the sound signal, referred to in Cubase VST as Audio events. Of course, once recorded, both kinds of data can be edited and processed as required. The audio side of things also includes the virtual studio features of mixing, routing, processing and adding effects to the material.

The MIDI and audio functions of the program are seamlessly integrated. For example, the recording of both kinds of data can take place in the Arrange window, the main window of Cubase VST, where MIDI recordings are displayed as simple graphic blocks and audio recordings are displayed similarly but with the addition of a waveform of the sound showing inside the block. However, upon leaving the Arrange window for editing or other processing purposes the system contains features which are purely MIDI or purely audio, and this divides Cubase VST into its two main areas of operation (see Figure 1.2).

On the MIDI side of matters, Figure 1.2 shows the main MIDI based editors, Key, Score, List and Drum Edit. These are often the first ports of call after the recording of MIDI data in the Arrange window. More distant

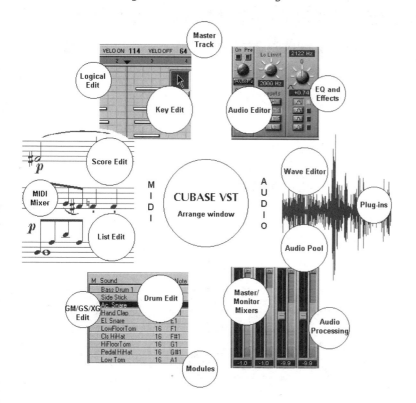

Figure 1.2 Cubase VST: graphic overview

from the central area of activities we find features like Logical Edit, the MIDI Mixer and the GM/GS/XG editor, and there is also a very comprehensive range of other features for the processing of MIDI data (not shown in the diagram).

In the audio domain, the Audio editor and the Wave editor form the main editing environments for audio material. There are also special processing features available in the Audio processing dialogue, and the management of the audio files themselves takes place in the Audio Pool. In addition to these elements, there are the all-important VST functions such as EQ and effects, mixing and plug-in technology.

Brief preview

Figure 1.2 (above) provides a graphic overview of the main parts of Cubase VST which is useful for an appreciation of what the system includes. But what does Cubase VST actually look like on screen, where is the main area of activity and how do you interact with the program?

You can actually change the appearance of Cubase VST to suit your own requirements but when the program is first launched you will normally see the Arrange window, with various default settings, and the Transport bar (similar to Figure 1.3).

Figure 1.3 Cubase VST's Arrange window and Transport bar

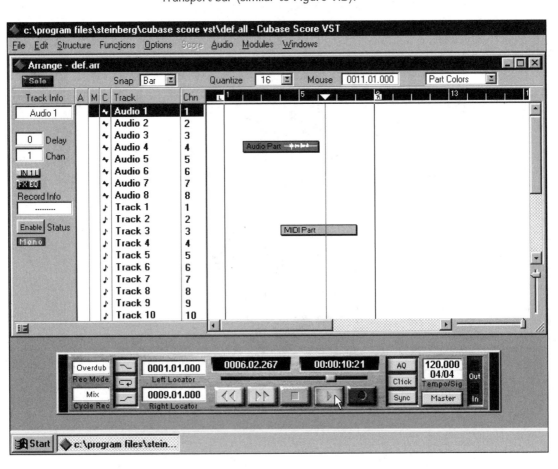

The Arrange window is where you see a graphic representation of your audio and MIDI material in the form of rectangular blocks known as 'Parts'. The Track names are displayed vertically in the Track column and time is represented horizontally. The Arrange window is the centre of activity for most Cubase VST operations.

The Transport bar features the normal rewind, fast-forward, stop, play and record controls and manages most playback and recording functions.

The current song position is shown by a triangular pointer and vertical line known as the song position pointer.

Cubase VST's user interface is intuitive and direct. It features a comprehensive set of menus, icon buttons, toolboxes and a large number of mouse functions, keyboard shortcuts, and drag-and-drop editing techniques with which to control operations in the Arrange and other windows. These are outlined in detail throughout the course of this book.

This chapter has provided a brief preview of the Arrange window and the Transport bar to help you become familiar with some of the main points of contact with Cubase VST. They are described in more detail in Chapter 4.

Patience, practice and understanding

After reading this chapter you will have an idea of the essence of Cubase VST, but before proceeding further it is worth being aware of the following. Cubase VST is the result of many years of research and development and represents the leading edge in integrated music software. However, this does not mean that the program is capable of instantly performing any task you may deem applicable. The program provides a logical and adaptable framework within which you can operate intuitively and creatively, but there are obviously techniques with which to become familiar and concepts to understand; this requires some initial effort from the user. Achieving the best results requires patience, practice and understanding.

2

Installing the software and setting up the system

This chapter describes what PC and Mac hardware you need to run Cubase VST, how to install the software and what kinds of overall system set-ups are suitable for the program. Experienced computer users who already have their Cubase VST system up and running may wish to move on to Chapter 3.

PC hardware requirements

PC processor and memory
In terms of processing power, Steinberg suggest that a 100 MHz Pentium with 24 MB of RAM is an *absolute* minimum for recording and playing back digital audio using Cubase VST. Although you could get results with such a system this book does not actually recommend it.

A Pentium 166MHz MMX machine with 32MB of RAM is recommended as a *minimum* setup. It is also important that the motherboard has a 2nd level cache memory, (preferably with a size of 512K), as this helps handle the flow of data.

These specifications might already be enough to describe the essentials of a PC computer if you were buying it for general purpose use but they would not describe matters in enough detail for use with Cubase VST and digital audio. The recording of multi-track digital audio puts special demands on a computer system and certain key components need to be considered.

Typical overall PC component requirements
The following specification describes *typical* PC component requirements for a Cubase VST system running 8 tracks of digital audio:

- Intel Pentium 200MHz MMX processor
- 512K 2nd level PB cache
- 32MB of EDO RAM (60ns)
- A large and fast hard disk drive (SCSI or EIDE ultra DMA with at least 3GB capacity and less than 9ms average seek time)
- A 16 bit stereo or multiple I/O audio card (Windows multimedia

compatible or with special ASIO driver. Should be capable of
recording and playing back digital audio using the hard drive for
storage of data and should support 44.1kHz sampling rate.)
- MIDI interface (on a separate card if not already built into the
audio card)
- A well-specified graphics card with 2-4 MB RAM
- 24 speed (or faster) CD-ROM drive
- 1.44MB 3.5 inch floppy drive
- Good quality mouse and keyboard
- Colour monitor (15 inch or larger screen)
- Windows 95 operating system installed on the computer

In order to use Cubase VST comfortably, it is recommended that you
choose a computer with similar or better components than those
described above.

A faster Pentium II or Pentium Pro processor, more and faster RAM
(e.g. SDRAM) and a faster and larger hard disk will increase Cubase VST's
performance and potential. The more audio tracks and effects you wish to
use, the more powerful your computer must be. The above specification
should be able to handle Cubase VST's internal effects and 8 tracks of
audio but if you intend to use high quality reverb and EQ plug-ins and 16
tracks of audio, you will need a faster processor and more RAM.

Currently, the Intel processor range gives better performance for audio
recording than its competitors. Cubase VST works with all of the following: Pentium, Pentium MMX, Pentium Pro and Pentium II.

Hard drives and audio cards, in brief
The two most important hardware elements for a computer intended for
Cubase VST, apart from the processor and the memory, are the hard
drive and the audio/sound card.

The audio card is particularly important for the sound quality and the
manner in which you can record digital audio. No matter how fast your
computer processor and no matter how much computer memory you
have, the actual sound quality is finally governed by your audio card.

The recording of digital audio also demands more than usual from the
hard drive. It must be particularly large and fast. You should also ensure
that you regularly defragment the hard disk and this should certainly be
carried out before you install Cubase VST. This optimises the drive's performance by re-organising the data already recorded on the disk and is
achieved using a special defragmentation program.

Audio card hardware is discussed further in Chapter 17. PC hardware
in general and hard drives are discussed in more detail in Chapter 18.
Although this is not essential reading in order to use Cubase VST, it helps
in the choice of hardware and in the understanding of which components
are particularly important for hard disk recording.

PC installation

Cubase VST is supplied on a CD-ROM and is easily installed onto a suitably prepared PC computer. The following steps outline what you need to do:

• Before installation ensure that you already have your chosen Windows operating system running on the computer (e.g. Windows 95) and that it appears to be functioning correctly.

• Ensure that the appropriate Steinberg copy protection key (sometimes referred to as the 'dongle') is plugged into the computer's parallel port. (Switch off the computer before plugging in the key!)

• Ensure that your printer is also connected if you intend to use one. (The printer connector must be plugged into the other end of the copy protection key and, once again, the computer must be switched OFF before doing this).

• Install your audio/sound card and its drivers according to the documentation supplied with it. Most cards are plug and play compatible so you will just need to follow the Windows prompts for the necessary drivers. These may be supplied on diskette or CD-ROM. If the card is supplied with a special ASIO driver (Audio Stream Input Output) then this must also be installed. Remember that audio/sound cards are supplied with various degrees of functionality. Some cards are audio only, some include audio with a MIDI interface and some feature audio, synthesiser and MIDI interface functionality. For this reason you may need to install more than one card if you are to have full audio and MIDI functionality.

Figure 2.1 Sound Recorder Accessory

• Test the audio functionality of the card outside of Cubase VST by playing a .WAV file. A simple way of doing this in Windows is to use a multimedia accessory like Sound Recorder (Figure 2.1) to play back any WAV file. Sound Recorder could also be used to record the output from an audio CD to test the recording functionality of the card. Alternatively use the accessories supplied with the audio card. Of course, this test assumes that you already have your card's audio outputs connected to an amplifier and loudspeakers (or headphones).

• Insert the Cubase VST CD-ROM. Normally, the first dialogue window appears automatically asking for confirmation to go ahead with the installation of either Cubase VST or the non-VST version of Cubase. Choose Cubase VST and follow the instructions in the subsequent dialogues. For a successful installation you must enter your name and the serial number provided on the registration card supplied with your copy of Cubase VST. It is also important to install the Acrobat Reader software as this is used to read the electronic documentation which comes with the program. Use the 'Next' button to proceed through the installation procedure which in total should only take a few minutes.

Figure 2.2 Cubase VST program group

• Once you have been informed that the installation was successful verify that there is now the Cubase VST group in the Programs sub-menu of the Windows start menu. This will be similar to Figure 2.2.

In addition you should find a Cubase VST icon (a red diamond shaped logo) on the main part of the desktop. Double clicking on this will launch Cubase VST, as will selecting Cubase VST from the start menu.

MIDI settings

• Before launching Cubase VST open the Setup MME application. Here you can verify the MIDI inputs and outputs of your sound card (or interface) which should appear in the MME (Multimedia Extensions) inputs and outputs, if the card has been correctly installed. It is possible to change the order of items in the lists , to de-activate items or to rename items (this is convenient if you wish to provide more meaningful names than those provided by your sound card). Those names which appear in the lists also appear in Cubase VST in the inputs pop-up of MIDI setup (Options menu) and in the output column of the Arrange window. Don't worry if this is all very unfamiliar at this stage, things will become clearer as you start to use the program.

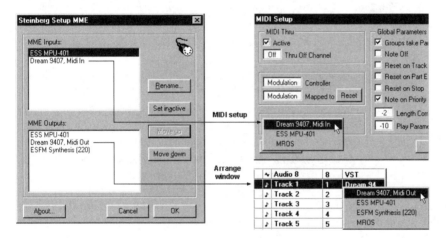

• Launch Cubase VST and verify that your MIDI card or interface appears as expected in MIDI Setup and in the Output column for each MIDI Track in the Arrange window. To see the Output column you may need to drag the split point at the left edge of the Part display. To see the available MIDI outputs click on the output name in the Output column of any of the MIDI Tracks. The verification of the MIDI inputs and outputs ensures that any MIDI data from your MIDI keyboard (or other MIDI instrument) is received by Cubase VST when it arrives at the MIDI input, and that any MIDI data transmitted from the program is directed to the MIDI output of the card.

• To make the basic audio settings which control the way in which Cubase VST communicates with your audio card, select System from the Audio menu. This opens the Audio System Setup dialogue.

Figure 2.3 The liaison between Setup MME and Cubase VST

Audio settings

• The setting up of the parameters which govern how your audio card performs with Cubase VST is vitally important but it can turn out to be a little complicated, especially if this is your first contact with the program. The advice here is to take things one step at a time and, if you run into difficulties, read the Troubleshooting section of the electronic documentation.

• For a standard stereo in/out card, ensure that the ASIO multimedia

Figure 2.4 The Audio System
Setup dialogue

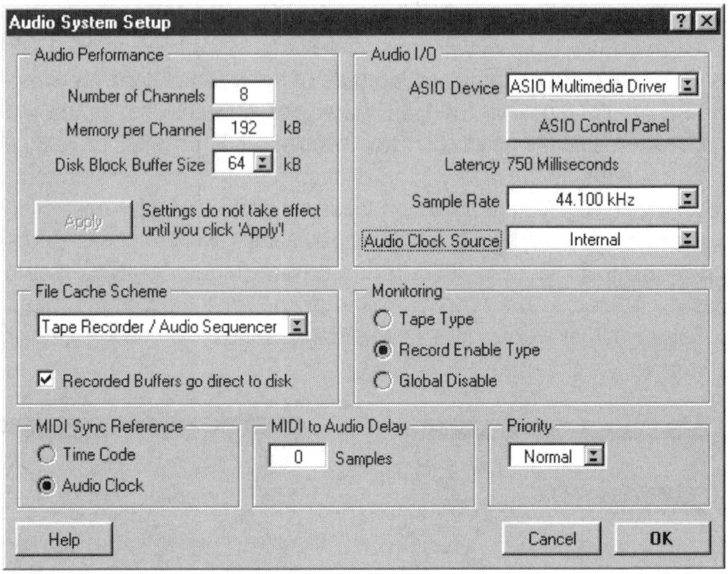

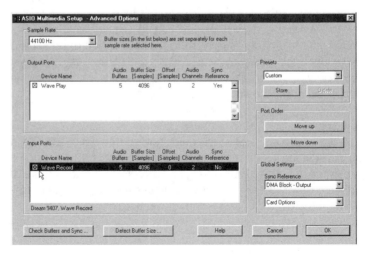

driver is selected in the ASIO device pop-up menu. The ASIO multimedia
driver is a default driver supplied by Steinberg which allows Cubase VST to
communicate with cards which have a standard MME driver. Alternatively,
you may need to install a special ASIO driver supplied with your card, (this
provides better performance than the ASIO multimedia driver).

• Click on the ASIO Control Panel button to open the basic Multimedia
Setup dialogue (Figure 2.5). This features a pop-up menu of presets for a
selection of sound cards. If your card is in the list, select it to configure
Cubase VST automatically, and at this point your card is ready to use with
the program, (you need not read the remainder of this installation guide).

• If your card is not in the list then you must configure Cubase VST's
ASIO settings manually. Click on the Advanced Options button to open the
Advanced Multimedia Setup dialogue (Figure 2.6). The input and output
device names for your audio card should already be displayed in the input
and output lists.

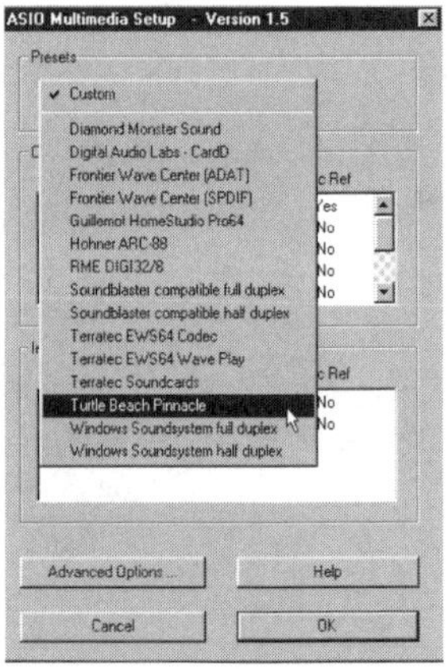

Figure 2.5 Basic Multimedia
Setup dialogue

Figure 2.6 Advanced ASIO
Multimedia Setup dialogue

• Click in the check boxes to the left of the device names to activate the required input and output devices, (a cross in the box indicates an active device). The buffer size in the Buffer size column for each device may also have to be adjusted. To automatically detect the ideal size click on the Detect Buffer Size button. There will also be special settings to make in the Global settings section.

Guideline settings for specific cards can be found in the Audio Card Issues part of the Troubleshooting section of the Cubase VST electronic documentation. Alternatively look for the latest technical information on the Steinberg knowledge base website at

http://metalguru.steinberg.de/sc/knowledge.nsf

or browse the main Steinberg website at

http://www.steinberg.net.

There is also specific information about selected audio cards in Chapter 17 of this book.

• Once all the parameters have been adjusted click on the Check Buffers and Sync button to open the Synchronisation Test dialogue (Figure 2.7). This tests the suitability of the settings. Click on the Start button to begin the test. In a satisfactory test, Sync lost and Buffer lost will read zero and upon completion a pop-up dialogue will inform you that the test was successful.

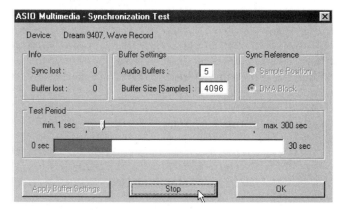

Figure 2.7 Synchronisation Test dialogue

• If you have a multiple I/O audio card then the set-up process may be slightly more involved. Some multiple I/O cards come with standard MME drivers that see the card as multiple virtual stereo cards and others come with special ASIO drivers. Multiple I/O cards with a special ASIO driver provide better performance than those with an MME driver.

If you have problems installing your system try reading the Troubleshooting section of the electronic documentation. Alternatively, try browsing the Steinberg knowledge base website at:

http:// metalguru.steinberg.de/sc/knowledge.nsf

or the PC Cubase independent website at

http://www.instanet.com/~thedusk

If your problems persist, try contacting the Steinberg helpline. (Before contacting the helpline always make sure you have your registration number, your system details and a precise explanation of the problem ready). But before you do any of this, try re-reading the above sections carefully.

Apple Macintosh hardware requirements

General Macintosh requirements

A Power Mac running at 120MHz with 32MB of RAM is an absolute minimum for running Cubase VST. The computer should also feature a 2nd level cache memory of at least 256K and a MacOS 7.6.1 (or later) operating system.

Recording multi-track digital audio demands more from your computer than other kinds of operations and a Power Mac with a fast Power PC 604e or G3 processor and at least 64MB of memory is recommended for high end audio applications.

It is also important to have a particularly large and fast hard drive (preferably a SCSI AV drive). The hard disk should be regularly defragmented using a defragmentation program and this should certainly be carried out before installing Cubase VST. This optimises its performance by re-organising the data recorded on the disk.

Macintosh computers have built-in audio inputs and outputs (on 1/8 inch mini jacks) but an additional PCI audio card is recommended for higher quality audio and digital I/O requirements. An additional MIDI interface is also normally required, and all standard Macintosh MIDI interfaces will function with Cubase VST.

Mac specifications summary

The following describes a typical Macintosh setup designed for *high end* audio applications:

- Macintosh PowerPC 604e (200MHz or more) or G3 (233MHz or more) processor
- 512K 2nd level cache memory
- 64MB of RAM (or more)
- A large and fast hard drive (preferably a SCSI AV drive of 4GB, or more, capacity with less than 9ms average seek time)
- A 16 bit stereo or multiple I/O PCI type audio card (compatible with the Macintosh and Cubase VST and preferably with a special ASIO driver).
- Macintosh compatible MIDI interface
- 24 speed CD-ROM drive
- 3.5 inch floppy drive
- high quality keyboard and mouse
- 17 inch (or larger) colour monitor
- MacOS 7.6.1 (or later) operating system installed on the computer

Apple Macintosh installation

Preparation

Cubase VST is supplied on a CD-ROM and is easily installed onto a suitably prepared Macintosh computer. Before installation you should:

- Defragment the hard disk
- De-activate File Sharing and Virtual Memory (File Sharing slows down the computer's performance and Cubase VST will not function if Virtual Memory is activated).
- Check that Modern Memory Manager is activated (if you are running System 7). This improves screen redraw speed.
- Disable AppleTalk, if you are using the printer port for MIDI.
- Select an audio input in the Monitor and Sound control panel, if you intend to use the built-in audio inputs and outputs.
- Install your audio card and its drivers according to the documentation supplied with it, if you intend to use an audio card.
- Test the audio functionality of the card outside of Cubase VST to ensure that it is installed correctly.
- Install your chosen MIDI interface and its drivers according to the documentation supplied with it.
- Ensure that you have a MacOS 7.6.1 (or later) operating system running on the computer and that it is functioning correctly.

Installation

Proceed with the installation as follows:

- Close all applications and disable any virus protection software
- Insert the Cubase VST CD-ROM. A window appears showing the contents of the CD-ROM. This includes various installers, a demo song, a 'Read me first' file, a 'Late changes' file, a folder containing the documentation for the program and a folder with additional utility and tutorial files.
- Read the 'Read me first' file and 'Late changes' files before commencing the installation. These may contain last minute information.
- Double click on the installer of the Cubase VST program for which you have purchased a licence and then follow the instructions in the dialogues which appear on screen.
- When installation is complete you will be asked to re-start your computer.
- The Adobe Acrobat Reader program is required in order to read the supplied electronic documentation. If this is not already installed on your system you can find the Acrobat installer in the Documentation folder. Double click on the Acrobat Reader installer and follow the instructions on screen.
- Now find the location of the Cubase VST icon on the hard disk and double click on it to launch the program.
- When requested, insert the Master diskette into the 3 1/2 inch floppy drive. This performs an authorisation check, after which your version of Cubase VST will appear on screen.
- Re-insert the Cubase VST CD into the CD-ROM drive and, when requested to do so, type in the CD authorisation number found on the card supplied with the program.
- You are now ready to start using the program.

MIDI and audio settings

In order to have meaningful communication with your MIDI and audio hardware you will need to make various adjustments within Cubase VST.

For MIDI, verify that the appropriate MIDI output port appears in the Output column for each MIDI Track in the Arrange window. To see the Output column you may need to drag the split point at the left edge of the Part display. Clicking in the Output column name field of a MIDI Track opens a pop-up menu containing the available output ports from which you should make the appropriate selection.

Ensure also that you have the MIDI Thru activated in the System dialogue of the MIDI Setup sub-menu (Options menu), and verify that Cubase VST is receiving and transmitting MIDI data by selecting a MIDI Track and monitoring the MIDI In/Out activity indicators as you play a MIDI keyboard connected to the system.

For audio, open the Audio System Setup dialogue (Options/Audio Setup/System) and select a device from the ASIO Device menu. If you are using the built-in audio connections with a PCI bus Macintosh the normal selection is 'Apple DAV'. For non-PCI Macintosh models select 'Apple Sound Manager'. If you are using an audio card with a special ASIO driver, select this device from the menu.

While in the Audio System Setup dialogue you could also adjust the number of audio channels for your system, in the Audio performance section, and you could choose the manner in which you monitor the input signal, in the Monitoring section. Tape Type and Record Enable Type allow monitoring of the signal via Cubase VST. This involves an unavoidable delay (latency) between the input and the output. Global Disable blocks monitoring via Cubase VST and should be selected when you are monitoring directly via the audio hardware or via an external mixer. For example, to monitor directly through the built-in audio hardware of the Macintosh, launch the ASIO device control panel and activate the 'play through' check-box (see 'Monitoring in Cubase VST' in Chapter 6 for more details about monitoring).

That's the nasty bit over! From here on things become more musical and slightly less technical. Inevitably, some of you will run into difficulties during the set up process, but do not despair since even the most experienced user can have problems setting up the system.

Overall system setup

The overall system used for Cubase VST may vary enormously and depends on the precise requirements of the user. By overall system we mean Cubase VST and all the peripheral MIDI and audio equipment which may surround it.

The simplest of set-ups

Unless you intend to monitor on headphones alone you will definitely need some kind of amplifier and speaker system. In the simplest of cases the stereo outputs from the audio card would pass directly to the amplifier and all playback from Cubase VST would be heard on the speakers. In

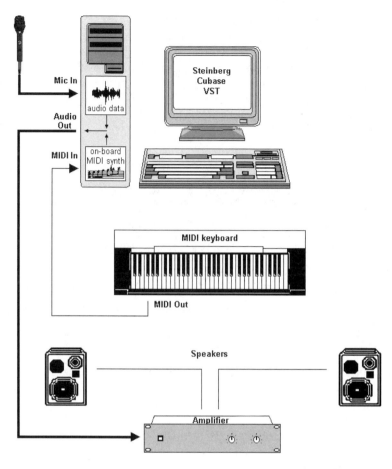

Figure 2.8 Minimum set-up for MIDI+audio recording and playback

order to make MIDI-based recordings you would also need some kind of MIDI input device such as a MIDI keyboard/synthesiser or a MIDI guitar. For audio recording the bare minimum might be a single microphone connected to the microphone input of the audio card. This describes the minimum set-up needed to record and playback both MIDI and audio material and is shown in Figure 2.8.

If you have chosen a similar system set-up then you should be aware of the variables involved.

Microphone matters

If you intend to use a microphone you must make sure that your card actually has a microphone input and you should endeavour to use a high quality model. Remember that the microphone is the very first stage in the recording path so, if you are serious about your recording, it is worth investing in a well specified model. A bad quality input signal cannot be corrected in Cubase VST and cannot be improved no matter how high the quality of the analogue to digital conversion of you audio card.

Microphone models from professional microphone manufacturers like Neumann, AKG, Shure, Beyer, Sennheiser, Sony, Calrec etc. give better results than cheaper models. Microphone choice is highly dependent on the application.

For connecting directly to the microphone input of an audio card a dynamic microphone is usually required although some cards do allow the direct connection of a capacitor (condenser) microphone. The microphone chosen could be one designed to record vocals (these are often also suitable for other live instruments) or a good all-round model. Note that the output impedance of the microphone should match the input of the card. There are two additional practical problems when using a microphone directly attached to a PC:

- *Fan noise.* Most PC's make enough fan noise to interfere with a microphone recording taking place in the same room. The best solution in this situation is to get as great a distance away from the fan as is practicable, or to use screening between the computer and the microphone. Never attempt to dampen the noise of the fan by blocking the ventilation of the computer case as this could cause your computer to overheat. Of course, the ideal solution is to make all recordings with a microphone in a separate room to the computer, as takes place in professional recording studios.

- *The choice of a stereo or mono microphone.* The microphone input on many audio cards is stereo, and if you intend to use a mono microphone some audio cards feature a jumper which allows the switching of the input for mono compatibility.

✦ TIP ✦

Most dynamic microphones are low impedance (200ohm) but, unfortunately, the microphone input of many sound cards is suited to high impedance microphones (600 ohm). To correct the mismatch, you could use a low-to-high-impedance converter, (usually an XLR to 1/4 inch jack device).

If you are on a tight budget, you could try using a hi-fi cassette deck as a mic pre-amp. It must have a mic input which will, in most cases, be high impedance. If your microphone is low impedance, use a low-to-high-impedance converter as described left. Feed the output from the cassette deck into the line inputs of the audio card.

Other input sources

If you are an electric guitarist or bassist, it is possible to record directly into the line inputs of the audio card via a guitar or bass pre-amp. This can be particularly useful for the small home recording set-up and for guitarists who wish to make use of this kind of technology, which has, until recently, been MIDI and keyboard centred.

MIDI matters

To make MIDI recordings the MIDI keyboard (or other MIDI device) should preferably be velocity sensitive and have at least a 5 octave key span. It should also be equipped with MIDI in, out and thru sockets. Other things to look out for are high quality on-board sounds and effects, ease of programmability and keys which are comfortable to play. It is difficult to recommend specific keyboard models since there are so many to choose from and a discussion of all the factors involved is beyond the scope of this book.

Monitoring tips

For convenience, you may want to try to monitor Cubase VST via your computer's own speakers. However, this is certainly not recommended and, given the bad quality of many computer speakers, is not appropriate for serious recording. It is acceptable to attach your audio output to a hi-fi system in a home studio situation and, depending on the frequency range of your speakers and how much they colour the sound, this solution could be adequate.

For semi-professional and professional applications it is usual to use professional audio monitoring equipment. This would normally include a high quality power amplifier and studio monitors which have been designed to give a clear, neutral sound so that the recording process can be judged more reliably, (discussed in more detail below).

A larger scale setup

Larger scale overall set-ups for Cubase VST involve a wide range of variables. Some of the things common to almost all set-ups are the inclusion of a mixing console, some kind of mastering machine (e.g. a DAT machine), good quality studio monitors and a network of MIDI devices. These items significantly improve the functionality of Cubase VST. An example set-up is shown in Figure 2.9.

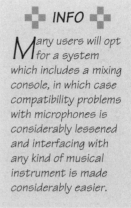

Figure 2.9 A larger Cubase VST system

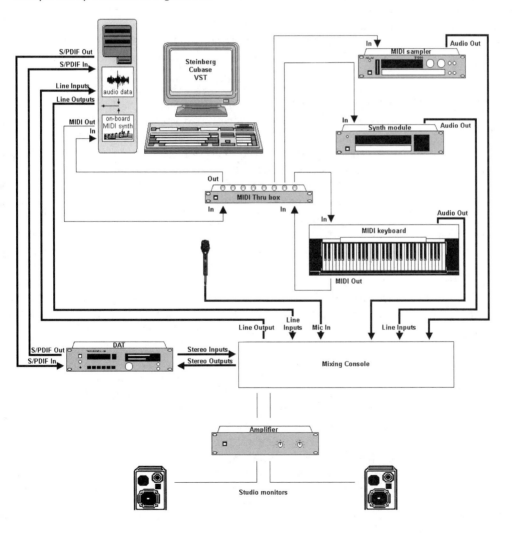

Do you need a mixer?

One of the first questions which might be asked is 'why do we need a mixing console when there is a virtual mixer in Cubase VST?'. The answer is that it all depends on the intended application, but most users will find it more convenient if an external mixing console is included in their system. Some users may decide that they do not need a mixing console at all. Others need a way of interfacing the wide range of equipment which is commonly used in the recording process. This might include one or more microphones, a lead or bass guitar, a keyboard or any other musical instrument, a multi-track tape recorder, a DAT (Digital Audio Tape) machine or any number of other sources.

The actual choice of mixer is also dependent on the application. A project studio may only require a small mixer, providing enough inputs for several microphone and line signals and enough I/O sockets to be able to interface to a DAT machine and Cubase VST (as shown in Figure 2.9). The mixing facilities of Cubase VST are most useful once the audio tracks have been recorded. The fact that the program can handle up to 32 virtual mixer channels means that you can cut down on the cost and extra space requirements of a large console. An automated mix can now take place within the computer and the stereo result can be routed to the external console or, if it is the final mix, this could be routed directly to a DAT machine.

DAT is useful!

Of all the peripheral equipment surrounding Cubase VST a DAT machine is among the most useful. The use of digital audio tape means that you have a convenient way of recording the final results of your endeavours onto a high quality medium, which is also an accepted standard in the professional audio industry. If the final mix is taking place in Cubase VST alone then, in order to maintain optimum sound quality, this can be digitally transferred directly to DAT via the digital output of the audio card. In addition, many DAT machines allow the switching of their circuitry into AD conversion mode so that any audio received at the analogue line inputs is converted to digital data which is simultaneously available at the S/PDIF digital output of the machine. The digital audio can then be routed directly into Cubase VST via the digital input of the audio card, allowing a high quality method of recording using the AD converter of the DAT machine (which is likely to be superior to that found on many audio cards).

More on monitoring

The use of good quality studio monitors is essential in order to be able to judge the quality and balance of the sounds being recorded. All professional installations use high quality studio monitors and, if professional results are required, then they are essential tools. Many home studio set-ups may only ever monitor at low volume levels and a pair of small nearfield monitors may be adequate.

Hi-fi speakers which produce noticeable coloration of the sound can lead to confusing results; i.e. a mix may sound excellent on these speakers in your own studio but when you play it on any other system it may be found to have lost, for example, much of its bass, or vice versa. Equally important is the positioning of the monitors. A good starting point is that of an equilateral triangle formed by the listening position and the two speakers.

Traditionally, the sound path from the two monitors produces a 60 degrees angle at the listening position. The distance between the two monitors should not exceed the distance from the monitors to the listener as this can seriously affect the perception of the stereo image. It is also desirable to have the monitors placed on a non-resonant, rigid surface which does not produce any vibrations in the actual structure of the room.

Also of primary importance is the use of a high quality amplifier which comfortably produces a clear, undistorted signal. The amplifier should not have to be driven to its maximum volume in order to achieve the desired listening level, so a model with sufficient headroom above the average listening level should be chosen.

MIDI networks

Many Cubase VST systems include some kind of MIDI network. Larger networks may feature a MIDI thru box (also called a MIDI splitter box) which enables the channelling of MIDI data to specific locations in the system. The MIDI network in Figure 2.9 features a master keyboard from which the MIDI Out is sent to the MIDI In of the computer. The MIDI input data passes through Cubase VST and is passed back out, along with any other data which has already been recorded, to the MIDI input of the MIDI thru box. The data is connected to the respective outputs of the thru box to be passed back to the master keyboard and to the other modules in the system. The audio card of the computer may also feature an on-board synthesiser which adds to the available sound palette. While some of the on-board synthesisers of popular sound cards are not suitable for serious music production some of the high end cards provide synthesiser sound quality and features which match those of their external counterparts.

Summary

The above has explained some of the variables involved in the setting up of a larger scale system for use with Cubase VST but readers should be aware that the art of sound recording and the science of studio design include many more parameters, which are beyond the scope of this book. It should also be apparent that any combination of the above elements might be included in a Cubase VST system, depending on the application. Some users might require a very comprehensive MIDI network with just one extremely high quality microphone for the recording of vocals. Others may opt for a very basic MIDI system of just one master keyboard and an on-board synthesiser, coupled with a large external mixing console and a comprehensive range of microphones and devices for recording audio into the program. And, of course, many professional applications would require all of the above and a whole lot more besides.

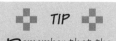

 TIP

*R*emember that the secret of setting up a recording system around Cubase VST is to have a clear idea of exactly what you will be using the system for and how you would like to incorporate Cubase VST into the recording process..

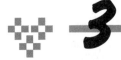

3

First steps

This chapter describes the basic steps involved in recording both MIDI and audio data and explores some of the general features of the system. Most users will be keen to make their first recordings as soon as possible and many will attempt to do this without ever having read the manual. This is certainly easy enough to do without any instructions and Cubase VST has, of course, been designed to make the recording process as trouble-free as possible. There is nothing to stop you making a recording simply by pressing the Transport bar record button, without any knowledge of the details involved. However, it is not always certain that things will go according to plan since the recording process is controlled by many parameters.

Let's start by recording some MIDI data. This first section demonstrates a simple step-by-step approach to the MIDI recording process in an attempt to avoid some of the grey areas which may arise for first-time users and it assumes that recording is taking place in the Arrange window (the default window which appears when Cubase VST is first started up and the usual location for MIDI recording).

If you are already familiar with basic MIDI recording then you should move on to the section about audio recording.

Your first MIDI recording

1 Connect your MIDI keyboard
You must first ensure that a MIDI keyboard, (or other input source), has its MIDI out connected to the MIDI In of your chosen MIDI interface/sound card. This can be verified by checking the 'IN' MIDI activity indicator on the Transport bar while playing the MIDI keyboard. Reasons for no activity indication include an interface that has been wrongly installed or a MIDI cable connected incorrectly. Ensure also that the MIDI Out of the computer's MIDI interface is connected to the MIDI In of the keyboard.

2 Choose a Track and Track class
The Arrange window includes a number of columns, one of which is marked with a 'C'. This stands for 'Class' and each Track can be assigned to a different type according to what kind of data is being recorded. In

this case, choose an existing empty Track in the Arrange window or create a new one by double clicking below the existing Tracks. Next, click in the Track's 'C' column and select 'MIDI Track' in the pop-up menu. A note symbol appears in the column.

3 Set Output port

The current Track should have its Output column set to the MIDI device being used. (The Output column is revealed by clicking and dragging on the Arrange window split point and pulling it to the right). This could be one of many devices with default names such as, for example, MPU401, AWE64, TBS Pro, Dream 9407 etc. Remember that there could be several output ports available, depending on the hardware which is installed in your computer. An appropriate MIDI channel should also be selected in the Channel column ('Chn').

4 Activate MIDI Thru

On all but the very rarest of occasions the MIDI Thru of Cubase VST should be made active. This is found in the MIDI setup dialogue of the Options menu and should be ticked. This ensures that any MIDI data received at the MIDI In of Cubase VST is echoed, or through put, to the MIDI Out.

5 Set Metronome

Before recording anything ensure that there is an appropriate precount and guide click by adjusting the status of the Metronome found in the Options menu. Try ticking Precount, Prerecord and MIDI click and set a precount of 2 bars. Set the MIDI click Channel and Output to an appropriate drum or percussion sound source if there is one available. (MIDI channel 10 is the standard MIDI channel for drums and percussion sounds and the selection of C#1 as the note for a MIDI click is the standard position for a rimshot sound). Ensure that Audio Click is de-activated. Click on OK to leave the Metronome dialogue.

6 Activate Click

Ensure that Click is activated and the tempo adjusted to the desired setting on the Transport bar. This provides a guide click from the computer's speaker or from a MIDI instrument, as set above. Leave all other Transport bar settings in their default positions.

7 Start recording

To record, select the record button on the Transport bar. Cubase VST will output a 2 bar count, as set in the metronome, before recording commences from the left locator position (a small box marked with an L found in the position bar above the Part Display). Anything played on the keyboard will be recorded by Cubase VST.

8 Stop recording

Stop recording by selecting the stop button on the Transport bar. At this

moment a graphic strip will appear in the Arrange window display with the same name as the Track upon which it was recorded. This graphic strip is known as a 'Part' and it contains the music which has just been played. It can be renamed by pressing the alt key (Mac: option) and double clicking on the Part.

9 Rewind

Rewind the song position in the conventional manner using the rewind button or, alternatively, select the stop button a second time which will take you back to the left locator position.

10 Now play it back

To play back the performance simply select the Play button.

The above ten steps should get you into MIDI recording with the minimum of fuss and you will notice that Cubase VST has been supplied with most of the parameters already sensibly set. Due to this fact, in most cases, only steps 8,9 and 10 are necessary to actually make the recording. Steps 1 to 7 ensure that the user is aware of some of the parameters and preparation involved. Once all the parameters have been set up successfully, steps 1 to 7 can be largely ignored in the routine recording process.

Figure 3.1 Resulting MIDI Part in the Arrange window

A	M	C	Track	Chn	Output				
		♦	**Audio 7**	7	**VST**				
		♦	**Audio 8**	8	**VST**				
		♪	**Test Track**	1	**ESS M..4**	FirstSteps			
		♪	**Track 2**	2	**ESS M..4**				
		♪	**Track 3**	3	**ESS M..4**				
		♪	**Track 4**	4	**ESS M..4**				

If you experience problems with this process you should, once again, ensure that:

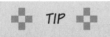

TIP

Be careful with your locator positions! Accidentally placing the left locator to the wrong side of the right locator (or vice versa!) will cause Cubase VST to block any attempt at recording.

- the MIDI cables are not faulty and have been connected correctly
- the MIDI Interface has been correctly installed and is selected in the Arrange window Output column of the Track which is being recorded
- the MIDI channel is appropriate in the Channel column
- any external equipment connected to the system is switched on and configured to receive MIDI information on the appropriate channel(s).

Your first audio recording

Audio recording is managed in a similar manner to MIDI recording and normally takes place in the Arrange window of Cubase VST. However, it is potentially more problematic than MIDI recording since there are more parameters involved. The following steps outline the basic procedure. It is assumed that an audio signal is being fed into the line input of a standard stereo in/stereo out audio card and that you are already familiar with MIDI recording:

1 Check your audio card

Before proceeding make sure that your audio card has been installed correctly. Ensure that the audio inputs and outputs of the card are connected to your sound system or external mixer. Test the card outside of Cubase VST by playing back an audio file using, for example, the Sound Recorder accessory supplied with Windows. Also try recording the signal from an audio CD using Sound Recorder or, if available, use the software supplied with the audio card to make a short recording. Switch on the audio through function of the card's mixer application so that you can monitor a signal when it is sent into the card's inputs. If everything functions normally then your audio card has been proved to be in good working order, regardless of the current settings in Cubase VST. This is important to establish before proceeding further.

2 Connect your audio signal and activate the VST inputs

Decide what you are going to record and connect the source signal cable to the line input of the audio card. This might be a stereo line socket or individual sockets for the left and right inputs. If it is a mono source connect the cable to the left input socket (if available separately). Select Inputs from the Audio menu. This opens the VST Inputs dialogue containing a list of the available input ports (right). Ensure that the green light is on (active) for the input pair of your audio card.

3 Choose a Track and select it as an audio track

Similar to the procedure for recording MIDI data choose an existing empty Track in the Arrange window or create a new one by double clicking below the existing Tracks. Click in its 'C' column and select 'Audio Track' in the pop-up menu. A sine wave symbol appears in the Track's Class column and 'VST' appears in the Output column.

4 Select the audio channel

Select an audio channel in the Channel column ('Chn') of the chosen Track. The default number of audio channels is usually eight (this can be increased according to the processing power of your system). For this exercise, choose channel 1.

5 Open the Inspector and select mono

Open the Inspector by clicking on the Inspector icon (a small square in the bottom left corner of the Arrange window). The Inspector is a narrow window opened at the left side of the Arrange window display which is used for managing various functions of the currently chosen Track. Select mono in the lower part of the Inspector display.

6 Select an audio input

Select Monitor from the Audio menu to open the Monitor mixer display. Hold down the Control key on the computer keyboard and click on the top button of channel 1 (this is the audio channel which was chosen in step 4). This opens a pop-up menu (left) containing the available inputs in your system. With a standard stereo in/stereo out card this might contain two menu items 'IN 1 L' and 'IN 1 R', the left and right line inputs of the card. Select the input to which you have attached the audio input signal (as described in step 2). Note that the Input select button is also available in the Inspector.

7 Select a folder for the audio files

Go back to the Inspector and click on the Record Enable button. The first time that you do this Cubase VST opens the file dialogue where you should choose or create a folder in which you wish to store the audio files of the current song. Thereafter, all recorded audio files in the same song are placed in this folder. If needed, you can change the default folder at a later stage by selecting 'Select Audio File Folder' in the File menu.

8 Monitor the signal

Select System from the Audio menu and ensure that Global Disable is selected in the Monitor section of the Audio System Setup dialogue. In this configuration, the monitoring of the audio input is achieved via the card or from an external mixer. To monitor audio via the card, make sure that any audio through function on the card's mixer is activated. This monitoring configuration is known as monitoring via the card. It is also possible to monitor via Cubase VST but, with a standard stereo in/stereo out card without a special ASIO driver, this involves an unavoidable delay (latency) between the input signal and the actual monitored signal you hear. If you wish to monitor via Cubase VST, select Tape Type or Record Enable Type in the Monitor section of the Audio System Setup dialogue and de-activate the audio through function on the card's mixer application.

To activate *visual* monitoring of the input signal in Cubase VST, click on the In button (just above the level meter) of channel 1 in the Monitor mixer (left). When the In button is illuminated, the meter shows the level of the incoming signal. When it is not illuminated, it shows the level of any outgoing signal which has already been recorded.

9 Adjust the recording level

The fader on the Monitor mixer channel is *not* used to adjust the recording level. Instead, the level must be adjusted using one of the following:

- your audio card's own input level controls
- the ASIO Control Panel of the Audio System dialogue if your card supports it
- a level control at the source of the audio signal, such as the output fader on your external mixing console.

Most users with standard stereo in/stereo out cards and an external mixer will set the record input level of their card's mixer application to an optimum level at the beginning of the session. Thereafter, finer level adjustments can be made using the output fader on the external mixer.

Whatever technique you use, carefully adjust the input level so that no overload occurs on the level meter of the chosen channel strip in Cubase VST's Monitor mixer (channel 1 in this exercise). The signal must never exceed 0dB. Signals which exceed this level produce an unpleasant audible distortion although very short bursts of overload may go unnoticed. If peak overloads are detected by Cubase VST, the red clipping indicator is illuminated, meaning that the signal has exceeded 0dB (click once to reset). The precise amount of headroom is also shown just above the channel fader (right).

Set the signal level so that there is a safety margin of around -2dB to -3dB. The final decision for the precise input level is a matter of judgement and experience and is highly dependent on the characteristics of the input signal. For example, a smooth signal such as slow synthesiser strings will be easier to predict and control than live vocals. While it is desirable to avoid distortion you need also to be careful not to record signals too low.

10 Record and playback

As with MIDI recording the Metronome can be adjusted to give the required pre-count before recording commences. It is possible to record audio with no concern for the current tempo but if you intend to record MIDI Tracks alongside then you should monitor the tempo to keep in time.

To make the recording, press the record button on the Transport bar. After the pre-count, commence the musical performance (or send the audio signal). Recording commences at the position of the left locator. When the performance is finished press the stop button. At this point a Part (a graphic strip) appears in the Arrange window similar to the MIDI recording process, but this time containing a waveform (see Figure 3.2). To play back the audio simply rewind the song position and press the play button.

As can be seen, the audio recording process relies on the correct setting up of a range of parameters associated with the software configuration and directly related to the audio hardware in use. In order to be successful it is essential to understand the operation of your chosen audio card and how Cubase VST communicates with it. Those readers experienc-

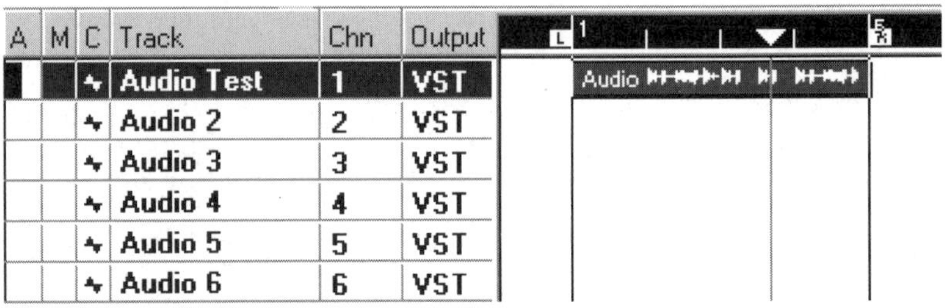

Figure 3.2 Resulting audio
Part in the Arrange window

A	M	C	Track	Chn	Output		
	↟	Audio Test	1	VST		Audio
	↟	Audio 2	2	VST		
	↟	Audio 3	3	VST		
	↟	Audio 4	4	VST		
	↟	Audio 5	5	VST		
	↟	Audio 6	6	VST		

ing difficulties with their first audio recording should not despair since system setup problems are not uncommon. If you are impatient to find out more about audio recording then go to Chapter 6 now.

First impressions

Any attempts to record with Cubase VST will have already revealed some of the features of the program but, before plunging more deeply into specific details, it is important to explore the system in a more generalised way.

Testing the controls

Many users have a tendency to ignore the peripheral features in their quest for a quick result. They may also become over-reliant on the mouse. Remember that there are a substantial number of keyboard commands which make navigating around the system faster and easier (Table 3.1).

When Cubase VST is started up the Arrange window appears on the computer screen with various default settings. From here we can use some of the keyboard commands to move around the system. We are not following any particular logic here, but just becoming familiar with the controls. It's rather like learning to drive a car – it's a good idea to get the feel of the controls before actually going out on the road. The table shows some of the most important keyboard commands.

So, without attempting to achieve anything musically constructive, let's try various combinations of the keyboard commands on the computer keyboard. Select a MIDI Track and then press ctrl + P (Mac: command + P) to create a new blank MIDI Part in the Arrange window between the left and right locators (two small boxes in the position bar display marked L and R). Parts are graphic blocks which appear in the working area to the right of the Track list. They would usually contain audio or MIDI data but they may also be empty, as in this case. Then try ctrl + E (Mac: command + E) followed by ctrl + L (Mac: command + L) which, in the case of a MIDI Track, opens Key edit followed by Logical edit. Pressing the escape key will exit from each editor and take you back to the Arrange window. Note that escape can be used to exit most of the editors and dialogue boxes without making any changes to the recorded data. Try the other 'ctrl plus a key' commands to move around the system.

Audio and VST shortcuts include ctrl + F (Mac: command + F) to open the Audio pool, ctrl + * (Mac: command + *) to open the Monitor mixer and ctrl + + (Mac: command + +) to open the Master faders. Shift + F12 hides or shows all VST windows (PC version).

Table 3.1 Computer keyboard shortcuts

| Typewriter keyboard | | Function |
PC	Mac	
ctrl + O	command + O	open file
ctrl + S	command + S	save song file
ctrl + Q	command + Q	quit program
ctrl + E	command + E	Key edit or the default editor associated with the Track's class
ctrl + G	command + G	List edit
ctrl + D	command + D	Drum edit
ctrl + R	command + R	Score edit
ctrl + L	command + L	Logical edit
ctrl + T	command + T	create a new Track
ctrl + P	command + P	create a new Part
ctrl + X	command + X	cut
ctrl + C	command + C	copy
ctrl + V	command + V	paste
ctrl + Z	command + Z	undo
ctrl + *	command + *	open audio monitor mixer
ctrl + +	command + +	open audio master faders
ctrl + F	command + F	open the audio pool
alt + ctrl + I	option + I	open/close the Inspector
alt + ctrl + P	option + P	move locators to start and end points of the selected Part
alt + ctrl + N	no default	open name entry box of the currently selected Track
F12	no default	hide/show Transport bar
shift + F12	n/a	hide/show VST windows
S	S	solo on/off
I	I	punch in on/off
O	O	punch out on/off
C	C	metronome click on/off
M	M	activate/de-activate Mastertrack
home	home	move song position pointer to start of current window
esc	esc	cancel (or leave a dialogue box)

Other immediately useful key commands include the C key for turning the guide click on and off, the S key for soloing the selected Track and the + and – keys of the numeric keypad to change the tempo.

The numeric keypad

The numeric keypad may be viewed as a kind of tape recorder remote control. Although all the controls are obviously already available to the mouse on the computer screen, their repetition on the keypad provides a handy alternative (see Table 3.2). Users will also find this indispensable after having used the hide transport option in the Windows menu.

Table 3.2 Numeric keypad shortcuts

Numeric keypad		Function
PC	Mac	
**	record	
Enter	Enter	play/continue
O or spacebar	O or spacebar	first time – stop
		second time – go to left locator
		third time – go to bar 1.1.0
PgDn	num lock	rewind
PgUp	=	fast forward
1	1	go to left locator
2	2	go to right locator
/	/	cycle on/off
+	+	increase tempo
–	–	decrease tempo

The mouse

Let's now go on to use the mouse. As well as operating such things as the Transport bar, the mouse is most useful for all the graphic elements of the system, such as dragging objects around the screen, changing values, using tools, fine editing in the editors and manipulating the VST elements of the program. It is useful for setting the song position by double clicking in the position bar above the Arrange window display or clicking once in the position bar in any one of the editors. It is also the preferred method of opening up what are effectively the contents pages of the system: the menus.

The menus

The menus are found under various headings at the top of the computer screen and Figure 3.3 shows all the menu contents.

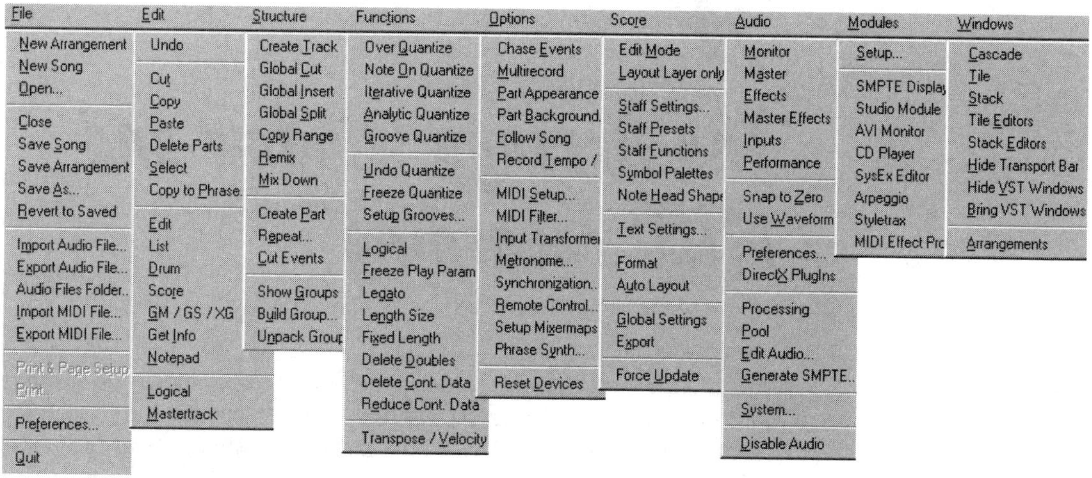

File	Edit	Structure	Functions	Options	Score	Audio	Modules	Windows
New Arrangement	Undo	Create Track	Over Quantize	Chase Events	Edit Mode	Monitor	Setup...	Cascade
New Song		Global Cut	Note On Quantize	Multirecord	Layout Layer only	Master		Tile
Open...	Cut	Global Insert	Iterative Quantize	Part Appearance		Effects	SMPTE Display	Stack
	Copy	Global Split	Analytic Quantize	Part Background	Staff Settings...	Master Effects	Studio Module	Tile Editors
Close	Paste	Copy Range	Groove Quantize	Follow Song	Staff Presets	Inputs	AVI Monitor	Stack Editors
Save Song	Delete Parts	Remix		Record Tempo /	Staff Functions	Performance	CD Player	Hide Transport Bar
Save Arrangement	Select	Mix Down	Undo Quantize		Symbol Palettes		SysEx Editor	Hide VST Windows
Save As...	Copy to Phrase		Freeze Quantize	MIDI Setup...	Note Head Shape	Snap to Zero	Arpeggio	Bring VST Windows
Revert to Saved		Create Part	Setup Grooves...	MIDI Filter...		Use Waveform	Styletrax	
	Edit	Repeat...		Input Transformer	Text Settings...		MIDI Effect Pro	Arrangements
Import Audio File...	List	Cut Events	Logical	Metronome...		Preferences...		
Export Audio File...	Drum		Freeze Play Param	Synchronization...	Format	DirectX PlugIns		
Audio Files Folder...	Score	Show Groups	Legato	Remote Control...	Auto Layout			
Import MIDI File...	GM / GS / XG	Build Group...	Length Size	Setup Mixermaps		Processing		
Export MIDI File...	Get Info	Unpack Group	Fixed Length	Phrase Synth...	Global Settings	Pool		
	Notepad		Delete Doubles		Export	Edit Audio...		
Print & Page Setup			Delete Cont. Data	Reset Devices		Generate SMPTE...		
Print	Logical		Reduce Cont. Data		Force Update			
	Mastertrack					System...		
Preferences...			Transpose / Velocity					
Quit						Disable Audio		

Figure 3.3 The menus

It is immediately apparent from here that Cubase VST is extremely comprehensive. Some of the most important elements include the various MIDI editors, the Audio editor, the Wave editor, the Audio pool, Audio processing, the Monitor and Master mixers, the quantize functions, the copy, repeat and transposition functions and, of course, the file save and load functions. Most of the important menu items will be dealt with during the course of this book but, before we jump too far ahead, it is important to understand what actually happens when Cubase VST is launched — this involves the auto-loading of a special file known as a definition file which sets certain key parameters of the system.

Definition Files

Cubase VST appears on the screen after having auto-loaded any 'Def' files found on the hard drive (Def.all, Def.arr, Def.set etc.). These are 'definition' files which contain user preferences for the setup, general handling and appearance of the system. This includes such things as the window size and magnification, button settings, last tool used, quantize value etc. for the Arrange window and editor windows. It might have seemed more logical to set up a definition file before recording any music but before any meaningful definition files can be created you must have a good understanding of the essential features of the program. (See 'System Preparation' in Chapter 10 for more details on defining the appearance and performance of your system).

4

The Arrange window and MIDI recording

This chapter provides information on the Arrange window, the Arrange window toolbox, the Transport bar, the Inspector and the MIDI recording process. The Arrange window is the centre of activity for many of Cubase VST's functions and, as such, this chapter is essential reading for those not yet familiar.

The Arrange window

The Arrange window (Figures 4.1 and 4.2) is divided into two sections by a moveable split point which can be dragged across to the left or right of the screen using the mouse. Pulling the split point as far as possible to the left maximises the working area for the Arrangement. This area is known as the Part display.

The layout of the Arrange window features time on the horizontal axis, represented as bars and beats, and Tracks on the vertical axis, which are named in the Track column. The current time position in the arrangement is shown by a moving vertical line known as the song position pointer.

Figure 4.1 The Arrange window columns

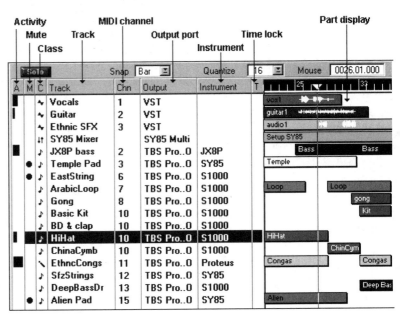

The Arrange window columns

Pulling the split point fully to the right reveals a number of columns which show the status of various settings governing each Track. These include:

- the activity column (A), showing the current activity of each Track in real time
- the mute column (M), where any number of Tracks may be muted
- the classification column (C), where Tracks can be designated as audio, MIDI, drum, mix etc.
- the Track column, where Tracks are named
- the channel column (Chn), where the audio or MIDI channel for each Track may be chosen
- the output column, where the MIDI output port may be chosen
- the instrument column, where any combination of the MIDI channel and output columns may be named. The instrument column has no function for audio Tracks.
- the 'T' column where Tracks may be time locked.

Remember that, in the case of MIDI Tracks, the output column contains the output port names of the driver(s) you have installed with your sound card and, in the case of audio Tracks, contains the letters 'VST'.

Note that the Arrange window also features a solo button in the top left corner. This is used to solo the currently selected Track.

Figure 4.2 The Arrange window, Inspector and Transport bar

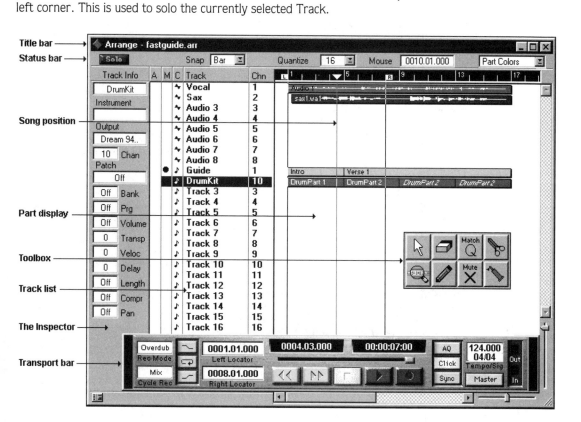

Some readers may have already noticed that there is a separate mini-window to the left of the columns. This is known as the Inspector and, for MIDI Tracks, is used to select sounds and change various parameters such as velocity, volume, delay and pitch. For audio Tracks the Inspector contains various controls for handling audio recording, such as a record enable button, a mono/stereo button and audio channel and delay parameters. The Inspector displays the parameters for the currently selected Track or Part in the Arrange window (the Track or Part which appears in black). It also contains the Track/Part name, the Instrument and Output port (for MIDI tracks), and the audio/MIDI channel. The Inspector can be shown or hidden by clicking on the small square shaped icon underneath it (See Chapter 10 for more details on the Inspector).

The current arrangement on screen can be one of several held in memory at the same time, (as found in the Arrangements list of the Windows menu). A new Arrange window may be created by selecting New Arrangement in the File menu or pressing ctrl + N (Mac: command + N) on the computer keyboard.

The Toolbox

To open the toolbox click with the right mouse button (Mac: ctrl + shift + mouse click) in empty space in the Part display, (see opened toolbox in Arrange window, Figure 4.2). This is for the manipulation and editing of Parts, and the main functions are as follows:

Pointer

The pointer is the default tool for the selection, moving and copying of Parts, and for the general manipulation of data anywhere on the screen.

Eraser

The eraser is for deleting Parts simply by clicking on one Part or by dragging over several.

Match Q

The match Q (match quantize) tool is used to impose the timing characteristics of one Part upon another by dragging and releasing a source Part over a target Part.

Scissors

The scissors are for splicing Parts into smaller portions. Parts will be split at the mouse position and according to the current Snap value.

Magnifying glass

The magnifying glass is for monitoring the contents of either MIDI Parts, by clicking and dragging it over the Part with the left mouse button, or audio Parts, whose contents will be played from the position at which the Part is clicked.

Pencil

The pencil is for lengthening or shortening Parts by grabbing and moving the start or end points of the Part. It may also be used to create new Parts anywhere on the Part display by clicking and dragging in blank space.

Mute tool
The mute tool (you guessed it) is for muting Parts.

Glue tool
The glue tool is used to join two or more Parts to make one longer Part.

The Transport bar

The Transport bar, usually located in the lower part of the screen below the Arrange window, features a number of important functions. Apart from the obvious tape recorder style controls there are the following:

The Record mode selector
This is for selecting whether Cubase VST adds to any existing music when recording (Overdub mode) or overwrites it (Replace Mode). The Record mode selector concerns MIDI data only and has no effect on the recording of audio. Recording over an existing audio Part never overwrites or merges with the existing audio; instead, a new audio file is created for each new recording, but only one single audio recording at a time can be heard when the audio is on the same channel (see Chapter 6 for more details).

The Cycle button
This is for cycling between the left and right locator positions.

The punch in and out buttons
For automatically dropping in and out of record mode at the left and right locator positions. Note that Cubase VST always starts recording from the left locator position and when it is put into record mode the punch in button is automatically selected. However, if Cubase VST is rewound to a point some bars before the left locator and put into play with the punch in button manually selected, Cubase VST will drop in to record when it reaches the left locator position. If the punch out button has also been selected, then Cubase VST will drop out of record at the right locator position. Otherwise it will remain in record mode until you stop the sequencer.

The left and right locator positions
These show the current positions of the locators.

The bar display
This shows the current position in bars, beats and fractions of a beat (ticks).

The Time code display
Showing the current song position in hours, minutes, seconds and frames.

The Click on/off button
To toggle on or off the guide click (as set up in the Metronome dialogue).

The sync button
For synchronising the sequencer to an external device such as a tape recorder.

The tempo and time signature displays

The Master button

For activating or de-activating the Mastertrack's tempo and time signature changes.

The automatic quantize button (AQ)

Used to automatically quantize a performance as it is recorded.

The position slider

Between the tape recorder style controls and the position displays, for quickly moving to new song positions within the current arrangement.

The Transport bar itself can be grabbed and moved to any screen position according to the needs of each user. All features may be updated or manipulated in some way using either the mouse or various computer keyboard commands. Remember that, normally, the left mouse button will decrease and the right mouse button will increase a value.

MIDI recording in more detail

Most readers will have Cubase VST connected to some kind of MIDI equipped synthesiser or piano keyboard and a network of MIDI devices such as rackmount synth modules, MIDI samplers, drum machines or effects units (see Figure 4.3).

It is usually desirable for the MIDI data received at the MIDI IN of the computer to be echoed to the MIDI OUT. So, open the MIDI Setup dialogue box of the Options menu and ensure that MIDI THRU is active

Figure 4.3 A typical MIDI network

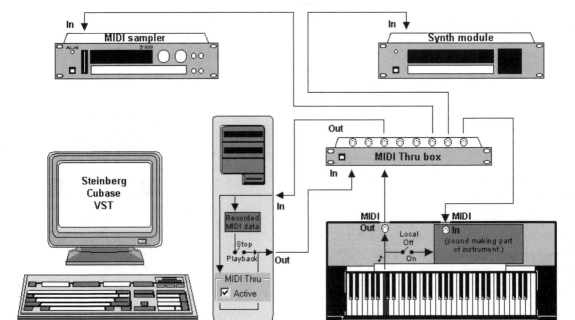

(ticked). Ensure also that SysEx and Aftertouch are filtered in the record and thru sections of the MIDI filter, also found in the Options menu. This will avoid recording any unnecessary data in the exercise outlined below.

It is also desirable, if possible, to set the master keyboard to LOCAL *off*. Local Off means that the keyboard is disconnected from the sound making part of the instrument. This avoids double notes and stops the master keyboard sounding while other instruments in the network are being played via MIDI.

It should now be possible to play any of the devices in the MIDI network by changing the MIDI channel in the channel column of the currently selected MIDI Track (using the left or right mouse buttons). If you experience difficulties at this point verify that the correct output device has been selected in the Output column.

You could start by recording a simple piano (or drum) Part. To prepare the system for recording proceed as follows:

- Set up the Metronome dialogue of the Options menu. This can be set to output a MIDI click to an appropriate sound, such as a rimshot. The pre-count before recording commences is also adjustable.
- Activate the Transport bar guide click button using the mouse or by pressing 'C' on the computer keyboard.
- Test the click and the tempo of Cubase VST by selecting the Transport play button with the mouse (or by using the Enter key on the numeric keypad). Adjust the tempo on the fly, if necessary, by clicking the left and right mouse buttons in the tempo box of the Transport bar or by pressing the + and − keys of the numeric keypad.
- Choose a Track and select the appropriate class in the C column. For this exercise choose MIDI.
- Double click on the Track name and enter an appropriate name into the pop-up box.
- Select the appropriate MIDI channel for the Track and find a suitable sound from one of the units in the system.
- Stop and return to bar 1.1.0 of the Arrange window. Set the left and right locators to bar positions 1.1.0 and 5.1.0 by clicking with the left and right mouse buttons in the position bar above the arrangement area.
- Select Cycle on the Transport bar using the mouse or by pressing the divide key (/) on the numeric keypad to put Cubase VST into cycle mode. Cubase VST will now cycle between the left and right locator positions (in record or playback mode).
- Ensure that cycle record mode is set to 'mix' in order to be able to add to the recording on each lap of the cycle. This mode ignores the setting of the Record Mode selector.
- Ensure that Automatic Quantize (AQ) is *off*.

Cubase VST is now set to record and cycle between the left and right locators. In cycle mode the punch in and out buttons can be largely ignored since the punch in button is auto-selected when Cubase VST is put into record mode and the punch out point (the position of the right locator) is never actually reached since Cubase VST cycles back to the left locator position. Recording is de-activated only when Cubase VST is stopped manually.

Many users prefer recording MIDI data in cycle mode since Cubase VST automatically remains within the segment of music which is being recorded upon without any further effort, and any recorded material can be instantly monitored on the next lap of the cycle. It is also useful for continually adding to the material without dropping out of record and is particularly convenient for building up a rhythm pattern.

You can, of course, set up Cubase VST to record without cycle. In this mode recording begins from the left locator position and ends when Cubase VST is stopped or, if the punch out button has been activated, when the song position pointer reaches the right locator position.

Remember that, without cycle, the setting of the Record Mode selector must be taken into account. For most applications this would be set to Overdub, when recorded data will be added to any existing MIDI material already on the same Track. With the Record Mode selector set to Replace, any existing MIDI material on the Track will be overwritten, and as such this mode should be used with more caution.

We are now ready to actually record something. Some readers may consider this preparation far too much trouble just to put the system into the correct configuration to record some music. After all, recording onto a multitrack tape recorder is comparatively instantaneous. However, we must bear in mind that most of the steps described here were actually already sensibly set in the definition files supplied with Cubase VST, and they are invariably set up only once, according to the preferences of each user. In addition, a sequencer of the power of Cubase VST has the capacity to fine tune and re-process recorded data beyond that of a multitrack tape recorder.

So, to record, proceed as follows :

Start recording
Click on the record button of the Transport bar or select the asterisk (*) on the numeric keypad. A pre-count will be heard according to what has been set in the metronome, and then the song position pointer should start to move.

Play something simple
Anything played on the keyboard will now be recorded into Cubase VST. Try recording something simple using, for example, simple chords or a bass drum and snare. Cubase VST will cycle between the left and right locators (as set above), and the recording may be added to on each lap of the cycle.

Stop the recording
Stop the sequencer when recording is complete and a new Part will appear on the screen between the locators.

Quantize it?
If the new Part has been played extremely accurately it may not need any further attention, but a large number of users will want to quantize their work. Quantization is a kind of timing correction; it exists in various forms in the Functions menu of Cubase VST. Selecting Over Quantize (or Q on the computer keyboard) hard shifts all notes to the nearest fraction of a beat, as set in the quantize box above the arrangement display. For example, if 16 is selected in the quantize box, Over Quantize shifts each note in the Part onto the nearest 1/16 division of the bar. If a quantize method with more feel is required then try Iterative Quantize (E on the computer keyboard). This shifts notes *towards* the nearest chosen beat according to a strength percentage, which can be set in Edit Quantize. Iterative Quantize tightens up Parts that were loosely played but retains the feel of the playing.

Un-quantize needed?
If necessary, the quantize can be undone at any time using 'Undo quantize' in the Functions menu or pressing U on the computer keyboard. The Part will be returned to its original state. Parts recorded using Automatic Quantize can also be returned to their unquantized state by pressing U. Remember that it is not desirable to have all the notes in all Parts occurring on exact divisions of the beat, so quantize should be used with some care. Too much quantize can result in music which is robotic and lifeless. Experienced MIDI musicians know that getting the right feel can mean the make or break of any piece of music.

Rename the new Part
Rename the Part by double clicking on it while holding alt (Mac: option) on the computer keyboard. Enter a name of your choice into the entry box.

Copy the Part
We could now immediately copy the Part. Click and hold the left mouse button on the Part while holding down alt (Mac: option) on the computer keyboard, (a small hand appears), and drag the resulting outlined Part along the same Track to let go of it next to the original (using the same manoeuvre without holding down alt would have simply moved the Part itself to the new position).

Rename the copy
If desired, change the name of the copied Part.

Create ghosts
Another method of repeating the Part is to use the Repeat function of the

INFO

A newly recorded Part always appears in black, ready for further processing.

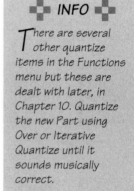

INFO

T here are several other quantize items in the Functions menu but these are dealt with later, in Chapter 10. Quantize the new Part using Over or Iterative Quantize until it sounds musically correct.

Structure menu, (ctrl + K on the computer keyboard). For example, try entering a count of 2 and tick ghost copies. Two ghost Parts appear on the Arrange display immediately after the original (see Figure 4.2 above). Ghost Parts are exact copies of one original and appear as italicised Parts on the display. Any changes to the contents of the original Part will be replicated in the ghost Parts.

Save, save, save
Once you are satisfied with the result, use save in the File menu to save the music to disk. Save as a Song file (.ALL extension) under an appropriate name. The file can now, of course, be recalled back into Cubase VST at any time using Open file.

Remember that the whole recording process as outlined above is a mere exercise and you should, of course, adapt things to suit your own needs. To help clarify the basic recording process Figure 4.4 summarises the essential steps:

Figure 4.4 The MIDI recording process

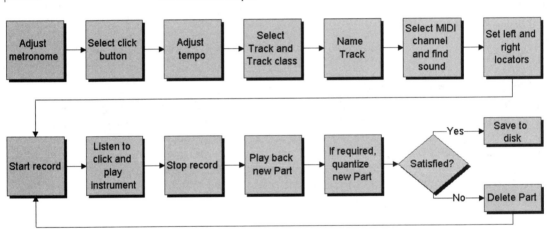

With a little practice you will quickly find your own preferred method of recording and, using the techniques outlined above, you can go on to build up a number of Tracks and Parts to make up an entire arrangement.

Saving and opening details

Cubase VST provides several ways of saving material to disk, and these should be fully understood before embarking on any serious projects. Files are handled using the options in the File menu. The type of file to be saved (or opened) can be recognised by its file extension and the following are the main possibilities available:

.ALL

This is the file extension for a Song file. This file type includes all the arrangements currently in memory, all audio file references, the audio pool, audio settings and the entire setup of Cubase VST, including most of the Menu, Dialogue Box and Editor settings and the Drum Map. This is like taking a snapshot of the current contents of the entire system. This is the recommended file format if you are working with audio.

.ARR

This is the file extension for an Arrangement. This includes the contents of the active Arrange window, the current tempo and the Mastertrack settings. An Arrangement file is all that is needed to save the current arrangement but it does not include the Audio pool. Therefore, it is *not* recommended that you use this file format if you are working with audio. However, this file type is fine if you are working with MIDI data alone. It also has the advantage of taking up less disk space.

.PRT

This is the file extension for a Parts file, containing individual Parts, several Parts or Tracks. When saving, the required Part(s) must be selected or, if no Parts are selected, all Parts in the current Track will be saved. Loading a Parts file will place its contents in the current arrangement beginning at the left locator position and onto the same Tracks as those from which it was saved.

.DRM

This is the file extension for Drum Maps (see the Drum edit section in Chapter 5).

.SET

This is the file extension for a Setup file. A setup contains all the important settings of the program other than the music itself. This is useful for loading different system configurations without affecting the music currently in memory.

.MID

This is the file extension for a MIDI file and is available by using the Import and Export MIDI file options. A MIDI file is a special file format designed to allow the transfer of music between different makes of MIDI sequencer and, sometimes, between different platforms, (depending on compatibility). MIDI Files usually come in two formats: Type 0 and Type 1.

Type 0 files always contain only one Track which plays back on many MIDI channels. Type 1 files contain the original Track structure of the material and include two or more Tracks on separate MIDI channels.

Cubase VST recognises both formats and normally saves as Type 1 unless only one Track is present, (or all but one are muted), in which case it is saved as Type 0. MIDI files imported into Cubase VST may be loaded into a new Arrange window or merged into the current arrangement at the left locator position.

✦ INFO ✦

All the moves are applicable to both MIDI and audio Parts so any skills learnt here will be useful when you come to record audio.

Part processing

Once any recording has been completed and further Tracks have been added, the role of the Arrange window starts to become more obvious. By sizing the window using the magnification sliders in the lower right corner, even the most complicated arrangement may be viewed as a single entity and the overall structure becomes easier to see. And, of course, the opportunity to restructure the music by zooming in and manipulating specific Parts is invaluable. Manipulating Parts is one of the major functions of the Arrange window. Check out the table.

Table 4.1 Part processing

Tool	Key(s) held		Mouse action	Result
	PC	Mac		
Pointer	–	–	double click between locators	creates a new Part
	–	–	click on Part	selects Part
	–	–	click/hold in white space and drag	opens rectangular selection box
	–	–	click/hold on Part(s) and drag	moves Part(s)
	alt	option	click/hold on Part(s) and drag	copies Part(s)
	ctrl	command	click/hold on Part(s) and drag	creates ghost Part(s)
	alt + ctrl	command + option	drag one Part on top of another	merges Parts
Eraser	–	–	click on Part(s)	erases Part(s)
	–	–	click/hold and drag over Parts	erases Part(s)
Scissors	–	–	click on Part	splits Part at mouse position
	alt	option	click on Part	splits Part into several smaller Parts
Magnifier	–	–	click/hold and drag over Part	plays Part's contents
Pencil	–	–	click in white space and drag	creates a new Part
	–	–	click/hold on start/end point and drag	lengthens or shortens Part
	alt	option	click/hold on end point and drag	repeats Part over distance dragged
Mute	–	–	click on Part	mutes the Part
Glue	–	–	click on Part	joins selected Part to the next Part
	alt	option	click on Part	joins Part to all following Parts

Be sure to become familiar with the manipulation of Parts using the toolbox. Try practising all the moves in the table on empty or test Parts. The ability to use the toolbox is among the most important skills in the confident handling of Cubase VST. Figure 4.5 clarifies the essentials of basic Part manipulation.

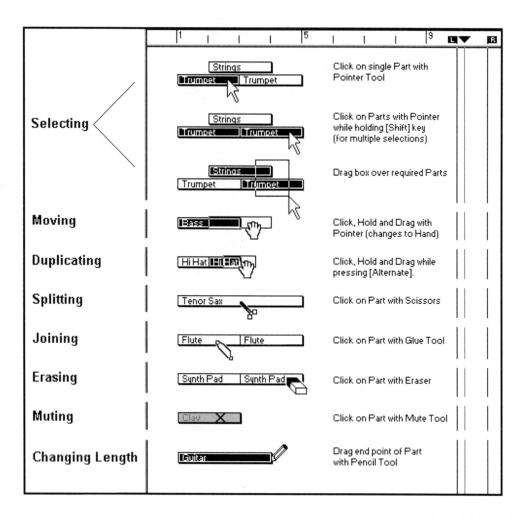

Figure 4.5 Basic Part
manipulation

Progress report

So, what have we achieved in this chapter? Well, not an awful lot musically, but then that was not the aim. Above all, this chapter has helped you become familiar with the Arrange window, which is of central importance to the successful handling of the program. It has also provided a general overview before we plunge into the more detailed aspects of the package. We have only just scratched the surface of the possibilities that are available with Cubase VST but we have armed ourselves with some of the essential tools and commands with which to go on to more musically meaningful pursuits.

In Chapter 5 we venture out from the Arrange window into the worlds of Key, List and Drum Edit.

5

Key, List and Drum edit

In Chapter 4 we explored the Arrange window and some of the main techniques associated with the recording and processing of MIDI based music. This allows you to record and manipulate MIDI data at the arrangement level. A wide variety of editing functions can be carried out on MIDI Parts while still remaining in the Arrange window but the Part's contents can never actually be looked at in detail. To look inside a Part we must go into one of the main MIDI editors. These editors are primarily designed for MIDI data but note that List edit also has the ability to display Audio events.

Key edit

Let's start with Key edit (Figure 5.1). To open the editor from the Arrange window select a MIDI Track or Part in the Arrange window and then select Edit from the Edit menu or ctrl+E (Mac: command+E) on the computer keyboard. If one or more Parts are selected then this is what will be available for editing, or if no Parts are selected then all Parts in the current Track will be available for editing. Parts from up to 31 different Tracks may be selected but most of the time you will probably edit single Parts.

Before leaving the Arrange window it is a good idea to use alt + ctrl + P (Mac: option + P) on the selected Part to set the left and right locators

Figure 5.1 Key edit

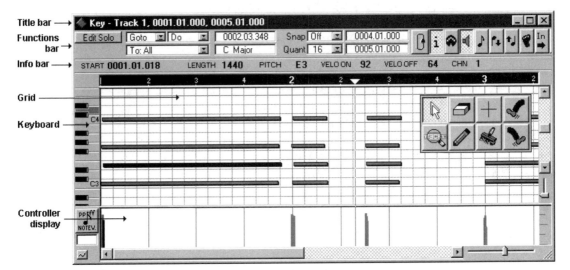

to the start and end points. Then select Cycle on the Transport bar, (the /
key on the numeric keypad). Cubase VST will now cycle continuously on
the selected Part (between the left and right locators) and, after going
into Key edit, the song position can be managed with the various numeric
keypad cue points such as 1, to go to the left locator, or 2, to go to the
right locator etc.

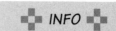

Key edit appears on the screen with a grid, where the horizontal axis
represents time and the vertical axis represents pitch displayed as a piano
keyboard. Directly above the grid there is a Position bar, showing the
numbered bars and beats, and below the grid there is the Controller display, where various non-note events, such as Pitch Bend and Modulation,
are displayed.

Key edit has a toolbox similar to the Arrange window but featuring
four new tools for specific use in the editor. The toolbox is opened by
clicking in empty space on the grid with the right mouse button (Mac:
ctrl + shift + mouse click) and it features the following :

Pointer
Similar to the Arrange window, the pointer is a general purpose tool but,
this time, for selecting, moving and copying notes and events.

Eraser
The eraser is for deleting by clicking on single events or dragging over
several while holding the left mouse button.

Line tool
The line tool is for changing values (usually Controller data), according to
a straight line drawn in the Controller display.

Kicker
The kicker tools are for jogging notes backwards or forwards by clicking
on each. Notes will be moved according to the current Snap box value.

Magnifying glass
The magnifying glass is for monitoring notes by clicking on single events
or dragging over several while holding the left mouse button.

Pencil tool
The pencil tool is for inserting notes, changing their lengths and for
changing the values of Controller events.

Brush
The brush is for pasting notes onto the grid.

Notes inserted or moved with the pointer, pencil, kicker or brush tools
will be shifted onto the nearest fraction of a beat according to the Snap
box value and the length of inserted notes will be governed by the Quant
(Quantize) box value. For insertion purposes, regard Snap as the position
and Quant as the length.

Notes are displayed as graphic strips on the grid. Once a note has been
selected, by clicking on it with the pointer tool (the note will turn black),
its characteristics can be seen on the information bar. These include the
start time, length, pitch, velocity on and off, and the channel. The info bar
can be hidden or shown using the 'i' button (info button) on the Functions

bar of the window. Similarly, the Controller display can be hidden or shown using the small icon in the bottom left of the window.

There are several other icons in the Functions bar governing the set up of a loop, the reception of MIDI data and the recording of data in step-time. In addition, there are three local menus : Goto, for moving the song position pointer to various points in the Track or Part, the Select menu, dictating which data will be targeted by any chosen functions, and a useful local Do menu containing items specific to Key edit.

A further display box beside the local menus shows the current mouse position when it is moved into the grid area. Clicking in this box with the left mouse button changes the Position display to Time code. Remember that the usual main Cubase VST menus are still available while in Key edit, so any of the normal functions, like the different kinds of quantize, repeat, cut, copy, paste etc., may be used on the chosen data. But how do we put all these very obviously powerful Key edit features to good use ? Let's look at some examples from a typical Cubase VST MIDI session.

Editing a bass line
You have just recorded a perfect bass line with a great feel but some notes are too long and some overlap. Key edit is the ideal facility to remedy the situation. Proceed as follows:

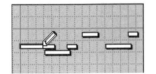

- Select the pencil tool from the pop-up toolbox.
- Click and hold near the end of each offending note and drag the length back to the desired shorter duration.
- The new length can be graphically monitored on the grid and will be set to the nearest Snap value as set in the Snap box. Setting Snap to Off allows the maximum subtlety of length change since the pencil may be dragged in ticks (the smallest units of time or resolution measured by Cubase VST).

Editing note entry times
The note entry time of the chords you just played are jumbled and misplaced. The simple answer is found in Key edit as follows:

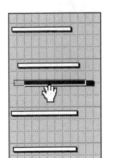

- Click and hold on the misplaced note using the pointer tool.
- The pointer changes to a hand.
- The whole note can now be dragged to a new position.

For this kind of operation the Snap value could once again be set to Off to facilitate the placing of notes with maximum subtlety on the grid. If very subtle changes in position are required try clicking on the notes with the kicker tools to shift the start time backwards or forwards one tick at a time.

Editing timing values
The repeated melody on one of your Tracks is perfect on the first and fourth bars but out of time in bars two and three. One answer is to go

into Key edit and repair the four bar Part using a select box and drag process. Proceed as follows:

- Set Key edit to an appropriate size to see all four bars.
- With the pointer tool selected, click and drag the mouse in empty space on the grid.
- A box will appear which can be sized around the appropriate group of notes in bars 2 and 3. The notes within the box will turn black when the mouse is released.
- Delete the notes using the backspace key on the computer keyboard or Delete events from the Do menu.
- Select the appropriate group of notes from the first bar which will once again turn black. Select and hold any one of the blacked notes while pressing alt (Mac: option) on the computer keyboard. A box will re-appear.
- Without releasing the mouse, drag this box, and the resulting copy of all the notes within it, to the appropriate position in the second bar. Remember that the notes will be dropped onto the nearest fraction of a beat according to the current Snap setting.
- The same procedure can then be applied to copy the repeated melody into the third bar.

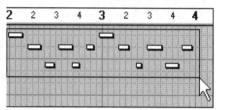
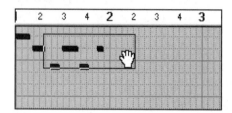

You will notice that many mouse/keyboard combinations exhibit the same behaviour in all the main windows. In other words, selecting and dragging will simply move the event(s) or Part(s) and holding down alt (Mac: option) while selecting and dragging will copy them.

Editing note velocities

The synthesiser sound you are using produces an unwanted percussive attack on certain notes which were played with a higher velocity. To correct the situation proceed as follows:

- Open Key edit and select velocity in the Controller display by clicking on the Controller icon to the left of the display.
- The velocities of all notes should now be visible in the display as vertical strips.
- The offending velocities can be singled out and adjusted using the pencil tool.

Producing crescendos

Following on from the last example, if any crescendos or decrescendos are required after the notes have been recorded then the Controller display of Key edit is one of the best places to create them.

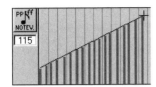

- Select velocity in the Controller display.
- Click and drag using the line tool to draw in a straight line at the desired angle.
- When the mouse is released a velocity ramp matching the straight line appears.
- This technique could be used for similar operations on other Controller data such as, for example, MIDI volume events.

To write new events into the Controller display for any chosen Controller, select the pencil tool or the line tool and click and drag in the display while holding alt (Mac: option). Events will be inserted at the resolution set in the Snap box.

General tips

That's a start in using some of the principal techniques of Key edit. As a general guide to moving around among the note data on the grid you may find the following tips useful:

Once one note has been selected, try using the left and right arrow keys to scroll through consecutive notes. This is often easier than using the mouse. In order to be able to hear each event as it is selected activate the MIDI monitor icon (loudspeaker symbol) in the top right icon panel.

Also useful is the MIDI In icon (5 pin DIN symbol), which, along with the Note and the velocity On and Off icons, allows the user to target data for updating via MIDI. For example, if the MIDI In and velocity On buttons are selected you can change the velocity On value of the currently selected note simply by playing any note on the master keyboard. Once updated, Cubase VST will automatically move on to the next note which can, in turn, be updated in the same manner.

Remember that any changes made in Key, or any other editor, need not be kept. Leaving Key edit using the escape key will return the Part back to its original state before entering the editor. A warning dialogue asks for confirmation of whether you wish to keep the edits or not. Pressing escape a second time leaves the editor without keeping the edits. To keep all edits press the return key to leave Key edit.

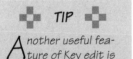

TIP

Another useful feature of Key edit is the ability to view data as it is being quantized. This provides excellent visual feedback of how the notes are actually being shifted in time.

List edit

And now let's move on to List edit. List edit (Figure 5.2) differs from the other editors in that all kinds of MIDI data and special Cubase VST events may be accessed and updated, including System Exclusive.

Open List edit using the Edit menu or select ctrl + G (Mac: command + G) on the computer keyboard. Similar to Key edit, List edit features a grid and a toolbox containing the same set of tools, but of far greater importance and far more useful are the columns hidden behind the grid which can be revealed by moving the split point to the right of the screen.

The columns contain information about each MIDI event including its start position, length, status and MIDI channel. There are also the value

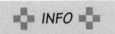

INFO

The general handling of Key, List and Drum edit are very similar and many of the important editing commands outlined above are common to all three.

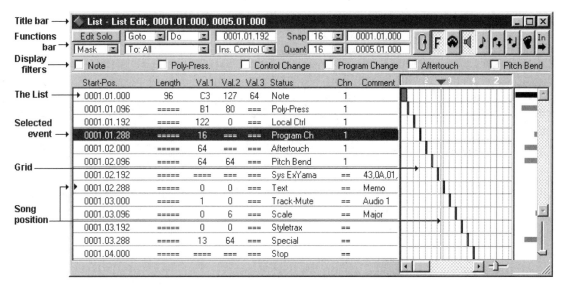

Title bar →
Functions bar →
Display filters →
The List →
Selected event →
Grid
Song position

Start-Pos.	Length	Val.1	Val.2	Val.3	Status	Chn	Comment
0001.01.000	96	C3	127	64	Note	1	
0001.01.096	=====	B1	80	===	Poly-Press	1	
0001.01.192	=====	122	0	===	Local Ctrl	1	
0001.01.288	=====	16	===	===	Program Ch	1	
0001.02.000	=====	64	===	===	Aftertouch	1	
0001.02.096	=====	64	64	===	Pitch Bend	1	
0001.02.192	=====	====	===	===	Sys ExYama	==	43,0A,01,
0001.02.288	=====	0	0	===	Text	==	Memo
0001.03.000	=====	1	0	===	Track-Mute	==	Audio 1
0001.03.096	=====	0	6	===	Scale	==	Major
0001.03.192	=====	0	0	===	Styletrax	==	
0001.03.288	=====	13	64	===	Special	==	
0001.04.000	=====	====	===	===	Stop	==	

Figure 5.2. List edit

columns, (Val 1, Val 2 and Val 3), which will be active or not active according to the event type. For example, ordinary note events will feature their pitch in the value 1 column followed by their Velocity On and Off values in the value 2 and value 3 columns but a Controller event will be active in the value 1 and value 2 columns only. Many events will have no entry in the Comment column. However, the Comment column for a System Exclusive event will contain the System Exclusive message itself.

Functions which are unique to List edit include the Mask menu, the Insert bar (Ins), and the Display filters. These are found in the Functions bar above the list.

The Mask menu may be used to force a display of all data of the same event type as the currently selected event or of all data with the same event type and the same values as the currently selected event. All other events will be hidden from view.

The Insert bar contains a pop-up menu for the selection of event types. Any chosen type of data may be inserted into the List by clicking with the pencil tool on the grid.

The Display filters are comprised of six tick boxes. These are hidden or shown using the Function bar's 'F' button and there is a box for each event type. When a box is ticked the corresponding event type is filtered out of the display.

In List edit, the events themselves may be edited by clicking and holding in the columns with the left or right mouse button on any of the changeable values of the chosen event. For example, it is a simple matter to change the Velocity value of a Note by clicking and holding in the Value 2 column of the chosen event. The right mouse button increases the value and the left mouse button decreases it. All values in the columns are changeable using the mouse buttons but it is not possible to change events from one type to another in the status column. Remember also the graphic display to the right of the grid. When the mouse pointer is moved into this area it is automatically changed to the pencil tool. The horizontal

◆ INFO ◆

The Display filters and the Mask functions are among the most useful features of List edit but they should not be confused. The Display filters hide the chosen data from view but, unlike Mask, they do not hide the data from editing. With the filters any global editing operation will still affect all events regardless of what is currently displayed. Mask, however, completely shields the hidden data from editing operations.

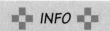
bars in the display represent the velocities of notes or the Val 2 values of most other MIDI event types. Here, events may be changed in much the same way as in the Controller display of Key edit.

As we can see, there is one essential difference between List and Key edit. Whereas Key edit is directed towards the graphic editing of note data on the grid and controller data in the Controller display, List edit is directed towards the somewhat more detailed editing of any type of MIDI event and its various values in the display list. So, as a general rule, List edit is probably most useful for the editing of non-note events, and, (particularly with the addition of the SysEx editor module), it is an essential tool for viewing and changing SysEx data. And there are, of course, those types of data which cannot be viewed and edited anywhere else, such as Track mute, text and MIDI mixer events. But let's look at some specific examples which may prove useful to a number of users:

Editing System Exclusive messages

For the editing of System Exclusive messages proceed as follows:

- Select the SysEx event, (which will appear in the list and on the grid as a single block), and click once in the Comment column.
- The message itself will then appear in a pop-up box on screen as Hexadecimal code.
- Edit the message as desired and press return to keep the data.

The SysEx editor Module allows access to longer messages. However, a good knowledge of System Exclusive is required to make any meaningful changes.

Finding unwanted Program Change messages

At some time in their lives most Cubase VST users will suffer from the problem of an unwanted or incorrect program change (or some other data such as a volume controller) embedded somewhere among the rest of the data. This is not always easy to find for deletion or editing. With the List edit filters the task is easy.

- Tick the filter boxes of all those event types you do *not* wish to see.
- The unwanted event(s) can now be found more easily among the remaining unfiltered data displayed in the list.

	Note	☑ Poly-Press.	☑ Control Change	☐ Program Change				
Start-Pos.	Length	Val.1	Val.2	Val.3	Status	2	3	4	2
0001.01.000	=====	2	===	===	Program Ch				
0002.01.000	=====	12	===	===	Program Ch				

Inserting a Local Off Controller event

Most users will have their master keyboard set to Local Off for use with
Cubase VST. One problem is that some synthesisers used as master keyboards power up with Local On. This means that the user must manually
set the keyboard to Local Off at the start of each session. However, using
List edit, a Local Off controller event may be inserted into a Part. This
could be included in the Def file which is first loaded into Cubase VST
when the program is launched. To insert the appropriate event, proceed
as follows:

❖ *INFO* ❖

*Unlike Key edit, only
one Track or
selected Parts from
one Track, may be edit-
ed in List edit at any
one time.*

- Select controller in the 'Ins' box.
- Select the pencil tool in the grid and click with the left mouse (at the beginning of the Part, for
  example). A new controller event with various default values will be inserted into the list.
- Click and hold in the value 1 column to change the controller number to 122, the Local On / Off
  controller.
- Set the controller to 0 in the value 2 column, which is the Off setting. (The On setting would
  have been 127).
- When the Part is played the target keyboard will be set to Local Off. This is assuming that the
  keyboard responds to this controller. Most modern synths do. This technique could be used for
  the input of similar controllers or any other event types.

Start-Pos.	Length	Val.1	Val.2	Val.3	Status	2	3	4	2
0001.02.000	=====	122	0	===	Local Ctrl				

Changing all settings to the same value

Sometimes it is appropriate to change all the settings in one column of
List edit to the same value.

- Hold 'alt' (Mac: option) while clicking and holding with the left or right mouse buttons on any
  value in the chosen column.
- Increase or decrease the value appropriately and when the mouse button is released, all values in
  that column (for the same event types) will change to the same setting simultaneously.

Start-Pos.	Length	Val.1	Val.2	Val.3	Status
0003.01.297	202	F#4	75	0	Note
0003.02.190	125	E4	75	0	Note
0003.03.001	274	F#4	75	0	Note
0003.03.295	241	E4	75	0	Note
0003.04.193	188	F#4	75	0	Note

Other aspects

Other aspects of List edit worth considering include the following :

- A further column may be added to List edit by clicking in the mouse position indicator bar. This changes the position display to Time code and List edit now features two columns showing the Time code start and end points for each event. In fact, the Time code end column replaces the length column. This is useful for circumstances when the precise timing of events is crucial.
- Remember that quantize works on notes alone, so other kinds of events will remain at their original positions.
- Audio mix automation events can be edited in fine detail in List edit (see Chapter 12).
- List edit can also show the Audio events from audio Tracks or Parts. The data is displayed in a similar manner to MIDI events but can only be moved or deleted. The audio cannot actually be heard while remaining in List edit. The start position for the Audio event is the only value which can be edited directly in the columns. Although providing limited audio editing options, List edit can help find Audio events which are obscured in the Audio editor since it always displays all the events.

Drum edit

And now let's move onto the third of Cubase VST's main MIDI editors, Drum edit (Figure 5.3). As the name implies, this is designed for the editing of drum or percussion data. Users should be aware, however, that it is not absolutely essential to view this kind of data in Drum edit. It could equally be viewed in any of the other editors. However, if a MIDI Track is converted into a Drum Track the data will be adapted for specific uses in Drum edit. This will become clearer as we go on.

Figure 5.3. Drum edit

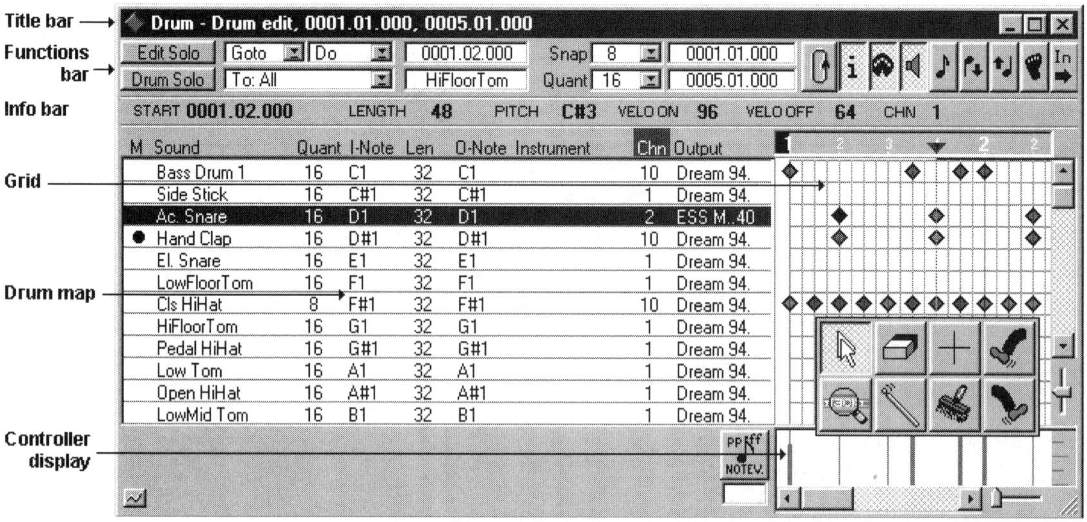

Title bar →	Drum - Drum edit, 0001.01.000, 0005.01.000						_ □ ×
Functions bar →	Edit Solo	Goto	Do	0001.02.000	Snap 8	0001.01.000	
	Drum Solo	To: All	HiFloorTom	Quant 16	0005.01.000		In →
Info bar	START **0001.02.000**	LENGTH **48**	PITCH **C#3**	VELO ON **96**	VELO OFF **64**	CHN **1**	

M	Sound	Quant	I-Note	Len	O-Note	Instrument	Chn	Output
	Bass Drum 1	16	C1	32	C1		10	Dream 94.
	Side Stick	16	C#1	32	C#1		1	Dream 94.
	Ac. Snare	16	D1	32	D1		2	ESS M..40
●	Hand Clap	16	D#1	32	D#1		10	Dream 94.
	El. Snare	16	E1	32	E1		1	Dream 94.
	LowFloorTom	16	F1	32	F1		1	Dream 94.
	Cls HiHat	8	F#1	32	F#1		10	Dream 94.
	HiFloorTom	16	G1	32	G1		1	Dream 94.
	Pedal HiHat	16	G#1	32	G#1		1	Dream 94.
	Low Tom	16	A1	32	A1		1	Dream 94.
	Open HiHat	16	A#1	32	A#1		1	Dream 94.
	LowMid Tom	16	B1	32	B1		1	Dream 94.

Grid

Drum map

Controller display

Drum edit features a grid with time on the horizontal axis and the drum or percussion instruments on the vertical axis. Pulling the split point to the right reveals a number of columns, most of which are unique to

Drum edit. If the Track to be edited is classed as a Drum Track, the columns will feature the following:

- the Mute column (M), for the muting of individual drum instruments
- the Sound column, for naming each drum sound
- the Quantize column (Quant), where each sound may have an individual Quantize value
- the Input Note column (I-Note), defining the Note value controlling each sound
- the Output Note column (O-Note), defining the target note departing from the MIDI Out of Cubase VST
- the length column (Len), defining a fixed length for each sound
- the channel column (Chn), for the selection of a MIDI channel for each sound
- the Output column, for the selection of the MIDI port for each sound
- the Instrument column, for the naming of combinations of the channel and Output columns
- the four level columns, where four preset velocity levels may be set for each sound when events are inserted using the mouse on the grid or in step time.

If the Track to be edited is a MIDI Track, the Output note (O-Note), Instrument and Output columns are omitted.

Using the grid is similar to the other editors. However, knowing how to manage the columns is probably the most important requirement for using Drum edit successfully.

Setting up the Drum Map

Before recording any drum data it is a good idea to have first set up the Drum Map. The Drum Map is simply a set of 64 drum sound names each with their corresponding values in the columns. It is not possible to have more than one Drum Map in Cubase VST at the same time. Here we will be considering the procedure for a Drum Track. This shows Drum edit in its most adaptable mode. Proceed as follows:

- Create an empty Part on a Track in the Arrange window and change the Track class to Drum Track. A small drumstick symbol appears in the class column.
- Open Drum edit by selecting it from the Edit menu, double clicking on the Part or use ctrl + D (Mac: command + D) on the computer keyboard.
- Let's update the I-Note (input note) and O-Note (output note) columns to the desired settings via MIDI, followed by entering the

appropriate names in the Sound column. Ensure that the master keyboard is playing the target drum or percussion sounds through Cubase VST. These could be, for example, the sounds of a drum machine.

- Select the MIDI In icon from the Functions bar in the top right of the window.
- Go to the first sound in the sound list by clicking on it once with the left mouse and then select the I-Note column.
- Play the first sound on the keyboard and this note value will be automatically entered into the I-Note column for the currently selected sound.
- Press the down arrow on the computer keyboard to go to the next sound.
- Enter the next note via MIDI and proceed similarly until all sounds have been entered.
- Follow exactly the same procedure for the O-Note column so that the input and output notes match. (Remember that, for more complicated Drum Maps, the input and output notes need not match at all. This is explained in more detail below).
- Double click on each sound and enter an appropriate name into the pop-up box.
- The channel column could also be changed accordingly if sounds are being targeted on more than one MIDI channel. However, for multi channel operation, 'Any' must be selected in the Track's channel column in the Arrange window.

So what is the point of having an I-Note (Input) and an O-Note (Output) column in Drum edit ? The idea is to facilitate the user's quick selection of drum and percussion sources while maintaining the kit in a standard position on the keyboard. In other words, if you are used to having the bass drum on C1 (36), but the bass drum in the target unit is on C2 (48), then you could set the I-Note column to C1 (36) and the O-Note column to C2 (48). It makes things clearer to view the I-Note column as a representation of where the sounds are being played on the keyboard and the O-Note column as a representation of where the sounds are found in the target unit.

The note positions in the O-Note column could be literally anywhere in the MIDI range and, by keeping the I-Note column notes static, we have avoided some of the complex mapping and transposition problems which are often associated with building a MIDI kit.

For example, imagine the current Drum Map is set to play a Roland TR808 drum machine but later it is decided that a replacement sound for the snare is required using a sampled sound from an Akai sampler. All that is needed is to change the appropriate snare sound O-Note column to the position of the replacement sound and the MIDI channel column to that of the sampler. Any music already programmed will be playing the new sound immediately. No more awkward re-arranging and transposition. The procedure is also excellent for quickly seeking and trying out alternative sounds for any drum or percussion set up. As time goes on users will establish a number of Drum Maps which relate specifically to the units in their set-up.

The current Drum Map is always saved as part of the song file (.ALL file), and Drum Maps can also be separately saved or loaded from the File menu using the Drum Map file type. All Drum Map files are given the file extension .DRM.

And now let's clarify the use of some of the other Drum edit features: The Length and Quant (Quantize) columns and level 1 to 4 columns apply when inserting events graphically on the grid or inputting notes in step time. Some users will have already noticed that Drum edit's toolbox differs slightly from the other editors in that the pencil tool has been replaced by a drumstick tool. Inserting involves the use of the drumstick.

The drumstick differs in that it cannot be held and dragged on the grid to adjust the length of a note as it is being inserted. Each Drum edit event's length is governed by the duration set in the Length column. However, if you click, hold and drag the drumstick horizontally along the grid, for one sound, events will be written in at the resolution set by the quantize column for that sound. This could be useful for quickly writing in some closed hi-hats at 1/16 note intervals. In addition, if clicked over an already existing event, the drumstick will delete that event.

When inserting notes with the drumstick their velocity level can be managed using the level 1 to 4 columns. Each of the level columns can be separately adjusted for each sound and the choice of level is selected by holding various keys on the computer keyboard. Holding no key when inserting an event selects level 1, holding 'shift' (Mac: command) selects level 2, holding 'ctrl' (Mac: option) selects level 3 and holding 'ctrl + shift' (Mac: command + option) selects level 4.

Like Key edit, Drum edit features an Info line, where existing events can be updated in terms of their note value, velocity and length etc.

Drum edit also has a Controller display but it differs from Key edit in that it shows the controller data for the currently selected sound only.

Also new is the Solo button which, as expected, mutes all sounds other than the currently selected one. Other mute configurations can be set up by clicking directly in the Mute column.

Smart Moves

That's it for Chapter 5. Its now up to you to experiment until the main editing moves become second nature. To this end Table 5.1 shows some principal mouse and keyboard moves which are useable in all three editors. Remember that, as well as going from the Arrange window to any editor, you can also go directly from one editor to another, which is often extremely useful for detailed work. In addition, several editors may be opened at the same time and tiled onto the screen, using the Tile or Stack options in the Windows menu.

Table 5.1 Smart Moves useable in all three editors

Tool	Key held PC	Mac	Mouse action	Result
Pointer	–	–	click on event	selects event
	–	–	click/hold on event and drag	moves event
	alt	option	click/hold on event and drag	copies event
	–	–	click/hold and drag on grid	opens rectangular selection box
	–	n/a	click/hold on value with left mouse	decreases value
	–	n/a	click/hold on value with right mouse	increases value
	shift	n/a	click/hold on value with left mouse	decreases value in tens
	shift	n/a	click/hold on value with right mouse	increases value in tens
	–	–	double click on value	opens pop-up input box
Eraser	–	–	click on event	deletes event
Line tool	–	–	click and drag in Controller display	changes values in straight lines
	alt	option	click and drag in Controller display	inserts new controller events
Magnifyer	–	–	click on note	monitors selected note
Pencil	–	–	click/hold on event and drag	changes length of event
	–	–	click on grid	inputs an event
	–	–	click on events in Controller display	changes values of events
	alt	option	click and drag in Controller display	inserts new controller events
Paintbrush	–	–	click/hold and drag	paints in events on one pitch
	alt	option	click/hold and drag	paints in events anywhere on grid
–	return	return	–	keeps edits
–	esc	esc	–	discards edits

6

Audio recording

Chapter 3 outlined the basic audio recording process. This chapter provides more detailed information about audio recording, routing and the general handling of audio data within Cubase VST.

Although this chapter is mainly concerned with the audio recording process within Cubase VST it was also considered useful to include brief information about digital audio and the larger recording process. Cubase VST does not exist in isolation from the rest of the sound recording world and it is essential to keep this in perspective when using the software to record audio material. The following section is for the benefit of those with little experience in sound recording. More experienced users may prefer to move on to the section entitled 'The audio path'.

Digital audio and the larger recording process

What is digital audio?

Audio recording in Cubase VST is of the digital variety. This means that the sounds you record are converted into a numerical representation of the signal using an analogue-to-digital converter (ADC). These numbers are stored in a data retrieval system (e.g. your hard disk), and you can hear the sounds again by converting the numbers back into the analogue domain using a digital-to-analogue converter (DAC). With a Cubase VST system these converters are found on your audio card or some other part of the audio hardware.

The quality of the audio is dependent on the general performance of the converters, the sampling rate and the bit resolution. The sampling rate is the number of times the analogue signal is measured, or 'sampled', per second. The bit resolution is a measure of the accuracy of the system. The greater the number of bits the more levels of resolution are available to measure the analogue signal. Popular bit resolutions include 8, 16, 20 and 24 bit. The standard bit resolution of Cubase VST is 16 bit. (Cubase VST24 is 24 bit).

So, Cubase VST normally functions at a sampling rate of 44.1kHz with 16 bit resolution which is the same as an audio CD. This means that, theoretically, you can achieve very high quality recordings with the system. However, there are many other factors which affect the sound quality and paramount among these is *how* you actually record things.

Some differences between analogue and digital recording

If you were recording onto an analogue multi-track tape recorder your approach to sound recording might be different to when using a digital system like Cubase VST.

For example, analogue systems are more forgiving of extreme peaks in the signal than digital systems. When recording onto analogue many sound engineers might record certain sounds with the level meters pushing up into the red on certain peaks in the signal. Although, strictly speaking, the sound is distorting, the kind of mild distortion produced is not displeasing to the ear. The extreme peaks alone are distorting and in the analogue system these will effectively be rounded off to closer to the level of the rest of the signal, bringing about a kind of natural compression effect and, some would say, adding a certain warmth to the sound.

This is not the case with digital audio. Once the level goes into the red, (above 0dB), the distortion produced is extremely unpleasant to the ear. There is also no graduated distortion response with digital systems; it sounds terrible whether you are 10dB or 0.1dB above 0dB. For this reason, when you record with Cubase VST you must ensure that no clipping occurs. At the same time, you must also ensure that you do not record the signal too low. The secret is to achieve the optimum record level without distortion (see 'Your First Audio Recording' step 9 in Chapter 3 for suggestions on how to set the record level in Cubase VST).

The nature of the digital medium tends to result in material which has been recorded at a lower average level than it might have otherwise been recorded on an analogue system. If you need to maximise the average level of a recording or control the extreme variations of a rapidly changing signal level then applying mild compression before the signal arrives in Cubase VST can help cut down the peaks a little. Alternatively, the average level of a recording can be increased after the signal has been recorded using, for example, a loudness maximiser plug-in (see Chapter 13 and the Normalisation topic in Chapter 11).

However, digital audio does have advantages. It suffers less from background noise and hiss, it has a better dynamic range than analogue, it can be conveniently stored on hard disk, it can be easily processed in the digital domain using digital signal processing techniques (as in Cubase VST's plug-ins), and exact copies of the original can be made with no loss of quality.

Regardless of the medium, all traditional sound recording begins with a sound source somewhere outside of the recording device and Cubase VST is no exception. The precise technique used to record the sound signal depends on the nature of the source, and it is the choice of technique which often governs the success or failure of a sound recording.

There are, of course, a whole multitude of sound recording techniques and there now follow two sections which provide a very brief outline of some of them.

Recording vocals and live instruments – microphone recording techniques

The first stage in making a recording of a vocalist or live instrumentalist is deciding where they are going to perform. The acoustic environment for

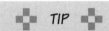

the performance plays a considerable part in giving the recorded sound its particular characteristics. In a professional recording studio this environment is often an acoustically treated performance area which is isolated from the control room and the outside world. If you are lucky enough to have a similar facility as part of your Cubase VST system then so much the better.

The second stage is deciding which microphone to use and where to place it in relation to the vocalist or instrumentalist. The inexperienced might think that you can just place a microphone anywhere in front of the source and then start recording. Unfortunately, it is not quite as simple as this, since even a change of a few centimetres in microphone position can affect the sound. It is wise, therefore, to experiment with the microphone position and, if you have several models, the microphone type. Do not be afraid to take a little time to get the right sound. This might also involve some EQ or compression using your external equipment. If you are recording vocals remember that a pop shield will reduce the 'explosives', (the 'p' and 'b' sounds which cause pops and low frequency rumbles), and can simultaneously help set the distance that the vocalist should be from the microphone.

Recording electric guitars, electric basses, synthesizers and samplers

The recording of electric guitars and basses presents a whole new set of potential problems and pitfalls to the sound recordist. Both instruments can be recorded using DI (Direct Injection) or microphone techniques or both simultaneously. You can also use a guitar or bass pre-amp which produces a convenient line level signal as output. This can be routed to the line inputs of your external mixer or directly into your audio card.

When placing microphones around a guitar speaker cabinet it is common practice to use two microphones, one placed close to the speaker and the other further back to pick up more of the room sound. A bass guitar cabinet is more likely to be recorded using a single microphone designed for lower frequencies and this signal is often mixed with a DI line signal from the bass amplifier or a DI box. One of the problems when recording these instruments is that of noise interference from the amplification equipment.

Once again, the sound from these instruments is often unpredictable as there can be significant changes in level from one note (or chord) to the next due to the instrument's resonant behaviour and changes in the player's technique and playing intensity.

Synthesizers and samplers tend to be easier to record since they are generally more predictable and, if they are controlled via the MIDI sequencer of Cubase VST, you can re-play the parts many times over until you are satisfied that you have set the optimum record level. They also have the convenience of line outputs which are easy to handle in your external mixer. However, synthesizer and sampler sounds can often seem lifeless and lacking in character when compared to 'real' acoustic instruments so care needs to be taken in how you record them. The use of effects and processing is a popular method of livening things up and some

TIP

Recording live sounds is generally more difficult than synthesizers and samplers since the sound is in a constant state of change and is likely to feature unpredictable peaks and lows in the amplitude of the signal. The level of difficulty is likely to be increased when you are using more than one microphone, as in the case of recording a drum kit.

INFO

See the 'Ten golden rules for recording and mixing' in Chapter 12 for more audio recording tips.

sound recordists will go as far as adding noise to the signal in order to give it more character.

The bottom line

The bottom line is to get the best possible sounding signal recorded into Cubase VST. This starts at source.

For example, is the vocalist singing in tune? Is the guitar in tune with the synthesizer you recorded on a previous session? Is everybody playing in time? Are you achieving the sound quality you require? etc. It is important to capture a good performance and to get the right sound at the time of recording; it is never advisable to expect to be able to 'fix it in the mix'. You should attempt to get the optimum signal level recorded whilst also avoiding distortion. Do not be afraid to take your time getting things right in the early stages of the recording process and do not hesitate to experiment with microphone placement before resorting to correcting the sound with EQ. Remember that EQ can also be used to filter out any hiss or other interference which does not form part of the required signal. Note that the use of EQ in this context would normally be that found on your external console and note also that many experienced sound engineers prefer to use no EQ or processing at the time of recording. Last but not least, use your ears and monitor your sounds through high quality loudspeakers.

The above topics have provided you with a very brief taste of what is involved in the larger recording process outside of the direct domain of Cubase VST. As you have probably realised, specific sound engineering skills are required if you intend to do a lot of audio recording using microphones. Microphone choice and placement is a big subject and it is beyond the scope of this book to cover it in detail.

The audio path

Part of understanding the manner in which a traditional recording studio functions involves knowledge of all the inputs and outputs of the mixing console and where the audio signals are going to and where they are coming from (otherwise known as routing). Things are similar with Cubase VST. Knowledge of how the signal path travels from the source into your audio card, through Cubase VST, and finally back out again can help you understand the audio recording process in more detail. This seems like common sense but it is surprisingly easy to get confused when there are a large number of inputs and outputs in an audio system.

The input path

Firstly, let's consider the input path. Figure 6.1 shows an example of the input path using a system with a standard stereo input audio card.

The signal is traced from its arrival at the physical inputs of the audio card through to its destination as a recording on one of Cubase VST's audio Tracks. Note that, in this example, it is the left input only which is being recorded. Although this is simple enough when presented in this

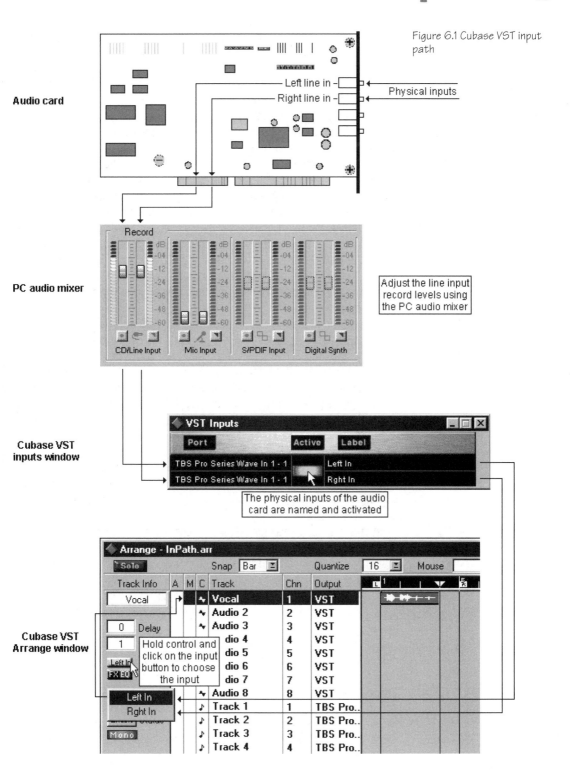

Figure 6.1 Cubase VST input path

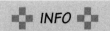 **INFO**

The details of how to monitor an input signal and set its level are described in the audio recording tutorial in Chapter 3 and in the Key Steps and Troubleshooting sections below.

graphical form it is perhaps not quite as easy when you are using the program. Looking at the signal path graphically allows you to stand back from the program and think about what is actually taking place.

In this example, the signal is connected to the line inputs of the audio card. It is first converted into digital form via the analogue-to-digital converters of the card. It then passes through the audio mixer associated with the card where the input level can be adjusted. (Note that the input level is not adjustable within Cubase VST.)

Next, the signal passes via the VST Inputs stage where the input ports are activated. Here, the inputs can also be renamed in the label column and, although this is not essential, it is strongly recommended since it can help clarify the source of the audio signal in other parts of the program. For example, the input source can be selected by holding ctrl (Mac: command) on the computer keyboard and clicking the input button found just above the FX/EQ buttons in the Inspector. This opens a pop-up menu containing the available inputs. If these inputs have been labelled with a suitably descriptive name then this will help clarify your choice in the routine recording process.

Finally, the signal arrives at the chosen Track for recording, which in this case is audio Track 1. Once recorded, the signal begins its journey back through the system to the outside world or, of course, if you are monitoring the input signal while recording then the input and output processes are performed simultaneously. It is also often the case that you are monitoring one or more audio Tracks while recording a new one, (normally referred to as overdubbing).

The output path

This leads us to the other half of the process; the output path. Figure 6.2 shows the output path for eight audio Tracks which are directed out through four outputs of a multiple I/O card (e.g.Event Gina, Midiman, Dman 2044 etc.).

In this example, the eight audio Tracks are assigned to eight consecutive audio channels in the channel column of the Arrange window. Note that it is the channel numbers which control where the audio signal is directed and *not* the Track numbers. It is perfectly possible to send Track 1 (or any other audio Track), to any audio channel. The audio signal then appears on its corresponding mixer channel strip in Cubase VST's monitor mixer.

For many applications, and in order to be less confusing, it may help to maintain the same Track and audio channel numbers in the Arrange window. Cubase VST cannot play several Tracks on the same audio channel at the same moment in time so we are not really wasting any resources by doing this. In addition, it helps clarify the process of mixing a song when each fader is dedicated to a specific Track or sound. A corresponding name could also be inserted into the name box at the bottom of each fader, which certainly helps in the mixing process.

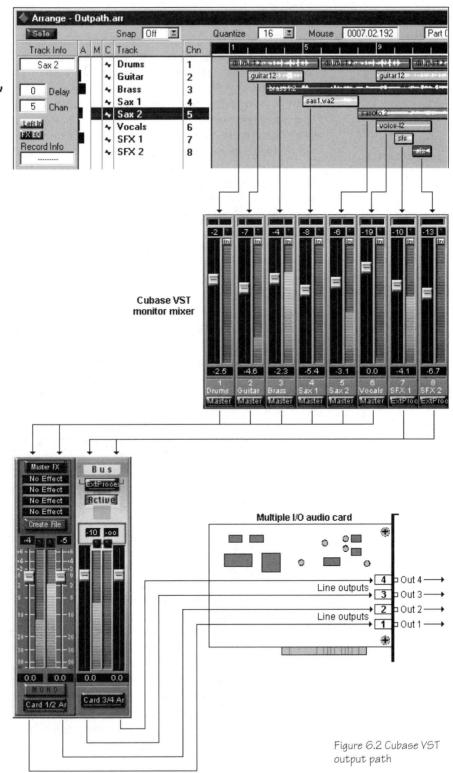

**Cubase VST
Arrange window**

**Cubase VST
monitor mixer**

**Cubase VST
master window**

Figure 6.2 Cubase VST
output path

However, if the number of audio channels in your system is limited, then it may be convenient to assign any number of Tracks to the same audio channel, but you must not forget that only one Track can be played back at any one time. This way of working, therefore, would require careful arrangement of the audio material (see Tracks, channels and Track priority, below).

After the monitor mixer stage the various audio signals are combined and directed to the Master mixer or additional bus(es). The signal is heard on the left or the right of the stereo image according to each channel's pan control setting. In Figure 6.2, the first six channels are assigned to the main master faders, (lower buttons assigned to 'Master'), and channels 7 and 8 are assigned to an additional bus (lower buttons assigned to 'ExtProcess'). In this case, the single additional bus is for outputs 3 and 4 on the multiple I/O card and this has been named as the external processing bus – this is just one possible example when you might wish to send out one or more channels separately from the rest of the mix. Note, however, that you cannot add a bus if you do not have the actual physical hardware installed in your system.

Extra buses for multiple I/O cards can be created in the ASIO multimedia setup panel by clicking on the appropriate box to the left of the device name in the output port list. A bus is present when there is a cross in the box. Cubase VST's Master fader bus is always present and active but, in order to use any additional bus(es), they must first be activated using their active button, found near the top of the fader strip.

Of course, if you are using a multiple output card of eight channels or more (e.g. the Event Gina or Korg 1212), then you have the possibility of a greater number of output buses than the setup shown in Figure 6.2. These could be directed to, for example, a multitrack recorder such as an Alesis ADAT or a Tascam DA88. In addition, the VST effects sends (or the output from a VST effect) can be routed separately to any of the buses. This means that the mixing facilities of Cubase VST can emulate the capabilities of a real multi-bus mixing console.

Once the signal arrives at the master bus it is then assigned to the actual physical outputs (output ports) according to the assignment buttons located below the faders. It is not possible to assign more than one bus to each output port. Names for the output ports can be chosen in the ASIO Multimedia setup panel output port list by clicking on the existing name and entering a new one into the pop-up box.

Finally, after being converted back into the analogue domain via the digital-to-analogue converters of the card, the composite audio signal arrives back in the real world where it can be amplified and monitored as required.

Viewing the audio system of Cubase VST in terms of the signal path as it passes through the program helps clarify the processes of routing and recording audio. The rest of this chapter is dedicated to solving some of the problems you may be having with routing and handling audio, and to outlining some of the key audio concepts of Cubase VST.

Key steps for routing an input signal onto an audio Track

This chapter assumes that you are already familiar with MIDI recording and that you have already attempted to make an audio recording using the tutorial in Chapter 3. This should have helped you understand the essentials but the audio recording process sometimes remains difficult to grasp. Among the most important elements and also among the most problematic is the input part of the process. For those readers who may still be having problems with audio recording, the following points outline the key steps to route an input signal onto an audio Track:

- Connect the audio signal to the appropriate physical input of the audio card.
- Activate the inputs of the audio card in the VST inputs window.
- Choose an audio Track and select the input in the Inspector by holding ctrl (Mac: command) and clicking on the input button. Choose the appropriate input in the pop-up menu.
- Open the monitor mixer and click on the input button at the top of the fader strip to activate monitoring for the audio channel of the chosen Track. This becomes illuminated if you have selected Record Enable or Tape Type monitoring in the Audio System Setup window. Ignore this step if you are monitoring via the card and have activated Global disable in the monitoring section of the Audio System Setup window.
- Make sure that the In button above the level meter is illuminated. In this mode, the meter shows the level of any input signal.
- Adjust the input level using either the output gain of the audio source, the input fader level in the the card's audio mixer or the input gain control of the ASIO device control panel (if available).
- Record the audio in the normal manner while in the Arrange window, using the record button on the Transport bar.

Troubleshooting the recording process

If you have not yet managed to get an input signal showing on one of the monitor mixer channel meters, then the following troubleshooting list may help solve the problem:

- Check that the input signal itself is not faulty and that the source is switched on/active. Check cables for faulty connections.
- Check that there is not an impedance mismatch between the source audio signal and the input you have chosen on your audio card.
- Check that the audio card has been correctly installed and is operational outside of Cubase VST. Test the card for audio

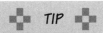

TIP

Normally, the default setting for a stereo audio card is for all odd numbered audio channels to be connected to the left input and all even numbered audio channels to be connected to the right input. The default settings should, of course, be modified according to how and what you are recording.

recording and playback using an accessory like sound recorder or media player.
- Check that the audio card is activated in the input and output port lists of the ASIO Multimedia Setup panel.
- It is possible to become confused about the left and right inputs of the card. Make sure that the inputs are clearly labelled in the VST inputs window and that the correct input has been selected on the chosen audio Track.
- Check that the inputs for the audio card are active in the VST inputs window. The green button should be illuminated.
- To see the signal on the level meter of the chosen monitor mixer channel make sure that the In button is activated (illuminated).

Monitoring in Cubase VST

The above troubleshooting steps should solve the majority of problems with the setting up of the input stage of Cubase VST. However, you may also be encountering difficulties and confusion due to the manner in which you are monitoring the input signal. There are three essential audio monitoring techniques, as follows:

1 Via an external mixer
If you have an external mixing console as part of your Cubase VST system then you may wish to monitor the signal directly from there. Most consoles have the facilities to do this.

2 Via the audio card
Audio cards usually function with a mixer application which allows the connection of the audio input to the output (audio through). If you intend to use this option then you should select Global Disable in the Monitoring section of the Audio System Setup window.

3 Via Cubase VST
It is possible to monitor the audio after it has passed through the input and output stages of Cubase VST. If you intend to use this option you should disable direct monitoring via the card and activate Record Enable or Tape Type monitoring in the Audio System Setup window.

The choice is yours but there are various advantages/disadvantages to each method. Option 1 requires a mixing console capable of routing a signal to the input of the audio card while simultaneously monitoring the signal. Both options 1 and 2 have the disadvantage of not allowing the monitoring of the record signal via VST as it is being recorded.

Latency

Option 3, although allowing the monitoring of the signal via VST as it is being recorded, suffers from an inevitable delay (latency) when using the standard ASIO multimedia driver (500 – 750ms, depending on the card). If you are using a special ASIO driver, the latency can be reduced to a more manageable level (around 40 – 70ms).

At the time of writing, the most convenient monitoring method for most Cubase VST users tends to be via the audio card. This avoids the latency issue and any timing problems when track laying and overdubbing.

Recording strategies

Hopefully, by this stage you will have understood the essential steps in recording an audio signal into Cubase VST. However, it is worth remembering that most of the settings you have made to route the signal through to the chosen channel do not have to be reset every time you record a new Track.

In the routine recording process, it is often sufficient simply to select an audio Track and press the record button. This will get your Track recorded but it is also useful to have visual feedback of what is taking place. To achieve this it may be necessary to have several windows open simultaneously on the same screen.

You need to be aware of the input you have selected for the chosen Track and this can be verified by looking in the Inspector. Hold down the control key and click on the Input select button if you need to change the input. The Inspector is best kept open during recording. If you wish to also visually monitor the level of the input signal, open the Monitor mixer window and click on the In button of the channel fader of the chosen Track. While recording, the Monitor mixer is also best left open and can be positioned on the screen next to the Arrange window. Note that you do not need to see the whole of the Monitor mixer window in order to monitor the recording of each Track; four visible channel faders is often sufficient.

Most users work out their own strategy and screen layout for dealing with the recording process, and much will depend on the actual hardware being used. Typical on-screen requirements might include the Arrange window, the Inspector, the Monitor mixer window and the Transport bar as shown in Figure 6.3. You may also occasionally need your card's audio mixer and this could be kept on stand-by in a minimised state.

Figure 6.3 Recording and monitoring the audio input signal in Cubase

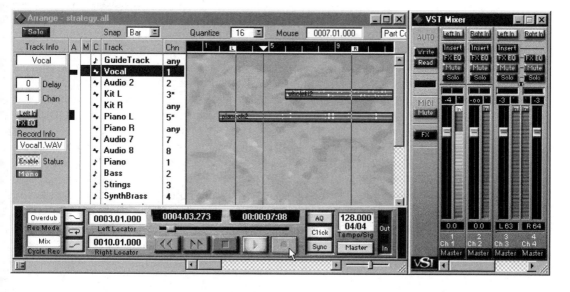

More about handling audio

Manipulating and arranging audio Parts in the Arrange window is much the same as with MIDI Parts. The MIDI Part processing techniques and use of the toolbox, outlined in Chapter 4, produce very similar results here. However, there are some aspects to the manner in which Cubase VST handles audio data which are fundamentally different.

Tracks, channels and Track priority

Two important concepts to understand when recording audio with Cubase VST are the difference between channels and Tracks and the idea of Track priority. In Cubase VST, there can be any number of audio Tracks but only a finite number of channels (up to 64, depending on available processing power and program version). Tracks can be assigned to any channel but an audio channel can only play back one mono audio recording at any one time. This does not prohibit the assignment of several Tracks to the same audio channel, but only the last played Track will be heard. In other words, the data from different audio Tracks cannot be merged together and then simultaneously routed through the same channel.

This has practical consequences when arranging the audio material in the Arrange window. Figure 6.4 shows an example of how the last played Parts in an arrangement take priority. The white areas show the sections which cannot be heard. Each time a new Part comes in on the same audio channel it takes precedence over the previous Part.

Figure 6.4 Audio playback priority in the Arrange window

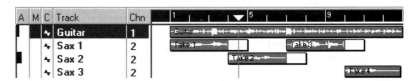

Dropping in

Playback priority also influences the behaviour of Cubase VST if you are recording over existing audio material on a single Track. This would often be achieved by dropping into record during playback. Remember that the Record mode selector (overdub or replace), on the Transport bar has no influence on the recording of audio and a new audio recording never overwrites the existing material. Upon dropping in, the new recording creates a new audio file and segment. The new segment takes precedence over the previously recorded material when the audio is played back, as explained above.

On a practical level, note that the best technique for manually dropping in and out of record over existing material is to start playback and click once on the record button when the drop-in point is reached. To drop back out of record, click on the record button a second time (Cubase VST drops out of record and continues in play mode), or simply click on the stop button to stop the sequencer. If you are not satisfied with the take, use ctrl + Z (Mac: command + Z) to undo and then try again.

If you propose to do a large number of drop-ins it is easier to keep track of the takes by recording in the Audio editor and separating each take onto different virtual lanes. At the time of writing, recordings made in the Audio editor do not appear in separate virtual lanes automatically, (except for cycle mode recording). In fact, recordings made on audio channel 1 always appear in the top virtual lane, those made on audio channel 2 always appear in the second virtual lane, those made on audio channel 3 always appear in the third virtual lane and so on.

Stereo recording

It is, of course, possible to record a stereo signal using Cubase VST but the process is governed by various rules.

Stereo recording is implemented in the Inspector using the mono/stereo button. When this button is illuminated it is possible to switch between mono and stereo. Only odd numbered audio channels can be selected for stereo recording. When stereo has been selected the left side of the signal is assigned to the odd numbered channel and the right side of the signal is assigned to the adjacent even numbered channel. For example, switching a Track on channel 3 to stereo assigns channels 3 and 4 as a stereo pair. This is reflected in the Inspector's channel parameter which now reads '3+4', and in the channel column which now displays a star next to the odd numbered channel and replaces the even numbered channel with the word 'Any' (as in Figure 6.5). Note that a stereo recording appears as a single Part (containing a stereo waveform) on the odd numbered channel.

Track Info	A	M	C	Track	Chn
Left				↝ Left	3*
0 Delay				↝ Right	any
3+4 Chan				↝ Audio 3	5
Left In / FX EQ				↝ Audio 4	6
Record Info / stereo.WAV				↝ Audio 5	7
Enable Status				↝ Audio 6	8
Stereo				♪ Piano	1

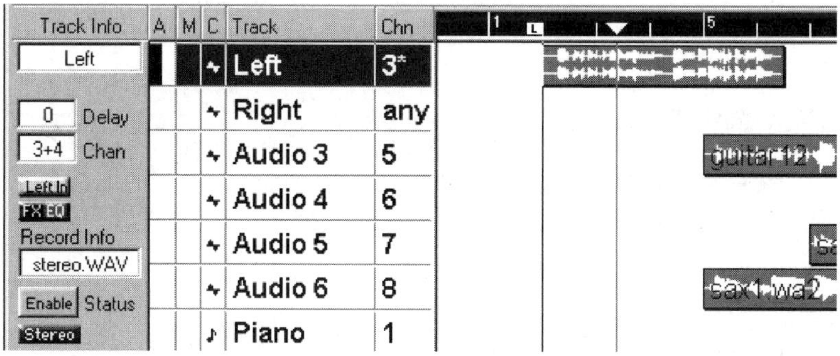

Figure 6.5 Stereo recording

If either one of the proposed stereo pair of channels already contains a mono recording then the pair cannot be selected for stereo. And, similarly, if a stereo pair of channels contains a stereo recording neither one of the channels can later be selected for mono recording.

Note also that a stereo pair will be latched together on the appropriate pair of channel faders in the Monitor mixer window and that adjusting either of the faders will move both. In addition, all EQ settings, effects sends, effects pre/post switches, mute and solo switches and monitoring on/off switches operate in stereo. Remember that after making a stereo recording it is invariably necessary to pan the left channel to the extreme left and the right channel to the extreme right using the pan controls in the Monitor mixer (the handle in the strip below the solo button).

Deleting audio

Deleting audio Parts in the Arrange window is not exactly the same as for MIDI Parts. There are two essential techniques for deleting audio:

- Select the Part and press backspace or click on the Part with the eraser tool. This deletes the Part but it does *not* delete the actual audio file or the segment, just the reference to it in the Arrange window.
- Hold ctrl and press backspace (Mac: command + backspace). The selected Part and the audio file associated with it are permanently deleted. A warning dialogue asks for confirmation since this kind of deletion is irreversible.

Audio files, segments and audio events

Audio files, segments and audio events are items within Cubase VST which need to be understood in order to appreciate exactly how Cubase VST handles audio data. The three things are inextricably linked in any audio editing or playback.

Audio files are created every time you record on an audio Track. Normally, these are rather large files which are written to the hard disk during the actual recording operation. However, when you play back the audio, Cubase VST is not designed to simply replay the audio file from beginning to end. Instead, the program is able to play any chosen part of the file for any chosen length of time. The manner in which this is performed depends on the concepts of audio events and segments.

The main properties of an audio event are:

- it contains a reference to a segment
- it has a start point relative to the Part in which it resides
- it has a Q point

The main properties of a segment are:

- it contains a reference to the actual audio file on the hard disk.
- it has start and end pointers to determine which part of the audio file is to be played.
- it has a name.
- it has volume and pan curves.

Much of this will become clearer in the next chapter which describes the Audio editor but, for now, it is helpful to think of an Audio Part as a box containing one or more Audio events (in much the same way as a MIDI Part is a box containing one or more MIDI events). Each Audio event can also be viewed as a box but, this time, containing a segment.

Audio events can be looked at and manipulated in the Audio editor and all changes performed there are non-destructive, i.e. the audio file on the hard disk is not changed in any way, only the references to the Audio file are changed. A simple example might be the changing of the start point of a sound. Here, it is simply the start reference of the Audio event which is dragged to a new position. The audio file on disk remains the same but playback begins from a new position.

The concepts of Audio events and segments will become clearer as you read through Chapters 7, 8 and 9.

7

The Audio editor

Similar to the editors for MIDI data, the Audio editor offers a way of looking at the audio data in more detail than is possible in the Arrange window. As was mentioned in the previous Chapter, audio Parts contain what are referred to as Audio events, comparable to MIDI events, and it is these elements which are available for editing. Manipulations of data in the Audio editor most often involves splicing, trimming and moving events and these kinds of actions are non-destructive. This means that the changes do not permanently alter the actual audio data on the hard disk.

The Audio editor window

The Audio editor is opened by double clicking on an audio Part or pressing ctrl + E (Mac: command + E) on the computer keyboard while an audio Part is selected.

Much of the time you will probably select single Parts for editing but it is also possible to select several Parts on different audio channels and edit these simultaneously.

Figure 7.1 The Audio editor

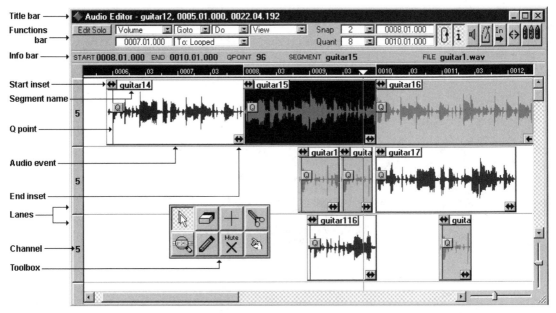

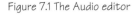

The editor features what are known as 'lanes' on the vertical axis and time on the horizontal axis. Each lane is labelled at the left of the window with the audio channel of the Part which is being edited. When editing audio which is on a single channel, all lanes will be labelled with the same channel number. Different Parts or takes on the same channel will appear on different lanes. When editing several audio Parts on different channels each lane will be labelled with different channel numbers. Lanes are particularly useful for manipulating multiple takes on the same audio channel, as occurs during cycled recording (see Audio recording in cycle mode, below).

The editor features a Functions bar at the top of the window which contains options specific to the needs of audio editing. There is also an optional Info bar displaying the details of the currently selected event, and the familiar scroll bars and zoom controls at the lower and right hand edges of the window. Audio events are shown as waveforms inside boxes. Each Audio event plays a segment, specifies a Q-point and shows where the segment should start. The segment determines the length of the Audio event and what part of the audio file should be played. The segment features a name, start and end insets and (if applicable), volume, pan and match point information.

Although it is largely the segment which controls exactly what is played, it is the Audio event which is the main point of contact when editing data in the Audio editor. This will become clearer as we go on.

Manipulating Audio events in the Audio editor is similar to manipulating MIDI events in the MIDI editors. However, the toolbox has a slightly different mix of tools and there are various editing techniques which are unique to the Audio editor.

Q-points

Each Audio event has a Q-point, marked by a 'Q' handle attached to a vertical line, which can be dragged to any point within the event. Once set at the desired position the Q-point is used by the Snap value to position the event whenever it is moved or quantized. When dragging the Q-point itself the Snap value is normally ignored, but if you press alt (Mac: command) on the computer keyboard while dragging then the Q-point snaps to the current Snap value.

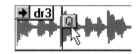

The Q-point allows you to find a musically significant moment within the event, such as the first downbeat in the bar or the precise hit point of a bass drum. This helps line up the audio material to existing MIDI Parts or to other audio material. The precise position of the Q-point can be seen on the info bar, given in ticks counting from the start inset. This variable can be edited directly by clicking on it with the left and right mouse buttons, enabling the editing of the Q-point position in fine detail.

Start and end insets

Each Audio event shows the start and end insets which specify the segment start and end points in the audio file. The start inset is found in the upper left corner and the end inset in the lower right corner. The insets can be moved in either direction to specify a new segment of the audio file. The Audio event box is like a window through which we can see the waveform of the audio file on disk. Moving either of the insets changes the size (width) of this window and reveals or obscures more or less of the audio file's contents. The audio file always remains intact regardless of the inset positions and any section which is obscured can later be revealed again simply by re-adjusting the inset positions.

The main function of the insets is to trim the Audio events to specific sections of the audio file. This might be as simple as trimming some unwanted noise off the start of a vocal take or isolating a snare drum for use in other parts of the arrangement. Whatever you need to achieve, there are a number of parameters related to the handling of the start and end insets which should be understood before getting into any serious audio editing.

If Snap to zero is enabled (ticked) in the Audio menu the positions of all changes to the insets will snap to the closest zero crossing point in the waveform. Zero crossing points are where there are the least amounts of energy in the waveform and editing here reduces the occurrence of audible clicks and makes for a good join when one Audio event is butted against another.

Any changes made to the insets do not snap to the current Snap value. In the Audio editor, the smallest shift in time possible for an inset position is one tick. There are 384 ticks per quarter note. If more precise edits are needed, the inset position can also be edited in fine detail by clicking the left and right mouse buttons on the start and end values on the info bar. If still more precise adjustments are required, sample accurate editing of the segment is possible in the Audio pool or the Wave editor.

There are four types of inset handles which give an indication of where the segment is located in the audio file. These are:

- A right facing arrow at the beginning of an Audio event means that audio playback commences from the very beginning of the audio file.

- A double arrow at the beginning of an Audio event means that audio playback commences at some point after the beginning of the audio file. This indicates that the start inset has already been adjusted or is the result of splitting an event.

- A left facing arrow at the end of an Audio event means that audio playback continues right up to the end of the audio file.

- A double arrow at the end of an Audio event means that audio playback stops at some point before the end of the audio file. This indicates that the end inset has already been adjusted or is the result of splitting an event.

Moving Audio events

Audio events can be dragged to new positions in the Audio editor in the same way that MIDI events can be dragged to new positions in the MIDI editors. You can select one or several events and, when released, the new position is snapped to the current Snap value using the Q-point. As you drag the event(s), the new position of the Q-point for the (first selected) event is shown in the mouse box.

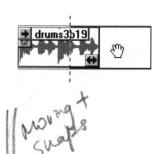

To move an Audio event in small steps try using the pointing hand tool found in the toolbox. When clicked on the first half of an event it is shifted forward according to the current resolution in the Snap box, and when clicked in the second half it is shifted back. Setting the Snap value to *off* allows the moving of events one tick at a time.

When dealing with multiple Audio events on the same channel whose start or end points overlap it is often desirable to view the data on separate lanes. Audio events can be dragged onto different lanes as needed. Pressing shift while dragging locks the horizontal or vertical position of the event according to the direction in which it is first dragged. When the Audio events in the Audio editor are found on different channels, dragging from one lane to another assigns a new audio channel to the event.

Duplicating

Duplication of Audio events is much the same as with moving except that you need to press alt (Mac: option) on the computer keyboard while dragging the event. To make a ghost copy of the event press ctrl (Mac: command) on the computer keyboard while dragging the event. Ghost copies are advantageous in certain circumstances since editing the audio in one of the ghosts will affect all the others simultaneously.

Repeating

Audio events can be repeated in a similar manner to MIDI events. Select the event(s) required for repetition and use the Repeat command in the Do menu. The chosen event(s) will be repeated up to the end of the Part.

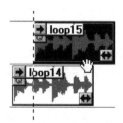

Deleting

The deletion of Audio events is similar to the deletion of audio Parts in the Arrange window. You can simply use the eraser tool or you can select the event(s) you wish to delete and press the backspace key on the computer keyboard. Alternatively, press ctrl + backspace (Mac: command + backspace) to delete the audio permanently. In this case, the audio file associated with the event is permanently deleted from the hard disk. Ctrl + backspace should therefore be used with caution!

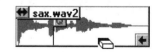

Another method of deleting Audio events is using the Keep function in the Do menu. To use Keep, select all those events in the editor that you wish to keep. Selecting Keep deletes all those Audio events in the editor which are not currently selected.

Quantizing

MORE

For more detailed information on the concept of quantizing see Chapter 10

Once a musically meaningful position has been found for an Audio event's Q-point it can be quantized in the same manner as with MIDI data. However, only Over quantize and Groove quantize in the Functions menu are available for quantizing Audio events. Quantize can be useful when, for example, a drum or percussion Part has been split into its constituent events. If the material was loosely played then using quantize could help tighten the feel.

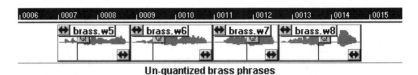

Un-quantized brass phrases

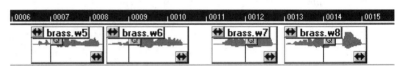

Quantized with quantize value set to 1 (all Q-points line up to bar lines)

Splitting

Audio events can be split using the scissors tool. An event is split at the current mouse position, the resolution of which is set by the Snap setting. More accuracy can be achieved by increasing the horizontal magnification. If Snap to zero (Audio menu) is enabled (ticked), the split occurs at the nearest zero crossing to the chosen split point.

MORE

See below for more details on M-points

Events can also be split using Snip at Song position, Snip at loop and Snip at M-points in the Do menu. Snip at Song position splits all events in the editor at the single point indicated by the song position. Snip at loop splits all events at the start and end loop positions. Snip at M-points conducts a multiple split of a single selected event at the position of each M-point.

Muting

Audio events can be muted using the mute tool. Muted events are displayed in grey. If, after working in the Audio editor, you decide that you would like to delete all the currently muted events then use Erase muted in the Do menu.

Looping

Loops can be set up in the Audio editor by dragging the pointer from left to right in the position bar. This simultaneously activates the loop button on the Functions bar and displays the start and end points of the loop in the loop position display. The loop start and end snaps to the current

Snap value. To de-activate the loop drag from right to left in the position bar or de-activate the loop button.

Matching tempo and audio using loops

Loops are particularly useful for manipulating the tempo of short rhythmic sections of audio material. Take, for example, a drum or percussion audio pattern which you need to fit to the current tempo or vice versa. Open the Audio editor and proceed as follows:

- De-activate Cubase VST's click to avoid confusion.
- Using the loop feature in the Audio editor find an accurate one bar section in the chosen Audio event. Try switching the Snap value to Off as you may need to make fine adjustments. Also try using the left and right mouse buttons to edit the loop start and end points directly in the loop display. At this stage ignore the meter position.

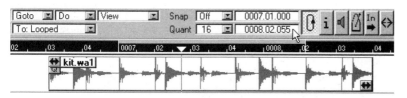

Find a 1 bar section of audio

- Once an accurate loop has been established select Snip loop in the Do menu. This cuts the event at the start and end points of the loop and creates a new event.

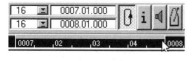

Snip at loop points

- Now, ignoring the length of the new Audio event, select an exact one bar loop in the position bar (meter position).

Select a 1-bar loop in the meter position display

- Select the new Audio event and click on Fit Event to Loop Range in the Do menu.

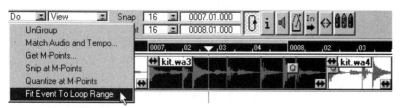

Fit event to loop range

• A dialogue appears with options to fit the audio to the loop by adjusting the tempo or by adjusting the audio. Choosing tempo finds a new bpm for Cubase VST so that the Audio event, as it is, will fit exactly within one bar. Choosing audio stretches or shrinks the audio itself so that it fits exactly into one bar at the current tempo. Changes to the audio file can be reversed for as long as you remain in the Audio editor. Once you leave the editor the changes become permanent.

Choose option in Fit audio to loop dialogue

• Make your choice of tempo or audio adjustment.
• Once processing is complete, re-activate Cubase VST's metronome click and verify that the audio is now synchronised with the tempo.

The audio event now fits into 1 bar at the current tempo

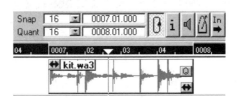

More sophisticated processing of tempo and audio is possible using M-points and the Match Audio/Tempo editor, outlined in the next section.

Creating a tempo map

The creation of a tempo map to match the timing subtleties of a real performance is a common requirement in the use of a MIDI+audio sequencer. Imagine recording a real piano as an audio Part in Cubase VST where the feel is among the most important elements in the performance. It would be pointless to try to straight-jacket this in a steady tempo but extremely useful to be able to adapt the tempo to the performance. This can be achieved using M-points and the Match Audio/Tempo editor. Proceed as follows:

• Select the audio Part in the Arrange window. For this exercise, let's use a test Part of 4 bars.
• Double click on the Part to open the Audio editor.
• Ignoring the meter position, trim the start of the Audio event to the first downbeat of the first bar in the audio material. Set the Q-point to the very beginning and move the event so that it coincides with the first beat of the bar (meter position) of the Part being edited. Set the tempo as near as possible to the starting tempo of the audio. Open the Mastertrack List editor and enter this tempo. Exit and then enable the Mastertrack by clicking on the Master button or pressing 'M' on the computer keyboard.

Trim the audio to start on the first beat

- Enable Dynamic events in the View menu and select M-points in the dynamic events choice menu (to the left of the Goto menu). With Dynamic events enabled, the Audio event display box changes into two horizontal sections, one containing the waveform and the other the dynamic events.

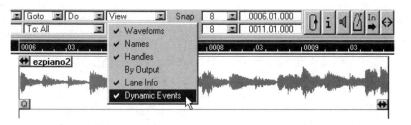

Enable dynamic events

- Select the Audio event and then select Get M-points in the Do menu. In the Get M-points dialogue try the default settings first (sensitivity 33%, attack 24%). You may need to change the sensitivity depending on the kind of audio material being processed. Higher sensitivities produce more M-points. Click the process button. Get M-points picks out the main rhythmic hits in the material.

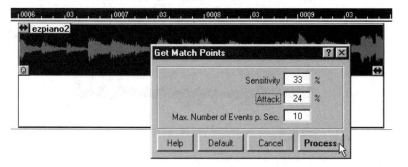

Get match points

- After processing the dynamic event display is filled with M-points at significant moments within the Audio event. For the purposes of this exercise we are going to delete all M-points except those on each beat of the audio material.

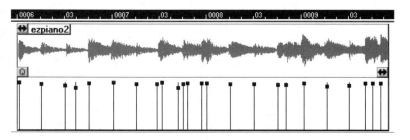

M-points after processing

- To erase the unwanted data use the eraser tool and click on the square shaped velocity indicator of each M-point. You should be left with 16 M-points, one on each beat of the 4 bars of audio.

Erase unwanted M-points

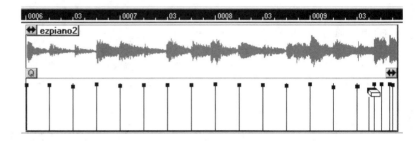

- Keep the edits made so far and return to the Arrange window. Set the left and right locators to the start and end points of the Part if you have not already done so.
- With the Part selected open the Audio editor again. Select the Audio event (the event box turns black) and then select Match Audio and Tempo in the Do menu. This opens the Graphic Mastertrack in a special mode, known as the Match Audio/Tempo editor. Here you can see the audio waveform and the M-points in the lower part of the window.

Select Match Audio to Tempo to open the Match Audio/Tempo editor

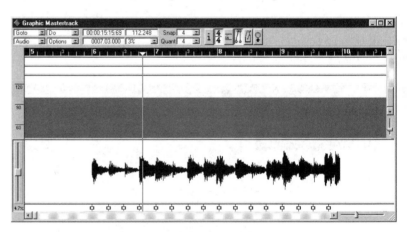

- Set Snap to 4 and enable Show Hitpoint Links in the Options menu. Select Fill Meter Hitpoints and then Link Hitpoints One to One in the Do menu.

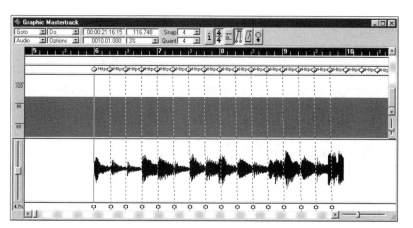

Link hitpoints one to one

- Finally, select Straighten up Hitpoints in the Do menu. A tempo change will be applied at each M-point to match any natural tempo variations in the audio. If more resolution is required then more M-points and hitpoints could be used, such as on every one eighth note, in which case Snap would be set to 8 in the above process. Note that for reliable results M-points should be placed throughout the Audio event at equi-distant spacings.

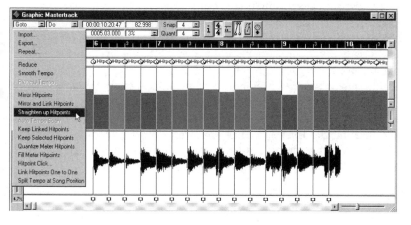

Straighten up hitpoints

This procedure is a complex affair but, once you have used it several times, it becomes easier. Remember that it is perfectly possible to create a tempo map for an entire piece of music and, more than anything else, this technique can inject that all important sense of feel into the MIDI parts of an arrangement.

For some audio passages it may be more convenient to insert time hitpoints 'on the fly' via MIDI in the Graphic Mastertrack. (See 'Using hitpoints to synchronise Cubase VST to music on tape' in Chapter 14).

When following the procedure described above, you can also find the 'Get M-points' option in the Audio menu of the Match Audio/Tempo editor. In addition, it is possible to save the M-points as a groove template using M-points to Groove. The template is saved under the same name as the Audio event.

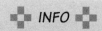

INFO

The ease with which you can create accurate M-points depends on the rhythmic complexity of the audio material. Complex passages are more difficult to process. The technique is also easier if you are already familiar with the Graphic Mastertrack, as described in Chapter 14.

Dynamic events

M-points, described above, are just one kind of dynamic event but there are also volume and pan. In the Audio editor, volume and pan information are special types of data which can be applied to an Audio event. They could be viewed as the audio equivalent to MIDI controller information as found in the Controller display of Key edit.

To use volume or pan you must enable Dynamic events in the View menu and select an event type in the dynamic event choice menu (to the left of the Goto menu). The Audio event box then divides into two horizontal sections, one displaying the usual waveform and the other showing any dynamic data.

Volume

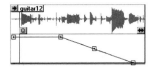

Volume is displayed as small square pointers known as 'breakpoints'. These are joined by lines which form a volume curve. To insert new breakpoints hold alt (Mac: option) and click in the dynamic event display with the pencil tool. To edit existing volume breakpoints drag the small squares with the pencil tool. The positions of newly created and moved volume breakpoints are snapped to the current Snap value. To erase a breakpoint click on the small square with the eraser tool.

The default value of the first breakpoint is 0.0dB and it is not possible to increase the gain above this level using dynamic volume events. The current level is shown to the right of the breakpoint as it is moved. The final level you actually hear is also influenced by the level of the fader in the monitor mixer. The current level of the fader is added to the dynamic events such that, for example, a dynamic event set to −4dB routed through a mixer fader set to −1dB results in a final level of −5dB.

Using dynamic volume events is a convenient and precise method of manipulating the level and, since the events are an integral part of the segment, has the advantage of remaining with the Audio event wherever it is moved and of repeatability when it is copied.

Pan

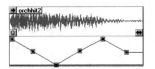

Pan dynamic events are handled very similarly to volume events. As would be expected, the mid-point on the dynamic event horizontal display represents the mid-point in the stereo image. The current stereo position (e.g. L15, R32 etc.) is shown to the right of the pan breakpoint as it is moved either side of the mid-point and the mid-point itself is represented by 0.

Creating auto-pan effects is easy with dynamic pan events. Dynamic pan events are also integral parts of the segment to which they belong which brings the same advantages as with dynamic volume events, as outlined above.

Audio recording in cycle mode

The recording of a live performer sometimes requires several takes before a satisfactory result is achieved. Rather than stop Cubase VST after each take it can often be more convenient to record continuously in cycle mode. In cycle mode the audio is recorded into one long audio file but when you open the Audio editor this will have been conveniently divided into segments and stacked onto separate lanes. Each segment matches the length and represents a different lap of the cycle. A perfect take can then be assembled by trimming and masking the material.

For example, if the vocalist is having trouble with the chorus, simply set up a cycle to repeat the chorus and record a number of takes in one go. Note that, although this can be a convenient and time saving way of capturing that elusive magical performance, audio recording in cycle mode can also produce lengthy audio files on the hard disk.

To record and edit audio in cycle mode proceed as follows:

- In the Arrange window, set the left and right locators to the start and end points of the relevant section of music. Activate the cycle button.
- Implement recording with Cubase VST in Stop mode, i.e. do not drop into record half way through one of the laps of the cycle.
- Record for as many laps of the cycle as required.
- Stop recording. A single Part appears between the left and right locators on the record Track.

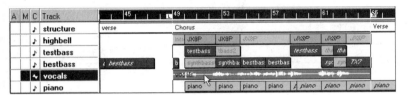

Record a multiple take in cycle mode

- Double click on the Part to open the Audio editor. Each lap of the cycle is represented in a different segment, stacked in the lanes of the editor (as described above). When playing back the audio, only one of the segments can be heard (usually the one in the top lane), since the events are all on the same channel.

Open the Audio editor

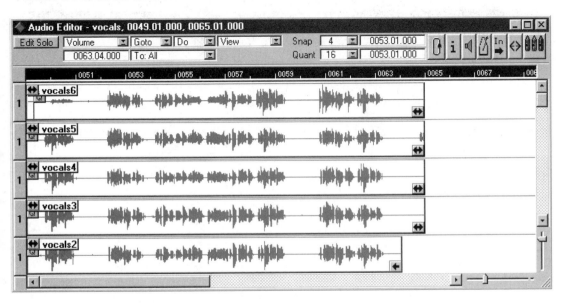

- Trim, mask or mute the segments as required in order to assemble the best composite take for the section. Remember that the most recently started Audio event is the one which is heard. Before editing, try enabling Snap to zero in the Audio menu as this may help cut down the audio clicks which can occur during the editing process.

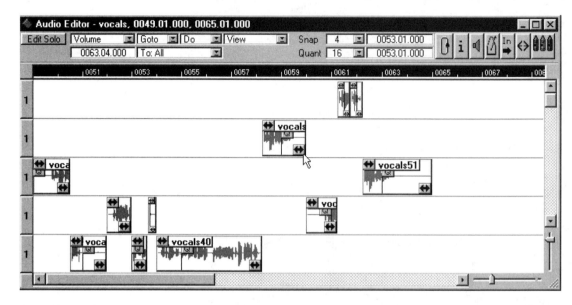

Assemble a perfect take

- To see the composite take on one lane, enable By Output in the View menu. Try also disabling Handles in the View menu to clarify the display.

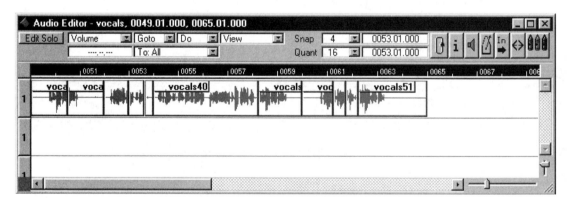

View the final result on one lane

Function bar buttons

On the right side of the Functions bar there are a number of buttons which have special significance in the Audio editor.

- The Loop button activates/de-activates the loop.
- The Info button activates/de-activates the Info bar.
- The Speaker button enables/disables the monitoring of a short section of the Audio event when the Q-point or start and end insets are adjusted. To change the length of the section you hear hold ctrl (Mac: command) and click on the Speaker button.
- The Meter Scale button decides whether the ruler should display time linearly or meter (bars and beats) linearly. When the icon is shown as a clock, the ruler displays each second in equal horizontal steps. When the icon is shown as a metronome, the ruler displays each bar and beat in equal horizontal steps. Note that this should be used in conjunction with the choice of ruler units (time code or bars and beats), which is chosen by clicking in the mouse box. The choice of Meter Scale depends entirely on what type of material you are working on. For musical material the default setting is to show bars and beats linearly and to have bars and beats as the units displayed in the ruler.
- The Scrub button enables/disables audio scrubbing using the magnifying glass tool. When the Scrub button is enabled, dragging across the waveform of an Audio event with the magnifying glass plays back the audio at the speed at which you drag. This is similar to rocking traditional tape back and forth across the playback heads of a tape machine and can be useful for lining up a specific moment in the Audio event. If you drag backwards the audio is played in reverse. When the Scrub button is disabled, clicking somewhere in an Audio event plays back the audio from that point at normal speed for as long as the left mouse button is held down.

Audio editor hints and tips

This chapter should have helped you become familiar with the main features of the Audio editor. The following points provide you with a few more final hints and tips:

- Note that the Audio editor is largely mouse-based and there are very few useful keyboard shortcuts.
- For working in fine detail try changing the horizontal zoom setting using the slider on the scroll bar. The horizontal zoom allows you to see the waveform up to a maximum resolution of one sample per pixel.

- Try leaving the Info bar displayed at all times. This helps see things clearly when moving an event or changing the start and end insets. In addition, by double clicking on the start, end and Q-point parameters in the Info bar a precise value can be entered directly into the pop-up box.
- Clicking once at any point in the position bar relocates the song pointer to that position.
- To help navigate while in the Audio editor, try using shift + 1 and shift + 2 (numeric keypad) to store the current song position to the left or right locators. This is convenient for placing the left and right locators around a specific section of audio and might be used in conjunction with cycle mode. Also remember shift + 3 to 8 for storing other song positions as cue points and note that cue points can be stored 'on the fly'.
- Remember that you can record directly into the Audio editor and, for some tasks, such as doing a large number of drop-ins, this might be preferable to recording in the Arrange window. (See 'Dropping in' in Chapter 6).
- To import audio directly into the Audio editor, select the pencil tool and click in empty space in a lane. This opens the file dialogue from which the desired audio file can be opened. Upon making your choice, a new segment containing the entire audio file is added to the display and also to the list of files in the Audio Pool.
- Remember that, although the Audio editor is non-destructive in most of its functions, there are certain processes which involve permanent change to the audio file on disk. This includes using Fit event to Loop range by adjusting the audio (Do menu). Here, either one part or the whole of the audio file undergoes time stretching. The changes to the audio remain reversible only for as long as you remain in the Audio editor. Also, be careful when using ctrl + backspace (Mac: command + backspace) to delete an event. This permanently deletes the audio file on disk.

8 ❖

The Audio Pool

The Audio Pool is Cubase VST's own file management window, designed specifically to handle audio files. It helps keep track of which audio files are currently in use and which segments are associated with each file. It also provides the means of importing, auditioning, replacing, renaming and deleting audio files and segments and finding out which Parts in the Arrange window are related to any chosen file or segment.

If you are unfamiliar with Cubase VST's concept of audio files and segments please refer to the section on audio files, segments and audio events in Chapter 6.

The Audio Pool window

The Audio Pool is opened by selecting Pool from the Audio menu or by pressing ctrl + F (Mac: command + F) on the computer keyboard.

The Pool displays a list of all the audio files and segments used by the current Song. This includes files and segments from all Arrange windows, if the Song contains several arrangements. Each file name is preceded by a small triangle. Clicking on the triangle shows or hides the segments associated with the audio file. Segments are preceded by a small speaker icon.

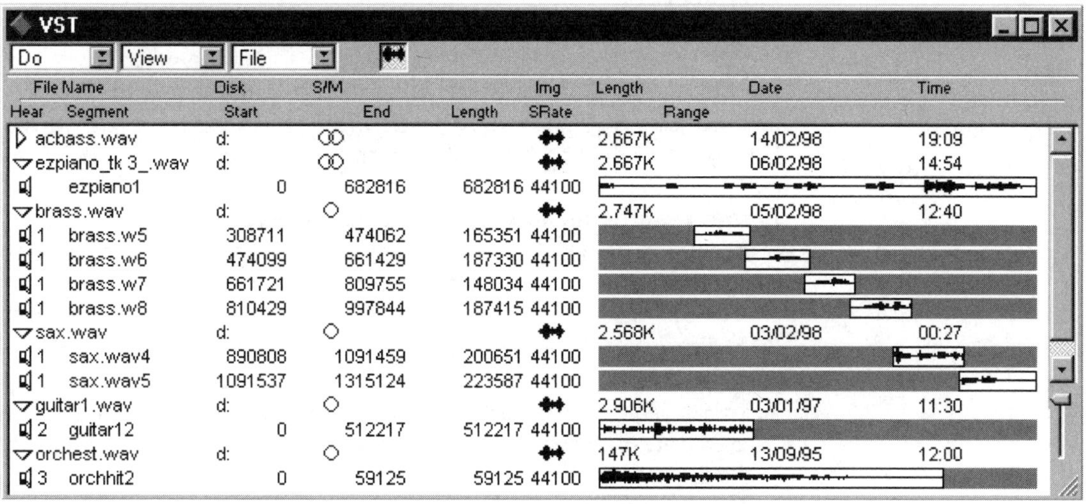

Figure 8.1 The Audio Pool

Hear	Segment	Disk / Start	S/M / End	Img / Length	Length / SRate	Date / Range	Time
▷ acbass.wav		d:	⬭	↔	2.667K	14/02/98	19:09
▽ ezpiano_tk 3_.wav		d:	⬭	↔	2.667K	06/02/98	14:54
🔈	ezpiano1	0	682816	682816	44100		
▽ brass.wav		d:	◯	↔	2.747K	05/02/98	12:40
🔈 1	brass.w5	308711	474062	165351	44100		
🔈 1	brass.w6	474099	661429	187330	44100		
🔈 1	brass.w7	661721	809755	148034	44100		
🔈 1	brass.w8	810429	997844	187415	44100		
▽ sax.wav		d:	◯	↔	2.568K	03/02/98	00:27
🔈 1	sax.wav4	890808	1091459	200651	44100		
🔈 1	sax.wav5	1091537	1315124	223587	44100		
▽ guitar1.wav		d:	◯	↔	2.906K	03/01/97	11:30
🔈 2	guitar12	0	512217	512217	44100		
▽ orchest.wav		d:	◯	↔	147K	13/09/95	12:00
🔈 3	orchhit2	0	59125	59125	44100		

As well as the name, the audio file's disk location, stereo/mono status, image status, length, date and time details are also shown, as specified by the top line of headings above the list. The next line of headings is related to the segments and, as well as the name, includes the start and end points, the length, the sample rate and a waveform representing the segment and its range within the audio file.

Getting to know the Pool

The first time you see the Audio Pool, the amount of information presented on the screen can seem rather bewildering. This section targets some of the key elements to help you become familiar with the Pool's main functions.

Showing and hiding segments
All audio files in the Pool will normally have at least one associated segment and, if no editing has been carried out in the Audio or Wave editors, then this will be one long segment lasting for the entire length of the file. To show or hide the segments associated with an audio file simply click on the small triangle which precedes the file name. A right pointing triangle indicates that the segments for the audio file are hidden and a downward pointing triangle indicates that they are showing. To show or hide all segments associated with all audio files select Expand or Collapse in the View menu.

The small speaker icon
To audition any segment which appears in the list click on the small speaker icon which precedes the segment name. There may also be a number next to the small speaker icon. This specifies the number of times the segment is used in the Song. If there is no number next to the icon then the segment is not currently used in the Song.

Find the Part
In a complex Song, it is easy to confuse exactly which audio file corresponds to which sound. To find out which Parts in the Arrange window use which audio file or segment, select the file or the segment in the Pool and then click on Find Parts in the Do menu. The Parts concerned will be highlighted (shown in black) in the Arrange window.

Purging segments and managing the display
If you have been doing a large amount of editing in the Audio editor this can generate a large number of segments in the Pool. It is not always the case that all the segments are in use. To clarify the list and keep the Pool up to date try using Purge segments in the Do menu. In addition, if you wish to simplify the overall display of the Pool try using Hide Info and/or Hide Headings in the View menu. Hide Info actually provides a more detailed view of the waveforms associated with each audio file or segment as the display area becomes wider.

The above sections have briefly outlined some of the common functions of the Pool but it is worth getting to know things in more detail.

File details

When inspecting audio files in the Pool, bear in mind that files are never used directly in the Song. It is rather the segments associated with them which are used. However, this does not imply that the segments are more important than the audio files themselves. Indeed, the majority of the Pool's functions are directed towards the audio files alone.

Audio file information

Once you get used to the layout of the Pool it is a simple matter to find out the status of any audio file in a number of important respects. Each audio file name is followed by a row of parameters and symbols. The first is the hard disk drive letter upon which the file was found so you know, at a glance, where it came from. It is also immediately apparent whether the file is stereo or mono by looking at the symbol under the S/M column. A single circle indicates mono and a double circle indicates stereo. The next symbol in the row indicates the status of the waveform image associated with the file. A black symbol indicates that the image is up to date, a

File Name	Disk	S/M	Img	Length	Date	Time
▷ acbass.wav	d:	⊙⊙	↔	2.667K	14/02/98	19:09

grey symbol indicates that the image needs updating and a symbol with a question mark indicates that there is no image associated with the file. Clicking on the waveform symbol updates the waveform image. Other information provided includes the size of the file in kilobytes and the date and time when the file was created.

File location

In order to find out more precise details of the location of the file on disk hold alt (Mac: command) on the computer keyboard and click on the file name with the left mouse button. This opens a pop-up box showing the drive letter and any folder(s) within which the file is located.

Re-find

There are occasions when you may wish to replace an audio file with an alternative file found elsewhere on the disk drive. Clicking on the drive letter of the file opens a dialogue (see below) asking if you wish to 're-find' the file. Selecting Yes opens the normal file selection dialogue from which you can choose the replacement file.

You are most likely to use this kind of operation when you are reverting to a backup file after having made some kind of processing error with the current file. Note that if the segments associated with the current file are still to be relevant, the replacement file must be of the same length as the original.

Renaming and duplicating

To rename a file double click on the existing name in the Pool and enter the new name into the pop-up box. To duplicate a file select it and then select Duplicate File in the File menu. Enter a suitable name into the pop-up box. Both renaming and duplicating are best achieved in the Pool rather than the Windows Explorer as Cubase VST can more easily keep track of the changes.

Deleting

Deleting audio files in the Pool is similar to other parts of Cubase VST. There are three methods of deleting:

1 To delete from the Pool alone, (and *not* from the hard disk), select one or more files in the Pool, (for multiple selections hold shift while clicking on each file), and press backspace on the computer keyboard. The audio file is removed from the Pool and any Parts in the Arrange window which used the file lose their contents and remain on the display as empty Parts. This operation cannot be undone.

2 To delete from the Pool and from the hard disk, select one or more files in the Pool and press ctrl + backspace (Mac: command + backspace) on the computer keyboard. This permanently deletes the chosen file(s) from the Pool and from the hard disk. This operation should be used with great care since it cannot be undone!

3 To delete all unused files in the current song from the Pool and from the hard disk, select Delete Unused Files in the local File menu. The files are deleted permanently from the hard disk and the operation cannot be undone! This function is useful after a long audio recording session when you may have accumulated a large number of takes, only some of which you have finally decided to use in the current arrangement. Make sure you do not delete any audio files which are used in other songs.

Deleting unused sections of audio files (Erase Unused)

As well as the normal delete functions outlined above, the Pool also offers the possibility of deleting all those sections which are unused in an audio file. This works by analysing those sections of the file which are currently used by the segments associated with that file. The idea is to crop the audio file down to its smallest size in order to save on disk space. It is particularly useful for clearing unwanted audio from the hard drive after assembling a composite take from a number of stacked segments recorded in cycle mode.

 **IMPORTANT**

All delete operations should be approached with great care, especially options 2 and 3 which involve the permanent deletion of audio from the hard disk.

To use this process select one or more audio files in the Pool and select Erase Unused from the Do menu. A dialogue informs you of the percentage of the original audio file which will be kept.

Selecting Compact purges all unused segments associated with the file

and then deletes the sections of the audio file which are unused. The sections of the audio file which remain are joined together with a short gap of silence between each and all remaining segments associated with the file are automatically re-adjusted so that they reference the appropriate audio material.

Multiple selections are possible but the files are processed one at a time. The changes to the audio file are permanent and irreversible. The use of Erase Unused should therefore be approached with extreme caution! If there is any possibility that you may need to revert to the original at some stage, or that the audio file may be used in another Song, you should make a backup of the file before proceeding.

Erase Unused should not be confused with Delete Unused Files, (explained above). Erase Unused trims the audio files according to the lengths of the segments which currently play them back and Delete Unused Files deletes whole audio files which are not currently used in the song. Both these functions involve permanent deletion of audio material on the hard disk and should be used with extreme caution!

The case of the missing file

Occasionally, when you open a Song, you may get a dialogue warning that there are one or more files missing. This often indicates that the files concerned have been moved, renamed, or deleted outside of Cubase VST since the last time you opened the Song. A file is also considered missing if you have changed the date outside of Cubase VST.

The warning dialogue gives you options to carry out an automatic or manual search for the missing file(s). Selecting cancel will open the Song anyway, without the missing file(s). A Song opened in this way still shows the missing file(s) in the Pool but a file which is missing is shown with three question marks in the disk column. If you have opened a Song with a missing file it is still possible to search for it by clicking on the question marks. You will be presented with the same missing files dialogue as when you first opened the Song.

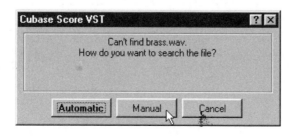

To automatically search for a missing file select Automatic. This searches the entire hard disk for a file with the correct name and creation date. Auto only works if the file has simply been moved to a different folder. If the date or size have been changed then this will not be accepted by Cubase VST, even if the name is identical.

If the auto search did not produce a result then you can manually search for the file by selecting Manual in the missing file dialogue. You will be warned if the name, size or date of the chosen file has been changed but you will still be able to proceed with locating the missing file.

Segment details

Segment information
Each audio file may have one or a number of segments associated with it. Each segment is a reference to a particular section of the audio file. A number of parameters are available for each segment including the name, the start and end points, the length, the sample rate and the range of the segment within the audio file, shown on the right of the display as a box containing a waveform.

Hear	Segment	Start	End	Length	SRate	Range
🔊 1	brass.w5	308711	474062	165351	44100	

Start and end insets
To change the start or end points, (insets), click on the values in the start or end columns with the left or right mouse buttons. The values are displayed in samples, meter position or time code according to which option has been enabled in the View menu. Alternatively, change the start and end insets graphically by dragging the start or end point of the box containing the waveform. This is similar to dragging the start and end insets in the Audio editor except that the display in the Pool is smaller and more awkward to use.

Hear	Segment	Start	End
▽ acbass.wav		d:	∞
🔊	acbass.1	20	682816
▷ dt03.wav		d:	○

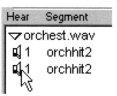

Auditioning a segment

To hear the contents of any segment click on the speaker icon which precedes the segment name or click in the waveform to the right of the display.

Renaming and duplicating

To rename a segment double click on the segment name and enter a new name into the pop-up box. To duplicate a segment select it and then select Duplicate Segment from the Do menu.

Deleting a segment

To delete a segment, select it and then press the backspace key on the computer keyboard. For multiple deletions press shift while selecting the segments. Deleting a segment removes it from the appropriate Part(s) in the Arrange window and the operation is irreversible.

Importing audio

Importing audio files into the Pool is convenient if you wish to use, for example, a sound stored on a CD-ROM or an audio file created in another Cubase VST Song. The file must be uncompressed, 16 bit stereo or mono and in WAV or AIFF format. The sample rate should also match that of the current Song, (normally 44.1kHz).

To import a file, select Import Audio File in the local File menu. The file dialogue appears from which you can search for and select the desired file. The chosen audio file is added to the Pool and a default segment lasting the length of the audio file is created. Note that audio files can be auditioned before they are selected by using the Play button which appears in the file dialogue. In addition, several files can be selected and imported at the same time.

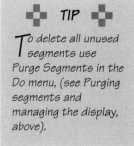

TIP

To delete all unused segments use Purge Segments in the Do menu, (see Purging segments and managing the display, above).

Dragging files and segments from the Pool

One of the most useful features of the Pool is the facility to be able to drag a file or a segment directly into the Arrange window, the Audio editor or the Wave editor. To drag a segment from the Pool into the Arrange window proceed as follows:

- Open the Pool and make sure that the Pool's window does not obscure the whole of the Arrange window's Part display. There must be at least one audio Track visible.
- Click the mouse on the chosen segment name and then drag. A dotted rectangle representing the segment appears.
- Drag the segment from the Pool into the Arrange window. Drop the segment onto an audio Track.

Drag the segment from the Pool

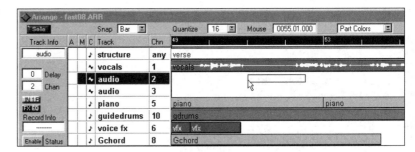

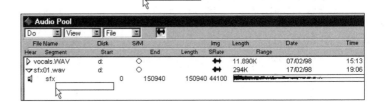

- A new Part is created containing an Audio event which plays the dragged segment. The Part is created at the position at which the mouse was released and is moved to the nearest beat according to the current Snap value.

Drop the segment in the Arrange window

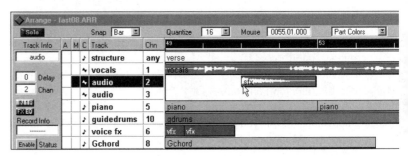

Dragging a segment from the Pool into the Audio editor follows a similar procedure. An Audio event is created at the position at which the mouse is released and the event is moved to the nearest beat according to the current Snap value.

A similar procedure also applies when dragging a segment into Cubase VST's Wave editor. A waveform representing the dragged segment appears in the editor window. Note that a new Wave editor window is opened for each dragged segment.

Other Pool functions

Prepare Archive

The Pool provides the option of automatically backing up a Song and all its audio files into a separate folder. To prepare an archive select Prepare Archive in the local File menu. A dialogue appears giving the option to archive all files in the Pool or only those which are referenced. Choosing 'All' copies all files, regardless of whether they are used in the Song or not. Choosing 'Referenced', copies only those files which are used in the Song. Upon making your choice a file dialogue appears where you can choose or create a new folder as the destination for the backup files. The Song file is also automatically copied into the backup folder. Note that this option copies the audio files alone. The files responsible for the waveforms you see in Cubase VST (.ovw files) are not copied. When restoring archived material into Cubase VST it will be necessary, in this case, to redraw all the waveforms by clicking on the waveform icons in the Pool or by re-selecting Use Waveforms in the Audio menu. Prepare Archive would normally be used for creating a safety backup of the Song while you continue to work on the material.

Prepare Master

The Prepare Master option in the local File menu is similar to Prepare Archive. The difference is that, in this case, only the used sections of the audio files are saved into the new folder. All those sections of the audio files which are not used are erased and a new version of each file is created. All segments and references to the audio are updated in Cubase VST and a new version of the Song is automatically saved alongside the new files. Before using Prepare Master make sure you have saved the Song in its current form since you may need to restore the original at some stage.

Prepare Master also includes the .ovw waveform files in the copying process and the final set of files is a complete set representing the Song in its current state. Prepare Master would usually be used when you have finished working on the Song and would like to prepare a final version which uses the minimum amount of hard disk space, or which will be used to make a backup. The original Song and audio files still remain intact in the original folder and, if you are sure that you will never need to update the Song again, the original files can later be deleted in order to free up some space on your hard disk.

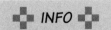

INFO

The Pool contains references to audio files and not the audio files themselves, so it is the references which are saved and loaded.

Saving and loading the Pool

The Pool is usually saved as an integral part of the Song but it can also be saved and loaded independently. This might be useful if you need to include a number of audio files from another Song in the current Song.

To save the Pool select Save Pool from the local File menu. Choose whether you wish to save all files or just the selected ones and then specify the name for the file in the file dialogue which appears. Pool files are given the extension .pol. To load a Pool file select Load Pool from the local File menu and select a Pool file from the file dialogue which appears. The audio files in the selected Pool file are added to any audio files currently in the Pool.

Time well spent

The Audio Pool is not the most musically inspiring part of Cubase VST but those tempted to avoid it should think twice. Unfortunately, not all aspects of the audio file management process can remain invisible. The Pool provides a necessary interface between the audio data as we see it within Cubase VST and the manner in which it is stored on hard disk, which we cannot really do without. Knowing how to handle the Audio Pool is essential for the routine management of your audio files and the time taken learning the details is time well spent.

9

The Wave editor

The Wave editor is used for the detailed editing and processing of the audio data itself, which is represented in the display as a waveform. Any editing affects the actual audio file on the hard disk and this is often referred to as destructive editing. For this reason, you must be careful when using the Wave editor and it is advisable to make a backup of any important material before editing commences. In addition, there is only one level of undo in the Wave editor i.e. you can undo the previous editing action but you cannot undo a whole series of editing actions.

The Wave editor window

The Wave editor (Figure 9.1) can be opened from a number of different locations. This is convenient since you may need to open the editor at any stage in your manipulation of audio data.

- If you are in the Arrange window select an audio Part and then choose Edit Audio in the Audio menu.
- If you are in the Audio editor double click on an Audio event.
- If you are in the Pool double click on the waveform display of any segment.

Figure 9.1 The Wave editor window

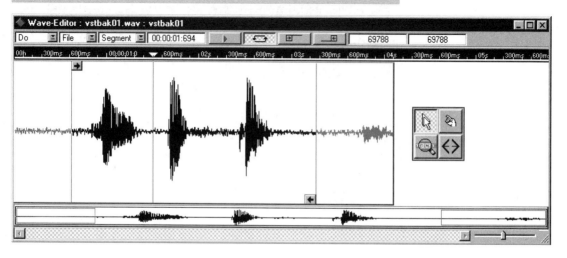

95

The Wave editor window features time on the horizontal axis and amplitude on the vertical axis. The horizontal ruler displays time in hours:minutes:seconds:milliseconds. The editor features a number of local menus, value boxes showing the current selection in samples, transport controls and a small toolbox, opened by clicking in the display with the right mouse button. Below the main display there is a thumbnail view of the waveform which helps navigate within the audio file.

If the editor is opened from the Arrange window the whole audio file is shown as a highlighted waveform (in black) and the first segment in the Part is marked with start and end insets. Otherwise, the chosen segment of the audio file is shown highlighted in black, with corresponding start and end insets, and the rest of the waveform is shown in grey. This helps you focus on the section of the audio file in which you are interested.

The contents of the Wave editor can be auditioned using the normal Transport bar play button or the editor's own special play button above the display. When clicked upon, this button plays back the current audio file in the Wave editor for as long as the mouse button is held down.

It is also possible to use an external Wave editor, such as Sonic Foundry's Sound Forge or Steinberg's Wavelab, and this is specified in the Preferences dialogue of the Audio menu (Figure 9.2).

Figure 9.2 The Preferences dialogue

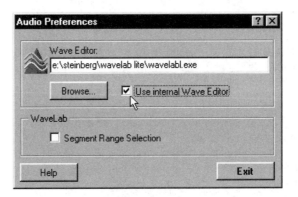

To use the internal Wave editor as the default editor tick the Use internal Wave editor box. In this configuration the commands outlined above for opening the Wave editor open the internal version. However, if you wish to open an external editor this is still possible by pressing the control key when opening the Wave editor.

Getting to know the Wave editor

Probably the best way to get to know the Wave editor is to experiment on a test audio file. Figure 9.3 shows the waveform of the spoken letters 'VST' and this makes good test material.

It is suggested that you take a microphone and quickly make a similar recording. Then proceed with the following tutorial:

Make a backup

Once you have made your test audio recording open the Audio Pool and select the new file. Open the local File menu and select Duplicate File. This is our backup file in case things go wrong in the Wave editor.

Open the Wave editor

While still in the Pool, double click on the segment associated with the original file to open the Wave editor. If you have recorded the spoken letters 'VST' the display should resemble Figure 9.3. You can clearly see the three letters as three significant peaks in the waveform.

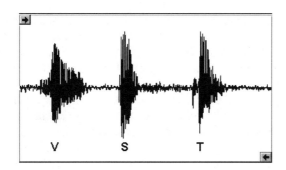

Figure 9.3 Test recording of the spoken letters 'VST'

Play back the audio

The first thing you might want to do is play back the audio. This is achieved by clicking on the play button at the top of the Wave editor window (the button with the green right-facing triangle). The audio plays back for as long as you hold the mouse button down. The manner in which the audio plays back depends on several factors. Try the following:

- Click once in the display area at any point in the audio file. When you press the play button the file plays back from this position to the end of the audio file.
- Click and drag across the display area. For example, try selecting the letter 'S.' in your audio recording. The selection is shown in reverse video.

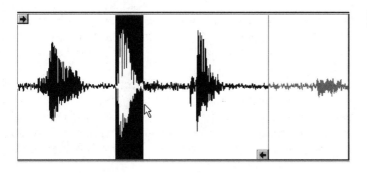

Figure 9.3b Select the 'S' of 'VST'

- Pressing the Wave editor's play button plays the selected section only. To de-select the section click once in the display area.
- Click on the loop button (next to the play button above the display).

When commencing from within the segment, the playback loops continuously between the starting point and the end of the segment. When commencing from outside the segment, the playback loops continuously between the starting point and the end of the audio file. When a section of the file has been selected, the playback loops continuously on this part of the audio file alone.

- Related to the playback of the audio material, try also using the segment start and end buttons. These move the song position to the start or end points of the segment and are particularly useful when you wish to loop a segment beginning at its exact starting point.

If the audio material being edited is contained within a Part in the Arrange window you can also use the normal play button on the Transport bar. The waveform in the display scrolls past during playback, as with the other editors. This provides a useful alternative to using the editor's own play button.

Audio processing in the Wave editor

Now that you are used to moving around inside the Wave editor, let's try some of the processing possibilities. The audio processing functions are found in the Do menu and these are the same as those found in the Processing sub-menu of the main Audio menu. Audio processing techniques are described in more detail in Chapter 11.

As an exercise, you could work through each function in the Do menu in vertical order. After trying each possibility the audio file can be returned to its original state by using the Undo Edit command in the Edit menu or by pressing ctrl + Z (Mac: command + Z) on the computer keyboard. Remember that the Wave editor has only one level of undo.

For example, the first option in the Do menu is the Reverse function. Before using Reverse you must decide which section of the audio file is to be processed. In this case, try selecting the whole segment by pressing ctrl + A (Mac: command + A) on the computer keyboard. The segment is highlighted. Upon selecting Reverse, the segment is, you guessed it, reversed !

To undo the edit press ctrl + Z (Mac: command + Z) on the computer keyboard. By selecting just the 'V.' of our 'VST' recording we would be able to reverse just this one letter. Of course, we do not have any real need to reverse our 'VST' recording but there are occasions when reversals can be useful. This and other audio processing techniques are described in more detail in Chapter 11.

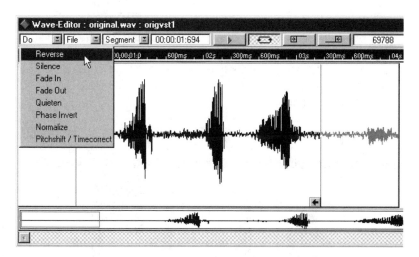

Figure 9.4 Audio reversal in the Wave editor

How to cut and paste in the Wave editor

To understand how to use the standard cut, copy and paste commands in the Wave editor try the following tutorial:

- If you have not already done so, take a microphone and quickly make a recording of the spoken letters 'VST' The aim of this exercise is to re-order the letters so that we hear 'T. V.' instead of 'VST'
- Select 'V.', (the first peak in the waveform), by dragging the mouse in the display. Copy the selection by pressing ctrl + C (Mac: command + C) on the computer keyboard.

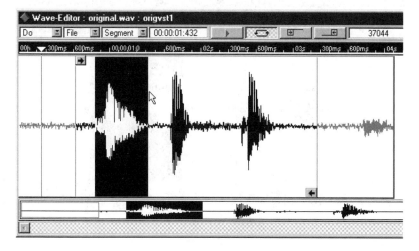

Select 'V' and copy

- Click on the point just after the 'T.' (the third peak in the waveform) and then press ctrl + V (Mac: command + V) on the computer keyboard. The contents of the clipboard are pasted over the existing waveform at the pointer position. Note that paste overwrites (replaces) any existing audio data. It is not possible to insert data using the internal Wave editor.

Paste 'V' onto the end of the waveform

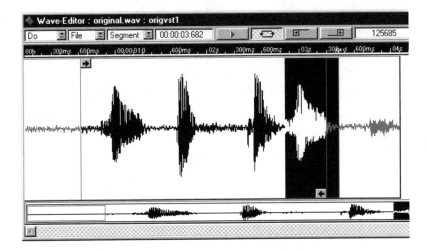

- Select the last two peaks in the waveform. Audition the selection which you should find to be the required spoken letters: 'TV'

Audition 'TV'

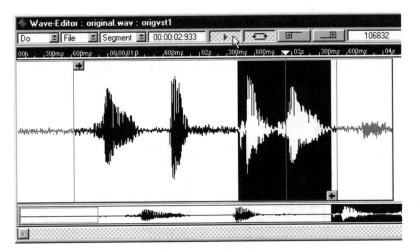

- If you are happy with the edit you could delete the first two peaks in the waveform, the original 'V' and 'S' Select the appropriate section of the audio file and press the backspace key on the computer keyboard.

Delete 'VS'

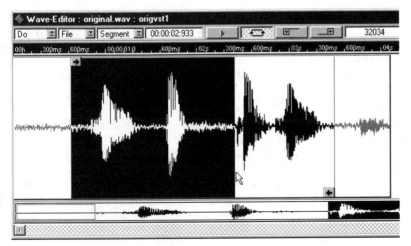

- Finally, adjust the start and end insets around the new waveform and audition the audio once more before leaving the editor.

Adjust the start and end insets and play back the final result

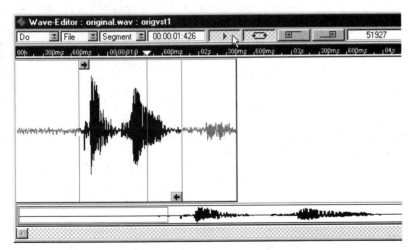

When you go back to the Arrange window the audio Part you recorded is now playing the new audio file. If you finally decide that you are not happy with the editing after all, you can revert to the original file in the Audio Pool. Simply click on the drive letter of the file you have just edited and confirm that you wish to re-find the file in the dialogue which appears. Choose the backup file you made prior to editing and this will replace your edited version. The Part in the Arrange window now plays back the audio file as it was originally.

More Wave editor features

The toolbox

The Wave editor features a small toolbox which deserves some explanation.

The pointer tool is for the general manipulation of items within the editor and for the selecting of menu functions. It is also used for graphically selecting sections of the audio file in the display.

When selected, the hand tool changes to an open hand in the display. This is used to move the segment frame or selected area (the selection in reverse video) within the audio file. With the hand tool selected, you can drag the segment frame or selected area left or right to encompass another section of the audio file. The length of the segment or selection remains identical.

The magnifying glass, also known as the audition tool, is used to play back the audio file by clicking on the display. As with other parts of Cubase VST the file plays back from the point at which it was clicked.

The scrub tool is used to play the audio file by dragging it backwards or forwards in the audio waveform. The playback speed is regulated by the speed of the mouse movements and when moving backwards the audio file is played in reverse.

The File menu

The first item in the File menu, Selection to File, allows the user to select any section of the audio file currently in the editor and save it as a separate file under a new name. This can be useful for making backups.

The File menu also contains a list of the audio files currently in the Audio Pool and any file can be selected for editing in the Wave editor. Upon selection, the current audio file in the editor is closed and the new file is opened.

The Segment menu

The first item in the Segment menu, Selection to Segment, changes the currently selected section of the audio file into a new segment, which is added to the segments associated with the audio file.

The remaining items in the Segment menu are all those segments associated with the currently open audio file. Selecting a segment in the list makes this the active segment (the segment highlighted in black, with start and end insets).

More about selecting

As has been mentioned above, any section of the currently opened audio file can be selected by clicking and dragging in the display. The size of the current selection can be adjusted by holding the shift key on the computer keyboard and clicking to either side of the selected area. It is also possible to select the whole active segment by pressing ctrl + A (Mac: command + A) on the computer keyboard. Pressing ctrl + A (Mac: command + A) a second time selects the whole audio file.

Magnification and using the thumbnail

To set the magnification of the display you could use the normal magnification slider in the lower right corner. This allows you to change the overall resolution of the display and zoom into specific sections of the waveform (see 'Detailed editing and click removal' below).

To select a specific section of the waveform to be shown in the main display, hold ctrl (Mac: command) on the computer keyboard and drag over the desired area in the thumbnail view. The main display then shows the selected section of the audio file. If you need to go back to displaying the whole audio file hold ctrl (Mac: command) and double click in the thumbnail view.

The thumbnail view always shows the whole audio file and the section shown on the main display is represented in the thumbnail as a rectangular box. This box can be dragged to any position in the audio file and provides a convenient method of navigating from one edit point to another (see 'Detailed editing and click removal' below).

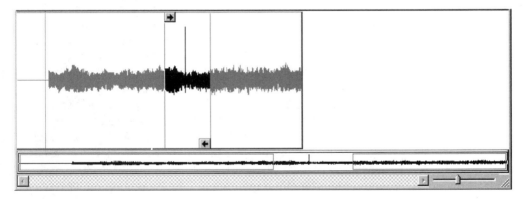

The Wave editor also features the thumbnail view which provides a convenient and adaptable method of navigating within an audio file. The thumbnail view is a narrow strip below the main display area.

Detailed editing and click removal

If you need to edit the waveform in extreme detail then you may wish to magnify the display to its maximum resolution. This allows the selection of a section with single sample accuracy i.e. if necessary, you can move the start or end points of a selection one sample at a time. Sample accurate editing can be achieved either graphically with the mouse or by changing the start and end sample value boxes above the display.

Editing in fine detail is best understood by example so let's imagine that one of your audio files contains an unwanted click, or some other interference. Here is one method of removing it:

- Select the Part with the unwanted click and open the Wave editor. Alternatively, open the Audio editor first and splice a new segment around the point where the click occurs and then open the Wave editor. Hopefully, the offending click will be visible in the display as a brief spike in the waveform. Note that many kinds of interference are not so obvious and could be far more difficult to locate. (The screenshots shown here are from a recording of a strings sound which has an unwanted click half-way through the file).

Find the offending click in the waveform

- Adjust the display to almost maximum magnification using the magnification slider. As you adjust the slider the rectangular black box in the thumbnail view becomes smaller, (indicating what section of the file is displayed).

Adjust the magnification

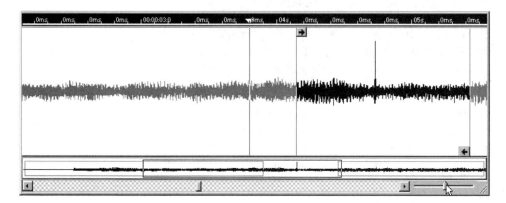

- Once you have chosen a magnification level move the rectangular box in the thumbnail view to the location of the click. If the magnification is not suitable re-adjust the magnification slider as required.

Move the rectangular box to the location of the click

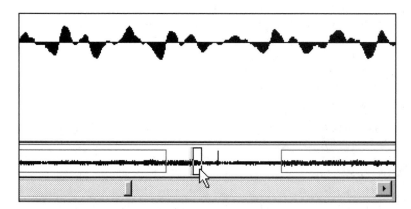

- Make sure that the thumbnail view rectangular box encompasses the area of interest. The offending click should now be visible in great detail in the main display. Note that, at this magnification the click may manifest itself as a small segment of the waveform with different characteristics to the rest of the audio. So, if you are having difficulty finding the click, look out for unusual characteristics in the shape of the waveform and this will generally lead you to the offending area. This could be something as obvious as the example shown here, it could be a variation in two or more cycles of the waveform or it could be a sudden dropout in the waveform lasting only 3 or 4 samples.
- Select what you judge to be the area of interest, attempting to keep the start and end points of the selection at zero crossing points. Also, attempt to ensure that the waveform before and after the selected points is on opposite sides of the centre line (as in the example below).

For maximum accuracy you might choose to edit the start and end
positions of the selection one sample at a time, by editing the values
directly in the sample value boxes.

Select the unwanted click

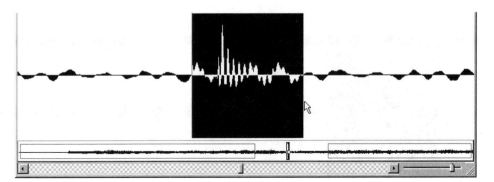

- Once selected, you may wish to simply delete the click, in which case
the remaining audio is butted onto the first section at the point of
deletion. (In the screenshot below, the join is indicated by the song
position pointer). Note that this means that the second part of the
joined audio has been moved in time.

Delete the click

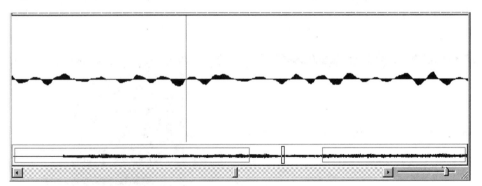

- Alternatively, you could try finding another section of audio to be
pasted over the click. This is the best option to avoid any timing
problems since the audio file remains exactly the same length. To
achieve this, select the hand tool and drag the selection area left or
right across the waveform.

Drag the selection area

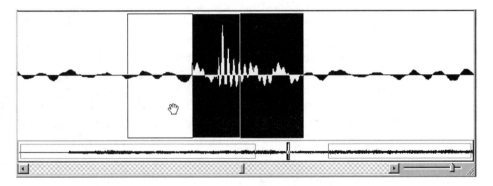

Choose another audio
section

- Look for a section of nearby audio which will fit neatly into the selection area. Once again, attempt to choose a section where the start and end of the waveform are at zero crossing points and on opposite sides of the centre line.

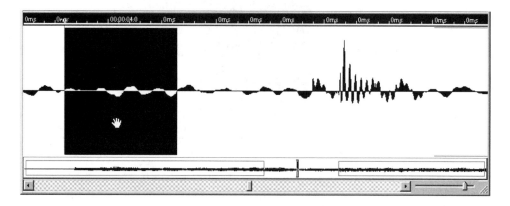

Copy and paste the audio
over the offending click

- If you are lucky enough to find some suitable audio, copy it using ctrl + C (Mac: command + C) and then paste this audio at the point where the audio click begins. The pasted audio replaces the click and the file should now play back without any interference.

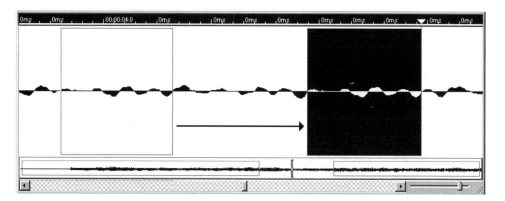

Investing for the future

Any knowledge you have gained throughout this chapter should help if you decide to also invest in an external Wave editor. The essentials of the procedures explained here are similar for many of the popular external Wave editors on the market, like Steinberg's Wavelab and Sonic Foundry's Sound Forge. Dedicated external editors like these also provide many more features than is possible with the internal Wave editor, including plug-in facilities, frequency analysis and multiple levels of undo, and they are especially useful for advanced audio processing and preparing material for burning to CD.

10

More editing and control functions

Up to now this book has explored the major working areas of Cubase VST but the program also includes a large number of smaller but equally useful features which help in the routine manipulation and control of audio and MIDI data. Many of these features are found in the main menus.

System preparation

Let's start with three menu items which are concerned with the general setting up and handling of the system: Preferences, MIDI Setup and MIDI Filter. Some readers may be thinking that these features should have been dealt with at the very beginning, but you cannot effectively update a system to your own settings if you do not first understand that system's structure.

Normally, Cubase VST is supplied with its important features already sensibly set in the supplied definition file (def.all). However, users, now more familiar with the program, will almost certainly wish to enter their own custom settings which can then be saved as a new def.all file. The def.all file is automatically opened whenever Cubase VST is launched and can be used to set up your own personalised default settings for the system.

Preferences

Selecting 'Preferences' in the File menu opens a dialogue box (Figure 10.1) where the user may select:

- 'Double click opens', to select the choice of editor,(Key, List or Score), when the user double clicks on a MIDI Part.
- 'Autosave', to automatically save the current song as 'Backup.All' at the time interval shown in the minutes box. This provides a safety copy which can be indispensable in the event of a system crash.
- 'Crosshair cursor', to show a crosshair comprising of a dynamic cross of vertical and horizontal lines which indicates the precise mouse position on the Arrange window grid. This is useful for the accurate positioning of Parts.
- 'Activity display', to show the activity column in the Arrange window.

- 'Play in background', to allow Cubase VST to play MIDI or audio material in the background behind another launched program.
- 'Dark rulers', to darken the appearance of the position bar in the Arrange window and editors.
- 'Fewer alerts', to disable the pop-up warning dialogues which appear for various editing operations. For expert users only.
- 'Leave MIDI File Track data as is', to leave the MIDI data of exported MIDI files exactly as it is found in the arrangement without including the MIDI parameters in the Inspector (ticked), or to include the Inspector's MIDI parameters which are converted into normal MIDI data and saved as part of the MIDI file (unticked).
- 'Plugins receive key commands', to allow key commands to be relevant for the currently active plug-in rather than their default Cubase VST function. However, the numeric keypad's stop (0), go to left and right locators (1 and 2), and play (enter) keys, and fast forward (page up) and rewind (page down) keys retain their function regardless of the active plug-in.

Figure 10.1 The Preferences dialogue

MIDI Setup

MIDI Setup is found in the Options menu (Figure 10.2). This is where users set up various global parameters which govern the manner in which Cubase VST handles MIDI. MIDI Thru is among the most important and, in most cases, this would be set to active so that incoming MIDI data is echoed to the MIDI Out. Cubase VST also offers the possibility to switch the THRU off for one unique MIDI Channel, (for those users with a master keyboard not equipped with a Local Off Function).

But why is it necessary to have the MIDI Thru activated in the first place? The answer is that to communicate with the MIDI units in the system the data from the master keyboard must travel *through* Cubase VST to reach them. When the MIDI Thru is de-activated the data stops inside Cubase VST. With the Thru function activated, the data arriving at the MIDI In is echoed to the MIDI Out, and the user may play any unit in the

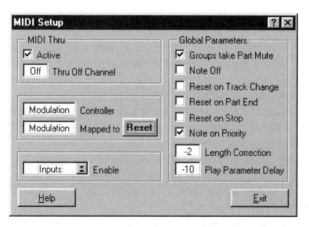

Figure 10.2 The MIDI setup
dialogue

system simply by changing the MIDI channel of the currently selected Track in the Arrange window. To avoid double sounding notes and other complications when playing the master keyboard, it is advisable to switch it to local off mode. This cuts the physical keyboard's feed to the synthesis part of the instrument such that it will only respond to the data received at its MIDI In via Cubase VST. (See also 'MIDI recording in more detail', Chapter 4).

MIDI Setup also allows the user to re-map any one controller to any other. For example, a Pan controller (controller 10) could be under the command of the master keyboard's modulation wheel (controller 1) by mapping Modulation to Pan in the Controller section of the setup window.

Running Status is a MIDI data compression technique in the MIDI protocol which is sent out from Cubase VST by default. Sometimes this causes problems with older synthesizers and this part of the window gives the user the opportunity to de-activate it for any of the output ports.

MIDI setup's global parameters section contains a number of miscellaneous features which affect the handling of various details of the software as follows:

- 'Groups take Part mute' toggles the ability to mute or not mute the Parts in a Group from the mute columns of the original Tracks.
- 'Note Off' toggles between sending real note off messages (ticked) and note off messages as note on with zero velocity (unticked).
- 'Reset on Track change' sends out a reset of pitch bend, modulation and channel pressure when changing Tracks.
- 'Reset on Part end' sends out a reset of pitch bend, modulation, sustain pedal and channel pressure when each Part comes to an end.
- 'Reset on stop' sends out a reset of pitch bend, modulation and channel pressure for all Tracks plus All Notes Off and Reset All Controllers messages when Cubase VST is stopped. (The reset options avoid such things as hanging notes and hanging pitch bends).

- 'Note On Priority' ensures that note on messages are always given timing priority over all other message types, resulting in a tighter mix during passages containing a heavy output of controller and other non-note messages.
- 'Length correction' attempts to ensure that there is always at least a short amount of time (measured in ticks) between a note off and note on message on the same pitch and MIDI channel in order to avoid lost notes.
- 'Play parameter delay' allows the user to anticipate or delay the time (in ticks) at which the play parameters of the Inspector are transmitted. Most often it will be set to a negative value in order to allow the target synth time to react to such things as bank or program changes.

Remember that MIDI Setup comes preset to sensible settings in the definition files supplied with the program but you may now wish to experiment with your own settings.

MIDI Filter
MIDI Filter, also found in the Options menu (Figure 10.3), is used to filter out unwanted MIDI data. The dialogue box allows the main types of MIDI data to be filtered from the record and thru paths of Cubase VST, and it allows the filtering of one or more MIDI channels and up to four different types of continuous controllers for data arriving at the MIDI input.

Figure 10.3 The MIDI Filter dialogue

The following flow chart should help clarify matters:

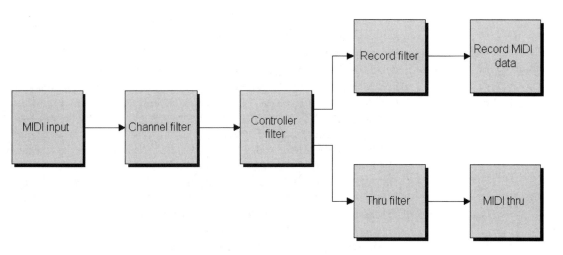

Filtering data during recording is particularly useful when, for example, the master keyboard is outputting unwanted aftertouch data, (especially if the target synth does not even respond to this kind of data). System Exclusive data may be equally unwanted. In fact, most users leave SysEx and aftertouch filtered as the default setting and only allow this kind of data into the system when it is specifically desired. You could equally filter SysEx and aftertouch from the Thru section. In addition, if changing the program number on the master synth causes undesirable program changes in one or more of the modules in the system, then temporarily filtering program change in the Thru section quickly solves the problem.

Whereas the record and thru filters provide for the blanket removal of all controller data from the incoming MIDI messages, the controller filter may be set to remove up to four specific continuous controllers. For example, this could be useful for discarding all modulation data but keeping all other controller data contained within the incoming MIDI messages. When required, each controller filter may be de-activated by setting it to 'no ctrl'.

The channel filter might be useful for transferring an arrangement from an external sequencer into Cubase VST when, for example, only the drums on MIDI Channel 10 were required. All other channels could be filtered and the drums alone would be transferred.

Figure 10.4 MIDI Filter flowchart

Cubase VST in colour

The use of colour in Cubase VST can be customised to suit the needs of each user. For example, try changing the background of the Arrange window using Part background in the Options menu. From here it is possible to load any Windows bitmap to appear as the background of the Part display. Several choices are supplied with the program and are found on the Cubase VST CD-ROM in Library\Textures. However, users requiring a simpler visual background, such as a single colour, might like to create their own bitmaps in a Windows image editing program like Paint. Simply open an existing small sized bitmap file and paint it the colour required. Re-save as a bitmap under a new name and load it as the Part background, as described above.

Of course, more elaborate bitmaps can be created if you have the time and patience. Those who need a simple white background should click the reset button in the Set Part Background file selector dialogue.

As for the Parts in the Arrange window, 16 user definable colours are available using the Part colors pop-up on the Status bar above the Part display. Select a Track or Part(s) and choose a colour from the menu. Colour coding Tracks and Parts in an arrangement can help identify specific instrument groups. For example, drums, brass, strings and piano Tracks could be colour coded in grey, yellow, green and light blue, which might help clarify a song's structure and contents. In addition to the colours there is, once again, plain white and this is very good for guide Tracks or those Tracks which mark the structure of the song. Audio Tracks could be left in their default red but, of course, the final colour scheme is a matter of personal choice.

Colour is also available in the editors by clicking on the colour palette icon found on the extreme right of the Functions bar. MIDI events may be white, or colour coded according to their channel, pitch, velocity or which Part they belong to. The chosen colours for channel, pitch and velocity may be customised using the last menu item (which appears when channel, pitch or velocity colours is chosen). In the Audio editor, the waveforms can be colour coded according to their Part or according to their channel.

The use of colour in the editors is excellent for clarifying the status of events and, in the case of MIDI velocity colours, provides a clearer impression of the velocity of the notes without necessarily showing velocity in the controller display.

Design your own workspace

Once you have prepared some of the performance and colour characteristics of you system you could also go on to set the size, magnification, quantize, snap and button settings etc. of the Arrange window and the editors, and you might wish to give your audio and MIDI Tracks your own start-up names. All this can then be saved as your own personalised def.all file which will be loaded each time Cubase VST is launched.

The importance of designing your own work space should not be underestimated since this can help optimise your productivity and creativity.

Structural editing actions

Cut, copy and paste

Cut, copy and paste will already be familiar to readers who have used a word processor. These functions are found in the Edit menu but may also be selected using the standard ctrl+X (Mac: command+X) for cut, ctrl+C (Mac: command+C) for copy and ctrl+V (Mac: command+V) for paste. Similar to a word processor, the chosen cut or copied data is stored in a temporary, invisible clipboard, ready to be pasted to a new location.

In the Arrange window, audio or MIDI Parts or whole arrangements may be cut or copied into the clipboard simply by selecting the Parts required and then choosing cut or copy from the Edit menu or from the computer keyboard. The chosen data may be pasted back into the same Arrange window at a new position, according to the song position pointer, or into a different Arrange window where new Tracks will be automatically created for the pasted Parts. Data may be pasted from the clipboard as many times as required since it is *copied* from the clipboard, not *moved* from it. Groups of notes, other kinds of MIDI data and Audio events can be similarly manipulated in the edit windows. Note, however, that MIDI data pasted in the editors may be selected from a number of different Parts but it is always pasted into the *active* Part at the song position pointer.

Cut, copy and paste are best for moving or copying data to positions many bars later in the song, for managing large amounts of data or for copying between separate arrangements.

Repeat

Also in the realms of moving data around, you should not forget Repeat. To repeat a single Part or a group of Parts in the Arrange window, select Repeat from the Structure menu or press ctrl + K (Mac: command + K) on the computer keyboard. This opens a small dialogue box where you may select the number of copies required and whether the copied Parts are to be ghost or real. The resulting copies will be automatically pasted onto the display, immediately after the original.

Repeat is the best option whenever Parts need to be repeated several times in a row and it has the added advantage of saving on memory when ghost copies are chosen. The repeat function works with both MIDI and audio Parts.

Global concerns

For the bulk manipulation of Parts in the Arrange window try Global cut, Global insert and Global split. Global cut and Global insert are best explained in terms of viewing the Arrange window as a length of recording tape.

- Using the left and right locators to mark the positions of the appropriate section of music, Global cut completely removes all data on all Tracks between these points and joins the remaining music together where the section has been removed. It is just like removing a section of recording tape with a razor blade.
- Global insert simply inserts a piece of virtual blank tape between the locators, using the left locator position as the point from which the existing music will be shifted forward to just after the right locator.
- Global split simultaneously splits all Parts at the left and right locator positions, similar to the action of the scissors tool used to split individual Parts.

In all three global cases, muted Tracks will not be subjected to the editing action.

The global functions provide invaluable editing power when the arrangement has become a complex affair, such as when last minute changes require the middle 8 to be a middle 16, (or vice versa), or when the Intro needs to be four bars longer!

Remix and Mixdown

Repeat, Global cut and Global insert can manipulate MIDI data in a linear fashion but what about splitting and mixing MIDI data vertically between Tracks? Remix and Mixdown, found in the Structure menu, provide the answer for certain structural editing requirements of this kind.

Remix

Remix is used to automatically extract a number of separate MIDI Tracks, based on the MIDI channel of events, from an original multi channel Part or Track. In other words, if a MIDI arrangement has been recorded into Cubase VST from an external sequencer and all the data has ended up on a single Track which has been set to 'Any', this data may be separated out onto different Tracks according to the MIDI channel of each event. Reasons for doing this might include the need to process or edit different parts of the arrangement separately, or simply to obtain a better overview of the actual structural content.

Before performing the Remix ensure that the left and right locators are set to the start and end positions of the target sequence. Upon selecting Remix from the menu, all data between the locators will be copied over to separate Tracks according to their MIDI channel, new Tracks being created automatically and the MIDI channel column being automatically numbered according to the MIDI channel of each Track's contents. Remix is also useful for separating the contents of Type 0 MIDI files.

Remix has no effect on audio Tracks.

Mixdown

Mixdown, also found in the Structure menu, performs the opposite function of Remix, i.e. the merging of all MIDI data on a number of Tracks into one single composite Part on a new Track. Simply set the left and right locators to the section of the song required, create a new Track and select it ready for the Mixdown Part. Then select Mixdown from the menu. All Tracks are merged into a new composite Part, entitled 'Mixdown', and the data assumes the appropriate MIDI channel values as found in the channel column for each Track.

Any Tracks not required should be muted in the mute column and they will not be included. To enable the new composite Track to play back normally, 'Any' should be selected in its channel column. Note that any of the Inspector's playback parameters, such as transposition or velocity changes, will be permanently written into the new mixdown Part.

Mixdown is useful for producing composite drum or percussion Parts, or bringing together disparate Tracks or harmony lines which are on the same MIDI channel. It can also simply help in tidying up an untidy arrangement.

Mixdown has no effect on audio Tracks.

The Inspector

The Inspector is found in the Arrange window to the left of the Arrange columns. It is opened and closed by clicking on the square shaped icon in the lower left corner of the screen. The Inspector contains a number of parameters which can be changed to affect the currently selected Part(s) or Track. The contents of the Inspector vary according to what type of Track or Part is currently selected (i.e. MIDI or audio).

For MIDI material, the Inspector resembles Figure 10.5 and features the following:

Figure 10.5 The Inspector (MIDI)

Bank and Program Change

The Bank and Program Change parameters simply change the bank or program number in the target unit. Note, however, that when the Bank select function is changed it also sends out the current Program Change. These functions are useful, firstly, for quickly searching for the desired patch on a synth by remote control from the comfort of the Arrange window and, secondly, for recording automatic program changes into Parts and Tracks. In addition, GM sounds may be selected by name rather than number.

Volume

Volume is useful for setting up a basic mix of the current arrangement by changing the relative levels of each Part or Track.

Transpose

Transpose is useful for trying out simple harmonies or shifting the octave for any given sound.

Velocity

Velocity affects the velocity dynamics of the MIDI data, in the sense of adding or subtracting a value.

Delay

Delay could be used for changing the feel of the chosen Part(s) or Track in relation to the others, by shifting the data backwards or forwards in time by a number of ticks. The actual amount of time in fractions of a second varies according to the current tempo. Possible uses might include adjusting a snare or hi-hat Track to be late or early to give the drum arrangement a special feel, or shifting a slow strings sound earlier to anticipate the beat and overcome the late feel of their slow attack time.

Length

Length might be used to increase the staccato feel of the Part by using a setting of 25%. To increase a Part's legato try a value of 150% or more.

Compression

Compression also affects the velocity dynamics of the MIDI data but by dividing or multiplying according to a percentage. Velocity and compression could be used together to flatten out the dynamics of an over-excited Part (try settings of +50 for velocity with 50% compression), or to add dynamics to a static sounding Part (try – 30 for velocity with 175% compression).

Pan

Pan is used to set up the position of each Track or Part in the stereo image and like Volume helps set up a basic mix of the MIDI arrangement.

The Inspector, therefore, provides an excellent facility for quickly experimenting with the data without the fear of irreversibly changing it. The immediately useful functions are shown in Table 10.1. This outlines the functions and range of each parameter, gives some example settings and shows their effect on the MIDI data.

Table 10.1 Inspector examples

Inspector parameter	Function	Range	Example setting	Result
Bank	bank change	(off) 0 – 16383	1	sends MIDI bank select 1
Program	program change	(off) 1 – 128	1	sends MIDI program change 1
Volume	volume controller (7)	(off) 0 – 127	100	sends MIDI vol. controller set at 100
Transpose	pitch change	– 127 + 127	–12	transposes pitch down by 1 octave
Velocity	velocity change	– 127 + 127	10	raises all note velocities by 10
Delay	time shift	– 256 + 256 ticks	–5	shifts selected Part slightly ahead in time
Length	changes note duration	(off) 25% – 200%	25%	cuts length of notes to $1/4$ of actual length
			200%	doubles the actual length
Compression	velocity compression/ expansion	(off) 25% – 200%	25%	current velocity values are divided by 4
			200%	current velocity values are doubled
Pan	pan position	(off) L63 – R63	R63	pans sound to the extreme right

The parameters in the Inspector for MIDI Tracks are usually referred to as the playback parameters. Beware of using too many playback parameters in an arrangement since, due to the fact that the changes are processed in real-time, this could lead to an unnecessary drain on the computer's processing power. Once absolutely sure that the changes made in the Inspector will never be updated, use Freeze Play Parameters in the Functions menu (alt + ctrl + F) to make them a permanent part of the data.

The Inspector assumes different functions when the currently selected Track or Part is audio. The only similarity with the MIDI Inspector is that the name of the selected Part or Track is displayed at the top and a delay parameter is available to shift the audio backwards or forwards in time. The audio Inspector's other features include an input select button for selecting the input when recording audio onto the Track, an FX/EQ button to open the FX send and EQ settings dialogue for the selected Track, a record enable button when monitoring via VST and a stereo/mono switch for choosing whether the Track is stereo or mono prior to recording.

The functions of the audio Inspector are described in more detail in Chapters 3 and 6.

Quantize

The quantize functions found in the Functions menu are among Cubase VST's most used features. These warrant detailed inspection. Far from being a mere timing correction function, with Cubase VST, quantize has become a creative tool in its own right.

It is apparent from the menu items that various different kinds of quantize operations are possible but the principle is the same for all of them; quantize shifts notes onto or towards the division of the bar set in the Quant (quantize) box. The rules of actually how this is done depends on the type of quantize chosen.

The following quantize descriptions are relevant to the quantizing of MIDI material. The use of quantize with audio is described in Chapter 7. If you are intending to quantize audio material this is best achieved while working in the Audio editor. Quantizing audio Parts in the Arrange window is not recommended. Note that only Over quantize and Groove quantize are available for the routine quantizing of audio but Match quantize can also be used to impose the timing of audio material onto MIDI data and vice versa (outlined below).

Over quantize
Over quantize (Q on the computer keyboard), shifts notes onto the nearest quantize value, but it also has the ability to detect if the playing is consistently behind or in front of the beat and it quantizes chords intelligently.

Note on quantize
Note On quantize (W on the computer keyboard), is the least musical quantize method. It uses the Note On element of notes to shift them onto the nearest quantize value with no regard for their particular context. The original note length remains unchanged.

Iterative quantize
Iterative quantize (E on the computer keyboard), takes things one stage further since the user can set up Strength and Don't Q (Don't quantize) parameters, (in the Setup Grooves dialogue), to govern the manner in

which notes will be shifted *towards* the quantize value. Don't Q tells Cubase VST the range *close* to the quantize value, (in ticks), within which no Iterative quantize action will take place, and the Strength percentage tells Cubase VST how far to shift notes that are not close enough to the quantize value. Due to its progressive nature Iterative quantize may be selected a number of times in succession.

Analytic quantize

Analytic quantize intelligently corrects timing errors according to an analysis of the music based on the quantize value and the actual characteristics of the contents. This is best suited to rhythmically complex input and solos and is worth trying if none of the other quantize methods give the desired result.

Match quantize

Match quantize is a special kind of quantize function provided in the Arrange window toolbox (Match Q). It is designed to impose the timing and accent characteristics (the feel) of one Part upon another.

For example, this could be used to tighten up the feel of bass line and bass drum MIDI Parts. Proceed as follows:

- Use the bass drum Part as the feel Part and simply drag it, using the Match Q tool, and let go over the target bass line Part.
- A dialogue box asks if the velocity values should also be matched. In this example, 'No' is probably the best option.
- The quantize value for this operation, (selected in the quantize box), governs the capture range. If a coarse quantize value has been selected, such as 4, then more data in the target Part will be dragged to the positions of the notes in the feel Part, (which, in this case, would probably not be desirable).
- Selecting a quantize value of 16 or 8 would ensure that the bass line remains intact, with most of the notes slipping through unchanged, and only those notes closest to those in the feel Part being shifted back or forth in time.

Match quantize also functions when dragging an audio Part onto a MIDI Part or vice versa. To match quantize a MIDI Part to an audio Part proceed as follows:

- Select the Match quantize tool from the toolbox.
- Drag and drop the audio Part on top of the target MIDI Part.
- This process requires Match points to be calculated for the audio Part and, if it does not already contain them, the Get Match points dialogue appears (Figure 10.6). Match points are generally used to pick out the main hitpoints in the audio material. If your audio Part contains rhythmic audio material try setting Sensitivity to

30%, Attack to 10% and the number of events per second to 10. This should pick out the bass drum and snare, for example, but all will depend on the precise characteristics of the audio material. Note that the Match points also register velocity information, matching the amplitude of each hitpoint.

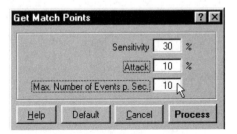

Figure 10.6 The Get match points dialogue

- Click on the Process button to compute the Match points for the Part.
- In the next dialogue which appears, (Figure 10.7), choose copy, to impose the velocity characteristics of the Match points upon the target MIDI Part, or merge, to influence the existing velocities with the new ones.

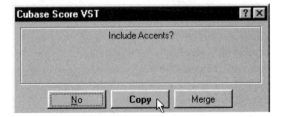

Figure 10.7 Choose copy or merge

- The quantize value for this operation, (selected in the quantize box), governs the capture range.
- Audition the result and, if unsatisfactory, use undo in the Edit menu to return the Part to its original state.

To match quantize an audio Part to a MIDI Part proceed as follows:

- Select the Match quantize tool from the toolbox.
- Drag and drop the MIDI Part on top of the target audio Part.
- In the dialogue which appears (Figure 10.8), click on Yes to proceed with dynamic time correction. When an audio Part is targeted for Match quantizing, this necessitates modification of the actual audio data and sections of the audio material may be time stretched.

Figure 10.8 Dynamic time correction dialogue

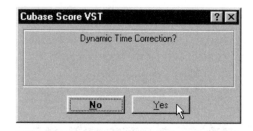

- If the audio Part does not already contain any Match points, the Get Match points dialogue appears (see Figure 10.6). Match points are used to find the main hitpoints in the audio material, as explained above.
- In the Get Match Points dialogue, try setting Sensitivity to 30%, Attack to 10% and the number of events per second to 10. Click on the Process button.
- Once the Match points have been computed the audio file undergoes time correction. This involves time stretching the material at the appropriate sections of the file according to the current quantize value in the quantize box, the Match points and the position of each event in the source MIDI Part.
- Audition the result and, if unsatisfactory, use undo in the Edit menu to return the Part to its original state. Remember that you have only one level of undo.

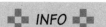 **INFO**

In both procedures involving audio Parts, the Match points are crucial to the success of the operation. It may be necessary to edit the Match points manually, and this is achieved in the Audio editor (see Chapter 7).

Groove quantize

Groove quantize (J on the computer keyboard), allows the user to create individual rhythmic templates known as Groove maps. Each Groove map is a timing template which may be imposed upon any chosen data. A selection of grooves are supplied with the program but these may be updated or completely replaced by new sets of grooves designed by the user or outside sources. Using the existing preset grooves on suitable material can produce startling results. (Pressing J on the computer keyboard repeats the most recently selected groove).

As with most Cubase VST processing, the final judge of whether the chosen quantize values are working or not is the ear. However, the maze of quantize parameters involved may obscure what is actually going on and what result is required. Visual feedback can help clarify matters. Figure 10.9 shows the results of various kinds of quantize on a simple drum Part in Key edit.

The snare drum (D1) and the hi-hat (F#1) on the second beat of the second bar have been recorded very inaccurately and the illustration shows how each quantize method changes the two notes. The direction in which each note is moved is indicated by an arrow.

The hi-hat has been recorded nearer to the third beat of the bar than the snare, and thus, for both Note on and Iterative quantize, gets pulled across to this beat rather than onto the desired second beat. Over quan-

Figure 10.9 Quantize results

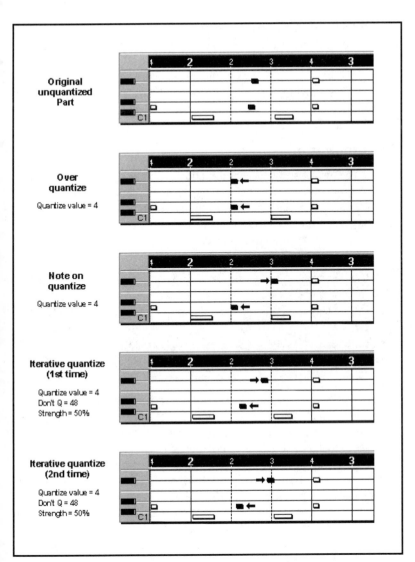

tize alone produces a satisfactory result, since this treats the snare and hi-hat events intelligently, (as a kind of chord), and shifts them back to the same position. Note also that Iterative quantize has no further effect on the data after the second selection because all notes are already within the chosen 48 tick Don't quantize zone. Of course, the quantizing of more sophisticated data may prove much more complicated and only experience, experimentation and understanding will help perfect the process.

You should be aware that, with MIDI Parts, quantize works on notes alone, leaving other kinds of MIDI messages unchanged. In addition, quantize does not permanently change the MIDI data, and except for Iterative quantize the original notes are always used for calculating subsequent quantize actions. Undo quantize, (U on the computer keyboard), will return a quantized MIDI Part to its original state. Remember also that

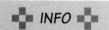

Cubase VST provides quantize values of any resolution between 1/64th and whole notes with triplet and dotted options for each. The choice of quantize value is crucial to a successful result.

Finally Freeze quantize makes the current MIDI quantizing status permanent. This should be used to permanently lock the quantize into MIDI Parts only when it is sure they will never need re-processing.

Synchronization

Cubase VST provides comprehensive and flexible synchronization features. The program can, of course, run by itself in synchronization with the computer's internal clock but, as with most computer-based sequencers, it can also be synchronized to external units.

The main possibilities are as follows :

- The synchronization of Cubase VST to an external device via MIDI Time Code (MTC).
- The synchronization of Cubase VST to an external device via MIDI Clock.
- The synchronization of Cubase VST with a tape recorder using MIDI Machine Control (MMC).

Selecting Synchronization in the Options menu opens a dialogue where the essential parameters may be adjusted (Figure 10.10). The various ports of your audio card or external device should already be available in the pop-up menus of the Sync Source section.

The Synchronization dialogue also features an MROS/System Resolution section. The value in the PPQN field (pulses per quarter note) defines the current resolution of Cubase VST. 384 is the maximum resolution available and is the default setting (PC version). System pre-roll defines a time in milliseconds that Cubase VST uses to prepare itself before playback commences. This creates a short delay after you have pressed the play button. If you are experiencing timing drift between your audio and MIDI Parts try setting the pre-roll value to the same value as the latency of your audio card. The latency time is found in the Audio I/O section of the Audio System Setup dialogue (Audio menu).

The default setting of the Synchronization dialogue when Cubase VST is supplied is to internal mode, where no synchronization to an external source is possible.

The synchronization settings are saved with each song file and, once the settings have been adjusted to suit your system, could be saved as part of the definition file which is loaded each time Cubase VST is launched.

Synchronizing Cubase VST to MIDI Time code (MTC)

MTC is a particular kind of Time code which can be transmitted through an ordinary MIDI cable. The device which sends the MTC to Cubase VST

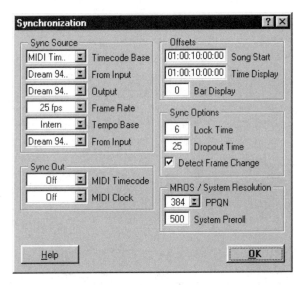

Figure 10.10. The
Synchronization dialogue

could be a SMPTE to MTC converter or, perhaps, another sequencer. A SMPTE to MTC converter is often used to provide an interface between a multitrack tape recorder and a computer based sequencer, like Cubase VST, and this forms the main subject matter of this section.

Before synchronization can occur with a tape machine, one of the tracks on the tape must be striped with Time code i.e.: some kind of Time code, (often referred to as SMPTE or EBU Time code), must be recorded onto it. This code, in turn, is played back to the interface which then drives the rest of the system. In this example the interface would convert the Time code into MTC, which would then be sent to the computer via a MIDI cable.

To set up Cubase VST with a SMPTE to MTC converter and tape machine proceed as follows:

- As just mentioned above, the first task is to stripe the tape with SMPTE code. For this task it is best to use Cubase VST's Generate SMPTE feature in the Audio menu (Figure 10.11). This generates an audio file containing 'perfect' Time code, with the specified start time, frame rate and length (in minutes), as shown in the dialogue. It is said to be perfect since it runs at the same speed as your audio hardware and is less likely to give synchronization problems with your MIDI data when Cubase VST is slaved to the

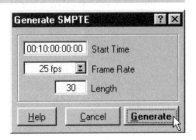

Figure 10.11 Generate SMPTE dialogue

*The MTC synchro-
nization option
does not dictate the
actual tempo of
Cubase VST. This is
still governed by the
tempo indicated on the
Transport bar or by
the tempo (or tempo
changes) in the
Mastertrack, when it is
activated.*

tape machine. When you have adjusted the settings, click on the generate button to create the file.

- Once created, send the file's signal to the SMPTE track of your tape machine and record it for the required length of time. When you have finished, the audio file can either remain on your hard disk or can be transferred to DAT for use in later sessions. It is strongly recommended that you always use SMPTE code which has been generated in this manner for synchronization purposes.

- Ensure that your SMPTE to MTC converter is correctly connected to the tape machine and that the MIDI out from the device is connected to the MIDI In of your card's MIDI interface. Remember that you may need a MIDI merge facility in order to be able to simultaneously connect your master keyboard (or other MIDI instrument) and the MIDI cable containing the MTC.

- In Cubase VST's synchronization dialogue, set Timecode base to MTC.

- Select the MIDI port which will be receiving MTC in the From Input pop-up.

- Set Tempo base to internal.

- Select the appropriate frame rate (the same as that recorded on the tape).

- Select the start time for the song in the Offsets section. This is the time in the received Time code which Cubase VST will treat as the starting point for the song. For certain uses it is appropriate to set the time display to the same as the song start. This causes Cubase VST's main time position on the Transport bar to match the Time code which is being received from tape. This is desirable if you would like all machines in the set-up to display the same SMPTE time.

- To activate synchronization, close the dialogue and click on the Sync button on the Transport bar or press X on the computer keyboard. Cubase VST is now ready to slave to any incoming MTC.

- Rewind the tape machine to before the start time of the song and press the play button. When the interface receives SMPTE code on or after the song start time, Cubase VST begins playback, in synchronization with the tape.

*The Offsets section
displays the time in
hours, minutes,
seconds, frames and
sub-frames.*

Those who have already used Time code will know that Cubase VST will now automatically chase and lock up to each new tape position selected. The sync options dictate exactly how Cubase VST will lock up to the incoming code, as follows:

- Locktime specifies the number of correct frames of Time code required before Cubase VST will lock to it.

- Dropout Time specifies the number of incorrect frames Cubase VST will tolerate before it drops out of synchronization.

- Detect Frame Change, when activated, will automatically recognise changes in the frame rate of incoming Time code.

Synchronizing Cubase VST to MIDI Clock

MIDI Clock data contains messages called song position pointers, as well as tempo information, to keep Cubase VST in sync with an external unit. The external unit could be a Time code to MIDI Clock converter or another sequencer. To synchronize Cubase VST to MIDI Clock, set up the Synchronization dialogue as follows :

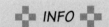

- Set Timecode base to internal.
- In the Tempo base pop-up select MIDI Clock.
- In the From Input of the Tempo base section, select the MIDI Input into which the MIDI Clocks are being sent.
- Close the synchronization dialogue and click on the Sync button on the Transport bar or press X on the computer keyboard. Cubase VST is now ready to slave to any incoming MIDI Clock data.

This time, the external unit governs the basic tempo and any tempo changes of Cubase VST. Therefore, any tempo changes programmed into the song will have to be re-programmed into the controlling device, which has become a kind of external Mastertrack.

Synchronization to MIDI Clock is rather awkward and inconvenient for slaving Cubase VST to external equipment when compared with other synchronization methods. It is advisable to only use it as a last resort and it should not be used for audio material.

However, MIDI Clock can have its uses when you need to slave a device to Cubase VST. For example, once Cubase VST is locked to an external device using MTC, MIDI Clock could be simultaneously transmitted using the Sync Out option to drive any slaved MIDI devices in the system, such as drum machines or synthesizers with on-board sequencers. It is advisable to drive a MIDI system where MIDI Clock is generated from only one source, (in this case, from Cubase VST), thus minimising the possibility of synchronization errors.

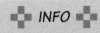

In addition, MIDI Clock may be the solution if you are directly recording the MIDI data from a non-MTC equipped drum machine or sequencer into Cubase VST. In this case, set Cubase VST as the master and the external unit as the slave. MIDI Clocks are transmitted from Cubase VST to the slaved device and the MIDI data from the external unit is sent back to Cubase VST. Activating record in Cubase VST records the incoming data onto the currently active Track.

Synchronizing Cubase VST with a tape recorder using MIDI Machine Control (MMC).

Cubase VST provides support for external devices which are able to send and receive MMC. MMC is a special part of the MIDI protocol which specifies MIDI messages for the control of such things as tape transports.

The use of MMC is, in fact, a two-way process, which involves both MMC messages and also MTC. It requires both the MIDI input and MIDI output of the tape recorder to be connected to Cubase VST. MMC messages are transmitted between the MIDI output of Cubase VST and the

MIDI input of the tape recorder, which controls the transport and other functions. The tape recorder transmits MTC to the MIDI input of Cubase VST and this locks the two machines in synchronization. The process usually requires the recording of SMPTE code onto one track of the tape recorder and this is converted into MTC during playback. In effect, Cubase VST becomes both the master and the slave in this process.

To set up your system and the Synchronization dialogue for use with a tape machine which supports MMC, proceed as follows:

- Ensure that the MIDI in and out cables are correctly connected between the tape recorder and Cubase VST and that SMPTE code has been recorded onto one track of the tape. Adjust the tape recorder set-up so that it is ready to send and receive MMC commands.
- In Cubase VST's synchronization dialogue set Timecode base to MMC.
- Select the MIDI port which will be receiving MIDI data from the tape recorder in the From Input pop-up menu.
- Select the MIDI port for transmitting Cubase VST's MMC commands in the Output pop-up menu.
- Select the appropriate frame rate, (the same as that recorded on the tape), in the Frame rate pop-up menu.
- Set Tempo base to internal.
- Select the start time for the song in the Offsets section. This is the time in the received MTC which Cubase VST will treat as the starting point for the song. Close the Synchronisation dialogue.
- Ensure that System Exclusive data is filtered (ticked) in the MIDI Setup dialogue (Options menu).
- Activate the Sync button on the Transport bar.
- Press the play button on the tape recorder and play the tape for a short section to allow Cubase VST to lock to the current Time code position.
- Stop the tape and then press play in Cubase VST. The tape should roll back to just before the current time position in Cubase VST and then commence playback. After a second or two Cubase VST commences playback in sync with the tape recorder and, thereafter, all Cubase VST transport controls, including stop, fast forward and rewind, as well as play, control the transport of the tape recorder.

Note that in order to use Cubase VST's record function to remotely activate recording on the tape recorder you must use one or more Tape Tracks. This is a special class of Track which is used to manage recording on the tape recorder. Each Tape Track in Cubase VST can be set to a channel number which corresponds to the same numbered track on the tape machine. Each Tape Track in Cubase VST can also be used to activate a record ready status on the tape recorder. All Tracks set to record ready will drop into record on the tape machine when the record button is activated in Cubase VST.

More about synchronization

Slaving Cubase VST to external units can have adverse effects on the precision of the synchronization when the arrangement contains audio Parts. The problem derives from the fact that the timing of the audio material is referenced to the audio clock of the digital audio hardware.

Under normal circumstances, when Cubase VST is not slaved to an external device (i.e. the Timecode base is internal), both the MIDI and audio data is locked to the same clock (the digital audio hardware's built-in clock, known as the audio clock). The choice of clock for MIDI is set in the Audio System Setup dialogue (Audio menu) in the MIDI Sync Reference section and, by default, this is usually set to Audio clock. Locking the MIDI data to the same timing reference as the audio data, (i.e. the audio clock), ensures that there is no timing drift between the two during playback.

However, when Cubase VST is slaved to an external device, the timing reference of the program is governed by the external clock, while the timing reference for the audio data is still locked to the audio clock. The clock for the MIDI data can be changed to the external Time code in the MIDI Sync Reference section of the Audio System Setup dialogue but the audio data cannot. Due to variations in tape speed and the fact that the speed of the external clock may be different from the speed of the audio clock, this can result in a timing drift between the audio recorded in Cubase VST and the audio on tape/MIDI data i.e. the audio on tape and the MIDI data in Cubase VST remain synchronised while the audio in Cubase VST does not.

As explained in Synchronizing Cubase VST to MIDI Time Code above, it helps to use Time code which has been generated by Cubase VST's Generate SMPTE feature, since this will run at exactly the same speed as that used by your digital audio hardware. Thus, when the system is locked to this code, it should match the speed of Cubase VST's audio clock and all should be in perfect synchronization. However, although this will certainly help, it is not the complete solution.

Steinberg recommend that, when using audio, if it is possible you should always use Cubase VST as the master device by sending MIDI Timecode out to drive other devices (Sync Out section in Synchronization dialogue). This ensures perfect synchronization.

The best solution to the problem, and one which is increasingly used in professional installations, is word clock. This is a method of keeping the sample rates of digital equipment in perfect synchronization by using a clock which ticks once for every bit of data transferred. In such a system, one digital clock provides the timing reference for all other digital units, which might include Cubase VST. To use this kind of synchronization, the installation of specialist hardware is required. Word clock is not generally available on standard audio cards but some of the more advanced hardware, like the Korg 1212 I/O card and the Event Layla, feature word clock in and out. Of course, if you wish to use word clock, the other units with which you wish to synchronize should also be similarly equipped.

Clearly, synchronization is a big subject and the finer points are beyond the scope of this text. Consult the electronic documentation for more details.

Modular matters

Modules are self-contained parts of Cubase VST which can be hooked on when required and jettisoned when not in use, in order to conserve memory.

The MIDI Effect processor is just such a module and serves as a good example for explanation purposes. Like all modules it must first be available and active in the Module Setup dialogue in order to use it.

Selecting Setup from the Modules menu opens the Modules Setup dialogue which features four columns indicating the module name, its size, its active status and its preload status (Figure 10.12). Modules will already be present if they have been put in the modules directory on the hard disk. The Modules are automatically added to the Modules Setup dialogue when Cubase VST is launched.

A typical PC modules list includes the Studio module, the AVI monitor, the CD Player, the SysEx editor, the Arpeggiator, Styletrax, the SMPTE display and the MIDI effect processor.

A module is not actually residing in memory until it has been activated. This is achieved by selecting the desired module and clicking in its Active column. You can also set modules to automatically load into memory each time the program is started by clicking in the Preload column. Those modules which have been made active then become available for selection in the main Modules menu.

Figure 10.12 The Modules Setup dialogue

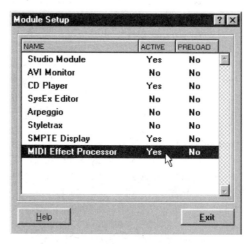

Setting up the MIDI effect processor module

First, select MIDI Effect processor in the Module Setup list and click in its Active column to activate the module. Note that, at this stage, the MIDI Effect processor itself is not actually being opened. Once activated, the MIDI Effect processor itself is selected from the extra items in the main Modules menu.

Selecting MIDI Effect processor from the Modules menu opens the MIDI Processor window (Figure 10.13). This processes MIDI data to produce delay, chorus and pitch-shift effects. The window has an On/Off status box, input and output selectors and six sliders.

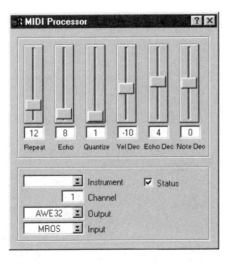

Figure 10.13 The MIDI Effect
processor

Switching the status to On, (ticked), activates the current effect but the result may not be immediately apparent if the input and output have not been sensibly adjusted. Set the input to that of the master keyboard, and the output to the MIDI channel and Output port of a synthesiser or rack-mount unit in the MIDI system.

For the initial testing of the effects it is suggested that a snare drum is targeted. Simply play the chosen sound and experiment with the Repeat and Echo sliders to produce echo and delay effects. The sliders may be directly dragged, moved coarsely by clicking above or below the slider control, or adjusted directly in each slider's value box.

- *Repeat* sets the number of repeats desired from each incoming note event.
- *Echo* sets the delay time between each repeat with one unit of the slider representing eight ticks.
- *Quantize* moves the repeats to the nearest set value (one unit, once again, representing eight ticks).
- *Echo Dec* adds or subtracts a set number (8 ticks per unit) for each subsequent repeat to produce accelerated or decelerated echo effects.
- *Vel Dec* adds or subtracts a set velocity value for each subsequent repeat to produce crescendo or de-crescendo echoes.
- *Note Dec* adds or subtracts from the note value of each subsequent repeat to produce arpeggio-like effects.

In order to guide the user, Table 10.2 shows various echo and quantize slider values and their corresponding note values.

That's a start in understanding the functions of the MIDI Effect processor, but how do we process a recorded Track? This requires a little knowledge of the possibilities of MROS (MIDI Real Time Operating System). Many Steinberg products run under MROS which provides synchronization and connection possibilities between different programs run-

Table 10.2 MIDI Effect processor slider values

MIDI Processor slider	No. of ticks	Note value
48	384	1 / 4 note
24	192	1 / 8 note
16	128	1 / 8 triplet
12	96	1 / 16 note
8	64	1 / 16 triplet
6	48	1 / 32 note
4	32	1 / 32 triplet
3	24	1 / 64 note

ning on the same computer. But it also provides the possibility of sending data to different parts of the same system.

If the Arrange window Output column of the target Track is set to MROS and the MIDI Processor's input is set to MROS, it will then receive and process the MIDI data of the chosen Track. It may also be necessary to reset the MIDI Processor output to send the processed data to the appropriate unit. It's rather like an internal patching system.

We could now take things one stage further and consider what needs to be set in order to actually record the output of the MIDI Processor. In this case, set the output to MROS and then go into the MIDI Setup dialogue box, (as described at the beginning of this Chapter), and set the Record From box to MROS. This patches the output of the MIDI Processor to the record input of Cubase VST and all data output from the MIDI Processor can be recorded on an appropriate Track. The MIDI Effect processor may be handy for those users not possessing vast numbers of effects units, but remember that it can also produce effects difficult to achieve on conventional units.

However, since the processing relies upon adding to existing MIDI note data, it could, in certain circumstances, produce undesirable hold-ups in the data flow of the rest of the music. It all depends on the density of the other events in the arrangement. Nevertheless, it is well worth spending some time exploring the possibilities. Try the settings in Table 10.3 as starting points for your own experiments.

That is just one of the modules available, but users requiring extra features should find the others on the list well worth exploring. For example, the SMPTE display module provides a very useable and practical large digit Time code display for time critical situations and the Studio module is a must for bringing a complex MIDI setup under central control.

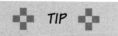

TIP

Remember that, once the MIDI Processor is On, it is possible to leave the window and work freely in other areas of the program ; the MIDI processor remains active.

Table 10.3 MIDI Effect processor starting points

Repeat	Echo	Quantize	Velocity dec	Echo dec	Note dec
8	12	1	−12	0	0
3	8	1	−30	−2	0
4	48	1	−30	−12	0
12	8	1	−10	4	0
3	12	1	6	0	5
4	12	1	0	0	12

Input transformation

The MIDI Setup and MIDI Filter dialogues control and transform the MIDI data as it arrives at the input of Cubase VST. The Input Transformer (Options menu) also operates on input data in real-time, but provides a more comprehensive range of possibilities.

The Input Transformer dialogue (Figure 10.14) closely resembles the Logical edit window in Easy Mode. Its functions are to either transform or filter incoming MIDI data according to the settings of the Filter and Processing sections. Transform and filter modes are found in the Functions box in the lower part of the window. Filter ignores the processing part of the window while transform takes all settings into account.

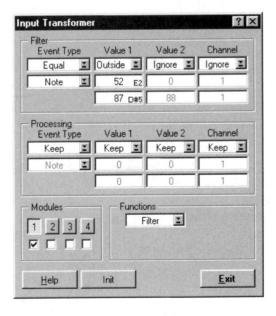

Figure 10.14 The Input Transformer

A statement in plain English describing a simple filtering action in the window might run as follows :

IF the input data contains aftertouch messages THEN filter them.

This translates into the window as follows:

- In the Filter section, set the event type column to read 'equal aftertouch' with all other columns being ignored.
- Ignore the Processing section.
- Choose Filter as the function mode.

In Filter mode the processing section is not active. The result of this setting is the stripping of all aftertouch messages from the incoming data.

Similarly a transformation setting might be described as follows:

IF the input data contains control change 1 messages, (modulation), THEN change, (fix), this data to control change 7 messages (volume).

This translates as follows:

- In the Filter section, set the event type to equal 'Control Change' and the value 1 column to 'equal 1'.
- In the Processing section. set the value 1 column to 'fix 7'.
- Set the mode to 'Transform' in the Functions box.

The result is the transformation of any modulation messages (control change 1) into volume messages (control change 7).

So, as we can see the logic of the window may be expressed as a kind of IF, THEN statement, as found in computer languages. Take a look in the pop-up menus of the various columns and it becomes clear that some very sophisticated filtering and transformation actions are possible. In addition, the window offers the possibility of four transformation set-ups in its memory at the same time (presets 1 – 4), and activating (ticked) or de-activating (unticked) any combination. Note that the data travels through each activated filter/transformation setup in its numbered order, so messages filtered out of setup number 1 do not reach setup number 2 and so on.

The contents of the Input Transformer are saved with the song. The four default presets which come with the program are useful for understanding the possibilities but users may also like to consider the following two examples.

Setting a filter to restrict the input range for a chosen instrument

For the playing range of a trumpet, for example, proceed as follows:

- In the Filter section, set the event type column to 'equal note' and the value 1 column to 'outside 52 (E2) to 87 (D#5)'.
- Set the mode to Filter in the Functions box.

The result is the filtering of any notes outside the chosen range. This kind of filter is excellent for keeping within the natural note range of an instrument, if a sense of realism is what your arrangement needs. It would also curb the dubious desires of the crazed soloist who insists on playing outside the instrument's natural range!

Changing pitch bend into pan data

To set a transformation which changes pitch bend into pan data:

- Set the Filter event type column to 'equal pitch bend'.
- Set the Processing section event type column to 'fix control change' and the value 1 column to 'fix 10' (pan controller).

The result is the immediate transformation of any pitch bend messages into pan data. This setup is excellent for the inspired real-time application of pan data using the synth's pitch wheel, which is a natural choice for manipulating pan.

Of course, many more configurations are possible and, by using two or more setups simultaneously, the user can design extremely complex filters and data transformations. And remember that any efforts made here will serve you well if ever you decide to venture into Logical edit.

Other useful features

Transpose/Velocity

Transpose/Velocity (selected in the Functions menu or with ctrl + H (Mac: command + H) on the computer keyboard), is for the manipulation of the pitch and velocity of notes. When selected, a small window presents options to change either the pitch or the velocity, or both at the same time (Figure 10.15).

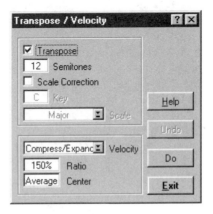

Figure 10.15 The Transpose/Velocity dialogue

Transpose

The Transpose section pitch shifts the chosen data up or down in semitones. Data may also be corrected according to a number of chosen scales using the scale correction option.

Velocity

The velocity options are slightly more complicated. These include the following:

- the addition or subtraction of a set velocity amount from all chosen notes.
- the limiting of velocities between a set lower and upper limit (this lowers or raises any velocities outside of the set range without affecting those within it).
- the compression/expansion of velocities according to a percentage and a centre point (Average). This requires some explanation. The compression/expansion ratio is in the range −100% to +300%. Ratios above 100% produce expansion and those below 100% produce compression. The Centre setting is used to calculate from where the expansion or compression occurs. It may be set to average, where the program finds its own centre value based on an average of the velocities of the chosen data, or it may be set to any user value. Velocities with exactly the centre value will not be affected by the operation.

On expansion, all velocity values lower than centre will be lowered and all those above will be raised, both according to the percentage amount.

On compression, all velocity values lower than Centre will be raised and all those above will be lowered, once again both according to the percentage amount.

Remember that Transpose/Velocity produces a permanent effect on the data but this may be undone as long as the edit remains in the clipboard. As a general precaution, it is probably best to work with Transpose/ Velocity from within one of the editors until the options have been mastered thoroughly. In this way, any updates to the data will only be committed to memory when keeping the data upon leaving the editor. In the case of an undesirable result, using escape to leave the editor will return the Part to its original form.

The Note Pad

The Note Pad (Figure 10.16), found in the Edit menu or opened using ctrl + B (Mac: command + B), is one of those Cubase VST features for which it is difficult to find a good use. But how many times have you loaded up versions of the same song which are subtly different but you can't remember why, and you can't remember which one is the definitive version?

Simply entering some explanatory text into the Note Pad could have saved a lot of time and ensured that the definitive arrangement had been

Figure 10.16 The Note Pad

loaded. The Note Pad is Cubase VST's own mini word processor and as well as entering guide text, as above, could also be used to note:

- Special settings or patches used in a song.
- The dates and times when the song was worked on.
- The Track listing for the multitrack tape tracks.
- The administrative details of the song, such as the names of the composer/writer or the record/publishing company.

The contents of the Note Pad are saved with each separate arrangement.

Part Appearance

Another miscellaneous function of Cubase VST is Part Appearance found in the Options menu. This provides several choices of how to show Parts in the Arrange window including: 'show names', 'show events', 'show frames' and 'show names and waves'.

'Show names' shows the Parts in the Arrange window with names, 'show events' shows the Events contained in the Parts as vertical lines, 'show frames' shows the Parts as blank strips and 'show names and waves' shows the names for all Parts and the waveforms for audio Parts.

Not only can all events be shown for MIDI Parts, it is also possible to visually filter the event types by ticking only those required. This is excellent for searching for specific events in a complicated arrangement. It is also useful for seeking out melodies and is invaluable in giving a more detailed overview of the actual contents of a MIDI arrangement.

The Windows menu

The Windows menu is another Cubase VST feature which is easily overlooked. It can, however, prove very convenient if you need to look at data in several windows at the same time. The ability to tile several editors onto the same screen can be invaluable when editing data in fine detail. Select the Tile or Stack options from the Windows menu to see two or more editors on screen simultaneously.

In addition, the Windows menu is where the user may select the arrangement from the listed arrangements currently in memory. The Windows menu also allows the user to hide or show the Transport bar (as does pressing F12 on the computer keyboard). This maximises the screen space for the Arrange window or the editors, and Cubase VST may still be controlled from the numeric keypad, where the Transport bar functions are replicated.

More smart moves

The features outlined in this chapter are often managed using the Mouse but there are still a substantial number of keyboard commands, particularly for the quantize functions, which help speed things up. The following table outlines some of the most useful keyboard moves (Table 10.4):

Table 10.4 More smart moves

Computer keyboard		Function
PC	Mac	
Q	Q	over quantize
W	W	note on quantize
E	E	iterative quantize
J	J	groove quantize
U	U	undo quantize
1 – 7	1 – 7	set quantize value
T	T	set triplet quantize value
.	.	set dotted quantize value
X	X	synchronization on/off
ctrl + H	command + H	open Transpose/Velocity dialogue
ctrl + K	command + K	open Repeat Part(s) dialogue
ctrl + B	command + B	open notepad
alt + ctrl + F	no default	freeze playback parameters

Having got this far, you should now understand most of the basics of Cubase VST. However, as many of you will be aware, we have hardly touched upon the VST and advanced audio aspects of the program. The next three chapters explore the wonders of digital audio processing, virtual studio technology and plug-ins.

11

Audio processing

This chapter describes the audio processing functions found in the Processing option of the main Audio menu. As well as providing a description of each function, there are explanations of how you might use them for creative and corrective purposes.

Important

Before you start any audio processing beware of the dangers! All the audio processing functions act upon the audio data on the hard disk and make permanent changes. There is one, and only one, level of undo. For example, if you reverse and then immediately pitch shift a file you will be unable to return the file to its original un-reversed state! Note also that leaving the Audio editor using Escape, after having used a processing function therein, does *not* undo the processing and return the file to its original state. Any processing conducted in the Audio editor which has affected the audio file on disk will be retained and, not only that, the undo buffer is cleared upon leaving, so you can no longer undo your last edit. If you are not an expert user, it is recommended that you make a backup before embarking on any serious audio processing.

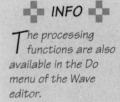

❖ *INFO* ❖

The processing functions are also available in the Do menu of the Wave editor.

The processing options
Cubase VST provides the following processing options: reverse, silence, fade in, fade out, quieten, invert, normalize and pitch shift/time correction. The function of the majority of these is self-evident but it is not quite so obvious how and why you might use them.

What gets affected
The processing functions act upon the following:

- One or more selected Parts in the Arrange window
- One or more selected Audio events in the Audio editor
- One or more selected files/segments in the Audio Pool
- A selection, segment, or file in the Wave editor

With multiple selections, all Parts/Audio events/segments have the same process applied in equal amounts. For example, if you select two consecutive Parts and apply fade out processing, the fade does not occur over the whole length of the two Parts but within each single Part.

Reverse

Reverse simply reverses the selection. In other words, after processing, you can play the audio backwards.

Great! But what could we use this for? Reversing certain kinds of audio material can produce a kind of crescendo, similar to a drum roll, and favourite material for this kind of effect includes snare drum hits, (preferably with a reverb tail), and cymbals. Reversals on any kind of audio material can sometimes produce startling results which are good for special effects, and shorter reversed segments can often find a place in a rhythmic pattern. The reverse function is also useful when used in conjunction with effects like reverb (see Combination processing below).

Reverse processing calls for experimentation so, if you do not want to risk losing the original file, make a backup.

Silence

The silence function overwrites the current selection with complete silence. This is most often useful in the Wave editor when working in fine detail.

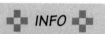

Much of the time you might clean up audio files in the Audio editor by splitting events and dragging the start and end points to mask the unwanted material but, if there are a large number of very small and precise sections which need to be silenced, it may be easier to select them in the Wave editor and use the silence function.

Remember that inserting absolute silence between the lyrics of a vocal Track or speech is *not* often an effective solution since it produces an unnatural effect where the silence actually accentuates the background noise in the remaining material. The technique may be adequate if you have recorded a vocal take with minimal background noise but, in general, it is better inserted between phrases and gaps in the lyrics and, if you have access to other corrective processing such as noise gate or expander plug-ins, these provide a better solution.

Audio files sometimes suffer from glitches at the very beginning or end of the file. Since the length of the section may be extremely short, the silence function in the Wave editor at high magnification often provides the easiest method of removal.

Fade in and Fade out

These functions apply a linear fade in or fade out to the selected material. They provide an alternative to using Cubase VST's automated mix functions for fading in or fading out an audio arrangement and are useful if you are assembling a sequence of completed stereo arrangements for later transferral to CD.

A Fade in Part and a fade out Part in the Arrange window could also be overlapped in order to produce crossfading effects.

In addition, Fade in and fade out can be used over the very beginning or end of an audio file for a *very* short section in order to mask any sharp transients which may be present. This would normally be achieved at high magnification in the Wave editor and results in an audio file which seems to start and end more smoothly.

Quieten

Quieten applies a −6dB cut to the selected audio, resulting in a file which has half the amplitude of the original. This function provides an alternative to the silence function when attempting to clean up the background noise between vocal lines and is likely to result in a final audio result which sounds more natural.

It might be used to quieten the audio in the middle of a vocal audio file when the vocalist has suddenly moved in closer to the microphone, resulting in one or more words sounding too loud. It can also be used to cut down sudden peaks in the audio material prior to normalization (see Combination processing below). Like the silence function, quieten is best used in the Wave editor, where precise selections of the audio to be treated can be made.

Since the amount of cut cannot be regulated, the quieten function may lack the precision many users require.

Invert

This inverts the phase of the selection. In effect, this turns the waveform upside down since all positive elements in the signal (those above the zero amplitude line) become negative, and all negative elements in the signal (those below the zero amplitude line) become positive. This is clearly demonstrated if you invert a small test selection in the Wave editor at high magnification.

Many mixing consoles feature a phase reversal button on each channel which produces the same result. The main purpose of reversing the phase of a signal is when it forms the left or right channel of a stereo image which has been recorded out of phase. With one of the signals out of phase the stereo image lacks clarity and there is a loss of bass frequencies. The situation becomes even worse if you try to mix the two out of phase channels into a mono signal. This can result in some of the frequencies disappearing altogether.

The invert function is Cubase VST's remedy for this potentially disastrous problem. If you suspect that a stereo file is out of phase try separating the two channels and applying invert to one of the files.

Normalize

Normalization allows you to increase the overall level of the signal. The process is available on most digital audio editors and traditionally involves the boosting of the overall signal up to a chosen maximum.

The process functions by finding the maximum peak in the chosen audio and establishing how many dBs it is below the required level. The whole signal is then boosted by this number of dBs. Selecting normalize in Cubase VST results in a scan of the selected audio file to find the maximum peak. A dialogue (Figure 11.1) then requests the maximum level

Figure 11.1 Normalize dialogue

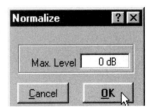

required for the resulting processing. Clicking on OK normalizes the file. The maximum level possible is 0dB.

Normalization can be used to boost the level of audio files which were recorded at too low a level. While this can help make up for a poorly recorded signal you should also be aware that the noise floor is also boosted by the same number of dBs as the rest of the recording. The best remedy for sounds recorded at too low a level is to record them again at a higher level.

It is also often desirable to boost the signal to its absolute maximum before transferring material onto CD. This is particularly true for rock, pop and dance material. However, there is more to normalizing than just simply boosting every file to the maximum 0dB possible and this is outlined in the Combination processing section below.

Lastly, normalize should not be used several times on the same audio file, for example, in between other processing since this can result in a noticeable degradation of the signal. Wherever possible, always use normalize once, after all other processing is complete.

Pitch shift/time correction

The pitch shift/time correction function allows the changing of the pitch of audio material without changing the length, or the changing of the length without changing the pitch. Nowadays, processing audio in the digital domain makes this kind of operation easier. Tape recorders suffer from the fact that pitch and length (duration) are inextricably linked; raise the speed of the tape machine and the pitch goes up while the duration becomes shorter, and vice versa.

To use pitch shift/time correction in Cubase VST proceed as follows:

- Select the audio which is in need of processing.
- Select pitch shift/time correction from the processing sub-menu of the main Audio menu. This opens the pitch shift/time correction dialogue (Figure 11.2).

Figure 11.2 Pitch shift/ time correction dialogue

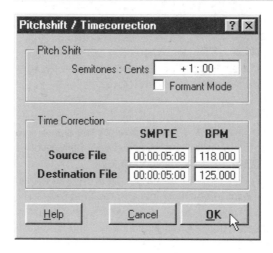

The pitch shift section features a pitch shift value, shown in semitones and cents, which can be increased or decreased to raise or lower the pitch, and a Formant mode option. To enter a single value directly, double-click on the current value. To change the value using the left and right mouse buttons, click and hold on the current value. The left mouse increases the value and the right mouse decreases it. The value normally changes in one cent steps but if you hold down the shift key the value changes in ten cent steps.

The Formant mode option should be activated if you are pitch shifting vocal material or other instruments with strong resonant characteristics. Formants are acoustic resonances which give vocal sounds their particular sonic identity and, with Formant mode activated in Cubase VST, the program takes these formants into account. This helps avoid some of the worst side-effects of pitch shifting which, without Formant mode, can very quickly go into 'chipmunk' territory.

- Decide on the amount of pitch shifting you require and whether you need to activate Formant mode. If you do not require any pitch shifting ensure that its value is set to '+0.00'. Note that time correction is no longer available when you activate formant mode.

The time correction section features the lengths of the source and destination files expressed in hours, minutes, seconds and frames or in terms of their tempos. The length field of the source file is non-changeable. To create a new length for the file, change the value of the destination file's length field.

The source file's tempo field can be set to the exact tempo of the source file, if you know it. This can then be used in conjunction with the destination file's tempo field to establish a new length and tempo for rhythmic audio material. Enter the new tempo required into the destination file's tempo field and the new length for the file is automatically adjusted.

- Decide on how you wish to time stretch/compress your chosen audio material and enter the appropriate values into the length or tempo fields.
- Click on the OK button to commence processing.

Pitch shifting is excellent for manually re-tuning the melody that the vocalist has sung out of tune and time correction can be used to great effect for establishing new tempos for rhythmic audio material. Both kinds of processing are also useful for creating sound effects.

However, both pitch shifting and time stretching can produce undesirable side-effects. The most common and easily recognised is pitch shifted vocals or speech which quickly begin to suffer a 'chipmunk' effect when the pitch is shifted upwards. When shifted downwards the human voice can take on an equally 'alien' character and may quickly become unintelligible. As mentioned above, this can be minimised by using Cubase VST's Formant mode but you should be aware that there are limitations. In general, vocal sounds which are pitch shifted up or down by more than 2 – 3 semitones begin to suffer undesirable side-effects.

When audio material is time stretched Cubase VST must build the audio data required to make the file longer. Depending on the type of material being processed, this may not always sound entirely natural. A similar problem occurs when the audio material is time shrunk. In general, stretching or shrinking a file by more than about 10% begins to produce undesirable audio artefacts.

With both pitch shifting and time correction the values you finally choose will depend upon the audio characteristics of the material being processed and the desired effect you require. For example, if you are producing sound effects, you may be searching for the very audio artefacts which somebody who is trying to transpose a vocal line is attempting to avoid.

Combination processing

One single processing function is not always enough to bring about the desired result. This section describes a number of processing techniques which employ the use of more than one function.

Increasing the average level of an audio file

As outlined in the normalize section above, the normalize function increases the overall level of an audio file based upon the maximum peak it finds in the waveform. This often bears no relation to the average amplitude of the signal, but it is the average amplitude which is important in our perception of loudness. The maximum peak can often be a transient spike in the waveform; this is a sudden extremely short burst of sound which is of significantly higher amplitude than the rest of the signal. It occurs so quickly that we do not perceive it when we listen to the music.

When the file is normalized the level can only ever be raised in relation to the maximum peak, so if the number of dBs between the peak and the required level is 3 dB, then the whole file is raised by 3dB, regardless of the average level of the rest of the file. This might seem OK, but imagine that you have another audio file with the same average level which has a peak significantly lower than the first example, so that normalizing the file results in a 6dB increase in level. This second file would be perceived as louder than the first. There is clearly a problem here.

Average level is particularly important if you are working on a number of stereo mixes intended for later transfer to CD. In many popular styles of music it is common practice to attempt to maximise the signal which will end up on the CD but, as you can see from the above, simply normalizing each of the files might lead to significant differences in the perceived loudness of each track.

One answer is to use a combination of the quieten and normalize functions. Remember that, in this exercise, we are looking for transient peaks which are significantly higher in amplitude than the other peaks in the waveform. Proceed as follows:

- Open the Wave editor and search through the audio material for any significant peak which clearly stands out from the rest of the waveform. This is usually obvious as a sudden spike (see Figure 11.3). In the example shown, using normalize results in virtually no increase in level since the spike is almost at 0dB already.

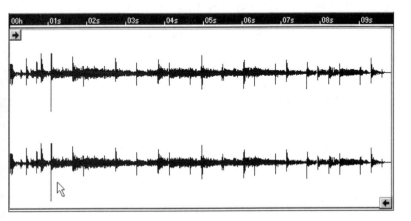

Figure 11.3 Search for any abnormally loud peaks

- Magnify the spike so that you can see it clearly in the display.
- Select the spike, taking care that the beginning and end points of the selection are at zero crossing points (see Figure 11.4).

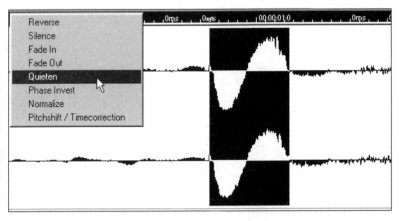

Figure 11.4 Select quieten to lower the amplitude

** INFO **

This kind of processing is not necessarily applicable to all styles of music and you should be careful not to ruin the natural dynamics of the sound. If you have more advanced processing in your system, such as Waves' Ultramaximizer plug-in, then this may be a better option (see Chapter 13).

- Select quieten from the Wave editor Do menu to lower the amplitude of the spike. This will have no audible effect on our perception of the sound since the spike is of extremely short duration.
- Search through the file for any other significant spikes and lower these too, using quieten. Remember that you are looking for transient spikes which are of significantly higher amplitude than the other peaks in the waveform.

- When you are satisfied that you have an audio file with no undesirable spikes, use the normalize function to raise the overall level (see result in Figure 11.5). If you compare Figure 11.5 with Figure 11.3 you will see that we have now succeeded in producing a considerable increase in the overall amplitude of the signal.

Figure 11.5 Use normalise to raise the overall level

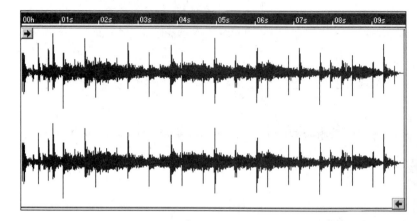

This process results in a higher average level than would have otherwise been possible and consecutive CD tracks treated in this way should end up at a more equal and higher average level. It requires a little more patience than simple one-function normalizing but the results are usually worth it.

Backward reverb and echo effects

This section describes a technique which was popular in the sixties and seventies for the production of 'psychedelic' effects, particularly with guitar and vocals. It was achieved by playing the multitrack tape backwards and adding reverb or echo effects to the target sound. The reverb or echo was recorded onto another track and the tape was then played in its normal direction. The result was a backwards reverb or echo occurring before each part of the original audio. This produced a characteristic other-worldly effect.

The same technique can be applied to audio material in Cubase VST using the reverse function and the supplied effects of the program. Proceed as follows:

- Select the audio material which you wish to process. For this exercise, it is best to work on a Part in the Arrange window.
- Select the reverse function. The selected audio now plays backwards.
- Apply a reverb or echo effect to the reversed audio. For example, try using the supplied Espacial or StereoEcho effects (see Chapter 12 for more details on how to use Cubase VST's effects).
- When you are satisfied with the effect, move the left and right

locators to the start and slightly beyond the end positions of the selected audio. You need to go slightly beyond the end point in order to capture the reverb tail (or the tail of whatever other effect you are using).

- Mute all other audio Tracks and select an empty audio Track.
- Select Export Audio File in the File menu (see Chapter 12 for more details on how to use Export Audio).
- In the Export Audio dialogue choose mono or stereo, (depending on the source file), and activate the channel or master effects (depending on how you have applied the effect to your audio file). Activate automatic import of the new file.
- Select a folder and a name for the new file and, after verifying that you have made the correct settings in the dialogue, click on the Create File button. A new Part appears in the empty Track you selected (above). This contains the new audio file with the reverb or echo effect included as part of the audio data.
- Select the new Part and use the reverse function. The original audio is now, once again, un-reversed and recognisable but the effect is reversed and flipped over in front of the audio material. This produces the other-worldly effect described above.

The first time you attempt this process it may seem rather involved and time consuming but after a few tries it becomes second nature. This kind of processing can be valuable to those searching for new sound effects and, used in a subtle fashion, it can become a valuable addition to the range of effects you can produce with Cubase VST. Remember that the effect need not always be the supplied reverb or echo, you could also try any of the plug-in effects you may have as part of your Cubase VST system.

That completes this description of Cubase VST's processing functions. All you have to remember is that using these functions makes changes directly to the audio data on the hard disk and, since there is only one level of undo in Cubase VST, you are taking a risk if you do not make a backup of the original audio file before processing commences. This is particularly true with the combination processing techniques.

12

Mixing, EQ and effects

Mixing audio in Cubase VST requires similar skills to those required in a traditional recording studio. You are provided with a virtual mixing console which includes EQ controls, auxiliary sends and insert points. You also have a virtual effects rack with various reverb, delay, chorus and other effects supplied as standard.

Mixing audio is a curious mixture of art and science and to achieve successful results can take years of experience and training. If you are completely new to the field and have just started mixing, then you should not be surprised to find that music production is not as easy as it sounds.

The quality of the recordings we hear every day on the radio or television is taken for granted but when you begin to attempt to achieve similar results, even with a tool like Cubase VST, it soon becomes obvious that there are an enormous number of parameters involved.

This is not to say that it is impossible to achieve a good result without any prior experience of music production and mixing, but simply that it will certainly require a lot of patience, perseverance and the extensive use of, sometimes, the most under-valued tool in your arsenal, your ears! If you do not know how to listen then you do not know how to mix.

We have already touched upon various aspects of audio recording, routing and processing in Chapters 2, 3, 6 and 11 and by now you will have certainly already explored many of the 'virtual studio' aspects of the program. This chapter describes all those functions relevant to mixing and EQ and outlines how to use the effects supplied with Cubase VST. It also describes various techniques which will help you in your own recording and mixing projects and explains how to get the best out of the VST parts of the system.

Preliminaries

One thing which must be appreciated when considering the idea of mixing multi-track audio is that the mix cannot be completely separated from the rest of the recording process. In the recording studio, it tends to become packaged as an entirely separate entity when all the 'track laying' is taking place during the first days of the project. Everyone involved starts to look forward to the magical day when the engineer will produce the 'perfect' mix.

However, it is not really quite like this. What really happens is that the producer/engineer is building the mix from the very first recording. As each musician is adding their part, the sound image of the final mix gradually takes shape.

Alternatively, in classical music the sound image often relies on the use of high quality, strategically placed microphones in, hopefully, an ideal acoustic recording environment. The mix is already largely decided at the moment of recording and any mixing which occurs is rather different from that which takes place with multi-track recordings in popular music.

In any kind of recording, mistakes made during the track laying stage will also be apparent when you come to do the mix, probably more so. Each stage in the sound recording chain contributes to the final result and great care should be taken when the signal is actually recorded.

What is mixing?

Having stated that mixing cannot be completely separated from the rest of the recording process, it remains the point at which the various elements of your recording endeavours come to fruition. The sounds you have carefully recorded are fine tuned, and reverb, EQ and other effects and processing are applied, all of which gives the music that polished, finished sound. Unfortunately, it is also the point at which a collection of well recorded tracks can be destroyed by a poor mix!

But how could we define what mixing actually is? Essentially, it is the setting of all the fader levels of a multi-channel recording in order to achieve a well-balanced stereo result. Balance is the key word for mixing. The stereo image must be carefully balanced so that it is not weighted too heavily to the left or right and different instruments might be mixed more 'forward' or 'back' in the mix (usually achieved using level, reverb and/or EQ), producing a sense of depth and focus. The mix should not be too 'boomy' at the bass end or too 'toppy' (harsh) in the upper frequencies. Despite careful attention at the track laying stage, some sounds may still need corrective EQ, and EQ may be used to carefully blend or highlight sounds, or for other creative purposes. The mix often incorporates reverb and other effects, which must be carefully mixed with the source sounds. Certain tracks also benefit from additional processing, like compression or noise gating, and the whole mix might be processed through a loudness maximiser to boost the final level.

Ten golden rules for recording and mixing

As a guide to achieving the best audio results and a successful mix with a Cubase VST system, remember the following guidelines:

1 Do not make recordings which sound bad and expect to 'fix it in the mix'. It is better to have recordings which already sound good and then you can improve them in the mix.
2 If you are using microphones to record any instrument take the time to ensure that they are placed in the best position to get the

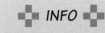

INFO

The mix itself can mean the make or break of the final product, and it deserves special attention.

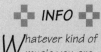

INFO

Whatever kind of music you are recording and mixing, the following section provides some general guidelines which should help in avoiding some of the pitfalls.

optimum sound quality. Be aware of the acoustic environment in which you are making the recording.

3 Use a good quality microphone and the right model for the job.

4 Make sure that you record at an optimum level whilst also avoiding distortion.

5 Monitor all recordings and the mix through good quality studio monitors.

6 When performing the mix, pan the sounds to appropriate positions across the stereo image and also attempt to achieve some depth in the sound field. Remember that the bass drum, snare drum, bass instrument and lead vocal in popular music are usually panned to the centre of the stereo image.

7 Do not over-use reverb.

8 Do not over-use EQ. When using microphones, attempt to get the right sound at the time of recording by experimenting with microphone position rather than immediately resorting to EQ. Remember that boosting frequencies is not the only way of using EQ, cutting frequencies is often preferable. EQ is best viewed as a way to improve (or creatively change) already well-recorded sounds and to provide a subtle means of balancing the sounds in the mix.

9 Use your ears and do not abuse them by monitoring at abnormally loud sound levels. Take plenty of breaks during the mixing session. After two to three hours of listening to the same sounds the ear becomes fatigued and is less sensitive to the upper frequencies.

10 As far as possible, know every aspect of the equipment you are using.

Remember that these rules only exist as a guide and, where appropriate, the rules can be broken. There are not always pre-set methods of achieving the desired results and some of the most important developments in sound production have occurred as a result of creative experimentation.

VST details

The Monitor mixer

In Cubase VST the Monitor mixer takes centre stage in the mixing process and, just like a real-world mixing console, it is important to know all of its functions to get the best results.

The Monitor mixer is laid out like a conventional console with a series of vertical modules (or strips), each of which controls an audio channel (Figure 12.1).

Cubase VST is supplied with the default number of channels set to 8 in the Audio System Setup dialogue, but this can be changed to any even number up to a maximum of 64 (depending on the processing power of your computer and program version). The monitor mixer expands accordingly.

Figure 12.1 The Monitor mixer

Stereo channels become a pair of linked channel strips for ease of use and for extra clarity when viewing the mixer layout. Normally the odd numbered channel in a stereo pair would be panned to the extreme left and the even numbered channel to the extreme right. Each channel strip contains the same set of controls and these are outlined in Figure 12.2:

Figure 12.2 Monitor mixer control functions

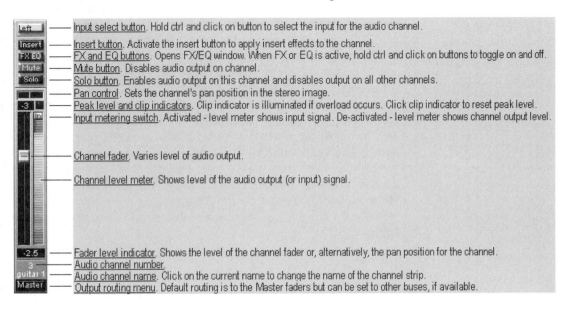

The Monitor mixer window also features a panel to the left of the channel strips which contains the mix automation read and write buttons, the MIDI mute button, to mute all MIDI Tracks in the current arrangement, and the FX button, to open the send effects window.

The Master window

By default, the Monitor mixer channels are routed to the Master faders (Figure 12.3). When needed and if they are available in your setup, a channel can be routed to other output buses using the Output routing menu. The Master faders are always present in the system and provide the normal output through which you send the final stereo mix.

Figure 12.3 Master window control functions

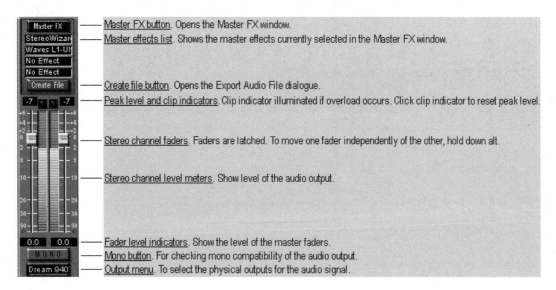

Master FX button. Opens the Master FX window.

Master effects list. Shows the master effects currently selected in the Master FX window.

Create file button. Opens the Export Audio File dialogue.

Peak level and clip indicators. Clip indicator illuminated if overload occurs. Click clip indicator to reset peak level.

Stereo channel faders. Faders are latched. To move one fader independently of the other, hold down alt.

Stereo channel level meters. Show level of the audio output.

Fader level indicators. Show the level of the master faders.

Mono button. For checking mono compatibility of the audio output.

Output menu. To select the physical outputs for the audio signal.

When mixing their music most readers will want to see the Monitor mixer and the Master faders simultaneously. Cubase VST allows a number of VST windows to be open at the same time and the Master faders might be placed at a convenient position to the right of the Monitor mixer.

In a multiple I/O system you may have configured more than one output bus and these become visible in the Master window (see Figure 12.4).

In order to see the extra buses, the devices associated with your multiple I/O audio card must be made active in the Advanced Multimedia Setup window (Audio menu/Setup). In order to actually use the buses they must be activated in the Master window by clicking on their active buttons.

Activating the extra buses uses processing power regardless of whether a signal is passing through them or not so, if you are not currently using them, they are best left de-activated.

The extra buses find many uses in a Cubase VST system including the following:

Figure 12.4 The Master window with additional output buses

- You can route any of the channels in the Monitor mixer to an output bus for external processing or mixing.
- In a multiple output system a number of audio channels could be simultaneously transferred to an external multi-track machine or they could be routed to separate channels on an external mixer for mixing operations outside of Cubase VST.
- Any of the FX sends may be routed to an output bus. The physical outputs of the bus can then be routed to any of the processing units you may have in your external rack. This means that you can use your FX sends to add external effects to the mix as well as the usual internal effects.
- The output from any of Cubase VST's send effects can be separately routed to an output bus for further external processing or mixing.

Channel settings window: parametric EQ

Cubase VST provides up to four bands of parametric EQ per channel. This is accessible by clicking on the FX/EQ button of the chosen channel strip which opens the Channel Settings window (Figure 12.5). The Channel Settings window can also be opened by clicking on the FX/EQ button in the Inspector.

The Channel Settings window features a replication of the channel strip as it appears in the Monitor mixer, an auxiliary FX send panel and between one to four parametric EQ modules. The four EQ modules are identical and can be switched in or out according to requirements. Each of the modules is displayed in two control strips and can be revealed or hidden using the arrows in the upper right corner of the window.

The EQ is available in standard or high quality mode according to the

Figure 12.5 Channel Settings window

setting of the high quality button. When the button is pressed (illuminated) all EQ modules for the channel switch to high quality mode giving an improved gain control range of -24dB to +24dB and a better sounding, more accurate EQ. When the button is not pressed (not illuminated) the gain range is between -12dB to +12dB (standard mode). It is recommended that you always use Cubase VST's EQ in high quality mode (unless you need to work on songs which already have standard EQ settings which you do not wish to change).

Figure 12.6 EQ control functions

To ease your understanding of the EQ functions, Figure 12.6 shows one EQ module as a single strip.

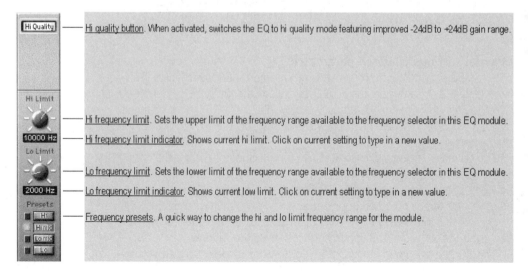

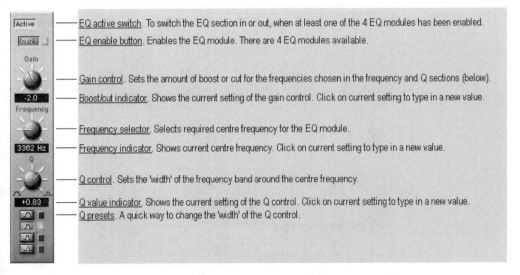

Figure 12.6 (Cont)

Parametric EQ may not be familiar to all readers so it deserves some explanation. The essential pre-requisites of a parametric EQ are a gain control, a centre frequency selector and a Q control. The frequency selector allows you to tune the EQ to the frequency band you wish to process and the Q control decides the 'width' of this band (otherwise known as the bandwidth). The gain control provides the means to boost or cut the chosen frequencies.

Parametric EQ is best understood by experimenting with a single Cubase VST EQ module. Try the following:

- Press the hi quality button and activate a single EQ module while playing a complex signal (such as a rhythm guitar or a drum part), through the chosen audio channel.
- Set the low and high limits to 20Hz and 2000Hz respectively.
- Set the gain control to −12dB to provide a cut in the chosen frequencies.
- Set the Q control to +0.56.
- Now slowly sweep the frequency selector from the maximum to the minimum position.

As you sweep the frequency selector you will notice the change in the sound as the cut frequency band sweeps down through the spectrum. As you reach the lower part of the frequency range the sound becomes more treble biased as the bass and lower mid frequencies are reduced in level. Using this kind of technique you can, for example, tune into unwanted frequencies to correct a sound which was recorded with too much middle, or too much bass.

To clarify the operation of the parametric EQ still further, the following diagram provides a graphic view of the main controls (Figure 12.7):

Figure 12.7 Parametric EQ
controls

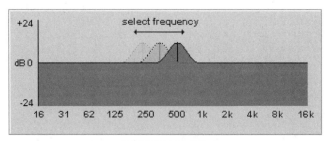

Frequency control

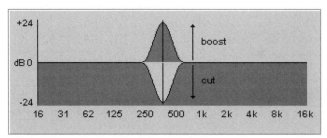

Gain control

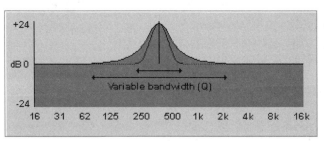

Q control

If you have not used it before, parametric EQ takes a little getting used to. However, it provides a very powerful means of shaping your sounds for both corrective and creative purposes. For further tips on using EQ see the 'Mixing decisions' section in this chapter and the Waves Q10 Paragraphic EQ section in Chapter 13.

Channel settings window: auxiliary send panel

The auxiliary send panel (Figure 12.8), is found to the right of the channel strip in the Channel Settings window. It features four sends which can be routed to any of the currently selected effects or to the Master bus (or to a separate bus if this has been activated in your system, normally as part of a multiple output audio card).

The available effects are chosen in the VST Send effects window (described below), and it is these which appear in the effect routing menu. Each send can be routed either pre or post fader. If it is pre-fader (i.e. with the pre-fader switch activated), then the signal is routed to the send before it arrives at the channel fader. If it is post-fader (i.e. with the

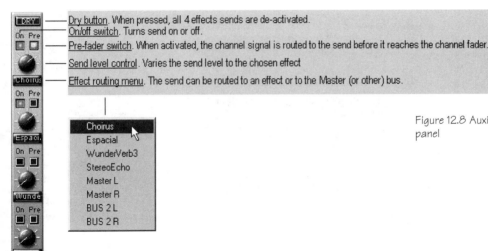

Dry button. When pressed, all 4 effects sends are de-activated.
On/off switch. Turns send on or off.
Pre-fader switch. When activated, the channel signal is routed to the send before it reaches the channel fader.
Send level control. Varies the send level to the chosen effect
Effect routing menu. The send can be routed to an effect or to the Master (or other) bus.

Figure 12.8 Auxiliary send panel

pre-fader switch de-activated), then the signal passes via the channel fader before it is routed to the send. You may wonder how this could be useful.

Practical uses include occasions when the channel fader has been set rather low and does not provide enough signal for the effect send; in this case the pre-fader signal provides more level. The pre-fader switch also allows you to fade a signal in the mix without also fading any effect applied to it. This can be used for special mixing techniques. For example, if you fade a sound which has pre-fader reverb added to it, the result gives the impression that the sound is disappearing into the distance as the dry signal diminishes whilst the reverberation signal remains.

There are also other creative applications for Cubase VST's auxiliary sends. If your Cubase VST system includes a multiple output card, an external effects unit and an external console then you can route one of the effect sends to an additional VST bus (activated in the ASIO Control panel and in the Master window). The physical output(s) associated with this bus can, in turn, be connected to the external effects unit. In this way you are able to route sounds out of Cubase VST to take advantage of any of the effects you may have in your external audio system.

VST Send effects

The effects that are available in the effects send panel are chosen in Cubase VST's Send effects window (Figure 12.9). This is opened by selecting Effects from the Audio menu or by clicking on the FX button found in the left-most panel of the Monitor mixer.

The Effects window is displayed in a silver-grey finish and is a virtual representation of an effects rack. Up to four effects can be included in the rack and different effects are chosen by clicking on the name of the current effect, shown in the top right corner. This opens a menu with all the available effects in your system, including the VST-native effects in the

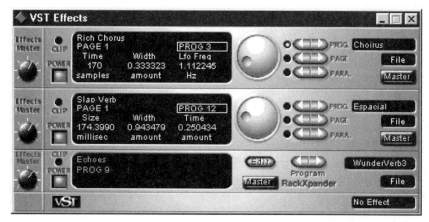

Figure 12.9
VST Send effects window

Figure 12.10 The
effects/processor choice
menu

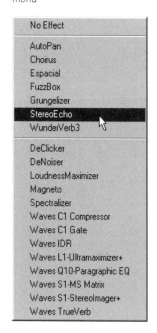

upper section, followed in the next section by any Direct X plug-ins you may have installed (see Figure 12.10).

Once an effect has been chosen, it appears in the rack and can be activated by clicking on its red power button. The layout of the rack unit front panel varies according to what type of effect has been chosen. There are three basic front panel types:

- Standard front panel. For standard VST-native effects like Espacial and Choirus. All editing takes place within the unit as presented on screen. There are no additional editing windows.
- Rack Xpander front panel. For VST-native effects and Direct X plug-ins which use additional editing windows to make effect settings.
- Empty front panel. This is an empty panel strip when the effect name box contains the words 'No effect'.

The routing configuration of the send effects is similar to a traditional recording studio. Figure 12.11 traces the signal as it is split between the 'dry' and the send signal paths. The 'dry' signal passes through the pan control of the channel strip, as usual, and is then routed to the Master faders. The send signal is routed (post-fader) via the send level and effects unit to the Master faders, where it joins the dry signal in the Master mix. The effect used in this configuration is mono in and stereo out.

With send effects the effect signal is *added* to the dry signal in the mix and by changing the send level the proportion of dry and effect signals can be controlled. Send effects are best suited to effects like reverb, delay and chorus where a stereo output signal from the effects unit is often the desired result and where you need to carefully balance the mix of the dry and effect signals.

Note that Cubase VST's sends are not numbered. This is because the system is more adaptable than most. Once the effects have been chosen in the Send effects window they can be chosen in any order on the send effects panel, and the send levels you set are unique for each audio chan-

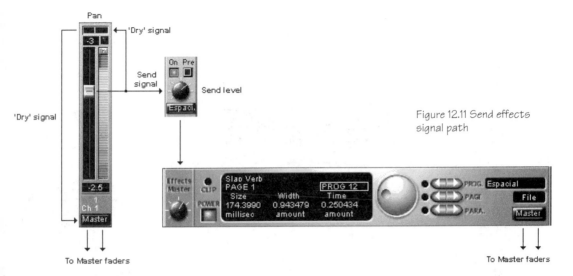

Figure 12.11 Send effects
signal path

nel. This means that, for example, the effects chosen in the send panel for audio channel 1 could be Choirus, Espacial, Wunderverb3, and StereoEcho (in descending order), while channel 2 could be simultaneously set to a differently ordered combination of the same four effects. In addition, all the send levels of the two channels can be set completely independently.

VST Insert effects

Cubase VST's insert effects are available on all audio channels in the Monitor mixer by clicking on the Insert buttons found at the top of each channel strip. This opens the Insert effects window (Figure 12.12) which is similar to the send effects window.

The Insert effects window is displayed in gold and up to four effects can be shown in the virtual rack. Once any of the four effects has been activated, the Insert button for the audio channel (Monitor mixer), is illuminated in blue.

The front panels vary in the same way as the send effects rack described above and the manner of choosing the effects is also the same. However, Insert effects differ in the manner in which the signal is routed. There is no separation of the dry and effect signals. Instead, the signal passes directly *through* the effect (see Figure 12.13). In addition, if there

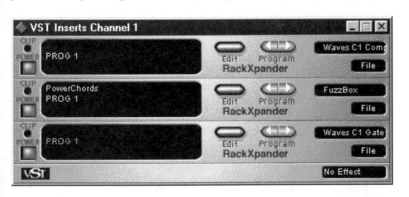

Figure 12.12 Insert Effects
window

Insert button activated

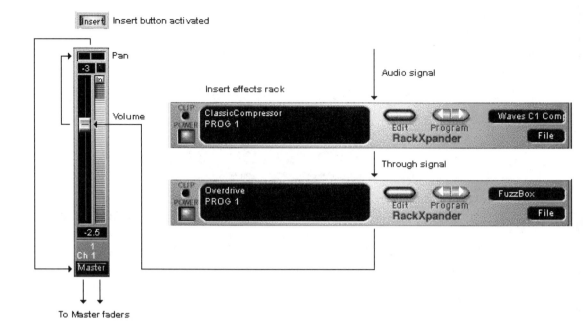

To Master faders

Figure 12.13 Insert effects
signal path

is more than one effect activated in the rack, the signal passes through
each in turn, in descending order. Note that the audio signal is routed
directly to the first insert effect's input (i.e. it has not yet passed via the
channel fader), and the output from the effect(s) is then routed via the
channel fader and pan control to the master faders. Therefore, unlike
send effects, the signal level going into the insert effect(s) is *not* affected
by the channel fader level.

The inserts are best suited to processing like compression, expansion,
noise gating, EQ, distortion etc.

The number of effects which are finally used is restricted only by the
processing power of your computer. Many high end compression and gating plug-ins use substantial amounts of CPU power so that, for example, a
Pentium PC running at 200 MHz and using more than four or five high
end plug-ins simultaneously could encounter a slowing down of the graphic performance and audio drop-outs much sooner than might have been
expected. Open the audio Performance window (Audio menu) to monitor
the current load on your CPU.

VST Master effects

The Master effects window is opened from the main Audio menu or by
clicking on the Master FX button at the top of the Master window (see
Figure 12.14).

The Master effects window is displayed in green and, similar to the
other effects windows, can display up to four effects in the rack. The
routing system is similar to that for Insert effects except that only effects

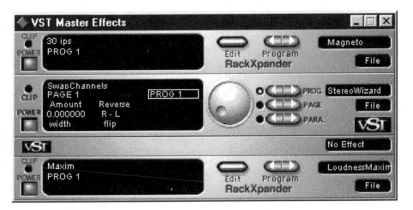

Figure 12.14 The Master Effects window

with a stereo input and stereo output can be used. As with Insert effects the signal passes through each effect in the rack in descending order.

The Master effects are primarily intended for processing which is suitable for a final stereo mix. This might include such things as limiters, compressors, loudness maximisers, noise reduction processors, de-noisers etc. These kinds of processors are often supplied as third party plug-ins (see Chapter 13). Steinberg supply 3 Master effects with the program, known as Grungelizer, Scopion and Stereo Wizard.

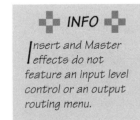

INFO

Insert and Master effects do not feature an input level control or an output routing menu.

What have we learnt so far?

The above sections have described the essential operational features of Cubase VST's virtual mixing environment. You now know where to make level and EQ adjustments and you know how to route signals to an effect (or processor). To get the most out of the system it is also important to know your effects rack.

Using the supplied effects

The supplied effects and processors are, in fact, plug-ins but they are of a type which can only be used within VST compatible programs. For this reason, they are often referred to as 'VST-native' plug-ins (or effects) and this differentiates them from Steinberg and third party developer Direct X plug-ins which can be used in any program which supports Direct X technology. Plug-ins are audio sound processing and effects modules which can be added to the effects rack of Cubase VST as and when you need them.

When using any kind of effect, it is important to remember that Send effects are usually mono in/stereo out devices, Master effects are always stereo in/stereo out devices and Insert effects can be in either category or mono in/mono out devices. All effects share some common operational features and these are summarised in Figures 12.15 and 12.16:

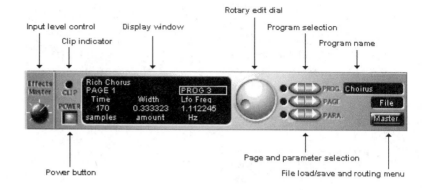

Figure 12.15 Standard front panel control features

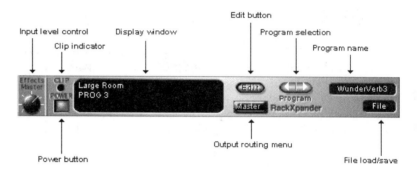

Figure 12.16 Rack Xpander front panel control features

There now follows a description of each of the supplied VST-native effects and how to get the best out of them.

Autopan

- Front panel layout: standard
- I/O: mono in/stereo out
- Number of program slots: 16
- Approximate CPU power used: 3% (200MHz Pentium MMX processor)
- Normal usage: as a Send effect

Description
Autopan is a 4 parameter device for producing auto pan effects. Parameters include an LFO (Low Frequency Oscillator), a width control, a waveform selector and an output level.

User guide
Autopanning is an effect involving the automatic panning of a signal back and forth across the stereo image.

Cubase VST's Autopan can be quickly set up to produce a standard autopan effect. The speed of the panning is regulated by the LFO setting and this is best set while listening to the treated signal until you have achieved the desired pan speed. The width control regulates the span of the effect in the stereo mix and this is important for achieving the required stereo image.

The character of the autopan can be adjusted using the waveform selector. The sine wave setting produces the smoothest pan while the pulse wave setting produces abrupt sweeps across the stereo image. The saw wave produces a sweep across the stereo image with a sudden return to the starting point and the triangle wave produces a pan similar in character to the sine wave.

If you need to exaggerate the autopan effect try taking down the mixer faders for the source sound and send the signal pre-fader. In this way the effect alone will be heard in the master mix.

Autopan can be used to add dynamism to individual instruments in static sounding mixes and is used to good effect on synth pads and riffs, percussion, and other ornamental sounds which have good definition in the upper frequencies.

Choirus

- Front panel layout: standard
- I/O: mono in/stereo out
- Number of program slots: 32
- Approximate CPU power used: 6% (200MHz Pentium MMX processor)
- Normal usage: Send effect.

Description

Choirus is a device which produces chorus and flanging effects. The parameters include:

- Time – controls the initial delay time (measured in samples).
- Width – controls the depth of the effect.
- LFO – controls the LFO frequency (in Hertz), which de-tunes the signal.
- Feedback amount – controls the amount of effects signal which is fed back to the input.
- Feedback balance – varies the proportion of direct and effected signal which is fed back to the input.
- Glimmer – animates and spreads the effect across the stereo image.
- Glimmer2 – animates and varies the effect in the centre of the

User guide

Chorus is an effect produced by taking a feed from the signal, slightly delaying it and then slightly de-tuning it. The effected signal is then combined with the original signal. The de-tuned signal is normally also modu-

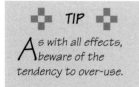

lated by a low frequency oscillator which further varies the amount of de-tuning. The result creates the illusion that there is more than one instrument producing the sound.

Flanging is produced in a similar manner. A feed from the signal is put through a delay and the delay time is varied with a low frequency oscillator. The effected signal is then combined with the original. This produces phase cancellation effects which are heard as the characteristic swishing or sweeping sound of classic flanging.

Cubase VST's Choirus provides the normal parameters associated with the creation of both effects.

To achieve flanging effects try the following initial settings: set time to a high value (more than 900 samples), width to between 0.75 – 1.0. and the LFO frequency to a low value (less than 0.15Hz), with feedback set to around 0.40 and feedback balance to 0. Set the other controls as desired, although the effect is more obvious with low glimmer control settings.

To achieve chorus effects try setting time moderately low (less than 200 samples), width between 0.5 –1.0, LFO frequency between 0.75 – 1.5Hz and the glimmer controls to between 0.5 – 1.0. Set the other controls as desired.

Chorus and flanging are versatile effects which can be used to good effect on a wide range of sounds. This versatility is apparent in the practical use of Cubase VST's Choirus effect since, although it is principally designed as a Send effect, it is also suitable as an Insert effect (but note that you may lose some of the effect when used in this manner). Chorus and flanging are excellent for thickening or sweetening sounds and are often used on bass, guitar, strings and organ in popular music. The effect shows up better with sounds which are rich in harmonics and tends to work well when used in combination with other effects (such as fuzz followed by chorus).

Espacial

- Front panel layout: standard
- I/O: mono in/stereo out
- Number of program slots: 64
- Approximate CPU power used: 6% (200MHz Pentium MMX processor)
- Normal usage: Send effect

Description
Espacial is a device for creating reverberation effects. The parameters include:

- Size – controls the size of the reverberant space.
- Width – controls the stereo spread of the reverberation.
- Time – controls the decay time of the reverberation.

- ER start – controls the delay time at which the early reflections begin.
- ER width – controls the stereo spread of the early reflections.
- ER gain – controls the proportion of early reflections and direct signal in the ER mix.
- ER decay – controls the decay time for the early reflections.
- ER output – controls the early reflection output level.
- Out level – controls the overall output level.

User guide

Artificial reverberation is among the most important and most used effects in popular music. In order to use Cubase VST's Espacial and Wunderverb3 (see below) it is helpful to understand some of the theory involved in reverberation techniques.

A sound signal with reverberation can be described in three distinct phases as shown in Figure 12.17.

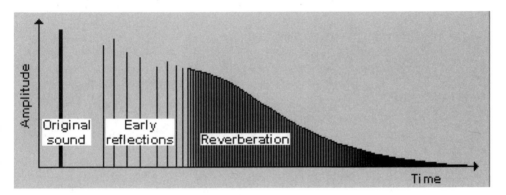

This approximates what takes place in a real reverberant space. Firstly, the original sound arrives directly from the source to the listener's ear. After a short pause the first reflections from the surfaces of the room (or other acoustic space) are heard; these are known as early reflections. This is then followed by a complex mass of multiple reflections as the reflected sounds continue to bounce off the various surfaces. The amplitude of these multiple reflections decays exponentially to form what is commonly known as the reverb tail. In real reverberant spaces (especially in large ones), the upper frequencies decay at a faster rate than the rest of the signal.

The idea with artificial reverberation units is to re-create the same kind of behaviour. However, the first thing you will notice when comparing different devices is that reverb units are not all created equal. Convincing reverberation remains difficult to replicate artificially and requires a large amount of processing power to achieve the best results. Cubase VST's Espacial and Wunderverb3 achieve very good results considering the small amount of processing power they use.

Espacial gives control over the size of the reverberant space, the decay time and the early reflections. To get to know the parameters, try setting the early reflection (ER) controls first. For example, set ER start to 20ms, ER width to 0.65, ER gain to 0.70 and ER decay to 0.35. Then use the first three parameters (size, width and time) to create the overall characteristics of the reverb. Try setting size to 63ms, width to 0.30 and time to 0.5. These particular settings add colour and presence to the source sound. Fine tune the proportion of early reflections in the effect by adjusting the ER output parameter and, lastly, decide the overall output level. As you become more familiar with Espacial you quickly find out its various strengths and weaknesses.

Espacial provides a reasonable quality reverb but suffers from an undesirably resonant reverb tail when used with longer reverb times. Overall it tends to work better with smooth string and pad sounds and is sometimes OK with vocals, though not to be recommended as a main reverb unit. More percussive sources may show up its defects more than other instruments.

FuzzBox

- Front panel layout: Rack Xpander
- I/O: mono in/stereo out
- Number of program slots: 16
- Approximate CPU power used: 2% (200MHz Pentium MMX processor)
- Normal usage: Insert effect

Description
Cubase VST's fuzz box is a Rack Xpander device for the creation of distortion effects. The parameters include boost, clipback and volume.

As with all Rack Xpander devices the interface for the unit is opened by clicking on the front panel edit button. Fuzzbox provides a virtual effects pedal with three rotary controls which can be graphically adjusted to create the desired fuzz effect (see Figure 12.18).

Figure 12.18 Cubase VST's fuzzbox

User guide
As a starting point try setting the controls to 0.33, 0.05 and 0.65 respectively. This produces a standard fuzz effect suitable for guitar sounds but the precise settings obviously depend on the characteristics of the source signal. The boost control regulates the amount of distortion, clipback regulates the feedback and intensity, and volume regulates the output level.

Apart from guitar solos and power chord applications, it is sometimes also worth trying mild distortion effects on sounds which are in need of some kind of animation. A common complaint with digitally recorded audio is that it is too clean and rather lifeless. This can be particularly true for synthesizer sounds and subtle distortion can sometimes provide the solution. Fuzz is also useful when applied in combination with other effects and processors for creating special guitar sounds and sound effects (e.g. fuzz followed by chorus).

Grungelizer

- Front panel layout: Rack Xpander
- I/O: stereo in/stereo out
- Number of program slots: 5
- Approximate CPU power used: 22% (200MHz Pentium MMX processor)
- Normal usage: Insert, send or master effect

Description
The Grungelizer is a device for producing noise, interference and ageing effects for your digital recordings. The parameters include:

- crackle – adds crackles and pops to the signal, as found on scratched vinyl recordings. The speed of the imaginary vinyl record can be changed between 33, 45 or 78rpm.
- noise – adds high frequency hiss to the signal.
- distort – mildly distorts the signal.
- EQ – filters the signal, progressively taking out the body of the sound as the control is increased.
- AC – adds 50Hz or 60Hz mains hum to the signal.
- timeline – accentuates all the other settings by a progressively greater amount as the dial is turned back in time to the year 1900.

The user interface for the unit is opened by clicking on the Rack Xpander edit button and features 6 dials on a retro style panel (see Figure 12.19).

Figure 12.19 Cubase VST's Grungelizer

User guide
The first question you might ask with regard to the Grungelizer is why would you want to add all this interference to your perfect digital recordings!? The answer is that the digital world is sometimes just too clean! Adding 'dirt' can sometimes give a sound more character. You may also need to artificially 'age' some element in a music production, such as a vocal, as a special effect or you might just want your guitar to sound as

dirty as possible. You may also need to replicate the sound of a vintage 78 record made in 1920.

For experimental purposes, try using just one of the dials alone in conjunction with the timeline dial. For example, used alone, the EQ dial is a filter which effectively takes out more of the body of the sound the higher it is set and this can be handy as a hybrid tone control. The distort dial provides a mild distortion effect which can be used to add subtle character to lifeless synth sounds. Used carefully, the Grungelizer can be a surprisingly welcome addition to your effects rack.

Scopion

- Front panel layout: Rack Xpander
- I/O: stereo in/stereo out
- Number of program slots: 4
- Approximate CPU power used: less than 1% (200MHz Pentium MMX processor)
- Normal usage: Master effect

Description
Scopion is a simplified virtual oscilloscope with 3 parameters. One dial controls amplitude, a second dial controls the horizontal zoom and a left/right lever selects which side of the stereo image is being monitored. The interface for the unit is opened by clicking on the Rack Xpander edit button (see Figure 12.20).

Figure 12.20 Scopion

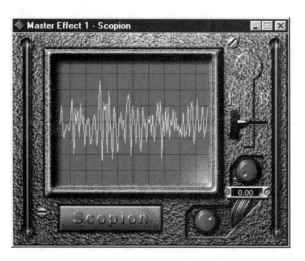

User guide
Try setting the amplitude control about half-way and the horizontal zoom at 0.00. At this setting you should be able to clearly see the waveform of most signals. Scopion would normally be used as a Master effect.

Scopion is a purely visual monitoring device and has no effect on the audio. It could be used to visualise the kind of waveform which is being produced by a steady state tone from a synthesizer or it might be useful as visual feedback while you make adjustments to the sound in other parts of the system.

Scopion can also be fun! Try viewing the input in real-time by selecting Record enable or Tape type monitoring in the Monitoring section of the Audio System setup dialogue and then activate the input select button of the current channel. You can now see a real-time display of your current audio input.

StereoEcho

- Front panel layout: standard
- I/O: mono in/stereo out
- Number of program slots: 16
- Approximate CPU power used: 3% (200MHz Pentium MMX processor)
- Normal usage: Send effect

Description
StereoEcho is a stereo delay device which has a standard front panel interface. The parameters include:

- Delay 1 – determines the amount of time (in milliseconds) the input signal will be delayed before being routed to the left output.
- Feedback 1 – determines the proportion of the delay 1 output which is 'fed back' to the input.
- Link 1-2 – links both channels so that the unit becomes a mono delay device.
- Delay 2 – determines the amount of time (in milliseconds) the input signal will be delayed before being routed to the right output.
- Feedback 2 – determines the proportion of the delay 2 output which is 'fed back' to the input.
- Delay 2 balance – set at 0, the input signal alone is routed to delay 2. Set at more than 0, a progressively greater proportion of the delay 1 output is mixed with the main input signal and routed to delay 2.
- Volume left – controls the output level of the left channel.
- Volume right – controls the output level of the right channel.

The maximum delay time in stereo mode is 1486ms and the maximum delay time in mono mode (linked) is 2972ms.

User guide
The concept of delay is easily understood by the majority of users but, nowadays, surrounded by ever more exotic effects, it tends to be undervalued. It is worth investigating delay in a little more detail.

In sound processing, delay and echo are terms which essentially refer to the same thing but, strictly speaking, an echo is a sound reflection separated from the original sound by more than 30ms. Before 30ms the ear perceives the reflections as part of the same sound i.e. they are fused into one. After 30ms the ear can begin to differentiate the original and the delayed signal. This is important to remember since it can help you achieve the desired effect when programming a delay device like Cubase VST's StereoEcho.

For example, ADT effects (Automatic Double Tracking) are usually achieved using delay times of around 30 to 60ms with no, or very little, feedback. This simulates the effect of doubling the sound, since the ear perceives the delayed signal as a separate event but the delay time is not great enough for it to become detached from the original sound. As you increase the delay time and the feedback other kinds of effects, such as 'slap-back' echo, are possible. Here we begin to more clearly differentiate the delayed and the original sound. If you also manipulate the stereo imagery by delaying one channel by a different amount to the other you can create pseudo-stereo effects. As you increase the delay time still further special effects such as 'ping pong' echoes and multiple echo effects become possible. 'Ping pong' is the term applied to an echo which 'bounces' a number of times between each channel in the stereo image. For longer delay times all kinds of special effects can be created and the timing of the echoes can also be tuned to the tempo of the music. If you have a calculator you can work out the delay times for any given tempo using the following equation:

delay (in milliseconds) = 60,000 / current tempo

This gives the delay time for one beat (or one quarter note). To work out the delay times for an eighth note or a sixteenth note divide the quarter note time by two or four respectively.

The best way of learning about delay is to try a few practical examples. Choose a suitable sound, such as a vocal or lead guitar, and try the following with Cubase VST's StereoEcho:

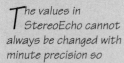

INFO

The values in StereoEcho cannot always be changed with minute precision so you may have to approximate some of the settings in the table. Using these as starting points, you could go on to create a wide variety of delay effects.

Table 12.1 StereoEcho delay effects

Effect	Delay 1 (ms)	Feedback 1	Link 1-2	Delay 2 (ms)	Feedback 2	Del 2 Bal.	Vol. L (dB)	Vol. R (dB)
ADT	40.00	0.08	linked	linked	linked	linked	–2.00	linked
Stereo spread	42.00	0.40	Off	40.00	0.20	0.00	–2.00	–6.00
Slapback	65.00	0.06	linked	linked	linked	linked	–6.00	linked
Ping pong	600.00	0.50	Off	300.00	0.00	1.00	–2.40	–2.40

It is not a good idea to actually record delay effects with the sound unless you are sure that the effect is an essential part of the sound's character. Delay is often best applied at the mixing stage. It can be used on almost any sound in the mix but is particularly suitable for lead guitar, saxophone and vocals and on featured elements in the mix, such as solos or special effects. Bass sounds do not generally benefit from delay treatment. Too much delay can result in a confused and messy mix so, as with all effects, it should not be over-used.

StereoWizard

- Front panel layout: standard
- I/O: stereo in/stereo out
- Number of program slots: 8
- Approximate CPU power used: 1% (200MHz Pentium MMX processor)
- Normal usage: Master or Insert effect

Description
The StereoWizard is a 2 parameter processor for stereo material and has a standard front panel interface. The parameters are width and L-R reverse.

User guide
This unit may be used as a Master or Insert effect and is designed to work exclusively with stereo audio. Since there are only two parameters it is very simple to operate.

As the value of the width control is increased above 0 the sound is progressively filtered and panned towards the centre. The filtering involves a reduction in bass and lower mid frequencies and, at its maximum setting, the sound is positioned in the centre of the stereo image. The effect at the higher settings creates an illusion of distance which gives the uncanny impression of listening to the sound from another room. The effect works particularly well on stereo drum material.

The reverse control flips the left/right stereo image. This is useful for those occasions when you have inadvertently recorded a reversed stereo image!

Wunderverb3

- Front panel layout: Rack Xpander
- I/O: mono in/stereo out
- Number of program slots: 10
- Approximate CPU power used: 6% (200MHz Pentium MMX processor)
- Normal usage: Send effect

Description
Wunderverb3 is a 3 parameter Rack Xpander reverb device. The parameters include size, decay and dampening.

To open the editing window of Wunderverb3 click on the edit button of the Rack Xpander front panel. The controls are displayed on a simple virtual rack as 3 rotary controls with value fields.

Figure 12.21 Wunderverb3

User guide

Despite its simplicity Wunderverb3 is capable of providing some convincing reverb effects. Its main asset is its damp control which approximates the kind of reverberant behaviour you might expect in a real acoustic environment, where the upper frequencies decay at a faster rate than the rest of the signal.

Size varies the dimensions of the reverberant space, *decay* controls the duration of the reverberation effect and *damp* filters the upper frequencies of the reverberation to produce bright or more mellow effects. Wunderverb3 comes pre-loaded with a good bank of sounds and it should present no difficulties when you need to program the effect yourself.

As with Espacial, it is difficult to recommend Wunderverb3 as a main reverb since it lacks the quality required for sounds such as vocals and drums. However, it has its own distinctive character and works well as a thickener for guitar and keyboard sounds. It is also quite good with brass and strings.

INFO

For more information on the theoretical aspects of reverberation see the Espacial section, above

Storing, saving and loading effects

All effects have program memory slots into which user settings can be stored. The number of program locations available varies with each unit. Once a new effect has been created it remains at the current program number until you exit the program. When the current song is saved the settings of all the effects are saved with it. However, if you wish to save the current program individually, or the current bank of effects, use the save effect or save bank options in the effect unit's File menu (lower right corner). Individual effects are saved with an .fxp file extension and banks are saved with an .fxb extension. Individual effects and banks are loaded by selecting the appropriate load options in the File menu.

Cubase VST is supplied with a number of effects banks and programs which can be found in the Steinberg\Cubase VST\Vstplugins folder. For convenience, it is suggested that you save your own effects creations in the same folder.

Adding VST-native effects

To add more VST-native effects to the system, new plug-ins must be placed in the 'VSTplugins' folder. Simply drag and drop the appropriate .dll file (e.g. Compressor.dll), into the folder using Windows Explorer. When Cubase VST is re-launched the plug-in will be available in the upper part of the usual plug-ins menu list.

General tips on using effects

There are some logistic problems to using a complex audio system and Cubase VST is no exception. For example, there can be some confusion as to how to set the Send effects level and the input gain of the effects unit. The answer is to avoid extremes.

For example, do not set the effects send to maximum and the input gain of the effects unit to 1 on the dial. Try setting both to around the 2 o'clock position and then fine tune the required level from there. On some units, there are also output level controls, and these also play a part in setting the final effects level.

If you have enough processing power you can achieve some creative effects by using more than one unit as Insert effects. Try the following combinations:

- Compressor followed by fuzzbox (typically used by guitarists to achieve more sustain).
- Fuzzbox followed by chorus/flange.
- Chorus/flange followed by chorus/flange.

Experimentation can yield some surprisingly good effects and if you are feeling really adventurous there is nothing to stop you using combinations of three or four effects/processors. In addition to using the Insert effects window, you could also simultaneously incorporate one or more Send effects but, as always, beware of over-using combination processing.

The figures quoted above for the CPU power usage of each effect are percentages of the whole power capacity of the CPU. Since it is also engaged in other tasks, you can generally use a Pentium 200 MHz CPU for audio processing in Cubase VST up to about 70% of its total power. After this point you will start to suffer from audio glitching and drop-outs. Faster CPUs will display smaller percentages. To monitor your current CPU usage, open the VST performance window (Audio menu).

When using the mouse to edit the parameters of an effect with the rotary control you may have noticed that it is difficult to set the values to precise amounts. This is the normal manner in which Cubase VST's native plug-ins function but you can improve the resolution slightly by moving the mouse a greater distance from the rotary control as you make adjustments.

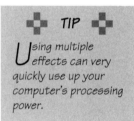

TIP

Using multiple effects can very quickly use up your computer's processing power.

Mixing decisions

At this point in the chapter you should have a good grasp of the parameters involved in the mixing process and how you might use the virtual mixing and audio processing features of Cubase VST. However, no matter how many channels or how many effects and processors you have, you still have to actually *do* the mix. Above all, this involves listening very carefully and making a large number of decisions based on what you hear.

More tips

The 'Ten golden rules for recording and mixing' (outlined in 'Preliminaries' above) should help with the basic decisions involved in the mixing process but here are a few more miscellaneous tips to help clarify matters further:

- If you have a lead vocal in your mix it should normally be in the centre of the stereo image and more 'upfront' than the other sounds. It would also normally be treated with reverberation. The correct balance of the 'dry' (original) and 'wet' (reverberant) signals of the vocal sound and their balance with the rest of the mix is crucial, as is the choice of reverb type. Beware of adding too much reverb.

- The vocal or other lead instrument may be difficult to hear because it is being masked by the frequencies from other instruments. Rather than trying to excessively boost the sound you wish to hear, try instead cutting some of the frequencies of the sounds in the same register. For vocals, try cutting some of the accompanying instruments at around 1.5kHz and slightly boosting the vocal itself in the same frequency range. To add still more presence to the vocal try also boosting at around 3kHz.

- Some instrumental and vocal performances can produce wildly fluctuating signal levels. These are difficult to mix since sometimes they are too loud and sometimes too soft. Applying mild compression can help control this type of unmanageable signal. The problem can also be resolved by riding the faders as part of a manual or automated mix.

- The perceived distance of a sound in the mix is determined by its level, its high frequency content and its reverberant characteristics. If you cut the high frequency content of a sound, reduce its overall level and add a little reverberation, the sound will be perceived as more distant than those which do not have this treatment. Using distance you can place some of your sounds 'back' in the mix and add depth to the sound field.

- If you are mixing pop or rock material, the bass drum, snare drum and bass instrument are invariably panned to the centre of the stereo image along with the lead vocal. The bass sounds tend to be mixed fairly dry (i.e. with little or no reverb). Carefully mixing the drum kit and bass first is a good way of laying the foundations for the rest of the mix.

- The different sounds in a drum kit should not be panned excessively wide as this can give the rather bizarre impression that the drummer has very long arms!

- As you add more sounds to the mix try to keep some kind of focus on the overall sound image you are trying to achieve. Many engineers listen to one or more mixes of established artists, before and during the mix session, as a point of comparison with their own mix.

- Do not try to achieve a mix by continually raising levels and boosting EQ frequencies since, not only will it sound like an aural battlefield, you will also quickly run out of headroom on the master faders.
- If the mix is sounding 'muddy' attempt to clarify the definition of the main instruments in the mix by slightly boosting their most prominent frequencies. However, beware of boosting all the instruments at the same frequency range; attempt to differentiate the sounds by giving each instrument its own EQ space. Your mix may also be sounding 'muddy' due to a confused and 'boomy' bass end. In this case, try using a little low frequency cut on the bass instruments.
- If the mix is sounding 'harsh' identify which instruments are producing this harshness and cut the offending frequencies. To add more 'warmth' try a moderate broad band boost centred around 250Hz on selected instruments.
- Use Cubase VST's mono button in the Master window to check the mono compatibility of your mix. If there is a problem, you will notice a drop in the bass frequencies and a lack of clarity in the sound.
- Judging the mix clearly, especially after having worked on it for some time, is not always easy. Some engineers recommend listening to the mix from outside the mixing room with the door open. This technique often shows up faults with the mix which were not obvious when you were in front of the speakers. Strange but true!
- As well as performing the mix in one take, do not be afraid to also try recording the mix in separate sections, which can then be edited together at a later stage.

The above tips should help solve a number of problems which may be encountered during the course of a mixing session but only knowledge, experience and practice will produce the 'perfect' mix.

Mix automation

These days, mix automation is considered a standard requirement in the best professional recording studios. It allows the producer and sound engineer more scope to produce the best possible mix and gives instant recall of a mix which was performed on a previous occasion. Automation normally includes all fader and control levels on the mixing console, and any adjustments can be overdubbed as many times as necessary in order to achieve the desired result. All mix data is recorded to a file on hard disk.

Cubase VST provides similar automation for all of the most important mixing parameters. These include the following:

Volume fader level
Pan position
Mute
Solo
EQ On/Off

Effect send On/Off switches
Effect send pre-fader switches
Effect send levels
Effect dry switch
All EQ controls
Send effect program selection
Send effect input levels
First 16 parameters for each send effect
First 16 parameters of each insert effect

Master faders
Master effect program selection
First eight parameters of each master effect

Create a test mix

In order to record mix automation events you do *not* have to be in normal record mode. All you have to do is activate the Write button found on the left panel of the Monitor mixer. You can now record any changes to the mixer controls whether Cubase VST is static, in which case the events are recorded at the current song position, or in play mode, in which case all events are recorded dynamically.

The best way of understanding how automation works is to record a short test mix. Try using the following test procedure:

- Open your definition file and ensure that Cubase VST has no audio or MIDI data recorded into the current arrangement. For this test we are beginning with a 'clean sheet' and exploring how the controls function with no actual audio involved.
- Set the left locator at bar 2 and the right locator at any point later in the song. We will use the left locator position as the point from which to begin our test mix.
- Open the Monitor mixer, leave all the settings in their default positions and activate the Write button. This writes the current settings of the Monitor mixer, Master faders, EQ settings etc. at bar 1.1.0. The data is stored in a special mixer Part called 'AudioMix' which is automatically created on a new Track in the Arrange window.

- Activate the Read button. Both the Read and Write buttons can be activated simultaneously and, when we play back the automation, the activated Read button allows us to view any changes we have made to the mix.
- Check that both the Write and Read buttons are activated. Move the song position to the left locator (2.1.0) and, with Cubase VST in stop mode, drag the fader of channel 1 to its lowest position. This writes the last set position of the fader at position 2.1.0. (A mix set up in this way is sometimes referred to as a static mix i.e. Cubase VST is not moving at the time of setting the controls).
- Now start playback and fade up channel 1 to around 0dB and stop playback.
- Rewind to position 2.1.0 and play back your fade. You should see the channel fader move on its own. If you are not happy with the fade select undo in the edit menu, or press ctrl + Z (Mac: command+Z), to undo the take and try again.
- When you are happy with the 'fade in', record a 'fade out' immediately afterwards.
- De-activate the Write button and leave the Read button activated. Rewind and play back the overall result. You should see the fader of channel 1 fade in and out on its own.

Edit the test mix

Once you have completed the test mix above you could go on to create a more complex sequence of automation but, before you do, it is useful to know how to edit the automation data.

As mentioned above the automation data is stored in a Part called 'AudioMix'. To edit the automation, find this Part in the Arrange window and proceed as follows:

View the fader movements in List edit's graphic display

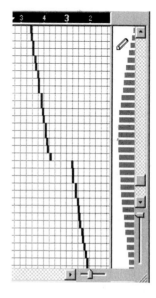

- Select the Audio Mix Part and open List edit (ctrl + G/Mac: command + G).
- All the default settings are stored at bar position 1.1.0 and these are shown in List edit as a long list of events with 'AUDIOMIX' marked in the status column. Dragging the split point to the right reveals the names of each parameter in the comment column. Move the song position to the left locator at bar 2.1.0.
- Look to the right of the grid and you should be able to see a graphic display of your fader movements in the controller display. The levels represented here are also found in numerical form in the value 3 column.
- Imagine that you want to boost the uppermost level of your fade in. Move the mouse into the controller display, at which time it automatically changes into the pencil tool. Dragging the graphic strips in the controller display changes the level. Try increasing the level at the upper extreme of the fade in. You can also change the level by adjusting the values in the value 3 column.

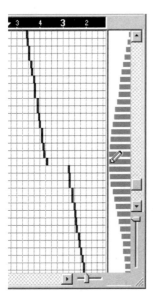

Boost the fade in

- Press return to keep the edits and verify the results by viewing the new fader movements in the Monitor mixer (make sure that the Read button is activated).

Organise the automation data

With a more complex automation Part, the data may be more difficult to view clearly. Also, if you have recorded, for example, a number of automated fader events on channels 1-8 and you later decide that channel 3 needs to be re-done, the data cannot be edited or deleted very easily.

For these, and other logical reasons, it is often better to separate your data onto different mix Tracks in the Arrange window as you proceed with each stage of the automated mix. To achieve this try the following:

- Open the Monitor mixer and activate both the Write and Read buttons and proceed to record, for example, automated fader and pan movements on channel 1. If you are not happy with the current take use undo in the Edit menu or press ctrl + Z (Mac: command + Z) to delete and try again.
- De-activate the Write button when the recording of automation for channel 1 is complete.
- Go to the Arrange window and find the 'Audio Mix' Part. Drag this Part to a new mix Track. Work at the bottom of the Track list and simply drag the Part below the existing Tracks. A new mix Track is created automatically for the dragged Part. Re-name the Track with an appropriate name e.g. 'Mix Ch.1'.
- Go back to the Monitor mixer and activate the Write button. This time record some fader and pan movements on channel 2.
- De-activate the Write button when the recording of automation for channel 2 is complete.
- Go to the Arrange window and find the 'Audio Mix' Part again. Drag this Part to another new Track and re-name the new Track as 'Mix Ch.2'.
- Proceed similarly to record automation events for channel 3 and as many channels as you require. When complete you will have the automation data for each channel on a separate mix Track. Should you need to go back and delete or edit any of the automation data at a later date it will now be easier to find. Remember also that the mix Parts can be spliced, moved and copied in the same manner as with MIDI and audio Parts.

The real thing

It is all very well conducting tests with automation but when it comes to automating a 'real' mix the procedure can become more complex. The following outlines one approach to automating a mix for a song you have already recorded:

- Open the song upon which you wish to apply automation.
- Do *not* start your mix from bar 1.1.0. If your material starts at bar 1.1.0 it is better to move it to bar 2 or later. This is because when you first activate the Write button all the current settings of the Monitor mixer etc. are recorded at position 1.1.0 and starting your mix at this same point can lead to confusion.
- With the Write button *de-activated* set up a basic mix manually. By basic mix we mean rough levels, pan and any EQ positions or effects settings for each of the recorded audio channels. At this point you may like to activate the MIDI mute button (Monitor mixer left panel) so that you are listening to the audio material alone.
- Activate the Write button. This records the basic mix you just created to song position 1.1.0. Also activate the Read button. Now whenever you rewind to the start of your material (at position 2.1.0 or later) it is this basic mix which will be showing. The rest of your mix can be developed from here.
- De-activate the Write button and play the whole mix through. Listen carefully and make some decisions about which sections of the mix need automation. You could mark these sections with the left and right locators and store them using shift+F2 to F12 (Mac: option+command+'typewriter' 1 to 0). Depending on the complexity of the material you may need very little automation or you may need to make drastic changes.
- Activate the Write button and work on each section separately. Organise the data as suggested in 'Organising automation data' above. Proceed carefully with one take at a time and always listen to the results. If you do not like the current take then delete it using ctrl+Z (Mac: command+Z) and try again.
- You may need to fade in or fade out the entire mix on the Master faders and, this too, can be treated as a separate section.
- If you have specific points in the mix which involve sudden changes or a series of non-dynamic settings then these are best programmed as a 'static mix'.
- If you are sure about the precise changes required for your static mix (for example mute buttons and other switches), move the song position to the point at which the changes should occur, make sure the Write button is still activated, and then simply move the switches etc. to their appropriate positions. The last set position of each moved control is recorded at the current song position.
- If you are not sure about the precise changes required and need to rehearse the changes, de-activate both the Write and Read buttons. Play back (cycle) the section which needs the static mix and manually adjust the volume, pan, EQ, settings etc. until satisfied. Take note of which controls you have changed (do not change too many at a time). Move the song position to the point at which the changes should occur, activate the Write and the Read button, and then nudge (move up and down slightly or switch on and off), the position of each of the controls you have changed. The last set position of each moved control is recorded at the current song position.
- Finally, when you have completed work on each of the sections which needed automation, rewind to the start of the song and replay the whole mix. Listen carefully for any mistakes or problems and redo or add automation as necessary.

The automation data is saved as part of the normal song file (.all extension). Thus, when the song is opened again at a later date, you will have convenient and instant recall of all the mixer, EQ and effects settings/movements you have made as part of the automated mix.

Mixing strategies

Design your own mix space in Cubase VST

The first thing you might like to do before proceeding with a mix is to set up Cubase VST's working environment so that it is optimised for the kinds of mixing tasks you will need to perform. This is rather like the traditional recording studio when the engineer may reset all the faders, knobs and buttons on the console before proceeding with mixing.

With Cubase VST you could open all the VST windows that you think you will be using during the mixing session, place them in convenient positions on the screen and pre-load the effects and processors required.

Figure 12.24 shows an 800 x 600 pixel screen optimised for mixing. Many Cubase VST users will be running at this resolution. If you have greater screen resolution then so much the better since you will be able to see more of the elements needed for mixing on a single screen. However, having less screen space is not a big disadvantage since you can use the scroll bars to quickly move around. For example, clicking once in the right hand part of the horizontal scroll bar in the setup shown moves the view across to reveal the Monitor mixer, the Master faders and the Master effects window (Figure 12.25).

Note that both the Master and Send effects windows are displayed below the Arrange and mixer windows for easy access. The Transport bar has been hidden since, during a mix, you can control transport functions from the numeric keypad. The SMPTE display module is activated and

Figure 12.24 Cubase VST
mixing session

Figure 12.25 Click on the scroll bar to reveal more 'mix space'

appears in both screens regardless of the scroll position. The VST Performance window is displayed in order to monitor the current CPU load as you add effects and processors during the course of the mix. And do not forget the Part background! Opening a Part background to suit the kind of music you are mixing can help inspire creativity and personalises your mix space.

Unfortunately, at the time of writing, the positions of all the VST windows are not saved with the song. When you load the song again at a later date the VST windows are not visible. However, selecting the Send and Master effects windows re-opens them at the same positions as when you saved the song.

Mastering decisions

Up to now we have mixed our audio within Cubase VST but, if the music is intended to be heard on other media such as cassette, mini-disk, DAT or CD, we have to make a choice about how it will be mastered.

In broad terms, a master is a final high quality recording from which copies can be made. If you wish to preserve the quality of your recording you must master onto the highest quality medium you have in your setup and, if possible, the audio should be transferred digitally.

DAT (digital audio tape) is among the most popular mastering mediums in the professional audio industry and, if you intend to have your work professionally duplicated, this is a good choice. The precise method you use to mix down to DAT depends on your audio card. If there are no digital outputs, you must use the analogue outputs of the card to mix down to the analogue inputs of the DAT machine. This involves a digital to analogue conversion as it leaves the computer and an analogue to digital conversion as it enters the DAT machine, which means a slight loss of quality. If you have digital outputs on the card, your mix can be transferred digitally to the DAT machine with no loss of quality, and this is the preferred option.

However, many Cubase VST users may prefer to master directly to an audio file for later transferral to CD using a CD-R drive (recordable CD). Recordable CD's are now increasingly popular for backup purposes and as a mastering and demo medium when only a small number of promotional copies are required. To mix down your material to an audio file, use Cubase VST's Export Audio file function (see below).

Integrating the MIDI tracks

When mixing your audio material you may also need to include a number of MIDI Tracks. The MIDI instruments are normally heard via an external mixer (as is the audio material), and there are two essential methods of including them in the final mix:

1 The audio Tracks are mixed within Cubase VST and the stereo result is routed to two channels of the external mixer. (If you have a multiple output audio card you may be routing more than two channels). The audio Tracks are then balanced with the MIDI instruments which also have their outputs routed to the external mixer. The final mixed result is then recorded onto DAT, or other mastering medium, via the analogue outputs of the mixer.

2 The sounds from the MIDI instruments are recorded onto one or more audio channels of Cubase VST (or onto a stereo pair). Next, the original MIDI Tracks are muted and the complete, all-inclusive arrangement is now audio only. The audio Tracks are then mixed within Cubase VST and the stereo result can be mastered in one of three ways: (i) via the analogue outputs of the audio card to DAT, or other mastering medium. (ii) via the digital outputs of the audio card to DAT, or other mastering medium. (iii) exported as an audio file within the computer using Cubase VST's Export Audio function (described below).

The process of recording the MIDI instruments onto one or more audio Tracks (option 2) deserves a little more explanation and there now follows a brief outline of the procedure:

• Decide how many audio channels you are going to use to record the sounds from your MIDI instruments. Depending on the complexity of your arrangement you may want to keep certain sounds separate but on most occasions you will probably use a stereo pair. For more than 2 channels you will need to record the material in more than one pass (unless you have a multiple input card).

• Prepare the mix of the MIDI material on your external mixer and route the master outputs to the audio inputs of your sound card.

• Before proceeding further ensure that any audio output from Cubase VST is muted on the external mixer in order to avoid feedback.

- Activate input metering on the appropriate channel(s) of the Monitor mixer in Cubase VST and verify that you have set the optimum record level by adjusting the level of the external mixer's output faders (or the input levels of the card's audio mixer), while playing the loudest section of the MIDI arrangement.
- Rewind to the beginning of the MIDI Parts and activate record. The sounds from the MIDI instruments are recorded onto the selected audio Track(s).
- When the recording is complete, mute the original MIDI Tracks. You can now play back your music as an audio only arrangement which can be automated, mixed digitally to DAT or exported as an audio file.

Export audio: Cubase VST's audio mixdown feature

The Export Audio feature provides the means for creating stereo files of a whole mix for later transferral to audio CD using a CD-R drive (recordable CD). It also provides a way of mixing down several tracks onto one audio channel or onto a stereo pair of audio channels in order to, for example, free up space in the audio arrangement (or on the hard disk), for more recording. In addition, it can help save processing power by including any effects in the audio file.

The Export Audio dialogue is opened by selecting Export Audio File in the main File menu (see Figure 12.26). It is also opened by clicking on the Create File button in the Master fader window.

Export Audio is similar in function to Mixdown for MIDI Parts. It allows the mixing of all unmuted audio Tracks between the left and right locators onto a single composite stereo or mono file, with or without audio mixer automation, channel effects and master effects.

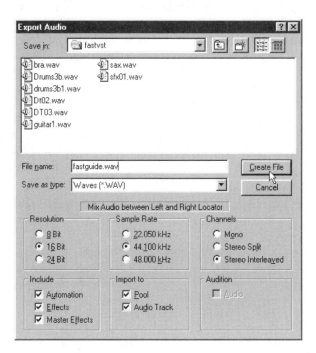

Figure 12.26 Export Audio dialogue

The basic procedure for mixing down any number of audio Tracks using Export Audio is as follows:

- Move the left and right locators to the start and end points of the section of audio you wish to mix down. This could be a short segment on one Track or an entire arrangement. Tracks which are not required should be muted.
- Audition the selected passage to make sure that the mix is exactly what you need and make any final adjustments.
- Open the Audio Export dialogue and decide the resolution, sample rate and channel status of the file to be created. If you intend to mix down to a stereo file to be used in Cubase VST the default settings of 16 bit, 44.1kHz and stereo interleaved (normal stereo) are the correct ones. If you need a mono file, select the mono option.
- Decide whether you wish to include any mix automation, channel effects or master effects and whether you would like the resulting file to be automatically imported back into the Pool and into a newly created Part on an audio Track in the Arrange window. When the file is imported into the Arrange window, a Part is written to the currently selected audio Track or, if no audio Track is selected, a new audio Track named 'MixDown' is created for the imported data.
- Select a folder and a name for the new file and, after verifying that you have made the correct settings in the dialogue, click on the Create File button.
- A new audio file is created and automatically appears as a new Part in the Arrange window (if you have activated the appropriate import option in the Export audio dialogue). Mute the original audio source Tracks used for the mix and audition the newly created mixdown Part to verify that all is as expected.

The above is also the procedure for creating a stereo file for a whole mix. Just make sure you have the left and right locators set at the appropriate positions (and take care that any reverberation tail which may occur after the audio tracks themselves does not get cut off due to the right locator being placed too close to the end point of the audio parts).

Using Export audio to create a stereo file of a whole mix results in an audio file which has not suffered any degradation due to being transferred from one medium to another and it is ready to be assembled with other similar files to create the tracks for a CD. If you have a CD-R drive then you can burn your completed sequence of audio files to an audio CD. In some ways this technique is more convenient than mastering to DAT, especially for demo purposes, but you may find that you quickly run out of hard disk space.

Other possibilities for exporting audio include the creation of:

- 24 bit Wave files for use in advanced digital audio software like Pro Tools, Wavelab, Sound Forge etc.
- 8 bit files for multimedia applications.
- AIFF files for use in the Macintosh version of Cubase VST, or in other software which does not recognise the PC Wave file format.
- Split stereo files, which results in two mono files, one for each side of the stereo image.

Export Audio uses the level of the Master faders to set the level of the exported file. However, if, for example, you have compressed or noise gated a mono sound via the Insert effects and you wish to export this to a mono mixdown file, keeping the file at the same level as seen on the Monitor mixer faders, you should boost the Master faders by 6dB before using Export Audio. This applies to any case of exporting single mono Tracks (with or without Insert effects), to a mono mixdown file.

Mixer moves

That completes our exploration of the essential aspects of mixing, EQ and effects. To help you in your various mixing tasks, the following table provides a practical summary of the main mixer moves:

Table 12.2 Mixer moves

Key(s) held		Mouse action	Result
PC	Mac		
ctrl	command	click once on fader	resets fader to 0dB
ctrl	command	click once on pan control	resets pan position to centre
ctrl	command	click once on EQ button	turns EQ on and off (if already active)
ctrl	command	click once on FX button	turns all FX sends on/off for channel (if already active)
alt	option	move fader, solo or mute in a stereo pair	moves one of the pair independently
alt	option	move fader, pan, solo, or mute of a mono channel	also moves corresponding control of adjacent channel
–	–	click on clip indicator	resets headroom indicator
–	–	click on channel strip name	opens name entry pop-up
ctrl + *	command + *	–	opens Monitor mixer window
ctrl + +	command + +	–	opens Master window
ctrl + F12	n/a	–	brings VST windows to the front
shift + F12	n/a	–	hides/shows VST windows

Remember that during mixing you are likely to concentrate on specific sections of the arrangement using Cubase VST's cycle function. Since the length of the cycle is regulated by the left and right locators, try storing the locator positions for the various sections of the song using shift + F2 to F11 (Mac: option + command + 'typewriter' 1 to 0). Each stored setting can then be instantly recalled during the mix process by pressing F2 to F11 (Mac: command + 'typewriter' 1 to 0).

More information

This chapter has provided you with most of what you need to mix and process audio using the VST features. However, outside of the direct domain of the program, there are many different techniques and approaches involved in mixing, effects and sound processing. It is beyond the scope of this book to cover the wider subject in full.

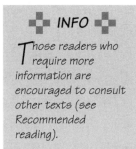

INFO

Those readers who require more information are encouraged to consult other texts (see Recommended reading).

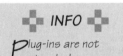

13

Plug-ins

✦ INFO ✦

Plug-ins are not stand-alone programs; they always require a host, like Cubase VST, in which to run.

Plug-in technology is one of the most attractive features of Cubase VST. As already outlined in the previous chapter, plug-ins are audio processing and effects modules which can be added to the effects rack of Cubase VST as and when you need them.

The plug-ins supplied with the program have already been described but it is also possible to incorporate additional Steinberg and third party plug-ins into the system. These might be supplied in VST-native format or they might be Direct X (described below).

Because of its open-endedness, the VST plug-in concept offers possibilities beyond the normal confines of the core program. Plug-ins open up whole new worlds of audio processing to the Cubase VST user and endow the program with a large degree of expandability and adaptability within a single software environment. This allows users to build their own virtual studio according to their budget and the kind of work they will be doing.

This chapter provides a description and user guide to the excellent Steinberg Spectral Design range of plug-ins and the superb Waves 'Native Power Pack' and AudioTrack (PC versions). This gives readers a good insight into the kinds of plug-ins which are available and how you might use them within Cubase VST.

Much of this chapter is aimed at the intermediate to advanced Cubase VST user and is not necessarily designed to be read in sequence. It may be of more value to skip to those sections which are of particular interest to your own requirements. Each plug-in is described in some detail in an attempt to give the reader something more than a quick review. This should help you get a real taste of what each plug-in incorporates. There is also a description of the theory of the important concepts of compression, expansion and gating included in the Waves C1 Compressor/Gate section. This complements the theory about EQ, reverberation and delay described in Chapter 12. In addition, there is information about EQ filter types included in the Waves Q10 ParaGraphic EQ section.

However, before we go on to explore the details of each plug-in, it is worth understanding a little more about the background of the plug-in concept.

Direct X

Direct X is a standard developed by Microsoft for the handling of audio, video and multimedia tasks in Windows 95 and Windows NT operating systems. When Cubase VST is installed, the latest version of Direct X is installed with it and this ensures the program's compatibility with Direct X plug-ins. Direct X is also sometimes referred to as Active Movie.

As mentioned above, a plug-in for Cubase VST may be of two types: VST-native or Direct X. VST-native plug-ins run only in Cubase VST, (or VST compatible programs), whereas Direct X plug-ins run in any host program which supports Direct X technology. Third party developers producing high-end effects and processors tend to use Direct X since their product will then instantly run on a larger number of host programs. These products also invariably incorporate an advanced user interface which runs in a separate window.

It is also possible to use your audio card's Direct X driver, rather than the usual ASIO multimedia driver, to play back audio from Cubase VST. However, this is for playback only since Direct X does not support audio recording. The main advantage of Direct X for playback in Cubase VST is that it cuts down the latency time. This helps when performing a mix, since there is not such a signifcant delay between mixer movements and hearing the result in the audio.

There now follows a series of descriptions of a selection of plug-ins from Steinberg and third party developer Waves.

Steinberg Spectral Design plug-ins

The plug-ins described here are from the high-end Steinberg Spectral Design range. They have been designed with audio restoration, broadcast and mastering in mind and are characterised by their distinctive red user interface, ease of use and superb audio processing quality.

The Steinberg Spectral Design plug-ins are Direct X and do not need to be located in the Vstplugins folder in order to be recognised by Cubase VST. Once installation is complete the plug-ins are automatically available in the plug-ins menu. To use any of the plug-ins in Cubase VST you must first open the chosen effects window and click on the name field of one of the front panels. This opens the plug-ins choice menu from which you should select the required Steinberg plug-in. In the Rack Xpander front panel which appears, click on the edit button to open the user interface for the chosen plug-in.

De-clicker

- I/O: stereo in/stereo out (operates in mono or stereo mode)
- Approximate CPU power used: variable 15 – 70% (200MHz Pentium MMX processor)
- Normal usage in Cubase VST: Insert or Master effect

Description

De-clicker (Figure 13.1) is a real-time click removal plug-in. It allows the removal of clicks, pops and other unwanted audio artefacts from audio recordings and also restores brief dropouts in the material.

Figure 13.1 The De-clicker window

The De-clicker user interface features the following parameters:

- Mode – sets the manner in which De-clicker analyses the incoming signal. 'Old' is for vintage vinyl recordings, 'Standard' is a general purpose setting for a wide range of input sources and 'Modern' is for digital and high quality material with a wide frequency range. When setting up De-clicker always try the 'Standard' setting first.
- Threshold – sets the amplitude level above which clicks will be detected. The lower the level, the more clicks will be be detected and removed. Range: 0 – 100%
- Deplop – sets the cut-off point for a special high pass filter which reduces the 'plop' noise which often appears when a click has been removed. Range: 0 – 150Hz
- Click reduction quality – provides 4 levels of click removal/audio restoration quality. The higher the level the better the quality. Range: level buttons 1 to 4.
- Audition – when activated, monitors the clicks and pops which are currently being removed. When de-activated, allows normal monitoring.

The central area of the De-clicker window is dominated by the DSP-performance and De-click performance displays.

The DSP-performance display shows the current DSP usage with a dynamic activity curve. The display scrolls past in real-time and the higher the curve the more DSP power is being used. If the curve reaches the top of the display, maximum DSP capacity has been reached and you may need to reduce the Click reduction quality number.

The De-click performance display shows the processed audio in green and the original signal in red. When no removal of clicks and pops is taking place the green waveform completely covers the red waveform; i.e. the output signal is the same as the input signal. When any clicks are removed, the corresponding part of the waveform is shown in red indicating that the output signal is now different from the input signal.

De-clicker also features peak level output meters which show the current output level.

User guide

When chosen as an Insert effect for a mono audio Track, De-clicker appears in mono format with one peak level output meter. When chosen as an Insert effect for a stereo Track or as a Master effect, De-clicker appears in stereo format with stereo peak level output meters.

De-clicker's parameter values are easily changed by dragging the two sliders and clicking on any of the buttons. All buttons are simple on/off switches and the current status of each is indicated by virtual LED's.

To set up De-clicker's parameters try the following:

- Play the audio material to be processed through De-clicker.
- Select the mode according to what kind of audio material is being processed. If in doubt, use Standard mode.
- Select the click reduction quality button required. Try starting with 3.
- Set the threshold to a starting value of 100 (its maximum setting).
- Activate the Audition button to listen to what is being removed.
- Reduce the threshold level until you are satisfied that the offending clicks and pops are being removed. The threshold can often remain fairly high since the De-clicker's algorithms are already very sensitive.
- Adjust the Deplop setting if required.
- De-activate the audition button and listen to the result.
- Fine tune the parameters as desired.
- Compare the original signal with the processed signal by switching on and off the power switch on Cubase VST's rack effect front panel.

Applications

De-clicker is ideal for re-mastering old or damaged recordings. This includes audio restoration of old vinyl recordings, the removal of digital clicks from digital recordings, the softening of digital distortion, the restoration of short dropouts and the removal of sharp audio artefacts like guitar pick noise. At extreme settings, De-clicker can also subtly soften audio material with sharp attack transients like drums, percussion etc. and it can be useful for audio forensics.

For more sophisticated audio restoration De-clicker can be used together with De-noiser (described below).

De-noiser

- I/O: stereo in/stereo out (operates in mono or stereo mode)
- Approximate CPU power used: mono 35%, stereo 65% (200MHz Pentium MMX processor)
- Normal usage in Cubase VST: Insert or Master effect

Description
De-noiser (Figure 13.2) is a real-time noise removal plug-in. It provides real-time broadband noise removal and incorporates an adaptive system which automatically tracks the noise as it changes in character and level.

Figure 13.2 The De-noiser window

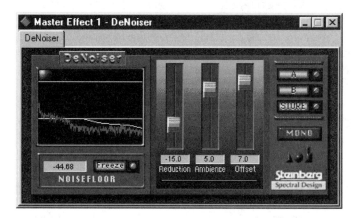

The De-noiser user interface features the following parameters:

- Reduction – controls the amount of noise reduction taking place. The lower the negative value, the more noise is removed. Range: 0dB to –20dB.
- Ambience – specifies a balance between the amount of noise reduction and the ambient characteristics of the input signal. Lower negative values increase the speed and intensity of the noise reduction action and tend to deaden the ambient qualities of the material, whereas higher positive values help maintain the ambient characteristics but provide less efficient noise reduction. Range: –10dB to +10dB.
- Offset – De-noiser is normally in auto-level mode i.e. the level below which noise reduction takes place is constantly updated according to the input signal. The Offset parameter provides an offset for the level at which noise reduction begins to take place. Higher positive values result in more acute noise reduction by increasing the overall threshold level below which noise reduction begins to take place. Lower negative values result in less acute noise reduction by decreasing the overall threshold level below

which noise reduction begins to take place. Range: –10dB to +10dB.

- Freeze – freezes the current calculated noisefloor of De-noiser to provide a spectral 'fingerprint' for special noise removal applications. When Freeze is activated, auto-level mode is de-activated but the Offset parameter remains operational.

De-noiser features a real-time graphic display of the on-going status of the device in relation to the user settings and the current input. This shows amplitude on the y-axis and frequency on the x-axis. It features three colour coded lines. The dark green line shows the spectrum of the incoming signal, the yellow line shows an estimation of the spectrum of the noise floor and the light green line shows the threshold level (noise floor) below which noise reduction is taking place. The noise floor is also shown numerically below the display.

De-noiser also features Setups A and B. These allow you to store two different setups for comparative purposes. To store the current settings click the Store button followed by your choice of button A or B. To recall the settings click once on button A or B.

To switch De-noiser to mono mode use the Mono button. In mono mode, the output from De-noiser will be mono, although it can still accept a mono or a stereo input signal.

User guide

All De-noiser's parameters are easily updated using the slider controls and buttons. De-noiser's sliders can be reset to their default settings by click-ing on a slider while holding shift, ('PlugIns receive key commands' must be activated in Cubase VST's Preferences dialogue).

De-noiser needs a short time to analyse the input signal before setting up its internal parameters. This short setup period is not meant to be included when you are recording the output so you should initialise the De-noiser before commencing. To do this, play a short section of the audio to be treated, so that De-noiser adjusts its internal parameters, and then stop and rewind to the beginning. De-noiser is now initialised and you can record its output.

Setting up De-noiser involves choosing a reduction level and offset which do not interfere with those parts of the signal which you wish to keep. A large amount of noise reduction is possible without undesirable side-effects. For live recordings and ambient sources the processing action can be fine tuned using the Ambience parameter.

Applications

De-noiser has a wide range of applications in re-mastering, audio restora-tion, audio forensics and analysis. It can improve noisy live recordings and can clean up speech in post production and broadcast applications. It is also good at reducing noise on heavily compressed electric guitar and bass (or any other noisy signal) when track laying.

Loudness maximizer

- I/O: stereo in/stereo out
- Approximate CPU power used: 25% (200MHz Pentium MMX processor)
- Normal usage in Cubase VST: Insert or Master effect

Description

Loudness Maximizer (Figure 13.3) is a real-time loudness optimiser. It provides dynamic enhancement of digital audio recordings, improving the perceived loudness and density of the signal and adding brilliance and punch to the sound. The algorithms driving Loudness Maximizer continually adapt to the audio material itself and the device achieves its effect without undesirable audio artefacts.

Figure 13.3 The Loudness Maximizer window

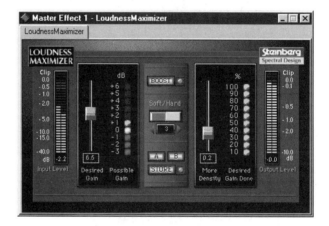

The Loudness Maximizer consists of three essential elements in its signal processing path. These are the continual real-time analysis of the input signal (which affects the overall response of the device), compression based on the Desired gain and Density settings, and limiting according to the Density, Soft/Hard and Boost settings.

The main controls available in the user interface are as follows:

- Input level meters – peak level meters showing the level of the input signal.
- Desired gain – sets the number of dB's by which the perceived loudness is to be increased. Range: 0dB to +12dB.
- Possible gain meter – shows the number of possible dB's by which the signal level can be increased. As the desired gain setting is increased, the possible gain meter is decreased. This meter should not fall below 0dB and, if it does, the desired gain setting should be reduced.
- Boost – provides a further 2dB gain to the perceived loudness.

Suitable for uncomplicated modern dance and popular music.
- Soft/Hard parameter – adjusts the limiter response, where higher values produce a hard, agressive response and lower values produce a soft, gentle action. In addition, higher values also allow a higher desired gain setting while lower values allow less desired gain. Range: –9 to 9.
- More density – affects the balance between the compressor and limiter elements of the device. The higher the value, the more the compressor is incorporated in the processing. Range: 0 – 1.
- Desired gain done – shows the percentage of desired gain which has currently been achieved. This should not register less than 50% continuously. Range: 0 – 100%.

Loudness Maximizer also features Setups A and B and peak level output meters. Setups A and B allow you to store two different setups for comparative purposes. To store the current settings click the Store button followed by your choice of button A or B. To recall the settings click once on button A or B. The output meters show peak levels with a very high degree of accuracy and can be trusted down to a headroom accuracy of 0.01dB.

User guide
The Desired gain and More density parameters are changed using the sliders. Boost is a simple on/off switch and the Hard/Soft parameter is a virtual rocker switch which is adjustable one value at a time by clicking on either side of the switch.

Loudness Maximizer is particularly transparent in its processing action and initial settings will usually revolve around the Desired gain and Soft/Hard parameters. Higher Soft/Hard settings are usually suitable for material with a lot of high frequency content and allow more Desired gain to be applied. Lower Soft/Hard settings may be required for mixes with a lot of bass or sub bass and allow less Desired gain to be applied. Once the basic settings have been established try using the More density parameter to fine tune the compressed quality of the output. Start with low values between 0 and 0.4.

Applications
All digital mastering applications requiring loudness maximisation. Loudness Maximizer's zero-overshoot limiting guarantees a clip free output. It is suitable for all music production, broadcast and multimedia applications where maximum output level, excellent sound quality and accuracy are required.

Spectralizer

- I/O: stereo in/stereo out (operates in mono or stereo mode)
- Approximate CPU power used: mono 36%, stereo 79% (200MHz Pentium MMX processor)
- Normal usage in Cubase VST: Insert or Master effect

Description

Spectralizer (Figure 13.4) is a real-time sonic optimiser. It provides spectral enhancement of digital audio recordings, improving their clarity and transparency without adding noise or undesirable audio artefacts.

Figure 13.4 The Spectralizer window

Spectralizer helps replace some of the original clarity and crispness which may be lost during routine audio processing. It can re-synthesize lost upper harmonics based on the signals which remain in the lower parts of the spectrum of the incoming signal. The result is a richer, brighter recording which retains the attention and interest of the listener. The harmonics are normally added at very low amplitude so the result often remains a psychoacoustic phenomenon rather than an obvious effect.

The Spectralizer user interface features the following parameters:

- Input – provides gain or attenuation for the overall input level. Range: –20dB to +6dB.
- Gain – adjusts the gain of the input signal before it passes through to the 2nd and 3rd harmonic generators. The input and gain parameters may need to be adjusted in relation to eachother in order to avoid clipping at the output. Range: 0 to 100.
- 2nd – sets the level of the second harmonics created by Spectralizer. The second harmonic is a spectral component at twice the frequency of the fundamental frequency. Range: 0 to 100.
- 3rd – sets the level of the third harmonics created by Spectralizer. The third harmonic is a spectral component at three times the frequency of the fundamental frequency. Range: 0 to 100.
- Mix – adjusts the balance between the processed and the unprocessed signal. The higher the value the more processed signal is present in the output. Range: 0 to 100.
- Frequency – controls the Spectralizer's sonically optimised high-pass filter which decides which part of the frequency spectrum is

affected by the processing. If Frequency is set to 2000, the 2nd
harmonic generator adds harmonics to the signal from 4000Hz
upwards, and the 3rd harmonic generator from 6000Hz upwards,
i.e. the higher the frequency setting, the higher the frequency of
the harmonics which are added to the signal. Range: 1000Hz to
7000Hz calibrated in 1000Hz steps.

- Density – modifies the amplitude envelope characteristics of the
  added harmonics. The higher the setting the more intense the
  harmonics. Range: 0 – 6.
- Solo – when activated, allows monitoring of the processed part of
  the signal alone. This is useful for analysing exactly what is being
  added to the signal.
- Kick – adds extra harmonics on the transients of the incoming
  signal in order to provide more presence and attack.

Spectralizer also features level meters to monitor the effect of the input
and gain settings. If these parameters have been set too high the internal
clip indicator is illuminated and the input level or gain should be reduced.
Click once on the clip indicator to reset.

User guide
The main parameters of Spectralizer are changed using the sliders. Solo
and Kick are simple on/off switches and the Frequency and Density
parameters are virtual rocker switches which are adjustable one value at a
time by clicking on either side of the switch.

To switch Spectralizer to mono mode use the Mono button. In mono
mode, the output from Spectralizer will be mono, although it can still
accept a mono or a stereo input signal.

To become familiar with the effect of Spectralizer, select it as a Master
effect and try the following exercise while playing a recording of drums or
percussion which are in need of spectral enhancement:

- Leave the Input slider at 0.0dB.
- Set the Mix slider to the maximum 100 position.
- Set all other sliders to about the 50 position.
- Set the density to 3 and the frequency to the maximum 7000 position.
- Now slowly reduce the frequency parameter and listen carefully to the timbral changes in the
  sound at each position. The lower frequency settings produce a more pronounced effect. Try a
  final setting of 4000 or 5000.
- Fine tune the gain and 2nd and 3rd harmonics as required.
- Reduce the Mix control to produce the desired proportion of the processed and unprocessed
  signal.
- Compare the original signal with the processed signal by switching on and off the power switch
  on Cubase VST's rack effect front panel.

Applications
Spectralizer improves the clarity and impact of masters and demos and puts back the frequencies lost through other audio processes. It adds interest and warmth to any recorded sound and increases the apparent width of the frequency range in a recording. As well as applications in mastering and re-mastering Spectralizer works well on selected sounds in multi-track recording. It adds attack to dull bass drums and bass guitars, provides extra 'sparkle' for strings and brass and injects brilliance and richness to lead vocals, helping them to stand out in the mix.

Magneto

- I/O: stereo in/stereo out (operates in mono or stereo mode)
- Approximate CPU power used: mono 18%, stereo 38% (200MHz Pentium MMX processor)
- Normal usage in Cubase VST: Insert or Master effect

Description
Magneto (Figure 13.5) is an analogue tape machine simulator. It produces the effect of analogue tape saturation, which adds warmth and punch to the processed signal, and helps eliminate the harshness often associated with digital recordings. The engineers at Spectral Design analysed the

Figure 13.5 The Magneto window

behaviour of a professional 24 track analogue tape recorder and incorporated the results into Magneto, but without any of the undesirable side-effects. Producers and engineers have long valued the mild compression action of tape saturation which adds subtle brilliance and smoothness to high quality analogue recordings. With Magneto this effect is now available in the digital domain.

The Magneto user interface features the following parameters:

- Input level – provides gain or attenuation for the input signal. Range: −12dB to +12dB.
- Tape speed – switches between 15ips and 30ips tape speed.

- Drive – controls the 'on tape' gain level. The higher this is set the more tape saturation occurs. Range: 0dB to +24dB.
- HF adjust – adjusts high frequency boost or attenuation for the treated signal. Range: –6dB to +6dB.
- Output level – adjusts the gain/attenuation and sets the ceiling for the output signal. Range: –12dB to +12dB.

✥ INFO ✥

For more information about Steinberg plug-ins see the Steinberg website at: www.steinberg.net.

The display is dominated by two large VU meters showing the current level of either the input, the 'on tape' sound or the output level according to which of the buttons of the same name is selected at the top of the window. The green LED's show which button is currently selected and also flash in red when a peak overload has occured.

To switch Magneto to mono mode use the Mono button. In mono mode, the output from Magneto will be mono, although it can still accept a mono or a stereo input signal.

User guide

To change the control values, drag vertically with the mouse on the dials or on the drive slider. Using the left mouse provides fine control over the dial values and the right mouse provides course control.

Most operations with Magneto centre around the setting of the relative levels of the input, drive and output controls. Once an optimum level has been set with the input level control, the required amount of tape saturation can be applied. No matter how high the saturation level 'on tape', the output signal cannot go beyond the level set with the output level control. Subtle or very extreme tape saturation effects are possible.

The saturation characteristics differ slightly between the 15ips and 30ips tape speeds and you can fine tune the high frequency content of the treated signal using the HF-adjust control.

Applications

Magneto is applicable to digital audio mastering where warmth, punch and brilliance is required for the finished product. It provides subtle attenuation of the peaks in the signal while raising the overall average level. It is excellent for re-mastering existing digital masters which are in need of more warmth and character. Whenever a digital recording has become too cold or harsh, Magneto can provide the antidote.

Magneto is also suitable for processing just about any instrument during multi-tracking, including drums, vocals, bass, guitars, strings, and it is especially good at enlivening samples and synthesizer sounds.

Waves Native Power Pack

The Waves Native Power Pack is a collection of 6 high-end plug-in processors and effects including TrueVerb, Q10 ParaGraphic EQ, C1 Compressor/Gate, L1 Ultramaximizer, S1 Stereo Imager and IDR (Increased Digital Resolution). The C1 comprises 2 separate plug-in modules; the C1 Compressor and the C1 Gate. The package also includes

WaveConvert, a stand-alone multimedia batch file processor. The Native Power Pack is a highly sophisticated set of audio tools designed for the advanced and professional user.

The Native Power Pack plug-ins are Direct X and do not need to be located in the Vstplugins folder in order to be recognised by Cubase VST. Once installation is complete the plug-ins are automatically available in the plug-ins menu. To use any of the plug-ins in Cubase VST you must first open the chosen effects window, (Send, Insert or Master), and click on the name field of one of the front panels. This opens the plug-ins choice menu from which you should select the required Waves plug-in. In the Rack Xpander front panel which appears, click on the edit button to open the user interface for the chosen plug-in.

TrueVerb

- I/O: stereo in/stereo out (accepts mono or stereo input)
- Approximate CPU power used: 28% (200MHz Pentium MMX processor)
- Normal usage in Cubase VST: Insert or Master effect

Description
TrueVerb (Figure 13.6) is a virtual room/reverb processor. As has been apparent in the descriptions of reverb in the previous chapter, producing convincing reverberation is among the most difficult tasks for any plug-in developer. With TrueVerb, Waves have succeeded in producing what is among the most convincing reverb plug-ins on the market. It is a true stereo in/stereo out device. The TrueVerb maintains true stereo processing throughout all of its internal operations, changing the reflections

Figure 13.6 The TrueVerb virtual room/reverb processor.

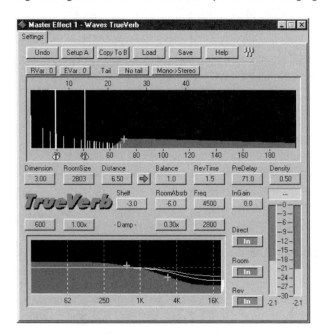

according to the position of the sounds in the input stereo image such that each element in the sound is treated with different reverberant characteristics. This is much like the behaviour of sound in a real acoustic space where the reverberation varies according to the position of the source in the room.

TrueVerb achieves its sound by the careful combination of the three essential elements of real reverberation: the direct sound, the early reflections and the reverberation. (See Chapter 12 for more information about the theoretical aspects of reverberation).

The user interface window is divided into two main sections: the Time Response display and the Frequency Response display.

The time response display

The time response display shows the direct sound as the first vertical line on the left, followed by a series of early reflections and then the reverberation. (For clarification, see Figure 12.17 in Chapter 12). The size of one dimension of the virtual acoustic space is shown above the display (in metres) and time is shown below the display (in milliseconds). The time response is governed by a number of parameters as follows:

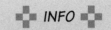

- Dimension – sets the number of dimensions for the virtual acoustic space, affecting the distribution and characteristics of the early reflections. Dimension affects the early reflections alone and has no affect on the reverberation. It also simultaneously changes Pre-delay when Link is active. Range: 1.00 to 3.99.
- RoomSize – varies the size of the virtual acoustic space (in cubic metres). Simultaneously changes Pre-delay when Link is active. Range: $50m^3$ to $20000m^3$.
- Distance – varies the apparent distance between the listener and the sound source. Simultaneously changes the reverb level when Link is active. Range: 0.5m to 40m.
- Link – links Pre-delay to the size and dimension of the room. When active (arrow showing), Pre-delay cannot be set independently. When inactive (no arrow), Pre-delay can be set independently.
- Balance – controls the balance between the direct sound/early reflections and the reverberation. When Link is active, the 0.0 position gives the natural balance that would be expected given the current settings of the other parameters. Range: –48dB to +12dB.
- Reverb time - controls the decay time for the reverberation. Range: 0.2secs to 100 secs.
- Pre-delay – sets the delay time before reverberation begins. When Link is active, Pre-delay cannot be independently adjusted. Range: 10.5ms to 200ms
- Density – controls the intensity of the initial reflections in the reverberation stage. Higher values mean more density. Range: 0.0 to 1.0.

The frequency response display

The frequency response display shows the frequency based characteristics of the early reflections and reverberation and is used to set up the absorption and dampening qualities of the virtual acoustic space. The frequency response is governed by a number of parameters as follows:

- Shelf – controls the amount of reverberation absorption in the acoustic space. Shown as a blue line in the display. Range: –12dB to 0dB.
- Room absorption – controls the amount of early reflection absorption in the acoustic space. Shown as a yellow line in the display. Range: –6dB to 0dB.
- Frequency – varies the cut-off frequency for both the shelf and room absorption parameters. Range: 1.6kHz to 21kHz.

and four dampening parameters:

- LF ratio – controls the decay time of low frequencies in the reverberation stage relative to the overall reverb decay time set in the time response display. Ratios lower than 1.0 result in more definition and less 'boomy' sounding reverb effects. Ratios higher than 1.0 result in more 'voluminous' and 'warmer' sounding reverb effects. Range: 0.1x to 2x.
- LF damp – sets the cut-off frequency for the LF ratio parameter. Range: 16Hz to 1.6kHz.
- HF ratio – controls the decay time of high frequencies in the reverberation stage relative to the overall reverb decay time set in the time response display. Ratios lower than 1.0 result in more 'mellow' sounding reverb effects. Ratios higher than 1.0 result in 'brighter' sounding reverb effects. Range: 0.1x to 2x.
- HF damp – sets the cut-off frequency for the HF ratio parameter. Range: 1.6kHz to 21kHz.

User guide

The user interface features the standard Waves system controls at the top of the window (see 'Waves system controls', below). To reset ALL the parameters to default values select 'TrueVerb default' from the Load menu. To change the parameters drag vertically or horizontally with the mouse in the value fields. Alternatively, press shift and the up/down arrow keys to change the values in small steps, ('PlugIns receive key commands' must be activated in Cubase VST's Preferences dialogue) , or double click on the value field to enter a value directly from the numeric keypad.

Reverb/early reflection balance can be changed directly by dragging the cross vertically in the time response display. When Link is inactive, dragging the cross horizontally affects the pre-delay value. The cut-off points and ratios for the low and high frequency damping controls can be changed in two dimensions by dragging the respective crosses in the frequency response display. To change the distance directly on the display drag the yellow double arrow and line. Note that the distance parameter allows the value to go beyond the theoretical maximum imposed by the size of the virtual acoustic space, expanding the palette of possibilities still further. The line turns red when this has occured, warning that the effect produced may not sound 'natural', (if a natural effect is what you require). To change the size of the acoustic space drag the blue double arrow and line.

The Direct, Room and Reverb buttons switch the direct sound, the early reflections and the reverberation in and out. When used as a send effect in Cubase VST you would normally switch the direct sound off. When used as a Master effect you would switch it on. These buttons are useful for monitoring each part of the reverberant effect when editing in fine detail. To regulate the input level adjust the InGain parameter. The current level is shown on the stereo level meters which feature peak hold numeric values below each meter bar and clip indicators above.

The time response display also features reverb and early reflection variation buttons above the display. These vary the characteristics of the reverb (Rvar parameter) and the early reflections (Evar), the results of which can be seen in the display. Also of interest are the Tail parameter and the mono/stereo button. The tail parameter can be set to 'Auto Tail', in which case the reverb stops when the level of the reverb tail gets to within 5% of the end of file level, or it can be set to a user time (in seconds) which will be in effect regardless of the reverb level. When set to 'No Tail' the parameter has no effect. The mono/stereo switch toggles the operation of TrueVerb between stereo and mono output when processing a mono input.

TrueVerb is supplied with a number of presets in the Load menu which make good starting points for your own settings. Also try the settings in Figure 13.6 above, which simulates a small concert hall. For comparative purposes, try switching the reverb in and out using Cubase VST's Rack Xpander power on/off switch.

Applications
Trueverb is particularly good at adding a sense of liveliness and stereo width to the treated sound(s). It produces excellent natural stereo reverberation, especially with stereo sources. Its unique distance parameter can place the listener at variable distances from the sound source with a startling sense of reality.

TrueVerb has applications beyond the traditional confines of many conventional reverb units. As well as any of the normal reverberation applications, such as adding reverb to individual mono or stereo tracks within a mix, TrueVerb is also suited to the processing of entire mixes when you need to place the instruments/performance in a 'natural' acoustic space. TrueVerb has the ability to simulate real acoustic behaviour in a truly stereophonic manner which allows the placing of sounds in a convincing virtual acoustic environment. In this application, it is important to imagine the kind of acoustic environment in which the musical performance might really take place. For example, a small hall might be suitable for a classical chamber music ensemble whereas a full orchestra would sound better in a large concert hall. A jazz group might be placed in a small club venue and rock and pop might be treated with anything between an intimate, 'up-front' small club effect to a large stadium.

Generally, TrueVerb has a wide range of mastering and re-mastering applications. In Cubase VST, it can be used on the whole mix as a Master effect or on certain chosen sounds within the mix as a Send effect. It is useful for re-mastering poor sounding demos and studio recordings, when the whole mix can be re-processed, as described above, to place the recording in a new, enlivened acoustic environment.

A major consideration to bear in mind when using TrueVerb is the fact that pleasant acoustic environments in the real world actually make it easier for us to listen to music and listening to sounds in an unsuitable acoustic environment quickly causes listening fatigue. Using Trueverb to apply the correct measure and type of reverberation for the given style of music, we can minimise listening fatigue, bring the performance to life and enhance and 'sweeten' the listening experience.

Q10 ParaGraphic EQ

- I/O: stereo in/stereo out (accepts mono or stereo input)
- Approximate CPU power used: 28% (200MHz Pentium MMX processor)
- Normal usage in Cubase VST: Insert or Master effect

Description

The Q10 (Figure 13.7) is a powerful EQ plug-in which can operate with up to 10 parametric EQ bands in mono or stereo. It features an excellent amplitude/frequency graphic display which makes this plug-in particularly easy and intuitive to use.

Figure 13.7 Q10 paragraphic EQ

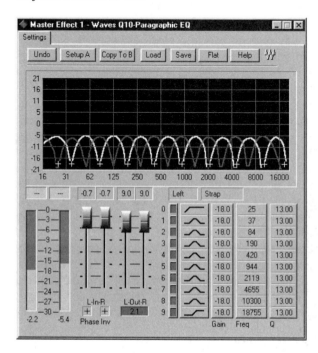

The Q10 user interface features the following parameters:

- Input faders – trim the input level. Range: –24dB to 0dB FS.
- Phase inversion switches – invert the phase of the chosen channel.
- Output faders – boost or attenuate the output level. Range: –24dB to +12dB FS.
- Left/Right channel selector – selects the left or right channel for individual EQ processing when the Q10 is in 'unstrapped' mode.
- Strap / Unstrap selector – links the left and right channels so that all EQ adjustments affect both channels ('strapped') or separates the left and rght channels so that each channel can be processed individually ('unstrapped').

and for each frequency band:

- Filter type selector – selects one of five different filter types for the chosen frequency band (see filter types, below).
- Gain – provides boost or cut for the chosen frequency band. (Has no effect with low and high pass cut-off filters). Range: –18dB to +18dB.
- Frequency – sets the filter's centre frequency (or cut-off and corner frequency with low/high pass cut-off and low/high shelving filters). Range: 16Hz to 21kHz.
- Q – sets the width of the chosen frequency band. (With parametric EQ filter type only). Range: 0.5 to 100, where 0.5 is the widest band and 100 is the narrowest.

User guide

The Q10 is available in modules with 1 to 10 bands of EQ which can be chosen according to the processing application. The greater the number of bands of EQ the more processing power will be required.

The interface features the standard Waves system controls at the top of the window (see 'Waves system controls', below) with the addition of a 'flat' button which resets the EQ to a flat response. To reset ALL the parameters select 'Q10 Full Reset' from the Load menu. To change the other parameters drag vertically or horizontally with the mouse in the value fields. Alternatively, press shift and the up/down or left/right arrow keys to change the values in small steps, ('PlugIns receive key commands' must be activated in Cubase VST's Preferences dialogue) , or double click on the value field to enter a value directly from the numeric keypad. Each EQ band features a button which activates/de-activates the band. An EQ band is active when the button is displayed in red.

In the routine setting up of the equaliser you will probably wish to do a comparison between the signal with EQ and the signal without EQ. This is easily achieved by clicking on the Setup A button which resets the EQ to Setup B. This acts as a bypass switch if you keep Setup B at its default values.

In the amplitude/frequency display, when a frequency band is active its marker appears as a cross in the graphic display; when a band is inactive it appears as a zero. The markers can be individually dragged to new positions in the display or several can be selected and dragged simultaneously. The response curve appears as a yellow line when it is at 0dB, as an orange line in strapped mode (when it is above or below flat response), and as separate yellow and green lines in unstrapped mode.

Filter types
The Q10 provides 5 types of filter as follows:

 Parametric (bell type filter). This is the default position for each band in the Q10 and provides parametric and notch filtering. Parametric EQ has already been described in Chapter 12 and basically involves a filter which boosts or cuts a range of frequencies between two cut-off frequencies. The bandwidth of the frequency range, the centre frequency and the gain (or cut) are all variable. One particular form of bell type filtering is known as a notch filter and this is when a narrow band of frequencies is filtered from the rest of the signal, usually for the purposes of hum and noise removal.

 Low shelf filter. Provides overall low frequency boost or cut in the frequencies below the cut-off point

 High shelf filter. Provides overall high frequency boost or cut in the frequencies above the cut-off point. The opposite of the low shelf filter.

 Low pass cut-off filter. Allows low frequencies to pass through while significantly reducing all frequencies above the cut-off point.

 High pass cut-off filter. Allows high frequencies to pass through while significantly reducing all frequencies below the cut-off point. The opposite of the low pass cut-off filter.

If you need to clarify your understanding of the filters this can be achieved graphically and aurally by using the Q10 in 1 band mode. This is also a useful exercise in simply getting to know the controls. Proceed as follows:

- Activate 'Q1 Paragraphic EQ' in the Master effects rack of Cubase VST and open the Q10 user interface.
- Choose an audio passage in Cubase VST and listen to it via the Q10 in cycle mode.
- Since you have activated the Q10 in one band mode you will have just one set of filter controls. The default filter type is the parametric or bell shaped curve. Click and drag in each of the gain, frequency and Q parameters to change their values (the gain is

changed by dragging vertically and the frequency and Q are changed by dragging horizontally). As you do so, the frequency response curve in the graphic display changes accordingly and, of course, the signal passing through the EQ changes aurally.

- Click on the filter type field once to change the filter to a low shelf type. Click and drag in each of the gain and frequency fields to monitor the effect. Note that Q is not applicable for this filter type.
- Continue in a similar manner for the remaining filter types. Note that neither gain nor Q is applicable in low and high pass cut-off filter types.
- Try selecting gain and frequency or gain and Q simultaneously (by pressing shift while selecting each value field). The X Y position of the mouse now controls the respective parameters in a two dimensional manner which is particularly useful for tuning into the desired frequency band you wish to boost or attenuate.
- Try also dragging the cross directly in the graphic display as a convenient alternative to the value fields.

Applications

The Q10 is an enormously powerful tool which can be used in any of the normal applications associated with EQ. As well as mastering and re-mastering applications in music, it is excellent for speech and multimedia processing. It is particularly useful for hum and hiss removal and band-limiting. It can also be used creatively to produce pseudo-stereo effects, comb-filter effects and such things as AM radio and telephone simulations.

C1 Compressor/Gate

The C1 is a high-quality stereo dynamics processor comprising two separate plug-in modules providing comprehensive control over compression, expansion and gating.

Compression, limiting, expansion and gating are important concepts in audio processing and, before we describe Waves' C1 Compressor/Gate in detail, it is worth considering some background theory.

In simple terms, when you compress a signal, loud parts become quieter and quiet parts become louder; compression converts a large dynamic range into a smaller dynamic range. When you expand a signal, loud parts become louder and quiet parts become quieter; expansion converts a small dynamic range into a larger dynamic range. Compressors and expanders are automatic gain control devices. Compressors start to reduce the gain of an audio signal when the level rises above a set threshold level and expanders reduce the gain as the level falls below a set threshold level.

The amount of compression or expansion is usually described in terms of a ratio, (e.g. 2:1, 10:1 20:1, infinity:1). When an infinitely high ratio of compression is applied to an input signal, the output does not increase above the threshold no matter how much level is applied at the input. This is a particular type of compression known as limiting. When an infinitely high ratio of expansion is applied to an input signal, the output reduces to zero as soon as the input drops below the threshold. This is a particular type of expansion known as gating, (also known as noise gating). Therefore, compression and limiting can be grouped into the same category, and expansion and gating can be grouped into another.

Compression and limiting – background theory

There are normally a number of standard controls which govern the compressor/limiter process and these are as follows:

- Threshold – sets the level at which compression begins to occur. When the input signal goes above the threshold, the output signal from the device is attenuated, (reduced in level), according to the ratio set with the ratio control.
- Ratio – varies the amount of gain reduction. A ratio of 2:1 indicates that for every 2dB the input level rises above the threshold level there will be a 1dB increase in the output level. A ratio of 10:1 indicates that for every 10dB the input level rises above the threshold level there will be a 1dB increase in the output level and so on. A ratio of 1:1 indicates that there is no change in gain between the input and output levels.
- Attack time – determines the rate at which the compressor attenuates the output level after the threshold has been exceeded.
- Release time – determines the rate at which the compressor returns to its normal output gain after the input signal has fallen below the threshold level.
- Gain makeup – since compression often involves an overall reduction in output level many compressors incorporate a 'makeup' control to increase the level after compression.

Compressor/limiters also generally feature soft-knee or hard-knee characteristics. Soft-knee is when compression begins gradually a number of dB's below the threshold, whereas hard-knee is when the compression begins more suddenly at the threshold level. Soft-knee compression tends to sound more natural and transparent to the listener whereas hard-knee compression produces a more obvious effect.

The relationship between the input level, output level and ratio is best viewed in diagramatic form as in Figure 13.8. Indeed, Waves' C1 Compressor resembles this same graphical format, as we shall see later.

Figure 13.8 shows the threshold set at –20dB. When the ratio is set at 2:1, an input level exceeding the threshold by 10dB results in a 5dB attenuation in the output level. When the ratio is at infinity:1 the output level remains at –20dB no matter how high the input level rises above the threshold.

Settings for the threshold and ratio vary enormously depending on the input signal but, as an initial starting point, a resulting gain reduction of

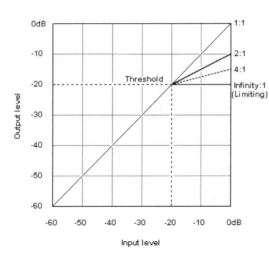

Figure 13.8 Compressor/ limiter input and output levels for different ratios

between 5 – 10dB might be expected. To achieve this the threshold might be set around 10 – 15dB below the maximum peaks in the signal and the ratio might be set between 2:1 and 10:1. The gain makeup might then be set to bring the output back up to the required level. The attack and release times are very important for the resulting characteristics of the compressed signal and can be used for a variety of creative effects.

For example, setting a slow attack time on a bass guitar or lead guitar allows the initial impact of each note to pass through unhindered before the compressor takes effect. This maintains the original attack character-istics while still compressing the rest of the signal, allowing it to cut through in the mix and adding more 'punch' to the sound.

Conversely, a slow attack time on a rock vocal sound, which you are attempting to level out, might not be appropriate. The slow attack may allow too many of the initial transients to pass through unhindered, negating the levelling effect you are trying to achieve, and perhaps pro-ducing an unnatural sounding vocal. For many vocal applications, a mod-erately fast attack time may be more suitable.

The choice of release time is also paramount in creating the desired effect. Too short or too long a release time can result in undesirable audi-ble 'pumping' or 'breathing' side-effects, so the release time must be set carefully. A fast release time can increase the perceived level of the natu-ral decay of an instrument. This can be used to increase the 'body' of, for example, a drum sound. Conversely, you may wish to emphasise the actu-al 'hit' of the drum, in which case you might set a slow release time com-bined with a moderately slow attack time.

Compressors are often used to increase the average signal level to make sounds and mixes seem louder and to even out the level of wildly fluctuat-ing signals so that they can be managed more easily in the mix (as with vocals, mentioned above). However, the parameters must be set very care-fully in order to avoid unwanted side-effects, especially when compressing a whole mix. This can sometimes result in one dominant instrument pro-ducing undesirable reduction in the level of the rest of the mix whenever it is playing. In addition, note that when you are using the gain makeup con-trol to increase the level after compression, you are also increasing the noise floor by the same amount. This is an unavoidable side-effect of compression which can sometimes become obtrusive, particularly if the original signal already contains high levels of background noise.

Compressors and limiters are often found in the same device but the applications of pure limiting are different from those of compression. Limiters are generally used to stop a signal passing above a set threshold, no matter how loud the input becomes, (sometimes referred to as 'brick-wall' limiting). Limiting devices are characterised by very fast attack and release times, so that fast transients can be detected and corrected very quickly. The threshold for limiting is normally set quite high, so that only the transient peaks are attenuated while the rest of the signal passes through unaffected.

Expansion and gating – background theory

As outlined above, expansion and gating are the opposite of compression and limiting and, once again, the precise characteristics are best viewed in diagramatic form (see Figure 13.9):

Although expanders have their uses, most of this section concentrates on the use of one particular kind of expander, commonly known as the noise gate. A noise gate is a very high ratio expander. If the input signal falls below a pre-set threshold the output is radically attenuated. This is extremely useful for eliminating the unwanted noise and interference which may be present in between the wanted sections of a musical performance. Figure 13.9 shows the behaviour of an expander/noise gate whose threshold has been set at –20dB.

Typically, expander/noise gates feature the following control features:

- Threshold – sets the level at which expansion begins to occur or the gate begins to close. When the input signal goes below the threshold, the output signal from the device is attenuated according to the ratio set with the ratio control.
- Ratio – varies the amount of gain reduction. A ratio of 1:2 indicates that for every 1dB the input level goes below the threshold level there will be a 2dB decrease in the output level. A ratio of 1:10 indicates that for every 1dB the input level goes below the threshold level there will be a 10dB decrease in the output level and so on. A ratio of 1:infinity indicates that as soon as the input goes below the threshold the output level is radically attenuated (i.e. switched off).
- Attack time – determines the rate at which the expander/noise gate opens (to allow the signal through) when the signal rises above the threshold.
- Release time – determines the rate of attenuation when the signal has fallen below the threshold.
- Hold time – controls the length of time for which the level of the signal is guaranteed to be held before attenuation occurs.

The attack control of noise gates should be endowed with very fast attack times in order to be able to cope with sounds which have rapid attack transients such as drum and percussion sounds. This ensures that the first part of the sound opens the gate quickly enough so that it passes through unhindered. However, sounds with slower attack characteristics benefit

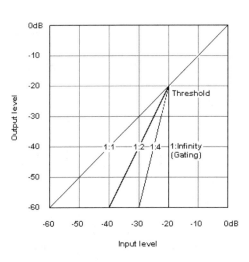

Figure 13.9 Expander/gate input and output levels for different ratios

from slower noise gate attack times in order to avoid the audible click which can sometimes occur when the gate is opened abruptly.

The hold time is used to determine how long the gate remains open and, once it starts to close, the release time determines the rate at which the signal fades away.

As well as their usual noise elimination function, noise gates can also be used creatively to modify the envelope of the signal. For example, special effects can be created by intentionally cutting off the attack portion of a sound using a slow attack setting, or the 'body' of the sound can be attenuated with a fast release time to produce staccato effects.

INFO

There now follows a description of the C1 Compressor/ Expander and Gate/ Expander plug-ins. These sections explore the C1 in its two main applications, as a compressor and as a noise gate.

C1 Compressor

- I/O: stereo in/stereo out (accepts mono or stereo input)
- Approximate CPU power used: 13% (200MHz Pentium MMX processor)
- Normal usage in Cubase VST: Insert or Master effect

Description

The C1 Compressor is a soft-knee, variable ratio, stereo compressor/expander. At maximum compression the module becomes a soft-knee limiter. It is operated via a user interface whose main features include a real-time display of the dynamic behaviour of the device using a level marker which moves along the compression/expansion curve in the input/output graph and a number of parameters and level meters to control the characteristics of the compression/expansion curve and monitor the output and gain reduction levels, (see Figure 13.10).

The C1 Compressor features the following main control parameters:

- Level reference control – switches the unit between LowRef mode (Low-level reference) and PeakRef mode (Peak-level reference). LowRef mode is the normal compressor mode where the output level falls as the threshold is lowered. PeakRef mode maintains the output at approximately the same level regardless of the threshold setting. The makeup control setting is modified according to which mode is chosen.

- Makeup – provides output level adjustment to compensate for changes in level due to compression/expansion. Range: –40dB to +40dB
- Threshold – sets the level above which the compression/expansion starts to act. Range: –100dB to 0dB FS (Full Scale).
- Ratio – sets the compression/expansion ratio for those parts of the signal which rise above the threshold. Range: 0.5:1 to 1:1 for high level expansion; 1:1 to 50:1 for compression (soft-knee limiting in the upper ratios); –50:1 to –5:1 to use the device in 'cancellation' mode for specialist applications.
- Attack – determines the rate at which the compressor/expander begins to act upon the output level after the threshold has been exceeded. Range: 0.1msec. to 1 second, calibrated in milliseconds.
- Release – determines the rate at which the compressor/expander returns to its normal output gain after the input signal has fallen below the threshold level. Range: 1msec. to 10 seconds, calibrated in milliseconds.
- PDR (Program Dependent Release) – varies the release time according to the characteristics of the input signal. When set at 0, the release time is that which is shown in the release field. When PDR is set higher than 0, the release time is shortened for transients which are shorter than the PDR value (shown in milliseconds), and all those which are longer are processed according to the release time specified in the release field. Range: 0 – 1 second, calibrated in milliseconds.

Figure 13.10 C1 Compressor

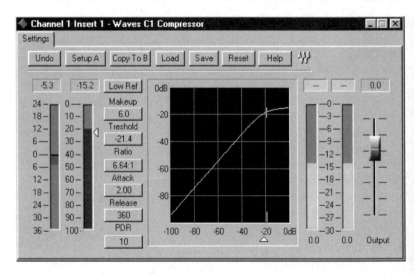

User guide

The user interface features the standard Waves system controls at the top of the window (see 'Waves system controls', below) with the addition of a reset button which resets the makeup, threshold and ratio values. To reset ALL the parameters select 'C1 compressor Full Reset' from the Load menu. Clicking on the level reference button toggles between Low level reference and Peak level reference mode. To change the other parameters drag vertically with the mouse in the value fields. Alternatively, press shift and the up/down arrow keys to change the values in small steps, ('PlugIns receive key commands' must be activated in Cubase VST's Preferences dialogue), or double click on the value field to enter a value directly from the numeric keypad. The threshold value can also be changed using the yellow markers beside the input level meter and below the input/output graph.

The interface also features 3 level meters to monitor the behaviour of the compressor. These include a gain reduction meter, a compressor control level meter and stereo output meters. The final output is also regulated with an output fader. Each level meter features a numeric peak level indicator which can be reset by clicking on the meter bar.

In the routine setting up of the compressor you will probably wish to do a comparison between the signal with compression and the signal without compression. This is easily achieved by clicking on the Setup A button which resets the compressor to Setup B. This acts as a bypass switch if you keep Setup B at its default values (i.e. with makeup gain and threshold set to 0, and ratio set to 1:1). You may also spend some time juggling the makeup gain with the threshold, attack and release controls, and, if you are working near maximum level, it is useful to view the headroom available on the stereo output meters.

Compressors are among the most important and powerful audio processors but they are also among the more difficult processors to use effectively. The C1 produces excellent results but only when it is set up with great care and subtlety.

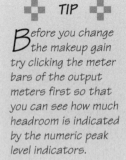

TIP

Before you change the makeup gain try clicking the meter bars of the output meters first so that you can see how much headroom is indicated by the numeric peak level indicators.

Applications

The C1 Compressor is supplied with a number of presets in the Load menu and these make good starting points for your own settings.

Some of the more general applications of compression have been outlined above. Other applications for the C1 Compressor include: increasing the presence, clarity and 'smoothness' of vocals, 'fattening' bass drum and snare sounds, 'thickening' electric pianos and acoustic guitars, lengthening the sustain of electric guitars and adding more 'punch' to just about any instrument. The C1 can breath life into dull sounding tracks and can provide subtle control over excessively dynamic passages.

C1 gate

- I/O: stereo in/stereo out (accepts mono or stereo input)
- Approximate CPU power used: 10% (200MHz Pentium MMX processor)
- Normal usage in Cubase VST: Insert or Master effect

Description

The C1 Gate functions as either a soft-knee expander or as a gate. It is operated via a user interface whose main features include a real-time display of the dynamic behaviour of the device using a level marker which moves along the gate/expander curve in the input/output graph and a number of parameters and level meters to control the characteristics of the gate/expander and monitor the output and gain reduction levels (see Figure 13.11).

Figure 13.11 *C1 Gate*

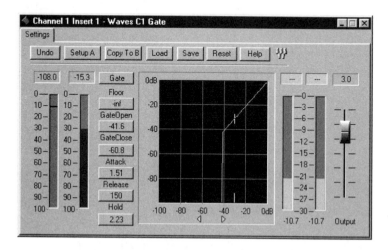

The C1 Gate features the following control parameters:

- Gate/Expander switch – switches between gate and expander mode.
- Floor – sets the level of the residual signal when the gate is closed or the expander is set to a high ratio. When set to infinity, the signal is completely cut at low levels. When set to 0dB, the signal remains unchanged at low levels. When set to a positive value the signal level is increased at low levels. In expander mode, the floor range also includes negative polarity values, indicated by the letter N after the value, and these can be used to completely cut a signal when it is the indicated number of dB below the Gate open threshold. Range in gate mode: -infinity dB to +12dB. Range in expander mode: −100 N to −10 N and −infinity dB to +12dB.
- Gate open – sets a threshold level above which the gate is opened to let the signal through or expansion begins to take place. When in gate mode this value is used in conjunction with the Gate close value to avoid the 'chatter' sometimes apparent when the signal is on or near the threshold level. Range: −100dB to 0dB (full scale).
- Gate close – sets the threshold level for the closing of the gate. When the signal falls below the threshold, the gate begins to close. The Gate close value is always equal to or less than the Gate open value. This parameter has no effect when in expander mode. Range: −100dB to 0dB (full scale).

- Attack – determines the rate at which the expander/noise gate opens when the signal rises above the Gate open threshold. Range: 0.1msec. to 1 second, calibrated in milliseconds.
- Release – determines the rate of attenuation when the signal has fallen below the threshold. Range: 1msec. to 10 seconds, calibrated in milliseconds.
- Hold – in gate mode, controls the time for which the level of the signal is guaranteed to be held before attenuation occurs. This parameter has no effect when in expander mode. Range: 0.01msec. to 5 seconds, calibrated in milliseconds.

User guide

The user interface features the standard Waves system controls at the top of the window (see 'Waves system controls', below) with the addition of a reset button which resets the floor, gate open and gate close values. To reset *all* the parameters select 'C1 Full Reset' from the Load menu. Clicking on the gate/expander button toggles between gate and expander mode. To change the other parameters drag up or down with the mouse in the value fields. Alternatively, press shift and the up/down arrow keys to change the values in small steps, ('PlugIns receive key commands' must be activated in Cubase VST's Preferences dialogue), or double click on the value field to enter a value directly from the numeric keypad. The gate open and gate close values can also be changed by dragging the blue markers found below the input/output graph.

The interface also features 3 level meters to monitor the behaviour of the gate/expander. These include a gain reduction meter, a gate/expander control level meter and stereo output meters. The final output is also regulated with an output fader. Each level meter features a numeric peak level indicator which can be reset by clicking on the meter bar.

In the routine setting up of the gate (or expander) you may wish to make a comparison between the gated signal and the un-gated signal. This is easily achieved by clicking on the Setup A button which resets the gate to Setup B. This acts as a bypass switch if you keep Setup B at its default values.

Applications

Gating can be used for a wide range of corrective and creative effects. The most obvious is the attenuation of noise during the unwanted passages of musical performances. It is also popular for the modification of the attack and release characteristics of sounds.

S1 Stereo Imager

- I/O: stereo in/stereo out
- Approximate CPU power used: 9% (200MHz Pentium MMX processor)
- Normal usage in Cubase VST: Insert or Master effect

Description

The S1 (Figure 13.12) is an advanced stereo image processor featuring four stereo image modifiers to expand the stereo width, enhance spaciousness and to seperately process sounds in the centre of the stereo image and those placed in other parts of the soundfield. The S1 is designed to work specifically with stereo signals and does not produce stereo imaging effects from a mono input.

Figure 13.12 S1 Stereo Imager

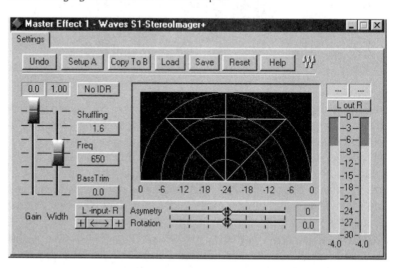

The S1 features the following controls:

- Gain – controls the overall gain without affecting the stereo image. Range: –24dB to 0dB.
- Width – expands or narrows the width of the stereo input signal. When the value is 1, there is no change in the width. Values less than 1 produce a narrower image which converges progressively towards the centre of the stereo soundfield until at zero the resulting output is mono. Values greater than 1 expand the width of the stereo image and, in the upper limits, produce a psychoacoustic effect which goes beyond the limits of the normal stereo soundfield. Range: 0 to 3.
- Shuffling – adds a sense of spaciousness and enlivens the stereo image by increasing the width of bass frequencies to compensate for the fact that the ear interprets the lower frequencies in a stereo recording as being more narrow than the higher frequencies. Shuffling enhances the stereo effect which is already present in the stereo input and it only has an effect on those sounds which are panned away from the centre. A value of 1 results in no shuffling and 3 results in the maximum increase in bass width. The best settings for normal stereo input are usually between 1.6 and 2.5. Range: 1 to 3.
- Freq – sets the frequency below which the shuffling effect takes place. For normal stereo input the best settings are usually between 600 – 700Hz. Range: 350Hz to 1400Hz.

- Asymmetry – adjusts the relative levels of the left and right sides of the stereo image without affecting the in-phase sounds in the centre. Range: –90 degrees to +90 degrees.
- Rotation – adjusts the left/right position of the stereo image without affecting the relative levels of the sounds in the mix. Range: –45 degrees to +45 degrees.

The S1 is dominated by the stereo vector display which shows the stereo soundstage and graphically represents the current settings of the gain, width, asymmetry and rotation values. It also features a stereo reversal button (double arrow) to reverse the left/right stereo image and phase reversal buttons (+/- buttons) for each channel.

User guide
The user interface features the standard Waves system controls at the top of the window (see 'Waves system controls', below) with the addition of a reset button which resets width, shuffling, bass trim asymmetry and rotation. To reset *all* the parameters select 'S1 Full Reset' from the Load menu. To change the value parameters drag vertically or horizontally with the mouse in the value fields. Alternatively, press shift and the up/down or left/right arrow keys to change the values in small steps, ('PlugIns receive key commands' must be activated in Cubase VST's Preferences dialogue), or double click on the value field to enter a value directly from the numeric keypad.

The values of the gain, width, asymmetry and rotation controls can be manipulated by dragging the mouse directly in the vector display. Dragging the mouse alone, simultaneously changes the gain and the rotation. Holding alt while dragging the mouse, simultaneously changes the width and the asymmetry.

When using the shuffling parameters, the sharpest stereo imaging is achieved when the shuffling value is set to around 1.6 and the shuffling frequency to around 650Hz. For more spaciousness try the shuffling level set between 2 and 2.5 and the frequency set at around 650Hz.

Applications
The S1 can be used to adjust the stereo image in a variety of creative and corrective ways. This includes expanding the width of the final stereo mix for a more spacious effect or narrowing the width to produce more punch in the centre. Recordings with an unsatisfactory stereo balance can be corrected and existing stereo masters can be enhanced and sweetened with no undesirable side effects. The S1 offers a high level of mono compatibility which makes it suitable for use in TV and radio broadcast. When the lines on the vector display representing the left, right and centre of the stereo image are within 45 degrees of being vertical the resulting mix will have good mono compatibility. As the lines are moved further towards the vertical position, so the mono compatibility is also further enhanced.

L1 Ultramaximizer

- I/O: stereo in/stereo out
- Approximate CPU power used: 23% (200MHz Pentium MMX processor)
- Normal usage in Cubase VST: Master effect

Description

The L1 Ultramaximizer (Figure 13.13) is a digital peak limiter combining look-ahead peak limiting with loudness maximisation and high-performance re-quantization. You can use the L1 to optimise both the perceived loudness and quality of your audio. It is intended for the final stage in the processing of digital audio files and is the perfect tool for mastering and multimedia applications.

Figure 13.13 L1
Ultramaximizer

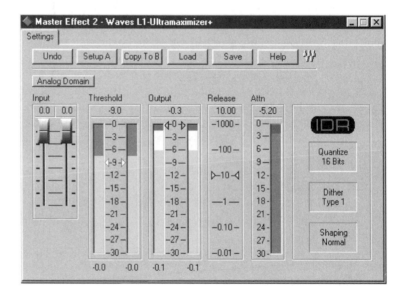

The L1 features the following controls:

- Analogue / Digital domain button – this is a complex issue but, in simple terms, the analogue domain position was implemented to allow for the deficiencies of poorly designed DAC's installed in consumer digital audio equipment which could cause digital overload in certain circumstances. However, in recent times, this is less of a problem and, although the analogue setting provides a safer option, the digital domain setting could now be used almost all of the time. If you are using heavy limiting with the output ceiling set at 0.0dB, (rather than the Waves recommended –0.3dB), then analogue mode might be a safer option. There is no difference in the perceived quality of the output between the two settings. Waves now recommend that you use digital domain all of the time unless you have a specific reason for using analogue domain. (For more information see the Waves documentation).

- Input trim faders – vary the level of the input signal as a linked pair or independently. Range: –20dB to 0dB FS.
- Peak limiter threshold setting and input level meters – sets the threshold at which peak limiting commences to take effect. Range: –30dB to 0dB FS. The input level meters show the peak program level of the input signal.
- Output Ceiling level setting and meters – sets the absolute ceiling for the audio output. The output level never rises above this setting, regardless of the input or threshold settings. Range: –30dB to 0dB FS. The output level meters show the peak program level of the output signal.
- Release control – controls the time it takes to return to normal gain after a peak above the threshold has been attenuated. Range: 0.01msec. to 1 second, calibrated in milliseconds.
- Attenuation meter – displays the amount of attenuation taking place. Range: –30dB to 0dB FS.
- IDR quantize resolution – sets the final bit depth for the output from the L1. Available in 20bit, 16bit, 12bit and 8bit resolutions. If your final audio is destined for DAT or CD then this should be set to 16bit.
- IDR dither type – sets the IDR dither type. Type 1 and Type 2 dither options are available.
- Noise shaping options – re-allocates the noise to different parts of the audio spectrum according to moderate, normal and ultra options. Normal and ultra are recommended for optimum results with Type 2 dither, and normal and moderate are recommended for Type 1 dither.

User guide

The L1 Ultramaximizer would normally be used as a Master effect (at the lowest position in the rack if there are other effects simultaneously present, since the L1 is designed to be used as the last stage in any processing before the final master). The user interface features the standard Waves system controls at the top of the window (see 'Waves system controls', below).

With the L1 Ultramaximizer, the final average signal level of an audio file can be significantly increased and its perceived quality at low levels can be enhanced with minimal audible side-effects. Once the peak threshold has been set (by dragging the yellow threshold pointers), the output ceiling can be adjusted to the desired final level for the output signal (by dragging the yellow output ceiling pointers). Waves suggest a final level of -0.3dB for mastering purposes.

Care must be taken with how low you set the threshold since a large amount of peak limiting at the faster release times can result in distortion of the signal. Try clicking in the input meter bar to see the current maximum peak of the input signal shown numerically below the meters and then, as a starting point, set your threshold around 6dB below this. As you lower the threshold you will notice that the output level rises towards the output ceiling and, if the final threshold indicates, for example, –9dB, then you have increased the average output signal by +9dB.

The release time should be adjusted to suit the input signal, although in most instances it might be set to around 1.0ms. Longer release times are appropriate for heavier limiting applications.

The load menu includes a number of useful presets which provide good starting points for your own settings.

IDR issues

IDR (Increased Digital Resolution) is particularly beneficial when the bit depth is reduced (e.g. 20 bit signals reduced to 16 bit, 16 bit signals reduced to 8 bit etc.) but it is also of benefit to Cubase VST users when their audio has gone through a number of stages of digital audio processing. Repeated processing can result in a significant loss in the definition of low-level signals which manifests itself as a particular kind of low-level non-linear digital distortion. The IDR process actually adds a small amount of controlled noise ('dither') to the audio signal which converts this low-level distortion into a more friendly linear noise or 'hiss'. Using a process known as noise shaping this noise is re-distributed to parts of the audio spectrum where it is less obvious to the ear. The result is an enhanced clarity and spaciousness in the audio material.

All the Waves plug-ins function at an internal 24bit resolution and are optimised with IDR to ensure that the processed output is of the best quality possible. However, IDR is available in its most sophisticated form in the L1 plug-in.

One of the best methods of understanding the actual effect of the IDR process is to actually listen to it. To achieve this, activate the L1 in the Master effects rack of Cubase VST and open the L1's user interface. Choose an audio passage in Cubase VST and listen to it via the L1 in cycle mode. Lower the input trim faders of the L1 to -20dB. The quantize value is normally set to the bit depth of the final media for which the audio is intended but, in this procedure, you should set the bit depth to 8bit in order to exaggerate the noise level. You may also need to reduce the level of the output ceiling. In this way, you can hear what is going on. Also set both dither and shaping to 'non'.

You should now be able to hear the low-level audio accompanied by non-linear distortion. This kind of noise is present to a greater or lesser degree in all digital audio. Selecting the moderate noise shaping option improves the clarity of the audio signal with a simultaneous slight increase in the level of hiss. Check out the distortion removing properties of the other noise shaping options and try listening to the effect of Type 1 and Type 2 dither and various combinations of both dither and noise shaping.

This test procedure should help you gain an appreciation of the action of dither and noise shaping but remember that it is an exaggerated example since the treated signal has been passed through the L1 at an unrealistically low level and you are listening in 8 bit resolution.

The dither and noise shaping options can be set in many different combinations but there are certain settings which Waves particularly recommended for specific applications. The most important of these are as follows:

- General purpose high-quality use: type 1, normal (20, 16 or 12bit). May be edited or EQ'ed at a later stage.
- Lowest noise (CD master): type 2, ultra (20 or 16 bit)
- Low noise/highest quality: type 1, ultra(20 or 16 bit)

Once again, remember that the bit depth you set relates to the output of the L1 and should be matched to the intended bit resolution of the final file or other destination. For DAT and CD mastering use 16 bit. For more information about IDR, additional recommended settings and other issues consult the Waves documentation.

Applications

As has been apparent in the above descriptions the L1 is designed primarily as a tool for mastering, digital editing, broadcast and multimedia applications. It is intended for the final stage in the processing of digital audio files and suits any application where strict level control, loudness maximisation and quality optimisation are required.

IDR (Increased Digital Resolution)

- I/O: stereo in/stereo out
- Approximate CPU power used: 16% (200MHz Pentium MMX processor)
- Normal usage in Cubase VST: Master effect

As well as being included in other Waves plug-ins, IDR is also featured as a separate simplified plug-in (Figure 13.14). As explained in the L1 Ultramaximizer description above, Waves' IDR is a noise shaped dither system which reduces quantization error and improves the perceived quality and dynamic range of the quietest sounds in your digital audio.

The IDR plug-in features one control for 20bit, 16bit or 12 bit requantization and has fixed type 1 dither and 'normal' noise shape settings. These are the most suitable settings for files which might be subject to further editing or EQ at a later stage. In Cubase VST, it might be used, for example, as the final effect in the Master effects rack after any other

Figure 13.14 IDR interface

processes, to improve the quality of quieter sounds and reverb tails prior to final mixdown to a file using the Export Audio File function. This is assuming that the L1 is not being used at the same time, in which case the IDR plug-in would not be needed.

More details of IDR are included in the section on the L1 Ultramaximizer.

Waves system controls

There are a number of controls which are common to each of the Waves plug-ins (except for the IDR plug-in) and these are displayed as a row of buttons in the top part of the interface window for each device, (similar to Figure 13.15).

Figure 13.15 Waves system controls

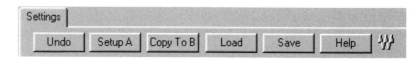

The buttons function as follows:

- Undo – provides one level of undo for any editing taking place in the interface window.
- Setup A – toggles between Setup A and Setup B. If Setup B is left at its default settings this provides what is effectively a bypass button for most of the plug-ins (when used in Cubase VST).
- Copy to B – copies the current settings into Setup B which could then be used for comparative purposes with Setup A.
- Load – opens a menu of library or user presets for the current plug-in.
- Save – saves the current settings of the plug-in to a file.
- Help – opens the Waves electronic documentation for the plug-in.

Clicking on the Waves logo to the right of the buttons opens an info window detailing the name of the plug-in and its version number.

Keyboard shortcuts

When 'PlugIns receive key commands' is activated in Cubase VST's Preferences dialogue various key combinations can change the values in the Waves plug-in windows. Holding shift with the up/down or left/right arrows changes the value of the currently selected parameter, holding shift and pressing the return key changes the value of the switch style parameters, holding shift with the tab key moves from one parameter to the next, and holding shift while selecting parameters with the mouse allows the selection of several parameters, the values of which can then all be changed simultaneously.

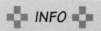

INFO

The C1 plug-ins also feature a reset button which provides a reset of the first three parameters of each module and the Q10 features a 'flat' button to reset the EQ curve to a flat response.

Recommended order of use

Waves emphasise the importance of the order in which you should use their plug-ins for traditional sound processing purposes. You might need to change this order for certain kinds of processing but in general the recommended order helps avoid undesirable interaction between the processes. The suggested order of use is as follows:

Gating (C1 gate)
Compression (C1 compressor)
Equalisation (Q10)
Stereo imaging (S1)
Reverb (TrueVerb)
Limiting (L1)

Waves AudioTrack

- I/O: mono and stereo modes
- Approximate CPU power used: mono 16%, stereo 24% (200MHz Pentium MMX processor)
- Normal usage in Cubase VST: Insert or Master effect

Description
For those Cubase VST users on a tighter budget, Waves also produce
AudioTrack (Figure 13.16). AudioTrack features paragraphic EQ, com-
pression and gating in one easy-to-use plug-in.

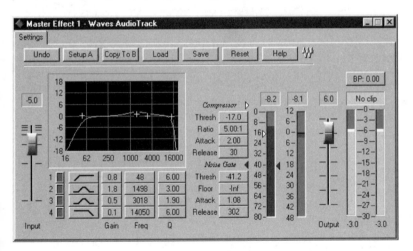

Figure 13.16 AudioTrack

The signal passes through four distinct areas; the input, the paragraphic EQ, the compressor/gate and the output. The signal is modified according to the settings chosen in the user interface.

The main AudioTrack parameters are as follows:

- Input fader – provides attenuation of the input signal. For example, this may be necessary after
  applying EQ which boosts the overall level of the signal. Range: –infinity to 0dB.

EQ section with 4 bands featuring:

- Filter type selector – selects a filter type for the chosen frequency band. Band 1 features a choice of bell type, low/high shelving and high pass cut-off filters. Bands 2 and 3 feature bell type and low/high shelving filters. Band 4 features bell type, low/high shelving and low pass cut-off filters (see Q10 paragraphic EQ section above for a description of filter types).
- Gain – provides boost or cut for the chosen frequency band. (Has no effect with low and high pass cut-off filters). Range: –18dB to +18dB.
- Frequency – sets the filter's centre frequency (or cut-off and corner frequency with low/high pass cut-off and low/high shelving filters). Range: 16Hz to 21kHz.
- Q – sets the width of the chosen frequency band. (With parametric EQ filter type only). Range: 0.5 to 30, where 0.5 is the widest band and 30 is the narrowest.

Compressor section featuring:

- Compressor threshold – sets the level above which compression starts to act. Range: –52dB to 0dB.
- Ratio – sets the compression ratio for those parts of the signal which rise above the threshold. Range: 0.5:1 to 1:1 for high level expansion; 1:1 to 40:1 for compression.
- Compressor attack – determines the rate at which the compressor begins to act upon the output level after the threshold has been exceeded. Range: 0.1msec. to 1 second, calibrated in milliseconds.
- Compressor release – determines the rate at which the compressor returns to its normal output gain after the input signal has fallen below the threshold level. Range: 1msec. to 10 seconds, calibrated in milliseconds.

Noise gate section featuring:

- Noise gate threshold – sets the threshold level for the opening and closing of the gate. When the signal rises above the threshold, the gate opens. When the signal falls below the threshold, the gate begins to close. Range: –infinity to 0dB.
- Floor – sets the level of the residual signal when the gate is closed. When set to infinity, the signal is completely cut at low levels. When set to 0dB, the signal remains unchanged at low levels. Range: –infinity dB to 0dB.
- Noise gate attack – determines the rate at which the noise gate opens when the signal rises above the threshold. Range: 0.1msec. to 1 second, calibrated in milliseconds.
- Noise gate release – determines the rate at which the gate closes after the signal has fallen below the threshold. Range: 1msec. to 10 seconds, calibrated in milliseconds.

and the output section featuring:

- Output fader – provides attenuation or gain for the output. Range: –24dB to +12dB.
- Output meters – monitor the peak level of the output signal. The peak level is also shown numerically below the meters. This can be reset by clicking in the meter bar.
- Clip indicator – displays 'EQ clip' for EQ section overloads and 'Out clip' for output overloads.

User guide

The user interface features the standard Waves system controls at the top of the window (see 'Waves system controls', above) with the addition of a reset button which resets the input and output faders, the compressor and noise gate parameters and switches off the 4 EQ bands. To reset ALL the parameters select 'Full AudioTrack reset' from the Load menu.

To change the value parameters drag vertically or horizontally with the mouse in the value fields. Alternatively, press shift and the up/down or left/right arrow keys to change the values in small steps, ('PlugIns receive key commands' must be activated in Cubase VST's Preferences dialogue), or double click on the value field to enter a value directly from the numeric keypad. Each EQ band features a button which activates/de-activates the band. An EQ band is active when the button is displayed in red.

The compression and gate thresholds can also be changed by dragging the blue and yellow arrows, and each band of EQ can be manipulated by dragging the crosses in the paragraphic EQ display, (see Q10 paragraphic EQ section for more details).

AudioTrack is supplied with a collection of presets which make good starting points for your own settings. For suggestions of how to operate the EQ and compressor/noise gate sections see the Q10 Paragraphic EQ and C1 compressor/gate sections above.

Applications

AudioTrack has a wide range of applications for multi-track processing, mastering and multimedia. It is particularly convenient for simultaneously processing a number of single tracks during the same session since it uses less processing power than other similar plug-ins. It can be used for corrective and creative EQ applications while simultaneously allowing the dynamic control and noise removal associated with compression and noise gating.

Plug-in summary

The above information has provided readers with an idea of the kinds of plug-ins which are available for use with Cubase VST. As you may have noticed from the statistics, many of the plug-ins reviewed require substantial amounts of CPU processing power.

For those users who intend to make regular use of high-end audio plug-ins, a minimum setup of a Pentium 200MHz MMX PC with 64Mb of RAM is recommended. Of course, if you have the option, a very fast Pentium II with still more memory is preferable.

As well as the high end products, there are also a number of excellent VST-native plug-ins which have been developed by Cubase VST enthusiasts and smaller companies. Although these are often much less sophisticated than the tools described above, they are well worth investigation and some of them are available for free via the internet. (See 'Useful websites' at the end of this book).

There are also a wide range of plug-ins from other manufacturers and users should check the press or the internet for the latest developments.

INFO

For more information about Waves Native Power Pack, Audiotrack and other Waves plug-ins see the Waves website at: www.waves.com.

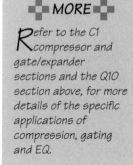

MORE

Refer to the C1 compressor and gate/expander sections and the Q10 section above, for more details of the specific applications of compression, gating and EQ.

14

The Mastertrack

The Mastertrack is Cubase VST's tempo and time signature manager. It is, in fact, another track like those in the Arrange window but it is specialised in its own kind of data. It comes in graphic or list form, each of which has its own unique display. It can be opened by selecting Mastertrack from the Edit menu, or by pressing ctrl + M (Mac: command + M), on the computer keyboard. It contains tempo, time signature and hitpoint information.

Cubase VST usually runs at the tempo set on the Transport bar but when the Master button is activated (by clicking on it or pressing M on the computer keyboard), Cubase VST follows the tempo(s) set in the Mastertrack. Even if the Mastertrack button has not been activated, all time signatures in the Mastertrack will be present in the Arrange window but tempo changes occur only when the button has been activated.

The Mastertrack List editor

The Mastertrack list display (Figure 14.1), is opened by pressing shift + ctrl + M and is managed using various commands in the local menus at the top of the window. The tempi and time signatures in the list may be changed directly by clicking on the values with the left and right mouse buttons, as can the positions of events by clicking on the values in the meter or time columns. The names of hitpoints can be changed by clicking on the current name in the value column. The Mastertrack always contains at least one initial tempo and one time signature at meter position 1.1.0. These cannot be erased or moved in time.

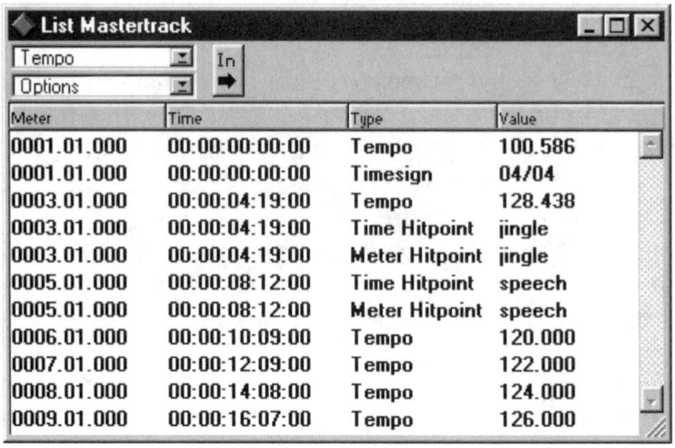

Figure 14.1 The Mastertrack list display

Meter	Time	Type	Value
0001.01.000	00:00:00:00:00	Tempo	100.586
0001.01.000	00:00:00:00:00	Timesign	04/04
0003.01.000	00:00:04:19:00	Tempo	128.438
0003.01.000	00:00:04:19:00	Time Hitpoint	jingle
0003.01.000	00:00:04:19:00	Meter Hitpoint	jingle
0005.01.000	00:00:08:12:00	Time Hitpoint	speech
0005.01.000	00:00:08:12:00	Meter Hitpoint	speech
0006.01.000	00:00:10:09:00	Tempo	120.000
0007.01.000	00:00:12:09:00	Tempo	122.000
0008.01.000	00:00:14:08:00	Tempo	124.000
0009.01.000	00:00:16:07:00	Tempo	126.000

List Mastertrack — Tempo / Options — In

Regardless of whether any tempo changes are required, it is always a good idea to enter the definitive tempo of the finished song into the Mastertrack, in case of accidental changes to the tempo on the Transport bar.

Typically, tempo changes might involve increasing the pace on all the choruses and going back to the original tempo for the verses. This could be achieved by manually entering the tempi into the list at the appropriate positions. Standard cut, copy and paste techniques can be used for the general manipulation of data in the Mastertrack.

To really feel what tempi are required in a more musical context try activating Record tempo/Mutes in the Options menu. If Cubase VST is then put into record and the tempo changed using the + and − keys of the numeric keypad, each change will be recorded into the Mastertrack. Note that, for this to function, the Mastertrack button must be de-activated at the time of recording. This process can result in tempo changes which feel more natural and musical. The data can be edited in the Mastertrack List editor, but the amount of entries in the list may prove unmanageable, particularly if 16 bars worth of tempi need to be deleted.

When things are just too complicated to handle in the Mastertrack List editor it may be time to use the Graphic editor, and many users will prefer the graphic version from the outset. Although the List Mastertrack provides a detailed, chronological view of the events, most editing can be accomplished with greater ease in the Graphic Mastertrack.

The Graphic Mastertrack

To open the Graphic Mastertrack press ctrl + M (Mac: command + M) on the computer keyboard or select Mastertrack in the Edit menu. The Graphic Mastertrack provides an environment where tempo can be edited graphically and where the relationship between time and meter can be conveniently manipulated.

The Graphic Mastertrack window

The default Graphic Mastertrack window appears with a large tempo display dominating the central area of the window. Tempo events are shown as colour-coded blocks. When there is only one tempo event present, this is shown as one continuous block spanning the whole display. To zoom in or out in the display use the magnification sliders. Above and below the display, there are meter and time position rulers and two strips known as the meter hitpoint and time hitpoint strips. Hitpoints are displayed as small circular pointers and these serve to mark important moments in the meter or time scale. There is also a time signature strip where any time signatures in the song are shown on small hangers. The rulers and strips can be shown or hidden using the buttons in the Functions bar.

The editor also features a toolbox which is used in much the same manner as in the other editors. Here the pencil tool has the most editing potential.

To quickly understand the essence of the Graphic Mastertrack, select the pencil tool and drag it up and down in the tempo display. This adjusts

Title bar
Functions bar
Info bar
Meter ruler
Time sig. strip
Meter hitpoints strip
Toolbox
Tempo display
Tempo scale
Time hitpoints strip
Time ruler

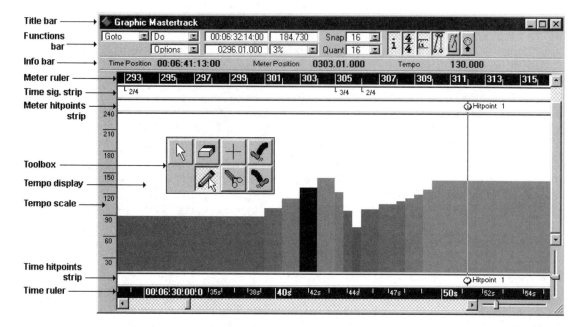

Figure 14.2 The Graphic Mastertrack

the tempo event at the current mouse position. As the tempo is increased, the event becomes more red in colour and, as it is decreased, the event becomes more blue. Simultaneously, the time ruler expands and contracts.

Getting to know the Graphic Mastertrack

There now follows a brief tutorial which will help you become familiar with the Graphic Mastertrack.

As with the list version, there is always at least one time signature and one tempo present at bar 1.1.0. These cannot be deleted. The following outlines some of the essential editing moves:

- To change an existing tempo event, drag it up or down using the pencil tool in the tempo display, as described above. Watch the tempo indicator box (Function bar), in order to verify the tempo of the edited event. The value in the box is updated as you move the pencil vertically.
- To insert a single new tempo event, press alt (Mac: option) on the computer keyboard and click once in the tempo display with the pencil tool. A new event is created at the mouse position, which is moved onto the nearest beat according to the current Snap setting. Once again, watch the tempo indicator box in order to verify the tempo of the inserted event.
- To insert a series of new tempo events, press alt (Mac: option) on the computer keyboard and click and drag the pencil tool across the tempo display. New tempo events are inserted according to the resolution set in the Snap box.
- To create a ramp from existing tempo events, click and drag the line tool across the display.

- To insert a ramp of new tempo events, press alt (Mac: option) on the computer keyboard and click and drag the line tool across the tempo display. New tempo events are inserted in a straight line at the resolution set in the Snap box. The line tool is particularly useful for inserting accelerandi and retardandi into an arrangement.
- To dynamically insert events as Cubase VST plays back, click in the tempo scale to the left of the tempo display while holding alt (Mac: no key required) on the computer keyboard. Events are inserted at the respective moments of each click of the mouse and are shifted onto the nearest beat according to the current Snap setting.
- To select a single tempo event click on it with the pointer tool. The selected event is shown in black.
- To select two or more tempo events drag a rectangular selection box over the required events in the tempo display using the pointer tool. All selected events are shown in black.
- To delete any events, use the eraser tool or select the events and press delete on the computer keyboard.

TIP

When inserting new tempo events, any events already located at the same time and meter positions will be overwritten. The Graphic Mastertrack is always in replace mode.

Time signatures can be inserted by clicking in the time signature strip with the pencil tool. The values of time signatures can be edited in the info bar.

A number of items in the Do menu also help in the routine manipulation of events. These include:

- Repeat, to copy the range of events within the left and right locator positions. All events within the range, including time signatures and hitpoints, are repeated in the Mastertrack beginning at the current song position.
- Reduce, to thin out the selected tempo events. This can be used in situations where the tempo events have become unnecessarily dense.
- Smooth tempo, to help in smoothing out any sudden changes in tempo in complex tempo curves.
- Split tempo at song position, to add a new tempo event at the current song position.
- Process tempo, to open the Tempo processor dialogue. This allows you to specify an overall reduction or increase in the time scale of a selection of tempo events according to a percentage or by adjusting the end time. For a successful result the last tempo event in the arrangement must not be included in the selected events.

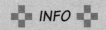

INFO

This chapter provides you with the essential information to be able to manage tempo, hitpoint and time signature events. The more advanced features of the Graphic Mastertrack are beyond the scope of this text.

The other items in the Do menu are for the manipulation of hitpoints and these are described in the next section.

Hitpoints and the meter/time relationship

In order to get the most from the Graphic Mastertrack, it is important to understand the concept and uses of hitpoints. Hitpoints are small markers which can be placed in the meter hitpoint and time hitpoint strips above and below the central display. Their purpose is to mark important moments in the meter or time scales of the music and to provide a link between these two elements.

In order to understand the concept further, try the following tutorial:

- Open the Graphic Mastertrack and select the pencil tool.
- Select a value of 1 in the Snap box.
- Move the pencil into the meter hitpoint strip and insert two hitpoints on bars 5 and 9 by clicking with the left mouse button.
- Select the pointer tool and click in blank space in the meter hitpoint strip to open a selection box. Select the newly created hitpoints. Open the Do menu and select Mirror and Link hitpoints. This creates two new hitpoints in the time hitpoint strip, linked to the meter hitpoints.

Insert two meter hitpoints on bars 5 and 9

Mirror and link hitpoints

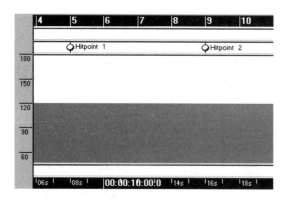
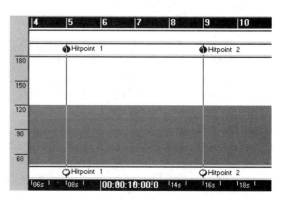

With the hitpoints in vertical alignment there is a direct relationship between the meter and time scales. In this example, at a tempo of 120 bpm, the meter range is 4 bars (5.1.0 to 9.1.0) and the duration is 8 seconds (from the 8sec. point to the 16sec. point). Each bar lasts for 2 seconds. Imagine that you now wish to make the same 4 bars fit into 10 seconds. Proceed as follows:

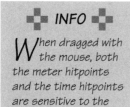

INFO

When dragged with the mouse, both the meter hitpoints and the time hitpoints are sensitive to the current Snap setting.

- With the pointer tool, drag the second time hitpoint to the right and let go of the mouse at the 18 second position on the time ruler. The hitpoints remain linked but this time by a dotted line.
- Open the Do menu and select Straighten up hitpoints. Upon selection, a new tempo of 96bpm is inserted into the tempo display and the link between the hitpoints is straightened up. 96bpm is the slower tempo necessary for the 4 bars to fit into 10 seconds instead of 8.

Drag the second time hitpoint to the 18s position   Straighten up hitpoints

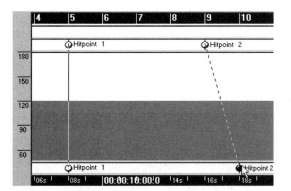   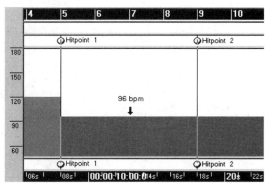

- Undo the edit using ctrl + Z (Mac: command + Z) on the computer keyboard. Now imagine that you want the same 4 bars to fit into a time segment of 6 seconds. Drag the second time hitpoint to the left and release the mouse at the 14 second point.
- Open the Do menu again and select Straighten up hitpoints. This time a new tempo of 160bpm is inserted into the display, the tempo necessary for the 4 bars to fit into 6 seconds.

Drag the second time hitpoint to the 14s position   Straighten up hitpoints

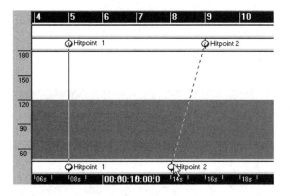   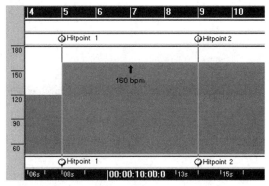

This simple example gives an idea of how the meter/tempo relationship can be manipulated using hitpoints in the Graphic Mastertrack, but what are the practical implications of this?

Among other things, it means that, by manipulating the tempo, the timing of musically meaningful events in the meter position can be matched to audio events which are fixed in time. Or, to put it another way, tempo changes can be used to pull the bars into alignment with hitpoints on the time scale.

Matching meter to time – a practical example

Imagine a short radio advertisement consisting of a recording of speech followed by a gap and then more speech. Let's assume that the recording is already on one of Cubase VST's audio Tracks. Your job is to fill the gap

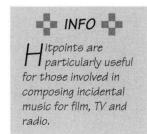

INFO

Hitpoints are particularly useful for those involved in composing incidental music for film, TV and radio.

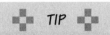

◆ TIP ◆

Hitpoints can be added while Cubase VST is in normal play mode; it is not necessary for Cubase VST to be in record mode in order to insert hitpoints via MIDI but the Graphic Mastertrack must be open.

in the announcement with a catchy musical jingle. Let's assume that you cannot alter the existing audio in any manner and that you have already written a two bar jingle on a number of Cubase VST's MIDI Tracks, which you have judged would fit into the duration of the gap in the audio. However, you have been asked to fit the music as tightly as possible into the gap and it is not easy to judge exactly where it should begin and what the exact tempo should be.

One way of approaching a solution is as follows:

- Activate the Master button on the Transport bar and open the Graphic Mastertrack.
- Activate the MIDI in button of the Graphic Mastertrack (left). This allows you to trigger hitpoints from a MIDI keyboard, which provides a convenient method of adding hitpoints at the required positions.
- Play back the audio and press a MIDI key at the beginning and end points of the gap in the speech. Hitpoints appear in the time hitpoint strip. Each hitpoint can be re-named by selecting it and double clicking on the current name shown on the info bar above the display. You now have two hitpoints indicating the position of the gap in time.
- Select both hitpoints and then select Mirror and link hitpoints in the Do menu. This creates two matching meter hitpoints in the meter strip, linked to the tempo hitpoints by a vertical line.

Insert time hitpoints via MIDI and name them   Mirror and link hitpoints

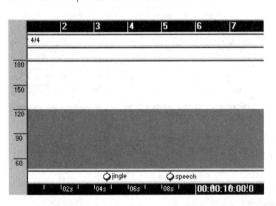
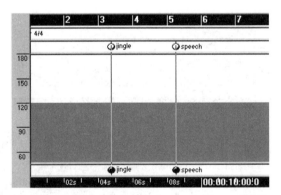

- Set Snap to 1 and move the first newly created meter hitpoint to the nearest bar line. The vertical link follows the hitpoint and becomes an angled, dotted line.
- Select Straighten up hitpoints in the Do menu. The linked hitpoints now line up and the tempo is split and adjusted at the position of the first pair of hitpoints. This lines up the beginning of the gap to the nearest bar line.

Move first meter hitpoint to nearest bar line

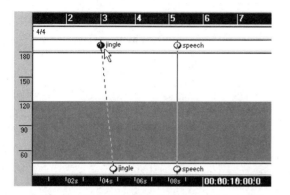

Straighten up hitpoints

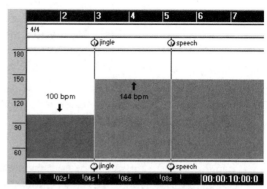

- Move the second meter hitpoint two bars to the right of the first meter hitpoint (to mark a 2 bar section).
- Select Straighten up hitpoints in the Do menu. This finds the tempo for the two bar section of music.

Move second meter hitpoint

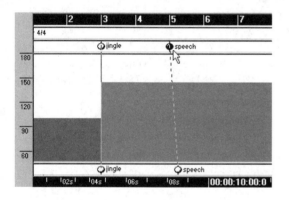

Straighten up hitpoints

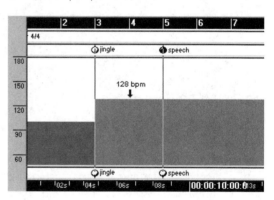

You could now go back to the Arrange window and move the two bar jingle to the chosen two bar segment. As long as the Master button on the Transport bar remains active, the two bars of music fit precisely into the gap. Of course, you may decide that the tempo has become too fast (or too slow) to suit the music, in which case you may have to find a different musical jingle or change the number of bars which fit into the gap.

The above procedure is a simple test example but when you become more familiar with the Mastertrack more elaborate manipulations of the time/meter relationship are possible.

Using hitpoints to synchronize Cubase VST to music on tape

This section explains how you can synchronize Cubase VST to music which has been recorded onto a multitrack tape which was not originally referenced to a Timecode track. The technique also applies to the situation when an existing Timecode track has been recorded over in error, or when it has suffered other damage which makes it unreadable (otherwise known as a lost sync track). In addition, the same technique can be used to freely create a tempo map while listening to an audio passage recorded in Cubase VST.

Proceed as follows:

- Stripe one track of the tape with fresh Timecode, starting before and finishing after the music to which you wish to synchronize Cubase VST.
- Play back the tape and attempt to find the approximate tempo of the first few bars of music by adjusting Cubase VST's tempo while listening to the metronome.
- Open the synchronization dialogue and make the necessary adjustments to slave Cubase VST to the code on tape (see Chapter 10 for synchronization details). Set the Song start so that Cubase VST starts one or two bars before the music on tape. Activate the Sync button on the Transport bar.
- Activate the Master button on the Transport bar of Cubase VST and open the Graphic Mastertrack.
- Change the first tempo event to the approximate tempo established above and activate the MIDI in button.
- Now run the tape and, with Cubase VST slaved to the incoming Timecode, insert a time hitpoint at the first bar of the music on tape, using a MIDI keyboard to trigger the insertion of the hitpoint. Note that Cubase VST is normally in play mode when hitpoints are inserted via MIDI; it is not necessary for Cubase VST to be in record mode but the Graphic Mastertrack must be open. Verify that the first hitpoint is precisely at the position of the first beat of the music. If not, delete and try again.
- When satisfied select the first hitpoint, open the Do menu and select Mirror and link hitpoints. A meter hitpoint is added in the meter hitpoint strip. Drag the meter hitpoint to the nearest bar line.
- Select Straighten up hitpoints in the Do menu. The tempo is adjusted to match the beginning of the music on tape to the chosen bar line in Cubase VST.
- Re-run the tape from the beginning and, with Cubase VST slaved to the incoming Timecode, insert hitpoints at equi-distant spacings, such as on beats 1 and 3 of each bar, using the MIDI keyboard, as before.
- Insert meter hitpoints at the same resolution as the time hitpoints using Fill meter hitpoints in the Do menu. Fill meter hitpoints adds meter hitpoints at the current Snap resolution, between the current positions of the left and right locators. For a satisfactory result, ensure that the left and right locators encompass the whole length of the song.
- Select Link hitpoints one to one in the Do menu. Select Straighten up hitpoints. At this point a large number of tempo changes are computed and, depending on the length of the music and the resolution of the hitpoints, this may take some time.
- Once complete, play the tape from the beginning and verify that Cubase VST's metronome remains in time with the music on tape. If dissatisfied, some of the hitpoints may need to be re-adjusted.

Inserting time hitpoints via MIDI can also be a convenient method of marking passages of audio in order to create a tempo map. Try inserting hitpoints via MIDI on every other beat of the bar and then use Fill meter hitpoints with Snap set to 2. Then use Link Hitpoints One to One and Straighten Up Hitpoints in the Do menu to insert the required tempo changes. This provides an alternative to using Match points, as described in Chapter 7.

15

A practical introduction to Score edit

More than most other parts of Cubase VST, Score edit is a world unto itself and is a major feature of the program. Yet, as you will have already realised, it is not necessary to understand Score edit in order to use Cubase VST. However, to use Score edit itself, an understanding of Score's particular way of functioning is essential, and some knowledge of musical theory is a pre-requisite. (This chapter outlines the features of the Cubase VST Score version of the program and other versions may vary in the options available.)

Background

Primarily, we will need to manipulate notes on a virtual score sheet but, unlike the other MIDI editors, we will also need to tell Score edit how to interpret the data. If the written score were to exactly follow the nuances of most musical performances, the result would be absurdly difficult to read. The design principle involves the MIDI data on one side and the score on the other, with the user in the middle ensuring that it all makes intelligent musical sense. Those not familiar with musical theory will obviously encounter some difficulty here and must read up on the subject elsewhere. Those who already know some of the basics should be able to manage by conducting their own visual and aural experiments in Score edit.

Score edit works with MIDI data alone and has no function with audio material. Similarly to the other editors, pre-recorded musical data may be viewed and updated, but Score edit is also designed for the direct scoring of arrangements within the window alone. Of course, by its very nature, Score edit is disposed towards the editing of notes but it also deals with special score events. Also, in complete contrast to any other part of Cubase, Score edit can print out the music as a full and professional score sheet. This could be anything from an entire orchestral arrangement to a basic lead sheet. Whatever your scoring needs, Score edit can usually fulfil them but, as with most things that are worthwhile, there is a learning curve.

Ways of using Score edit include the following:

- To produce a printed version of the recorded musical data.
- To act as the main editor for the recorded musical data with no regard for any potential printout of the material.
- To enter notes directly onto the score (in step-time or by adding to a blank score), to be printed out at a later stage.
- To enter notes directly onto the score, (in step-time or by adding to a blank score), to be played back via MIDI at a later stage.

Data may have been recorded in Score edit via MIDI or via the manual writing of notes onto the score. The manually entered case would often be tested by sending the data out via MIDI. This is excellent for testing complex pre-written scores and allows the orchestral arranger the luxury of testing the work before presenting it to the live orchestra. Whichever way Score edit is being used, there are some essential elements which mark it apart from the other editors: it has two modes, 'Edit mode' and 'Page mode' and it features something called 'Display Quantize'.

Before going on to explanations of these let's first get to know the Score edit window in Page mode. Page mode has the same editing features as Edit mode but provides additional functions for the printing and visual processing of the score.

A quick look around

Choose a simple Part or several Parts in any arrangement and open Score edit by selecting it from the Edit menu or pressing ctrl + R (Mac: command + R) on the computer keyboard. Once Page mode has been selected from the Score menu, the window should resemble Figure 15.1, (without the help boxes, of course). Score edit toggles between Edit mode and Page mode. Remember that the appearance of the page will also depend on what was initially selected in the Arrange window. Staves are arranged as a grand staff featuring the names of each Track (corresponding to the chosen Parts) in the same order as they were found in the Arrange window Track list.

Working down the screen (Figure 15.1), there is the usual title bar, showing the name of the Part and its bar range, a two line function/status bar, an Info line, a toolbar, and the Score display. There are the usual horizontal and vertical scroll bars at the bottom and right of the window plus an additional scale selector, a page selector, a show/hide toolbar icon and a show/hide status bar icon in the bottom right area.

Note also the pop-up toolbox (click right mouse) which features new tools unique to Score edit and the comprehensive range of features for the manipulation of all kinds of score data in the main Score menu which becomes active when Score edit is selected. Some of the most important features are reproduced on the toolbar found just below the usual Info line.

The toolbar includes, (from left to right):

- 'Voice select' when working with polyphonic voicings.
- 'Note value select' with triplet and dotted options.
- 'Enharmonic shift' for selecting appropriate accidentals.
- the 'Get info' button for opening a suitable pop-up dialogue for selected score items.
- the 'Flip stem' button for reversing the direction of the stems of selected notes.
- the 'Auto layout' button for automatically formatting the score and layout according to the 'Global' and 'Staff Settings' dialogues.
- the 'Group beam' button for joining or breaking the beam between quavers, semiquavers etc.
- the 'Hide item' button for hiding any chosen item(s) in the Score.
- the 'Make chords' button for automatic chord creation.
- the 'Force update' button to force a screen redraw.

The Score window obviously normally includes the staff with the Track name, default clef and the current time signature. The key would normally have to be manually selected by the user in the 'Staff Settings' dialogue, at which time some of the accidentals on notes in the default staff might disappear. The staff could also include a tempo indication, bar numbers and a variety of layout symbols and dynamics and accent markings.

Figure 15.1 *Score edit overview*

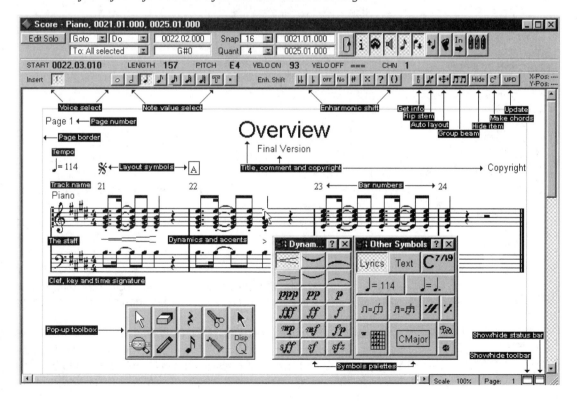

In addition, the Page mode screen would feature a page number and page border, and standard title, comment and copyright headings at the top of the first page. Some of these may not always be visible since the page is formatted according to the way things have been set up in 'Global Settings'.

The modes of operation and Display Quantize

Edit mode and Page mode

That completes a quick look around but before proceeding further let's take some time to understand the differences between Edit and Page mode and the meaning of Display Quantize.

The essential difference between the two modes is that Page mode was designed with a final *printed* version of the score in mind whereas Edit mode does not deal with this aspect at all. Page mode has more functions and possibilities but still performs all the editing operations available in Edit mode. The main differences are as follows:

- The Score edit window scrolls horizontally in Edit mode but scrolls vertically and flips from page to page in Page mode.
- The layout symbols palette is not available in Edit mode.
- The layout pointer tool is not available in Edit mode's pop-up toolbox.
- 'Hide' does not function in Edit mode.
- 'Auto layout' is not applicable in Edit mode.
- There is no title, comment and copyright in Edit mode.
- Magnification is not available in Edit mode.
- Printing is not possible in Edit mode.

Display Quantize

As well as the two modes Score edit also features the concept of 'Display Quantize' (found in the 'Staff Settings' dialogue or managed with the display quantize tool). In general, Cubase VST is concerned with an aural result but Score edit, particularly in Page mode, is also concerned with a quality visual representation.

You may already be familiar with the term WYSIWYG, meaning 'What you see Is what you get'. This could be applied to Score edit in Page mode since what you see is, more or less, what you get. However, if you attempt to apply WYSIWYG to Score edit in an aural sense then things become confusing. Most finished scores produced from an actual musical performance do not sound the same as they appear. This is due to 'Display Quantize'.

Display Quantize adjusts the graphic positions and values of the notes in the score without affecting the aural result. This preserves the musicality of a performance which, if displayed exactly as played, would be intolerable in the written score sense. Display Quantize is explained in more detail below.

Becoming familiar

There now follows a very brief tutorial on some of the basic aspects of Score edit. At this stage, we do not need to be particularly concerned about creating a meaningful score since we are just becoming familiar with what is available. So relax and let yourself go. However, always work on a *copy* of the Song or Arrangement until Score edit becomes more familiar.

Select Page mode
First, select Page mode from the main menu, and switch back and forth with Edit mode to become familiar with the differences. For example, it will be noticed immediately that Edit mode presents the score without a title.

Title, comment and copyright
Stay in Page mode and double click with the left mouse button on the title. This opens the 'Title, comment and copyright' dialogue where the appropriate information may be typed in. Type something for each section and click on OK to go back to the score.

Select tempo
Next open the 'Symbol Palettes' from the Score menu. Select any palette. At the top of the palette is the name of the current group of symbols, click on this to view the menu of the other available palettes. Select 'Other', and then select the Tempo symbol (represented as a crotchet followed by the tempo) which will already be set to the current tempo of Cubase VST. Upon selection, the mouse pointer will change into the pencil tool and by clicking in the appropriate area at the beginning of the staff the tempo icon will be inserted into the score.

Insert symbols
Try inserting symbols from any of the palettes and position them appropriately into the score, (each time the pointer will change into the pencil). The symbols which are note specific, such as accent, staccato and dynamic ornamentation, may be attached to specific note positions by clicking upon the chosen note itself. If a note is not chosen, the symbol will be placed at the nearest note found along the staff. Most text, layout and other symbols may be placed virtually anywhere on the page. After entry, any symbol may be later dragged to a new position, updated, deleted or copied in standard Cubase VST fashion.

Locate specific score segments
Also, try re-locating the song position pointer by clicking with the right mouse button while holding alt (Mac: option) . This is useful for locating and playing specific segments of the score.

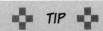

If a finished printed version of the score is required it is recommended that a copy is always used which is loaded and saved under a different filename.

The toolbox

You will already be familiar with some of the tools in the toolbox, which is opened in standard Cubase VST fashion by clicking in white space with the right mouse button. Score edit contains more tools than the other editors and the function of each is as follows.

The pointer tool

Used for selecting, dragging and manipulating specific notes or events (or several at the same time using a selection box) and the general selection and control of menu items, staves, bar lines, button controls, scroll position, dialogue boxes etc.

The eraser tool

Predictably, behaves like the real physical version, deleting several items if passed over them with the left mouse button held or deleting one at a time with single clicks. It may also be used to delete connecting bar lines between staves.

The rest tool

Used to insert rests into the score at the current value shown in the quantize box. i.e. a value of 4 will insert crotchet (1/4 note) rests. Note that inserting rests in the middle of a score pushes all events which come after it to the right, regardless of the status of the Insert button on the status bar.

The scissors tool

Used to divide a tied note into two separate notes by clicking on the second note head. It may also be used to send the last bar of one staff to the following staff by clicking on the penultimate bar line.

The layout tool

Available in Page mode, may be used to affect the score purely graphically, such as to move a clef without affecting the positions of notes on the staff, to move the graphical order of notes without affecting the order in which they are played back via MIDI, or to adjust the graphical position of slurs and ties without affecting their relationship with the notes to which they are attached.

The magnifying glass

Similar to the other editors, is used to inspect the notes of the score by playing them via MIDI when the tool is passed over them with the left mouse button held or clicked.

The pencil tool

Used to write in all text, ornamentation and other symbols (everything except notes) onto the score and is auto selected when certain symbols have been chosen.

The note tool

Used to write notes onto the score and is auto selected when a note value selection is made. The note tool itself changes to the appropriate note symbol (minim, crotchet, quaver etc.) according to the note value selection.

The glue tool

Used to join consecutive notes of the same pitch as in the other editors. It may also be used to connect bar lines between staves and to bring a bar up from the following staff by clicking on the last bar line of the upper staff.

The display quantize tool

Used to insert new display quantize settings at specific positions along the staff when processing particularly complicated passages within a score. This gives complete control over the score appearance and overcomes almost all difficulties encountered in the display of complex material.

The handling of notes

Obviously, among the most important elements of any score are the notes (and rests) themselves. Score edit provides for just about any possible note editing requirement. Notes are usually manipulated using the mouse and various tools from the toolbox. This manipulation comes in six essential forms: selecting, moving, copying, deleting, updating (editing) and adding (inserting) as follows.

Selecting

Notes may be selected one at a time by choosing the pointer tool and clicking on each with the left mouse button. Multi selections may be made by holding the shift key while doing this. A single note among a multi selection may be de-selected by holding 'shift' and re-clicking on it.

Several notes may be simultaneously selected by drawing a selection box over the desired events by clicking and dragging in white space (similar to the other editors) and then stretching the graphic box over the desired note heads. Double clicking with the left mouse while holding alt (Mac: option) selects all notes of the same pitch on all octaves. Double clicking with the left mouse while holding ctrl (Mac: command) selects all notes of the same pitch and the same octave.

In addition, notes may be stepped through using the left and right arrows of the computer keyboard with or without 'shift' to multi select or not. Selections may be made on one or several staves at the same time. The heads of selected notes change to reverse video and may be easily recognised on the screen. As in the other editors, if individual notes are to be played via MIDI as each is selected then the loudspeaker icon in the status bar should be highlighted.

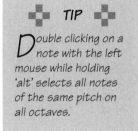

TIP

Double clicking on a note with the left mouse while holding 'alt' selects all notes of the same pitch on all octaves.

Moving

Notes may be moved individually by clicking, holding and dragging with the left mouse button or in groups by clicking, holding and dragging on one of the selected group. As usual, notes will be dropped at their new destination according to the current Snap value.

Notes may be moved up or down in pitch, or left or right along the staff, or between staves, as desired. Before releasing, notes will be magnetic to the current Snap value and, if 'ctrl' is held down, changes in pitch will only be within the scale of the current key signature (Mac: activate 'keep moved notes within key' in Preferences dialogue). Cut, copy and paste actions are useful for moving larger blocks of data around. Data moved to the clipboard using cut may be pasted to the current song position pointer in the active staff.

Copying

Notes may be copied in standard Cubase VST fashion by pressing alt (Mac: option) on the computer keyboard while clicking, holding and dragging on a note or group of notes with the left mouse button. The copy which appears may be manipulated in position and pitch, as with 'Moving' above, and, once again, notes will be dropped at their new destination according to the current Snap value. The 'copy' of cut, copy and paste may also be used to copy notes in Score edit.

Deleting

Notes may be deleted by making the appropriate selection using one of the above methods and then pressing delete or backspace on the computer keyboard. Alternative delete actions include clicking on one or more notes with the eraser tool and using delete from the Do menu, after having selected the appropriate notes. Remember that when notes are deleted they are automatically replaced in the score by the appropriate rest.

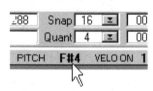

Updating

Note selections may also be updated and edited in a number of other ways. Similarly to the other editors, the characteristics of the selected note appear on the Info bar near the top of the screen. Any of the parameters may be decreased or increased using the left and right mouse buttons. This obviously includes changing the position in time or the length and pitch of the note. Selections may also be updated via MIDI if the MIDI icon and the appropriate combination of note, Note On velocity and Note Off velocity icons is selected. Cubase VST automatically steps on to the next note after each entry.

Other editing techniques include the joining together of consecutive notes of the same pitch using the glue tool and separating tied notes using the scissors. Holding alt (Mac: option) while clicking on a note head with the note tool will change its length to the current quantize length in the quantize box.

Adding

Notes may be added anywhere on the score using the note tool. The note tool will be automatically selected when one of the note value symbols is selected on the toolbar and the note may be inserted anywhere on the staves. The note value may be selected using the mouse or numbers 1-7 on the computer keyboard.

Click on the staff with the note tool and do not release until the desired pitch and position have been found. The unreleased note will be magnetic to the current Snap value and the precise pitch may be verified in the 'Pitch' parameter of the Info bar. Notes may be restricted to the current key if ctrl is held down at the time of entry (Mac: activate 'keep moved notes within key' in Preferences dialogue). Notes are always *added* to the score unless the Insert icon of the status bar is selected, in which case all notes which come after the entry will be pushed to the right.

That covers most of the possibilities with notes in Score edit. Rests are managed similarly but when they are entered onto the score the data which comes after them is *always* pushed to the right regardless of the status of the Insert icon.

Project 1

Creating a piano score

Let's start using Score edit in earnest by creating a simple piano score. The object of this exercise is to finish up with a well presented, readable score on a split staff with some kind of ornamentation or markings suggesting how it should be played. The score will then be printed. *Always* work on a copy, to avoid any danger of destroying valuable material.

Figure 15.2 Piano score before editing

Select a Track or a Part in the Arrange window which is for a piano or a related keyboard instrument. To illustrate the procedure here a very simple 4 bar piano part playing chords was chosen (see Figure 15.3). With the Part selected, open Score edit from the Edit menu or use ctrl + R (Mac: command + R). The notes will almost certainly appear in a format which is not acceptable for a piano score, with no split staff and perhaps an inappropriate display quantize setting (see unedited score Figure 15.2). Also, if the music is in any key other than C major there will invariably be some accidentals.

Figure 15.3 Piano score after editing

Taking the illustrated piano part as an example, the following steps need to be taken to make things acceptable:

Set title details

Change the mode to Page mode and double click on the title. A dialogue box will appear where a suitable title, comment and copyright may be entered (Figure 15.4). It is also possible to change the size and font of the text from within the dialogue.

Figure 15.4. The Title, Comment and Copyright dialogue

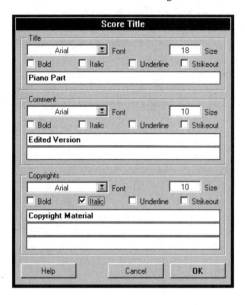

Set staff details

Open the Staff Settings dialogue (Figure 15.5). This provides the most important parameters for obtaining a legible score. The first item in the dialogue box is 'Staff mode'. Set this to 'Split' and ensure that the split point is set to C3 (middle C). Click on OK to approve the changes and go back to the score. Things should already be looking a little better.

Figure 15.5. The staff settings dialogue with the staff options dialogue

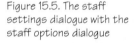

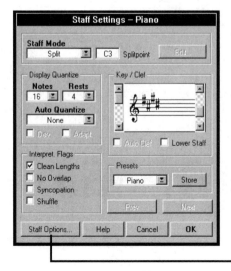

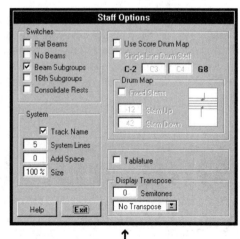

Set other symbols

Open the Symbols palette and select 'Other'. Select the tempo indicator and either drag it onto the score and release at the appropriate position on the staff, or select it and click on the appropriate position using the pencil tool (which automatically appears when certain types of symbols are chosen).

Figure 15.5(a) Other symbols palette

Select Global settings

Open 'Global settings' and select 'Bars' from the topic list (Figure 15.6). Set the 'Bar numbers every' box to 'Off' so that bar numbers will not be displayed on the score. Set 'Default bars across the page' to 4 – Score edit will display four bars across the page, if it is practical. While in Global settings select 'Page Numbers' from the topic list and ensure that the active box is *not* ticked. In this case, page numbers will not be displayed. Click on OK to leave the dialogue box. You may need to use the Auto Layout button to take into account all the new global settings.

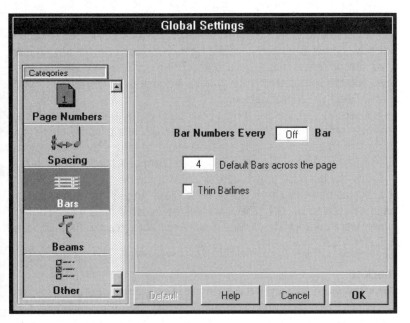

Figure 15.6 Global Settings Bar dialogue

Some confusion may arise with 'Default bars across the page' in Page mode since, unlike Edit mode, changes in the default number are not automatically registered when leaving the global settings dialogue. Clicking the Auto Layout button takes into account the changes.

However, in Page mode, yet another control, 'Number of bars' is also available (Figure 15.7). It is best to use this *after* most other editing has been completed. The Number of Bars dialogue allows the chosen number of bars across the page to be imposed upon either all staves (All), the active staff and all those following (Following), or the active staff only (This). Thus, varying numbers of bars across the page may be imposed at any point in the score.

Figure 15.7. Number of Bars dialogue

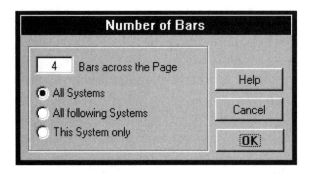

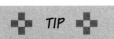

TIP

To change the time signature of a piece simply double click on the existing time signature and enter the new values into the pop-up box. To enter a new time signature use the Clef symbol palette.

Change the key

The page layout itself is probably now looking much better but, if the score is anything like the example in Figure 15.2, the notes themselves will still be in some disarray. There are many tied notes, awkward dotted rests, short semiquaver rests and numerous accidentals.

The first step to remedy the situation is to insert the correct key. The example is in E major. To change the key, open the Staff Settings dialogue and adjust the key/clef section. The left scroll bar is for clef selection, which we do not need here, and the right scroll bar is for the key. The up scroll arrow selects flat keys and the down scroll arrow selects sharp keys. For the split staff the key will be automatically inserted onto both staves. Select the appropriate key.

The second step, before leaving Staff Settings, is to update the Display Quantize section. This contains note quantize and rest quantize boxes, and a first step to getting the score readable might be setting the note quantize to 16 and the rest quantize to 4, with Auto Quantize set to 'off'.

Below the quantize boxes there are also a number of flags which may be activated by ticking their boxes. Tick 'Clean lengths' and leave the dialogue by clicking on OK. The score will be updated and, if the settings chosen were appropriate, it will be more readable (see the finished score in Figure 15.3).

Check it

Check the score for any incorrect notes. For example, keyboard players sometimes touch the wrong keys when playing chords and, although they are not always audible, they are visible on the score. Bar 2 of the piano part example contains a D# in the E chord which was certainly not intended but did not show up audibly. Such notes should simply be deleted.

Add ornamentation

Add any desired ornamentation from the Symbols palettes. This might include dynamics and accents, and text comments could also be added where appropriate.

Auto format again

Finally, click on the Auto Layout button to reformat the page for a last time and, if all has gone well, the score should resemble the same standard of presentation as that in Figure 15.3.

Printing the score

When you are satisfied with the result, try printing the score. The printed version should turn out to look as good as what can be seen on the screen.

Before printing, make sure that Cubase VST is set up correctly with the choice of printer and that the printer setup options are correctly adjusted. PC users should already have an appropriate default printer selected as part of their Windows setup.

Printer setup

Make your printing setup adjustments using the 'Page Setup' and 'Print' dialogues in the main File menu. The default printer chosen elsewhere in Windows is normally found in the 'Printer' section and the usual page orientation, paper size, margins and other options may be chosen in standard Windows fashion. Figure 15.8 shows the Page Setup' dialogue.

When everything has been correctly set up and the printer is on line and ready to print, go to the File menu and select Print. Note that the File menu's 'Page Setup' and 'Print' options are available only when Score edit is open and in Page mode.

Figure 15.8 Page Setup dialogue

Print the score

Click on OK in the print dialogue to activate printing and, if all is set up correctly, the printer should jump into action.

Display Quantize in detail

Readers who successfully managed to process and print a score in Project 1 will feel they have made progress but, undoubtedly, some aspects of Score edit will still seem somewhat mysterious. Display Quantize is probably one of these.

Display quantize is sufficiently important to warrant special attention. If the normal quantize functions of Cubase VST are already understood then Display Quantize will be a little easier to grasp.

Testing Display Quantize

The Display Quantize values, in the Display Quantize section of the Staff Settings dialogue, set the smallest note or rest allowed in the score display. The values are purely for the display and have no effect on the actual MIDI data, which remains as recorded. Without an appropriate setting the display of the notes and rests may appear over complicated and confusing. For example, try recording the following melody into Cubase VST:

Figure 15.9 Test melody

Once recorded, select the new Part in the Arrange window and open Score edit. Assuming that the Part has not been quantized, has been reasonably played, and has display quantize set to 16 for notes and 16 for rests with auto quantize set to 'none', the melody may initially be displayed more like the following.

Figure 15.10. The melody with Inappropriate Display Quantize

This apparent confusion in the display will be due to the player's particular manner of expressing the music, such as playing in front of or behind the beat, and possibly real timing errors. Most of the problems will probably revolve around the triplets in bar two. However, if the aural result is satisfactory, changing the note data itself is not a good solution. Display Quantize provides a way of interpreting the playing so that the notes are clearly displayed on the score without disturbing the aural result.

Firstly, let's try entering a note display quantize of 4. As before, do this in the Staff Settings dialogue and make sure that Auto quantize is set to 'none'. This tells Score edit that the smallest note in the score is a crotchet (1/4 note) and so, in keeping with this, the editor will shift, purely visually, all notes to the nearest crotchet (1/4 note) beat and the score will now resemble something like the following:

Figure 15.11. *Too much Display Quantize*

The editor has no problem with the first, third and fourth bars since, indeed, the smallest note intended was a crotchet (1/4 note). However, the triplets in bar two now look like chords, and the quavers and semi-quavers in bars five and six have also been transformed. The solution might have been to set the note display quantize to the smallest value note which, in this case, is a semiquaver (1/16 note). If there were only 'straight' notes in the passage then this could have worked, but each group of triplets would tend to be displayed as two semiquavers (1/16 notes) and a quaver (1/8 note) because Score edit has been given no guidance on how to interpret them correctly. Before we can find a solution we need to get to know Display Quantize in more detail.

The kind of Display Quantize settings chosen depends on the kind of note data to be processed, which can essentially be divided into two groups:

- that which contains a mix of 'straight' AND triplet notes together.
- that which contains 'straight' notes only OR triplets only.

Auto Quantize

One way of processing music containing triplets and 'straight' notes, like the example, is to use 'Auto quantize'. Auto quantize is found in the Staff Settings dialogue just below the main Display Quantize settings. It is either set to 'none' or in one of two active modes: 'Distance' and 'Position'.

- 'Distance' means that the display quantize will use the distance between the notes to calculate how they should be displayed, without specific regard for their position in time (such as when the playing is behind or ahead of the beat). This is more forgiving of passages which were inaccurately played.
- 'Position', however, is better suited to material which was played more accurately or entered manually. When 'position' is selected, two other options 'Deviation' and 'Adapt' may be toggled on or off. Selecting 'deviation' allows normal detection of notes even if they are not precisely on the beat. This should be turned off for material which has been tightly quantized. 'Adapt' detects the surrounding triplets after one triplet has been found.

Any of these settings could have an undesired effect on the score, so, in all cases, it is better to find out the best option by experimentation.

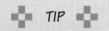

Before using auto quantize always choose the note quantize value first, based on the smallest triplet (for triplet dominated pieces), or the smallest 'straight' note (for pieces containing mainly 'straight' notes).

Using the Display Quantize tool

As an alternative to auto quantize, specific sections of the score could be manually 'display quantized' using the display quantize tool as follows:

- With the display quantize tool selected, (a Q appears on the screen), simply click at the appropriate position along the staff and enter the desired settings into the pop-up box.
- Click on OK to return to the score where the display quantize setting will be shown with a Q followed by the chosen quantize value, such as Q16, for example. This is assuming that display quantize events have not been hidden in 'Show invisible ...' (Global Settings). In addition, if auto quantize has already been used on the staff and a new display quantize setting is later entered with the display quantize tool, any display quantize changes that were invisibly imposed by auto quantize will now be transformed into ordinary visible display quantize settings. This avoids confusion.

Interpretation flags

In addition to the display quantize settings, the 'Interpretation flags', also found in the Staff Settings dialogue, are particularly useful for various musical styles:

- 'Clean lengths' extends the length of short notes to the next note or rest quantize position and is useful for eliminating the short rests which sometimes appear inappropriately between notes.
- 'No overlap' prevents undesirable strings of ties which sometimes join notes in certain circumstances. Experiment with 'No overlap' whenever unwanted ties become a problem in the score.
- 'Syncopation' may be a better solution than 'No overlap' if ties on long notes which cross the beat have become a problem. Score displays these as two tied notes with 'Syncopation' unticked and a single note with 'Syncopation' ticked.
- The 'Shuffle' flag is designed for a jazz score where 'straight' notes would be used to represent a shuffle beat, in order to make it more legible. A shuffled crotchet triplet (1/4 note triplet) followed by a quaver triplet (1/8 note triplet) become 'straight' quavers (1/8 notes) and a shuffled quaver triplet (1/8 note triplet) followed by a semiquaver triplet (1/16 note triplet) become 'straight' semiquavers (1/16 notes).

Remember that the Interpretation flags may not always be the appropriate solution for display problems on a staff, particularly a long and complicated one. Experimenting with the flags on a trial and error basis is probably the best approach, and always verify the score carefully after use.

The best solution

So now, with all this knowledge in mind, let's go back to the example above. The passage contains triplets *and* 'straight' notes so we could use Auto Quantize or insert display quantize settings using the Display Quantize tool.

A note quantize value of 16, with Auto quantize in 'position' mode and 'deviation' and 'adapt' selected, might be appropriate. Set the rest quantize value to 4, even though there are no rests, and tick the 'Clean lengths' interpretation flag. Some scores may read correctly as in Figure 15.9 above.

However, probably the best method in this case is to set Auto quantize to 'none' and use the display quantize tool. Enter display quantize values of 16 to all but the second bar, which should be set to semiquaver triplets (1/16 note triplets). Tick 'Clean lengths', enter any other appropriate settings and the score should, once again, read correctly (see Figure 15.12).

Figure 15.12. Corrected melody showing display quantize symbols

Project 2

Scoring a four part string arrangement

Processing a four part string arrangement in Score edit presents problems not encountered in the first tutorial. Figure 15.13 shows an example of an arrangement before editing. As usual, always work on a duplicate copy of the arrangement to avoid losing important material. It is recommended that you load from, and save to, a file with a different name to the original. This file is used purely for preparing the piece in Score edit. For the purposes of this exercise use Score edit in Page mode.

Figure 15.13 The unedited string arrangement

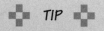

Arrange instruments in order

The first task is to arrange the instruments into the correct order in the Arrange window. Simply click, hold and drag the Tracks in the Track list until they are in the correct order. Tracks will appear in Score edit in exactly the same vertical order. Select the Parts required for the score.

The piece could be a short arrangement, as in the example, or an extended score. The example strings arrangement is comprised of four staves; violin I, violin II, cellos and basses in the order in which they might normally be found in an orchestral score. Note that, by default, the staves are displayed as a grand staff with the staves joined by common bar lines.

Decide on the clefs

Next, decide on the clefs required for each staff. The default clef when first opening Score edit is the treble clef. The violins would normally remain with this but the cellos and basses would need to be changed to bass clefs.

This may be achieved in one of two ways. Double click on the clef itself and adjust the clef type in the pop-up window or open Staff Settings, select the appropriate staff with the 'Previous/next' buttons and change the clef in the 'Key/clef' section.

Set the key
Decide on the key and then open Staff Settings and set the key in the 'Key/clef' section for each staff.

Set bars across page
Open the Global settings dialogue. Select 'bars' from the topic list and enter the desired default bars across the page (initially four bars suits most circumstances) and select bar numbers to appear every four bars. Consider also ticking 'Thin barlines', which will tend to help the notes stand out on the finished printed score.

Select page numbers as active by ticking the 'Active' box in the 'Page numbers' section. Click on OK to leave the Global settings dialogue. Open 'Page mode settings' and tick 'Real book' and 'Staff separators'. 'Real book' means that the clef appears only on the first line of the page and 'Staff separators' puts in an automatic staff separator symbol between each grand staff as it appears down the page.

Enter title details
Double click on the title to open the title, comment and copyright dialogue and enter the appropriate details, as described in the first tutorial.

Musicians' directions
Any number of directions might be required in the score to help the musicians understand how the piece should be played. To this end, Score edit provides four types of text.

Regular text ('Text' in the 'Other' symbols palette)
Regular text is tied to the bar and staff position. If the bar or staff is later moved, the regular text will be moved with it.

Page text ('Page text' in the 'Layout' symbols palette)
Page text is not attached to the staff or bar position and will remain at its original location regardless of changes on the staves. It is treated as part of the general layout (known in Score edit as the 'Layout layer', meaning all non-note specific details of the page).

System text ('System text' in the 'Layout' symbols palette).
System text is also part of the layout layer but, unlike page text, may be tied to a specific staff and bar position. System text is also handy when used in conjunction with the empty graphic box symbol found in the layout palette.

The box may be sized appropriately and will be added to the screen on top of all other objects and staves except system text. The two together provide an excellent facility to highlight particularly important information or directions on the score.

Lyrics ('Lyrics' in the 'Other' symbols palette)
The adding of lyrics is explained in the next project.

All text is input by selecting the appropriate symbol from the Symbols palette and clicking at the desired page or bar position with the pencil tool which appears. A pop-up input box is opened into which the text should be written. Any text may be dragged to a new position using standard click and drag procedures. Similarly to other objects found on the Score, text may be aligned using the align functions found in the Format menu.

Enter Layout symbols

Add any Layout symbols appropriate to the score as found in the Layout palette. This might include some rehearsal markers (like the A and B markers in the finished example, Figure 15.14) or perhaps a coda symbol or sign. If the score includes violins I and II, or other related instruments, try linking the staves with the brackets provided. If part of a larger orchestral score then all the strings could be linked with one large bracket. In addition, try indicating a repeated passage using Repeat Barlines.

Figure 15.14 The final version of the string arrangement

Double click on the appropriate start and end barlines and select the new style bar line from the Bar Lines pop-up window (Figure 15.15). If a better view of the layout in isolation is required then try selecting 'Layout layer only' from the Score menu.

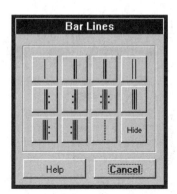

Figure 15.15 Bar Lines pop-up menu

Add accents etc.

Finally, add any desired accents, dynamics, slurs and ties to the score and double check that there are no incorrect notes. Accents, slurs and ties etc. are found in the various palettes.

All symbols in the 'Note Symbols' palette are note specific and are always tied to the selected note. Simply select the symbol and, as usual, the pencil tool will appear automatically on the screen. Then click on the desired note and the symbol will appear automatically positioned at a set distance from the note head.

The symbols in the Dynamics palette are selected in a similar fashion but the crescendo and decrescendo (diminuendo) symbols, for example, are entered onto the score at specific positions along the selected staff and are not linked to notes. Similarly, the ppp to fff dynamics are entered at positions along the staves and are also not linked to notes.

Both accents and dynamic symbols may be made to have a real effect on the actual MIDI data. Accents may be given a MIDI meaning by selecting 'MIDI Meaning' from Global settings (Figure 15.16), or if MIDI Meaning is already active a double click on any relevant accent opens the dialogue box. The accents and marks may be given a percentage increase or decrease in velocity or length which will affect the notes to which they are attached (assuming that active is ticked in the dialogue). It is probably best to set up all MIDI Meaning values *before* entering the symbols onto the score, since the results may become confusing if notes are edited and re-edited several times.

Double clicking on any of the dynamic symbols found in the score, like crescendos and diminuendos, opens a dialogue box where the range and percentage of the effect may be adjusted. For example, a crescendo may be given a start and end position and a velocity range, which will effect the target notes accordingly (Figure 15.17).

There is one important difference between MIDI Meaning processing and crescendo/diminuendo and ppp to fff dynamics processing. MIDI

Figure 15.16 The MIDI
Meaning dialogue

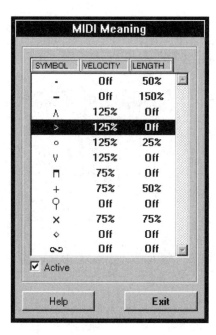

Meaning is reversible, i.e. if an accent is later removed the note in question will go back to its original length and velocity values; dynamics processing, however, brings about permanent changes to the MIDI data which cannot be reversed. When processing a score with MIDI Meaning or dynamics remember the importance of working on a *copy* to avoid confusion or loss of important material .

That completes the treatment of the strings arrangement, which should resemble the same standard of presentation as that in Figure 15.14. Comparing the before and after scores of Figures 15.13 and 15.14 shows the enormous visual improvements which can be achieved using Score edit. If required, print the score, as described above.

Figure 15.17. Programming a
crescendo

Project 3

Creating a lead sheet

This example is concerned with creating a Lead sheet comprised of chords, melody and lyrics. The order of events would usually be the input or editing of the melody line followed by the lyrics, which need the melody to latch onto, and lastly the chords, which could be created automatically from an existing chord track or entered manually.

Many readers will already have song arrangements containing the musical accompaniment alone. Some of the existing arrangement may be suitable in the creation of some elements of the Lead sheet but, very often, to achieve something presentable, the melody, and often the chords, will need to be entered into Cubase VST separately (manually or via MIDI), and the lyrics will always have to be added manually. The procedure for creating a lead sheet, as shown in Figure 15.18, is as follows:

Figure 15.18 A Lead sheet created in Score edit

Start with the melody

While in the Arrange window, make a copy of the melody Part(s) for the Lead sheet, select it and open Score edit. If a melody does not already exist then it will have to be recorded onto a new Track or the notes written manually in Score edit. The latter case might require the creation of a new empty Part of suitable length which could then be selected and worked upon in Score edit. Or the notes could be input in step-time.

Even if the melody already exists, it is often the case that, once the singer has worked on things and perhaps the lyrics have been updated, the melody as it originally existed is no longer accurate. This is certainly the case in the example where the melody started out as in Figure 15.19. Note that bars 15, 16 and 17 have been considerably updated in the final version (Figure 15.18). Updating the melody may involve moving the pitch or position of individual notes or changing the melodic content of entire passages. This kind of editing is best achieved in Score edit. Since we are aiming at a printable version of the Lead sheet start working in Page mode immediately.

Figure 15.19. The Lead sheet melody before editing

Set up Staff Settings and Global Settings

Use the information in the previous tutorials to set up the Staff Settings and Global Settings dialogues to achieve the correct key, bars across the page, display quantize and the overall initial look of the Layout. Use Auto Layout to format the page accordingly.

Add lyrics

Once the melody has been suitably corrected and the page layout is looking acceptable the lyrics can be added. Lyrics are entered using the 'Lyrics' symbol found in the Other symbols palette. Proceed as follows:

- Select the symbol and click on the melody note corresponding to the first word of the lyrics with the pencil tool (which will appear on the screen automatically). This opens a pop-up input box.
- Enter the first word or syllable but do not press return. Instead press the tab button which will automatically step to the next note in the melody, whereupon the next word or syllable of the lyrics may be entered into a new pop-up input box.
- Use the tilde symbol (~) between syllables; Cubase VST will use this to display correctly centred dashes between adjoining syllables.
- Press return after entering one line of lyrics, for example, in order to manage the results on the page. The freshly entered lyrics should already be clearly displayed in reverse video (blacked) attached to the corresponding melody. They may need to be re-

aligned. As with other elements of the score, use the align functions in the Format menu to line up the lyrics (usually in a straight line under the corresponding staff).

In most respects the lyrics may be treated like any other type of text, including formatting the text font, size and style. However, if a note is moved the attached lyric is moved with it. In addition, when lyrics are first entered certain words may be grouped too closely together. This can usually be remedied using the Auto Layout button which will move both the notes and the lyrics to the appropriate spacings.

Tidy up the spacing

Despite the use of Auto Layout to correct untidy spacings with the lyrics, some spacings may still be inappropriate. In these instances, notes may be graphically moved using the layout tool and, in so doing, the attached lyric will be moved with it. Simply select and drag the note. Movement is restricted to horizontal only, and changes in position will be entirely graphic with no effect on the MIDI data. Of course, the layout tool may also be used to move the note data for any other reason, to improve the graphic appearance and readability of the score.

Add the chords

The next task is to add the chords which, like the creation of the melody, may be achieved in a number of ways. The first and most obvious is simply to enter the chords manually using the chord symbol found in the Other symbols palette. The default chord symbol is shown as C 7/b9 and, when selected, the pencil tool appears on the screen as for the other symbols. Click on the staff at the appropriate bar and beat using the position indicator on the Status bar as a guide. This opens the Edit Chord Symbol dialogue (Figure 15.20), where the characteristics of the chord may be chosen as follows:

- The 'Root note' box selects the essential chord name.
- The chord name may subsequently be updated to minor, dominant 7th, major 7th etc. in the 'Type' menu.
- Any tension may be added by ticking the 'Tensions' boxes.
- Selecting 'Enharmonic shift' produces the flat version of the same chord i.e. : A# major becomes Bb major.
- An alternative bass note may be chosen from the 'Bass note' menu.
- Clicking on OK enters the chord symbol above the chosen bar and beat of the selected staff.

The actual style and appearance of the chord symbols may be further updated in the 'Chord font' section of the Global Settings dialogue. Here, the actual manner in which major 7th, minor, diminished and half dimin-

Figure 15.20. The Edit Chord
Symbol dialogue

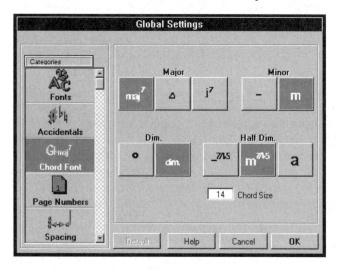

ished are displayed may be chosen, as well as the size of the symbols (Figure 15.21).

In addition to doing everything manually there is an alternative in the 'Do' menu called 'Make chords'. This feature automatically enters chord symbols onto the currently active staff. All notes on all staves are taken into consideration or the user may select specific groups of notes. There must be at least three notes at the same position in time for Cubase VST to interpret them as a chord. The user could use the chords from an existing Track or, if not available, a special chord Track could be quickly created. Both could be used to calculate the chord symbols.

Figure 15.21(a). The Global
Setting Chord Font section

It is always a good idea to heavily quantize chord tracks so that 'Make Chords' can interpret clearly where each chord is meant to be. The analysis produces inversions of chords when detected (a bass note is added to the symbol) but, if ctrl (Mac: command) is held while selecting Make Chords

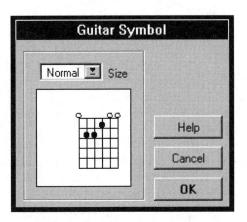

Figure 15.21(b). Edit Guitar
symbol dialogue

the essential chord name alone is entered. Make Chords is not always accurate and more complex chord shapes may need manual attention.

You may wish to include guitar style chord symbols on your scores. This is a purely graphic symbol, also found in the 'Other' symbols palette. Clicking with this symbol chosen enters a standard chord box representation of the six strings of the guitar onto the screen. Double clicking on the box opens the 'Edit guitar' dialogue.

Here, the size of the symbol, 'Regular' or 'Large', may be chosen and by clicking on the various fret positions of the strings, the fingering of any chord may be displayed.

By clicking outside of the box to the left of the first fret position, a fret number from 1 to 10 (in roman numerals I to X) may be added, and, by clicking at the top of any string, a O or X may be entered to denote that the string is either open or does not form part of the chord. These symbols are efficient and easy to use and look excellent on the score printout. Once the chord shape has been finalised the completed symbol may be dragged to the required position on the score.

The completed Lead sheet should resemble the same standard of presentation as that in Figure 15.18. If required, print out the score, as described above.

Having come this far, you should now have Score edit under control and be able to go on to explore most other aspects of the editor. However, before ending the Chapter, we need to look at one other important Score edit concept, the Layout layer.

The Layout Layer

Broadly speaking, a Layout is all those elements of a score which are not note specific. In other words, take away the notes and all things related to them and you are left with the Layout. The Layout Layer may be viewed by selecting 'Layout Layer Only'. However, the Layout does not include such things as the title, comment and copyright or page numbers, and Layouts are available only in page mode.

Each Layout consists of a specific group of Tracks which were chosen in the Arrange window. For example, if you selected trombone, saxophone and trumpet Tracks, worked on them in Score edit and then used 'Keep' to exit, a new Layout would be created. This Layout would be specific to these three Tracks and, if the same combination is reworked at a later stage, the previous Layout is overwritten if the return key is used to exit. However, if the trumpet Track only is selected for editing in Score edit, then a new Layout would be created if the return key is used to exit the editor.

A list of Layouts is found in the 'Page Mode Settings' dialogue of the Format menu (Figure 15.22). By default, Layouts are provisionally given the name of the first Track in each combination and these may be renamed by double clicking on the current name. The Layout currently residing in Score edit is indicated by a star and the Track combination used in each Layout is indicated in the Track list on the right. The display of Tracks is purely for reference and cannot be changed in any manner. The Layout names are also found in the main Edit menu in the 'Score layout' sub menu of 'Select'. This is excellent for finding the Track combination for different Score layouts within a complex arrangement.

Figure 15.22. Page Mode Settings dialogue

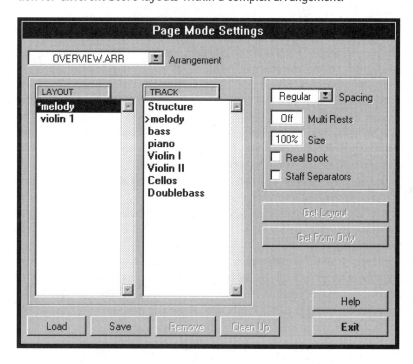

So, how can Layouts be useful? Theoretically, any Layout could be applied to any score but this would not usually be very constructive. One way of using Layouts is when a single instrument or group of instruments is extracted from a completed full score. By taking the Layout of the full score and imposing it upon the single instrument score, all rehearsal, repeat, segno, coda marks etc., along with various spacings and bar line settings, now appear on the single instrument staff.

To achieve this, with the single instrument Track in Score edit, simply select the Layout required, ('Full score', for example), from the Layout list in the 'Page Mode Settings' dialogue and select 'Get Layout' or 'Get Form Only'. The selected Layout will replace the current Layout. After using the 'Get' buttons, the return key should be used to leave Score edit in order to retain the new single instrument Layout. The new Layout can later be renamed and saved.

Different Layout elements are applied to the score according to which 'Get' button is selected, as in the following table:

Get button selections

Layout elements	Button selected	
	Get layout	Get form only
Symbols from layout palette	all symbols	'rehearsal, segnos, codas and endings'
Bar line types	yes	yes
Bar number offsets	yes	yes
Staff settings dialogue values	all	None
Page mode dialogue values	all	None
Vertical spacing of staves	yes	no
Bar line spacing	yes	no
Staff spacing	yes	no
Broken bar lines	yes	no

Layouts are saved and loaded within the 'Page Mode Settings' dialogue and are given the file extension '.LAY'.

Final comment

That completes this practical introduction to Score edit. Expert users will realise that not absolutely all aspects of the editor have been covered. However, the aim of this chapter was to provide an easy and practical way into Score's secrets. Those aspects not covered tend to be the more esoteric and less used options and many readers will only ever need the essentials. In any case, armed with the practical information provided here, the user will feel confident to go on to explore any other aspects of Score edit.

You will quickly establish your own way of working with Score edit and, of course, methods will vary according to your own needs. As with the other editors, there will be a tendency to become heavily reliant on the mouse, but remember that various keyboard commands and keyboard/mouse combinations can help in manipulating things quickly and easily. The following table outlines some useful smart moves for Score edit:

Smart moves for Score edit

Key		Mouse action	Result
PC	Mac		
alt + D	option + D	–	opens print dialogue
alt + B	option + B	–	hides selected item(s)
alt + E	option + E	–	opens Enharmonic shift dialogue
alt + G	option + G	–	groups selected notes under one beam
alt + X	option + X	–	flips stems of selected notes
→	→	–	selects next note
←	←	–	selects previous note
↓	↓	–	selects next staff
↑	↑	–	selects previous staff
keys 1 – 7	keys 1– 7	–	selects whole to 1/64 note values
T	T	–	selects triplet values
.	.	–	selects dotted note values
alt	n/a	click right mouse	moves song pos. pointer to mouse position
ctrl	n/a	click right mouse	opens current Symbols palette at mouse pos.
ctrl	n/a	input notes on staff with note tool	restricts notes to scale of chosen key sig.
alt	option	click on existing note with note tool	changes note length to current note value
alt	option	add note symbol from Symbols palette	adds symbol to all currently selected notes
shift	shift	double click on note	selects this and all following notes in current staff
ctrl	command	double click on note	selects all notes of same pitch from all staves
alt	option	double click on note	selects all octaves of same pitch from all staves
shift	shift	double click on symbol	selects all symbols of the same kind
–	–	double click on almost any score item	opens dialogue box relevant to that item

16 ♦

Logical edit

Logical edit in theory

While it helps to have some knowledge of the theory of MIDI and basic mathematics, Logical edit is within the grasp of all users. It requires some initial effort but, once mastered, Logical edit provides some extremely fast methods of manipulating any kind of MIDI data. This chapter deals with the subject by practical example. Real situations likely to be met during the course of a typical Cubase VST session are outlined, as well as some of the more elaborate possibilities.

Before looking at Logical edit itself let's take some time to think about the logical aspects of music in general. Most users will already be aware that many aspects of music can be expressed as mathematical data. With MIDI, numbers are given to all the notes within the normal pitch range, numbers express the intensity (velocity) of these notes and MIDI based sequencers express their durations in terms of numbers of pulses (or ticks). So, if three of the fundamental elements of musical expression (pitch, velocity and duration) are being expressed as numbers then it should be an easy matter to carry out logical operations upon them.

Of course, there is no purely logical element in the making of good music but this is not the point of Logical edit. Logical edit is a tool which reduces certain kinds of otherwise extremely laborious edit operations to one or two clicks of the mouse.

You cannot, however, *see* any musical data in the Logical edit window, as you can in the other editors. Therefore, Logical edit could be regarded as a very elaborate, user changeable 'function', similar to those already found in the Functions menu but adaptable to each user's needs. It provides a facility with which custom designed processing tools can be assembled to fulfil a wide range of tasks.

Many potential Logical edit operations can be expressed in plain English. For example:

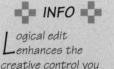

INFO ♦

Logical edit enhances the creative control you have over your music and, more than anything else, Logical edit saves time.

- 'IF the MIDI event type is a note THEN add ten to the velocity' or
- 'IF the MIDI event type is a note THEN fix the duration at 96' or
- 'IF the MIDI event type is a note and is equal to 36 THEN extract this note from the track and put it onto a new track'.

❖ **INFO** ❖

*Here we will be
exploring Logical
edit in expert mode.
Easy mode was
considered to be just a
little too easy for
most users and lacked
some of the more
useful functions
available in expert
mode.*

These statements are easy to understand and they describe actual Logical edit functions which are regularly used. If you can understand these statements then the next step is simply to translate their logic onto the Logical edit window of Cubase VST.

The Logical edit window

Logical edit is opened from the Edit menu or by selecting ctrl + L (Mac: command + L) from the computer keyboard (Figure 16.1). Note value (pitch), velocity and duration are found on the expert Logical edit window as the Value 1, Value 2 and Length columns. These are clearly marked in the Filter and Processing sections. So we already know where to find some of the most important musical parameters in the Logical edit window. It is now simply a matter of knowing how to manipulate them.

Why call the columns vague names like Value 1 and Value 2 ? This is because Logical edit can be made to act upon data other than notes, such as pitch bend and modulation, when the value columns assume different meanings. For the moment we are going to limit ourselves to note data alone.

The Filter and Processing sections may be regarded as equivalent to an IF, THEN statement as found in popular computer languages. Those already familiar with a computer language will understand the logic of this. Essentially the logic of the Logical edit window can be simply expressed in the following statement:

IF condition is true (or not true) THEN do the following calculation

In the Filter section, one or a number of conditions are set which 'filter' the type of data going through and, in the Processing section, one or a number of calculations/actions are specified to take place on the data.

Figure 16.1 The expert Logical edit window

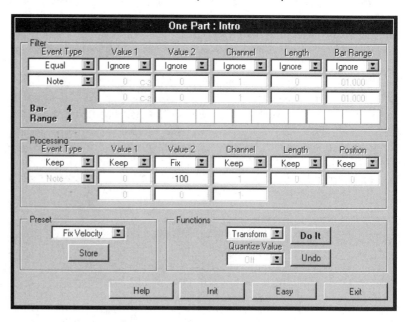

Opening the contents of the pop-up menus which are marked with downward pointing arrows reveals the myriad of possibilities available in Logical edit. However, things may have already become a little too complicated so let's get straight on to three introductory examples.

Logical solutions

Increasing the velocities of notes

Problem
The feel of the bass line you have just recorded is perfect but it was played too softly.

Solution

- While still on the Arrange window make sure the Part or Track in question is selected. Open Logical edit by selecting it from the Edit menu or use ctrl + L (Mac: command + L) on the computer keyboard.
- Ensure that the screen is in expert mode and initialise it by clicking on the 'Init' button.
- Adjust the Filter section so that the Event Type (column 1) reads 'Equal Note'. Leave all other Filter columns in 'ignore' mode.
- Set the Processing section Value 2 column (velocity) to 'Plus 10'.
- If the screen has been correctly initialised Logical edit should already be in the default 'Transform' mode (see Figure 16.2).

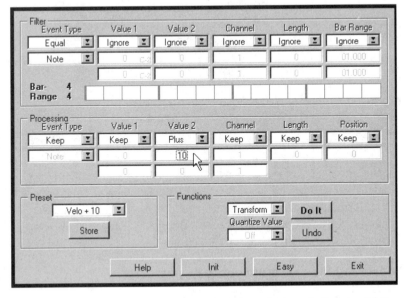

Figure 16.2 Adding 10 to the velocity

Clicking on the 'Do It' button adds 10 to the velocity of all notes in the chosen Part or Track thus making the result louder.

To verify the result try playing the Part while adding the velocity and click more than once if more velocity is required. Why 10 ? MIDI specifies a range of 0 – 127 for the velocity of notes and 10 makes a reasonable audible difference. But please note that not all synths react in the same way to velocity information and some are not velocity sensitive at all.

Making a part more staccato

Problem
You have recorded a repeating synth melody which is perfect except that you would like it to be more staccato. (i.e. notes with short durations).

Solution

- Select the Part or Track in question in the Arrange window and open Logical edit. Initialise the screen.
- Set the Filter section Event Type to 'Equal note'.
- Set the Processing section Length column to 'Fix 96'.
- Ensure that the Function mode is in 'Transform' (see Figure 16.3).

Figure 16.3 Setting all notes
to short durations

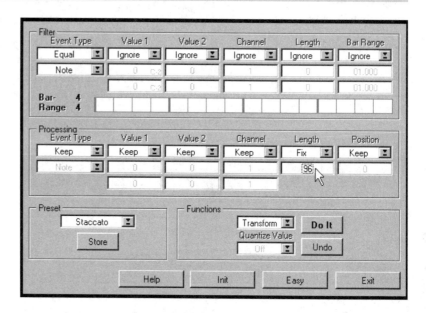

Clicking on 'Do It' will change the length of all notes in the chosen Part or Track to semiquavers i.e. short notes. Why 96 ? Cubase VST has a resolution of 384 pulses (ticks) per quarter note. There are four semiquavers in a quarter note. 384 divided by 4 equals 96. If this is not staccato enough then try 48 or even 24 in the Length column.

Separating the bass drum out to its own Track

Problem
You often program drums as MIDI tracks instead of Drum tracks and the Part you have recorded includes the bass drum, snare and hi-hat on the same Track. You would like to separate the bass drum onto its own Track in order to do some detailed editing.

Solution

- Open Logical edit from the Arrange window (since the Extract function is *not* available if you enter Logical edit from one of the editors).
- Set the Filter section Event Type column to 'Equal note', and the Value 1 column to 'Equal 36 (C1)'.
- Select 'Extract' in the Function mode pop-up menu.
- Leave all the columns in the Processing section in 'Keep' mode (see Figure 16.4).

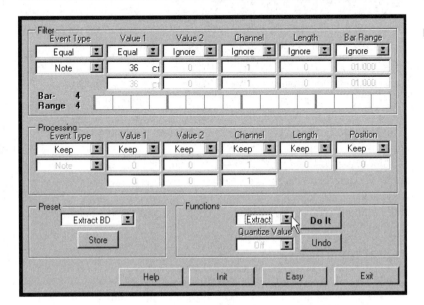

Figure 16.4 Extracting a bass drum

Clicking on 'Do It' will extract note number 36 (or C1) from the Part and automatically create a new Track on the Arrange window within which to store the extracted notes.

Why note number 36 ? The range of the full piano keyboard is expressed in MIDI as note numbers 21 to 108. As many readers will already know, the standard position for the main bass drum happens to be 36. This is also usually the first key of the keyboard found on most modern synthesizers.

There are other ways of dealing with the above problems but these examples have been used as a simple way in to Logical edit. Things have been kept at a deliberately basic level to take into account those who have never used Logical edit before and those who maybe don't know too much about the theory of MIDI. Of course, Logical edit is capable of very much more elaborate and exciting functions.

Further exploration

The first example above considered increasing the velocity of *all* notes within the Part. This is not particularly subtle and the requirements of musicians are often a lot more elaborate than this. So how do we treat a

Part where just a few notes are getting lost in the mix but the velocity level of the majority are OK. ?

It is simple really. A threshold is set below which the offending events alone will be subject to a set velocity increase. Or, in the language of Logical edit:

- Set the Filter section to 'Equal note' in the Event Type column and 'Lower (than) 30' (or some other threshold) in the Value 2 (Velocity) column.
- Set the Processing section Value 2 column to 'Plus 50' (or some other chosen level).
- Set the function to 'Transform'.

In this example, clicking on 'Do It' will search for all notes with a velocity (value 2) lower than 30 and add 50 to them. The result is that all previously inaudible notes will have been brought up to a reasonable level. Of course, the threshold set in the Processing section and the velocity added to the chosen notes depends on the user's judgement as to which notes should be affected and by how much. Each Part's treatment will obviously vary.

Things are becoming a little more elaborate but so far only the Transform and Extract functions have been used. However, there are also possibilities with quantize, delete, insert and copy, and, rather than use single columns to process the data, multiple columns could be employed.

Logical quantize

Imagine a composite drum Part where you wish to hard quantize just the bass drum leaving the feel of the rest of the kit intact. Simple:

- In the Processing section, select 'Equal note' in the Event Type column and specify the bass drum note in the Value 1 column.
- Select Quantize as the function and enter the required quantize value in the quantize pop-up menu.

Clicking on 'Do It' quantizes the bass drum to the desired value using Over quantize.

Logical delete

Users of GM compatible MIDI files are often delighted when all the program change messages embedded in the song call up the correct patches on their favourite GM modules and synths. However, many users will possess non-GM equipment and the program changes may wreak chaos when playing back the song. The simple answer is to delete them and put in your own program changes for each Track or Part.

There are several ways of deleting program changes but Logical edit probably provides the quickest:

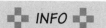

INFO

The main quantize functions of Cubase VST work upon note data alone but, using Logical edit, you may also quantize other kinds of data. This could be used, for example, to reduce pitch bend data. In the Processing section, simply select 'Equal pitch bend' in the Event Type column, choose a quantize value in the quantize pop-up and select the quantize function. This is a good alternative to 'Reduce continuous data' found in the main Functions menu which performs a similar thinning out of the data.

- Select *all* Parts in the Arrangement using ctrl + A (Mac: command + A) and open Logical edit using ctrl + L (Mac: command + L).
- In the Filter section, set the Event Type column to 'Equal program change'.
- Set 'Delete' in the functions pop-up menu.

Clicking on 'Do It' deletes all program changes in the arrangement. This kind of operation could equally be applied to a single track or used to perform blanket deletions of other kinds of data. Remember, however, that program changes contained within the Inspector will not be included in the deletion process.

Logical insert

The Logical 'insert' function 'adds' notes to the Part or Track. For example, if you needed to double up the snare drum with a handclap in a drum part, Logical edit provides an easy way to do it:

- In the Filter section, select 'Equal note' in the Event Type column and the note of the snare drum in the Value 1 column.
- In the Processing section, select 'fix' and the note of the handclap in the Value 1 column.
- Select Insert as the function.

When used, the result is that for every snare drum that Logical edit finds in the Part or Track a handclap will be inserted at the same position. Using the other four columns of the Processing section the velocity, the MIDI channel, the length or the position of the handclap could also be changed.

Logical copy

'Copy' is similar to 'Extract' in that it is available only when entering Logical edit from the Arrange window. It is best used for situations requiring the selective copying of events onto a new Track. Simply set the Filter section Event Type, Value 1, and/or other, columns to the values of the data to be copied and select the 'Copy' function. A new Track will be automatically created in the Arrange window containing the copied data. Note that the Processing section is non-operational in 'copy' and 'extract' mode.

The processing possibilities

To get an idea of what else is available in Logical edit consider the wealth of functions available in the pop-up menus of the Processing section. There is the possibility of adding or subtracting, multiplying or dividing the chosen data by a given value, fixing the data type to a set value, setting a velocity ramp between two values, and random operations on data.

Certain of these functions are better suited to specific data types and operations. For example:

- It is possible to raise the values of notes by one semitone using 'multiply by 1.02' ! but it is far easier to simply use 'plus 1'.
- The multiplication function is far better used in the Position column; if the position is multiplied by two this will halve the tempo of a given Part and if we divide by two this will double the tempo. These two functions are already saved as presets in the ten presets which come with Cubase VST.
- The dynamic function (dyn) can be effectively used in the Velocity column (Value 2) to produce crescendos and diminuendos. i.e. sequences can be faded in or out between two user defined values. This is effective for snare or timpani rolls and all other musical situations requiring dynamic ornamentation.
- It is probably irresistible to use the random function on note values at least once but random can be used to better effect with note velocity. If you have a Part that seems rather lifeless or a repetitive synth Part into which you wish to inject a little variation then entering, for example, a random variation between 85 and 100 in the Velocity column (Value 2) may be the answer.

A common problem in MIDI based music is the lifeless hi-hat, and this could be dealt with in a similar way to the previous example. However, introducing something a little more musical than randomness requires some Logical edit know-how and this leads us on to the next set of practical examples.

Hi-hat and rhythm processing

A lifeless hi-hat may be due to the choice of sound and/or the feel of the playing. The feel or the groove is dictated by the position and the accent of the notes. Position is better dealt with using Cubase VST's groove quantize, but accent can be processed very efficiently using Logical edit. A real drummer would obviously accent certain beats and these accents would also relate to what else is going on with the kit. It is almost impossible to recreate the feel of an excellent drummer but, using Logical edit, we can make up for some of the deficiencies of something that was badly played or input in step time.

This tutorial assumes that the hi-hat Part to be processed is very simple, i.e. continuous 1/16th notes occurring throughout a four bar pattern in 4/4 time. Only closed hi-hats are being taken into consideration. The aim is to accent the first and third beats of each bar and to make all the down beats a little stronger than the up beats. Once the technique has been mastered in its basic form the user can go on to experiment with more elaborate procedures.

Select a hi-hat Part in the Arrange window that is in need of livening up and open Key edit, (or Drum edit if preferred). While in the editor select the Mastertrack list editor from the Edit menu. Double click in the 'Signature' column and change the time signature of the passage being processed to 4/16.

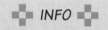

INFO

This section describes how to get some life back into an uninspired hi-hat part. This procedure could also be adapted for any kind of rhythmic material.

Why change the time signature? Because we need to prepare the scene for Logical edit to accentuate certain notes within each beat. 4/16 is equal to one quarter note beat in 4/4 time. This is a temporary change which will be reversed when processing is complete.

Now open Logical edit. Let's start by setting all the hi-hats to velocity values of between 70 and 80:

- Set the Filter section to 'Equal note' in the Event Type column.
- Set the Processing section to a random value of between 70 and 80 in the Value 2 column.
- Set Logical edit to 'Transform' and click on 'Do It' (see Figure 16.5).

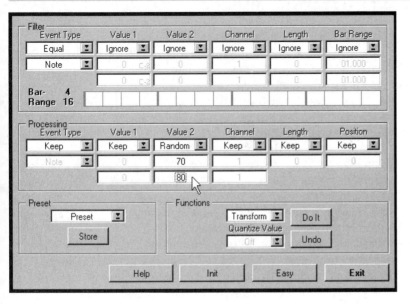

Figure 16.5 Hi-hat variations

Each stage of the process can be saved as a preset for future use or some users may feel comfortable working on the fly. Presets are stored by holding alt (PC version only) while selecting an existing preset which is to be overwritten. Clicking on 'Store' saves the current values under this preset name. Double clicking on the name opens an input box where a new name may be entered.

Next, a stress is required on all the down beats of the Part. A real drummer might do this but it depends on the style of the music. It is achieved in Logical edit by using the 'Bar Range' function of the Filter section. Without changing the previous Logical edit settings proceed as follows :

- Set a filter for all notes 'inside' the range '1.0 to 1.48' in the bar range column. This can be selected directly in the Bar Range column or the range can also be adjusted using click and drag in the graphic bar range found between the Filter and Processing sections.
- Set the Processing Value 2 column to plus 20 and click on the 'Do It' button (see Figure 16.6).

Figure 16.6 Using bar range
to target the down beats

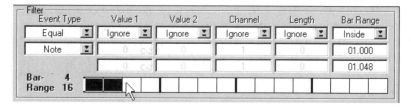

The graphic bar range is a graphic representation of a time segment of the music. With the current time signature set to 4/16 this time segment is equal to one beat. If the hi-hat Part contains continuous 1/16 notes then each successive group of four such notes will be acted upon according to how things are filtered.

A slightly lesser accent could be put on the third of each group of 1/16 notes (as in Figure 16.7), this time setting the Value 2 column to plus 10. The Bar Range filter should read 'inside 3.0 – 3.48'. Click on 'Do It' and play the hi-hat Part while still in Logical edit. Things should be sounding slightly more musical already.

Now exit Logical edit to get back to Key edit. Open the Mastertrack and change the time signature back to 4/4. Escape and return to Logical edit. Accents on the first and third beats of the bar will finish the exercise.

Figure 16.8 shows the accenting of the first beat of the bar, i.e. notes 'Inside 1.0 – 1.48' in the Bar Range column of the Filter section are processed with a 'plus 10' in the Value 2 (velocity) column of the Processing section. Finally the third beat of the bar is treated similarly but with a subtle velocity increase of 'plus 5'. As an alternative try accenting the second and fourth beats of the bar instead.

When you are satisfied with the results, go back into Key edit and 'keep' the changes to go back to the Arrange window. The hi-hat Part should sound more lively and musically expressive, but if more 'feel' is required then using one of the grooves in Groove quantize may be the answer.

Figure 16.7 A slightly lesser
accent

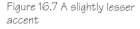

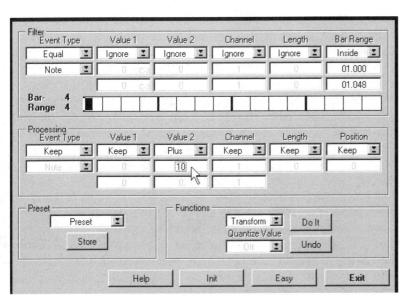

Figure 16.8 Accenting the first beat of the bar

If the results are not to your liking then you may need to experiment with the velocity values used in each preset. Not all hi-hats respond equally to velocity data, and subtle changes may not register at all in some drum machines. In order to achieve a satisfactory result, knowledge of how the target machine responds to velocity is as important as any knowledge of Logical edit.

The use of the Mastertrack with Logical edit greatly enhances the power of the Bar Range column. For example, if every other note needs to be selected in a Part consisting of equi-distant 1/16 notes, then using Logical edit with the Mastertrack time signature set to 2/16 makes the process easy. The Bar Range can be set to filter through either the first or the second of each pair of 1/16 notes. Experimentation with other time signatures can also prove fruitful. Try changing the time signature to 3/16 and then put an accent of 'plus 20' on the second 1/16 beat of each 3/16 bar. The result is a kind of continuous 'off the beat' feel. Remember to put back the original time signature into the Mastertrack after processing is complete.

The procedure for hi-hat parts described here can obviously be adapted to other kinds of musical data. But before going too wild remember that while it is easy to improve a very poor sounding part, it is also fairly easy to ruin a reasonably good sounding part. So tread carefully and always work with Logical edit out of Key Edit or one of the other edit windows. Only when you are completely satisfied should you keep the changes and go back to the Arrange window. This is particularly important if you have decided to process an entire Track.

Controlling the controllers

The so-called continuous controller type of MIDI data is a non-note part of the MIDI Specification used for controlling the notes themselves or other non-note parameters. Most readers will be familiar with pitch bend and modulation and the wheels that control them found on many synthesizers.

Pitch bend is not actually classed as a continuous controller but assumes its own special data type within the MIDI Specification. Modulation is usually classed as Controller number 1. These controllers could be processed in Logical edit but, it has to be said, that they are probably best left to the dedicated wheels and other parts of Cubase VST.

However, there are a number of more exotic controllers in the MIDI specification for which it is not always practical nor desirable to use the wheels. Logical edit can manipulate this kind of controller data in a way which would be difficult to achieve in real-time. In some instances, it is the only sensible method to achieve the desired result.

Imagine trying to record a fast, accurate MIDI auto-pan effect in real time; nearly impossible. But with Logical edit this kind of thing could be tackled reasonably quickly. What we need is a Logical edit controller tool-box. The examples outlined below show, above all, ways of 'inserting' controller events after the notes have been recorded. Let's start with auto-pan, but we will also be going on to explore tremolo and key gate effects, all created with the help of Logical edit.

Common to some of the tools will be the need to pre-fill the Part with a dummy controller. Why? Because when the 'Insert' function of Logical edit is used, the data to be inserted needs something to latch onto. 'Insert' adds new events to a Part only in relation to events already in existence in that Part. If a Part is empty 'insert' has no function. Hence, pre-filling the Part with dummy events ensures that new events can be added at the required resolution. All will become clearer as we go on.

Before going on to specific examples, let's just take a moment to understand some theory. When the Event Type is set to 'Control Change' in the Filter or Processing sections of the Logical edit window, the Value 1 and Value 2 columns assume different meanings. Instead of the MIDI note number, the Value 1 column corresponds to any one of the available controllers in the MIDI specification (modulation is specified as Controller number 1, volume is Controller number 7, pan is Controller number 10 and so on). Instead of velocity, the Value 2 column defines the setting of the chosen controller. Both columns may assume values of between 0 and 127.

Auto-pan

Now let's get down to business. To pre-fill the Part with dummy controller data proceed as follows:

- Choose or create a Part on the Arrange window and open List edit.
- Set the insert line to Control Change and set Snap to 8.
- Use 'fill' in the Function menu to insert dummy controller events at 1/8 note intervals. Leave the controller events at their default value of 0. Controller 0 should have no effect on the rest of your data but if it is not convenient, change it to one of the general purpose controllers between 16 and 19, for example, using Logical edit.
- 'Keep' the Part and then open Key edit.
- Open the Controller display and select the appropriate controller icon; a line of dummy controller

events should be visible. These events should have no effect whatsoever on the actual music; they are simply used as the framework upon which we can attach other controller data which *will* have an effect on the music. The dummy events will be deleted after editing has been completed.

The auto-pan effect requires the creation of five Logical edit presets. These will be named as follows:

- pan L to R
- pan R to L
- select pan
- speed up
- slow down

The use of these presets requires the Part to have been filled with dummy controller events, as just described.

MIDI specifies Controller 10 as Pan. A value of 0 for this controller pans the sound to the extreme left and a value of 127 pans to the extreme right. The first preset, pan L to R, does simply that, it pans the chosen Track from left to right in the stereo image.

Inserting a ramp of left to right Pan events
To create the first preset proceed as follows:

- Open Logical edit in Expert mode.
- In the Filter section, set the Event Type to 'Equal control change' and the Value 1 column to 'Equal 0'.
- In the Processing section, 'Fix' the Value 1 column to 10, set the Value 2 column to a 'Dyn' setting of 0 to 127 and set the Position column to 'Divide' by 2.
- Set Logical edit to 'Insert' mode and store as a preset under the appropriate name (see Figure 16.9).

This preset inserts an ascending ramp of Controller 10 events for every dummy controller event it finds.

Inserting a ramp of right to left Pan events
For the second preset, pan R to L, proceed as follows:

- In the Filter section, set the Event Type to Control Change and the Value 1 column to 'Equal 10'.
- In the Processing section, 'Fix' the Value 1 column to 10, set the Value 2 column to 'Invert' and set the Position column to 'Plus' 768.
- Once again, set Logical edit to 'Insert' mode and store as a preset under the appropriate name (see Figure 16.10).

Figure 16.9 Inserting a ramp of left to right pan events

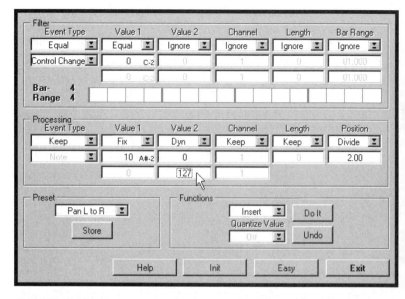

Figure 16.10 Inserting a Right to Left Pan

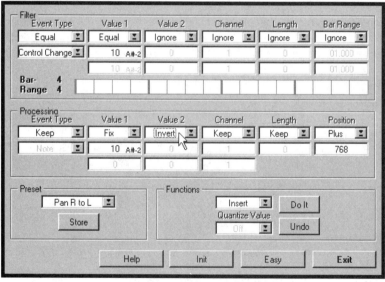

This preset will use the controller data created by the first preset to insert an inverted version of the events half a bar (768 ticks) later.

Select Pan

For the Select pan preset proceed as follows:

- In the Filter section, set the Event Type to 'Equal control change' and the Value 1 column to 'Equal 10'.
- Ignore the Processing section, set Logical edit to 'Select' mode and store as a preset (see Figure 16.11).

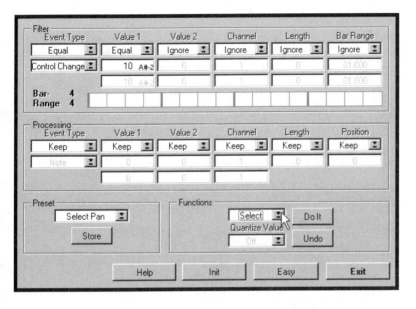

Figure 16.11 Selecting Pan data

This preset simply selects all Pan data in the Part. Note that the Select function is available only if Logical edit has been opened from one of the other editors.

Speed up preset

For the speed up preset proceed as follows:

- In the Filter section, set the Event Type to 'Equal control change' and the Value 1 column to 'Equal 10'.
- In the Processing section, set the Position column to 'Divide' by 2.
- Set Logical edit to 'Transform' mode and store as a preset (see Figure 16.12).

Figure 16.12 The speed up preset

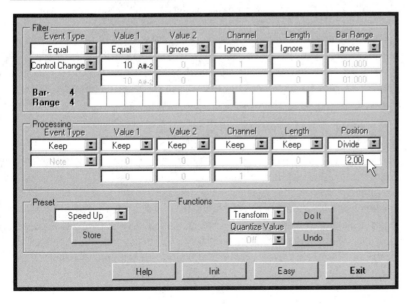

Slow down preset

The slow down preset is created in the same manner except that multiply by 2 should be entered in the Position column. The speed presets double or halve the speed of all Pan events they find in the Part.

DelDummy preset

Finally, before using the presets we must create one more general purpose preset which will be used to delete the dummy controller data initially recorded into the Part. We will name this as DelDummy and it is created as follows:

- In the Filter section, set the Event Type to 'Equal control change' and set the Value 1 column to 'Equal 0'.
- Ignore the Processing section.
- Set Logical edit to 'Delete' mode and store as a preset.

Of course, this preset must be adapted if a different number dummy controller has been used.

Using auto-pan tools

That completes the creation of the auto-pan tools. To use them, proceed as follows:

- Create a new two bar Part on the Arrange window and fill it with dummy controller events as described above.
- Set the Track of the new Part to the appropriate MIDI channel i.e. the same MIDI channel as the Track to which you wish to apply an auto-pan effect.
- Select the new Part and open Key edit. Select the Pan Controller from the menu in the Controller display by clicking on the controller icon.
- Set a one bar loop by clicking and dragging the mouse pointer in the position bar. Make sure that the pop-up event 'Select' menu, (next to the Goto menu), is in looped mode.
- Action the first auto-pan preset, Pan L to R, from the pop-up logical presets menu found in the main Functions menu. A number of Pan events will be inserted into the first half of the selected bar.
- Go back to the logical presets menu and action the second preset Pan R to L. This takes care of the second half of the bar with an inverted copy of the first half.

The first two presets have been designed to work with a looped 1 bar section in 4/4 time. You should now have a 'pyramid' shaped pattern of Pan events visible in the controller display (Figure 16.13).

This pyramid is the essential building block of the auto-pan. At the moment it will smoothly pan a sound from left to right and back to left again over a length of one bar. What is needed now is a way of repeating the pan over the length of the Part and of managing the speed of the auto-pan. This is achieved with a combination of the Logical edit auto-pan tools and other functions of Cubase VST as follows:

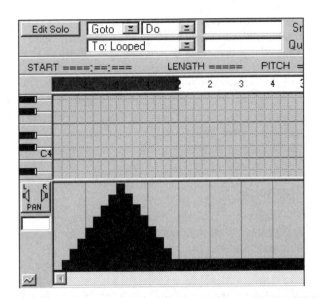

Figure 16.13 The pan pyramid

- First, select all Pan events using the 'Select pan' preset.
- If you have created a Part of four bars or more, make sure that the pop-up edit 'select' menu is in 'Selected looped' mode and use 'Repeat' found in the pop-up 'Function' menu of Key edit. The selected looped section, (i.e. the Pan events alone), will be repeated up to the end of the part.
- If you have created a two bar Part, as recommended, it is easier to use the copy and paste functions found in the Edit menu to repeat the data.
- To change the speed of the auto-pan, de-select the loop and use the speed up and slow down presets.
- Continue to use Key edit's 'repeat', or 'copy and paste', with the Logical edit speed presets to arrive at the desired result. Very fast, perfectly formed auto-panning is possible (see Figure 16.14).

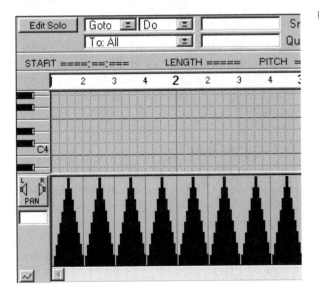

Figure 16.14 The Final Result

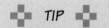

This kind of effect is difficult to achieve without the Logical edit auto-pan toolbox. Finally, when completely satisfied with the result use the 'DelDummy' preset, as described above, to delete all the dummy controller events that were input at the beginning of the operation and leave Key edit using the return key to keep the edits.

Remember that a very long Part full of pan data should not be created as this quickly becomes very memory hungry. A two bar Part is usually sufficient. Once back in the Arrange window, ghost parts of the original can be created and the auto-pan repeated for as long as desired.

Tremolo

The creation of Logical edit presets to create a MIDI tremolo effect is really very easy since the presets required are almost exactly the same as the auto-pan presets.

Tremolo is the rapid variation of the volume of a signal at a fixed rate and depth – the rate and depth are usually adjustable to produce the desired intensity and effect. So, to create this effect with MIDI, we will need to manipulate Controller 7 (Volume) data.

Proceed as follows:

- Load in or create the auto-pan presets (if they are not already in memory) as described above, and go into Logical edit.
- Every time you see a 10 (Pan) in the Value 1 column of either the Filter or the Processing sections of each preset, change this to a 7 (Volume).
- Store the new settings under new preset names and then follow the procedure for use as described for the auto-pan operation.
- This time you will be working on Volume data and not Pan data so you will need to be looking at Volume data in the Controller display of Key edit.
- Remember that, in order for things to work properly, you must prefill the Part with dummy Controller 0 events (or another dummy controller number if 0 is not suitable).

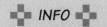

Alternatively, take an existing Part containing auto-pan data and simply convert the Pan data to Volume data using Logical edit. Remember, however, that the rate of the tremolo effect will invariably be faster than that of an auto-pan. The result, in both cases, is a very convincing and effective tremolo effect.

Key-trigger gate

Logical edit is good at converting one data type into another, and this feature can be used to simulate a key-trigger gate effect. But before creating the necessary presets we must first understand exactly what is meant by a key-trigger gate.

Most readers will know what a noise gate is; it is an audio device which opens or closes the signal path according to various threshold, ratio and envelope settings found on the unit. Among its simplest functions might be to close the signal path when the sound level falls below the threshold in order to block out unwanted background noise (in between the sung lines of a vocalist, for example). The signal path from the microphone would only be open when the vocalist is actually singing. Thus the opening and closing of the gate responds according to the characteristics of the input signal in relation to the user settings on the unit.

However, the gate can also be set to respond to a secondary input source. This is usually known as the key input. In this mode, for example, a sustained chord sound (main signal) could be gated in and out according to the rhythm of a hi-hat (key input signal).

A simple key-trigger effect can be mimicked using MIDI Volume data. The aim of the exercise would be to control the volume level of one Track according to the rhythm and intensity of another. The notes and the velocities of the chosen key source Track would be translated into Volume data. When there *is* a note the MIDI gate would be open and when there is *not* a note it would be closed.

With Logical edit it is easy to translate notes into Volume Controller events. The note values themselves need not be translated. Each note event can be simply fixed as a Controller 7 (Volume) event in the Value 1 column of Logical edit. The velocities of the notes in the Value 2 column can be directly translated into the actual Volume level for each Controller 7 event.

So the opening of the MIDI gate presents no real problem but the closing of the gate is not so simple. Logical edit does not allow access to the Note Off element of note events. It is, therefore, not possible to use the end of a note as the point in time to close the gate, by inserting a zero Volume event. The solution involves the creation of four Logical edit presets which will become part of our ever expanding Logical edit controller toolbox. They are named, in the order in which they will be used, as KeyGate 1, 2, 3 and 4.

For the purposes of this exercise, reference will be made to 'zero volume' and 'volume up' events. Zero volume refers to MIDI Controller 7 events with their levels set to 0, and volume up refers to MIDI Controller 7 events with their levels set to anything between 1 and 127.

Creating KeyGate 1

KeyGate 1' involves the insertion of zero volume events and is created in Logical edit in expert mode as follows:

- In the Filter section, set the Event Type to 'Equal note' and the Length column to 'Lower than 144'.
- In the Processing section, 'Fix' the Event Type to 'Control Change', 'Fix' the Value 1 column to 7, 'Fix' the Value 2 column to 0 and the Position column to 'Plus 40'.
- Set Logical edit to insert mode and store as a preset under the appropriate name (see Figure 16.15).

Figure 16.15 KeyGate 1

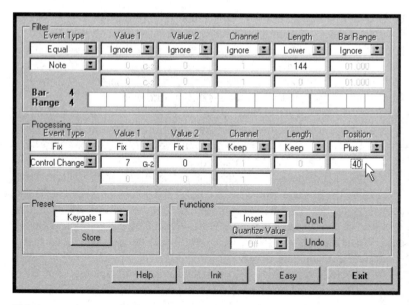

This preset inserts zero volume events at just under 1/32 (40 ticks) of a note after the onset of each note it finds within the Part whose length is less than a dotted 1/16 note (144 ticks). Or to put it more simply, this preset produces the closing of the gate at a very short period after the onset of each very short note it finds in the Part.

Creating KeyGate 2

The Logical edit settings for KeyGate 2 are similar to KeyGate 1 except that the Length column of the Filter section should be changed to 'Inside 144 – 240' and the Position column of the Processing section should be changed to 'Plus 88'.

This preset works in the same way as KeyGate 1 but is concerned with notes of slightly longer duration.

Creating KeyGate 3

KeyGate 3 is, once again, similar to the first two presets except that the Length column of the Filter section should be changed to 'Higher than 239' and the Position column of the Processing section should be changed to 'Plus 136'. This preset inserts zero volume events for all the remaining longer notes within the Part.

You may be asking why three presets have been created when one would have been sufficient. It's true that we could have regulated the length of the gate with one simple preset but an attempt has been made to create something a little more musical which, after exhaustive tests, was found to simulate more closely the actions of a real key-trigger gate effect. In any case, those readers requiring something very simple could use a single preset for the purposes of the zero volume Part of this exercise and, of course, the settings of each preset could be changed for experimental purposes and other effects.

Creating KeyGate 4

Finally, KeyGate 4 is created as follows:

- In the Filter section, set the Event Type to 'Equal note' and ignore all other columns.
- In the Processing section, 'Fix' the Event Type to 'Control Change' and 'Fix' the Value 1 column to 7.
- Set Logical edit to 'Transform' mode and store as a preset under the appropriate name (see Figure 16.16).

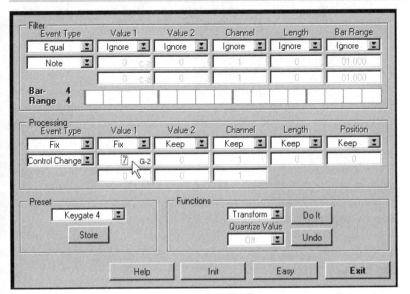

Figure 16.16 KeyGate 4

This preset is the volume up part of the procedure. It transforms all notes in the Part into volume up events. At the same time, the velocities (Value 2) of these notes are transformed into the actual volume level for each event. In this way, not only do we have a key-trigger gate effect which is sensitive to the length of the notes (thanks to the first three presets) but we have one which is also sensitive to the intensity (velocity) of the playing.

Using the Keygates

To use the presets proceed as follows:

- Copy the Part, or mix down the Parts, that you wish to use as the source for the key-trigger gate effect. A hi-hat Part or a bass drum and snare are good for testing the effect.
- Select the new Part and open Key edit.
- Select Volume in the Controller display and use the four Logical edit presets in their numbered order from the pop-up logical presets menu found in the main Functions menu.

The first three presets insert zero volume events so there will be no changes particularly visible in the Controller display window, but the moment KeyGate 4 is used all notes in the Part will disappear and be replaced by a corresponding series of Volume events. Figure 16.17 shows

Figure 16.17 Before and after using the KeyGate tools

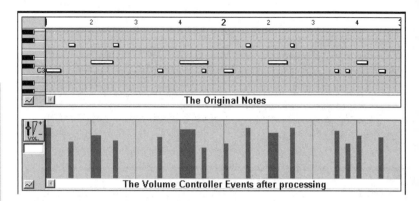

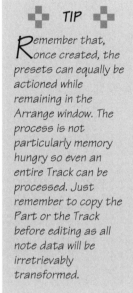

TIP

Remember that, once created, the presets can equally be actioned while remaining in the Arrange window. The process is not particularly memory hungry so even an entire Track can be processed. Just remember to copy the Part or the Track before editing as all note data will be irretrievably transformed.

two Key edit windows displaying the original Part at the top, and the same Part, after processing, below it.

When you are satisfied with the results, use 'Keep' to go back to the Arrange window. Change the KeyGate Track to the desired MIDI channel and the Volume data will be imposed upon any music already on that channel. Alternatively, try playing a sustained chord on the chosen channel while cycling on the KeyGate Part.

The settings of the presets were established after tests with various rhythm patterns and, if the source Parts are well chosen, there should be no problems. The KeyGate presets may be saved as part of a Set up or Song file and loaded back into Cubase VST when required.

Logical conclusion

The examples presented here provide a useful companion to the Logical edit section of the Cubase VST documentation, and those readers who re-created these examples for themselves will have benefited most.

Logical edit is best understood in the actual doing rather than in the theory. It is hoped that this chapter has helped de-mystify Logical edit and that you will be encouraged to explore the Logical edit window further.

Knowing Logical edit can lead to a more complete understanding of MIDI and Cubase VST itself. By combining the strengths of different parts of the program with the power of Logical edit, the user is encouraged to understand the real capabilities of the whole system. And, if Logical edit has been mastered, then Cubase VST's 'Input Transform' function in the Options menu becomes child's play.

Lastly, as a general rule to using Logical edit, always initialise the screen before setting up an edit or changing Presets. Also remember that, if Logical edit is opened from one of the other editors after having select-ed a note, the Filter section will display the note value and velocity of that selection. This increases the speed with which users can target specific data for Logical edit processing.

17

Choosing a PC audio card

Finding a suitable audio card/sound card is very important for the successful operation of Cubase VST. The basic Cubase VST requirements for an audio card are outlined in Chapters 2 and 18. This chapter explores the features of a number of popular audio cards which were available at the time of publication. Each was tested with Cubase VST and are rated in terms of their ease of installation, compatibility with the program and their audio sound quality. The information provided should help in the choice and installation of your own card.

It is emphasised that the cards have been tested specifically with Cubase VST in mind. Cards are supplied with various software applications and other features/options which may or may not be desirable to the user. To comment on the entire range of features for each card is beyond the scope of this chapter.

All cards were installed into the same computer (as specified at the end of Chapter 18) and, in the case of the ISA type cards, in the same slot at the extreme edge of the motherboard. This position maximised the card's distance from the graphics card and the other components of the computer and thus minimised noise and interference.

Manufacturers provide signal-to-noise (S/N) ratios which give an indication of the noise floor of the card (the level of noise present in the electronic circuitry). The S/N ratio is a measure of the difference between the loudest and the quietest sounds without there being any interference from the background noise in the system. The quoted figures are often 'A weighted'. 'A weighted' figures are those tuned to the frequency response of the human ear and, although they look good on paper, they can sometimes confuse the issue. If all cards were measured in exactly the same way then there would be no problem but unfortunately different manufacturers quote figures which have been measured in different ways. The rule when comparing the specifications of cards is to make sure that the S/N ratio has been measured in the same way.

The signal-to-noise ratio tests presented below were identical for all cards and provides an indication of the noise performance which can be expected. Similar tests in other PC systems may yield a different set of results since audio performance varies according to the location of the card inside the PC and the other components which are present. The results presented provide an unweighted reference which makes a good point of comparison with the manufacturer's A weighted figures.

Note that standard audio cards which use the supplied ASIO multimedia driver suffer from an inevitable delay ('latency') between the input and output, when monitoring via Cubase VST. This is not a drawback for most users since they can monitor via the card itself or via an external mixer. The latency also causes a time delay between hearing the audio and fader and control movements in the Master window, Monitor mixer window etc. Special ASIO drivers, available for a number of cards, reduce the latency to more acceptable levels.

Other factors to bear in mind when choosing a sound card include the frequency response, the dynamic range and the distortion figures.

Frequency response

The frequency response indicates the range of frequencies the card can handle and usually includes a measure in decibels of how flat this response is across the whole spectrum. A typical frequency response figure might be: 10Hz - 22kHz (+/- 1dB). This indicates a wide frequency response across the whole audible spectrum with deviations of up to 1dB. This gives a very wide and flat frequency response. A good frequency response should be as wide as possible and the deviation should be as small as possible, indicating that there is no undue colouration of the sound.

As a reference point, note that the human ear has a frequency range of approximately 20Hz – 20kHz (this range reduces with age, particularly in the upper frequency limit).

Dynamic range

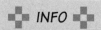

The dynamic range is the total usable range of audio level between the background noise of the system, at the lower extreme, and the point just before distortion ('clipping') sets in, at the upper extreme. This is measured in decibels and typical figures for a 16 bit digital system fall between 85dB to 95dB. The theoretical maximum dynamic range for a 16 bit system is 96dB. The greater the dynamic range, the better the performance of the system.

Distortion

Distortion is usually indicated by the letters THD; Total Harmonic Distortion. This is a measure of undesirable harmonic multiples of the original waveform which can be introduced into the signal. This is measured with a percentage figure and good distortion performance should be below 0.1%.

There now follows a description of a number of audio cards which were tested with Cubase VST.

Guillemot Home Studio Pro64 sound card (with daughter board)

General specifications

The Home Studio Pro64 sound card consists of a main board and a digital daughter board (see Figures 17.1 and 17.2).

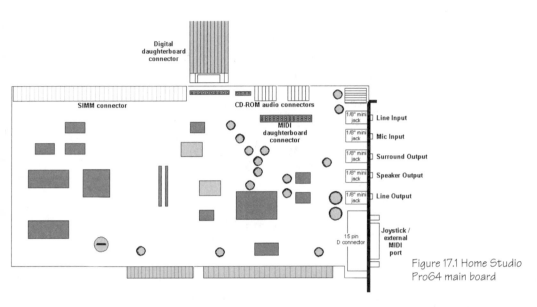

Figure 17.1 Home Studio Pro64 main board

The basic specifications of the main board are as follows:

Card type: ISA
Audio features:
    16/18 bit analog-to-digital (ADC) and digital-to-analog converter (DAC)
    sampling rate: 4kHz to 44.1kHz
    signal-to-noise ratio: >=91dB (A weighted figure for digital daughter board)
    full duplex operation
    on-board RISC based DSP, 50 million instructions per second (MIPS)
    microphone input (for high impedance 600ohm microphone)
    CD audio input on card
    stereo line in
    stereo amplified output (also suitable for headphones)
    standard stereo line out
    (all external inputs/outputs on 1/8 inch mini-jacks)
The specifications of the digital daughter board include:
    S/PDIF digital in/out on gold plated RCA phono connectors
    direct to digital signal processor stereo line in on gold plated RCA phono connectors
    direct from digital signal processor stereo line out on gold plated RCA phono connectors
Wavetable synthesiser featuring:
    64 note polyphony
    16 channel multi-timbral operation
    GM/GS compatibility
    128 instruments with 97 variation sounds
    200 percussion sounds
MIDI:
    MIDI in/out connectors (via 15 pin D connector, cable supplied as standard)
    separate drivers for wavetable synthesiser and external MIDI device
    comprehensive MIDI implementation

Figure 17.2 Home Studio
Pro64 daughterboard

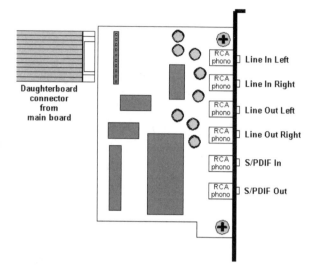

Figure 17.3 Basic ASIO
Multimedia setup dialogue

Installation

The physical installation of the card into the PC presented no real difficulties. However, attaching the cable connector for the daughter board required the use of considerable force since the socket was very tight. It is preferable, therefore, to attach the cable before fitting the card into the ISA slot and securing it onto the back plane. The daughter board is best installed in the next slot position.

The Home Studio Pro64 card is plug and play compatible and, upon switching on the computer, the card was recognised and driver installation proceeded with no problems.

Setting up for use with Cubase VST

- Select System from the Audio menu. In the Audio System Setup dialogue which appears click on the ASIO Control Panel button. This opens the basic ASIO Multimedia setup dialogue (Figure 17.3).
- The top of the dialogue features a pop-up menu of presets which, at the time of writing, did not feature the Home Studio Pro64. Therefore, you must set the parameters manually, as follows.
- Click on the advanced options button to open the Advanced Options dialogue.
- Activate 'Dream 9407, Wave nb 1' in the output port device list and 'Dream 9407, Wave Record' in the input port device list by clicking on the small boxes to the left of the device names. These are the WAV drivers for the card's digital signal processor. (When the box contains a cross it is activated).
- De-activate all other devices in the lists.
- Set the following values in the appropriate columns:
     Audio Buffers: 5
     Buffer size: 4096
- Adjust the Global settings sections as follows:
     Sync reference: DMA Block - Output

Card options
Activated: Full duplex, Open all devices before start
De-activated: Start input first

- Click on the store button and enter an appropriate name into the dialogue which appears. Click on OK to leave the Advanced Options dialogue. Your new preset should be selected in the basic ASIO Multimedia Setup dialogue and your card is now ready to use with Cubase VST at 44.1kHz.
- If you need to use Cubase VST at other sampling frequencies select a sample rate from the pop-up list near the top of the window and click on the Detect Buffer Size button for each frequency on both the input and output ports. This should find the correct buffer size for each sampling rate and the new information can all be saved as part of the same preset.

Using the Maxi Sound 64 mixer application

It is essential to run the supplied Maxi Sound 64 mixer application in order to have meaningful contact with the card since the standard Windows mixer (sndvol32.exe), does not provide the facilities for switching between the main board and the digital daughter board.

The Maxi Sound 64 mixer application is found on the CD supplied with the card in the Quartz Audiomaster folder under the name 'sndvol95.exe' or similar. If you have installed the Quartz Audiomaster SE application then you will find the Maxi Sound 64 mixer application in the Quartz Audiomaster folder (Qamms64) under the name 'sndvol64.exe'. Double clicking on this file opens the mixer application (Figures 17.4 and 17.5).

When running Cubase VST it is recommended that the Maxi Sound 64 is also run and is minimised when not in use (and never actually closed). If it is closed the sound card reverts back to its default main board configuration. In any case, it is useful to have the mixer application on standby ready for any changes needed in the audio configuration.

It is recommended that the digital daughter board is used for all serious recording applications. The main board's inputs and outputs are adequate for small demo projects but the signal-to-noise ratio of the daughter board's line inputs are significantly better. Among other things, this is because the daughter board provides a direct line input and output to and from the digital signal processor. In addition, the daughter board provides SPDIF digital in/out connectors which are invaluable for mixing

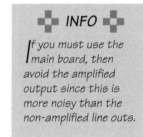

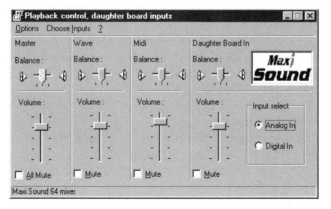

Figure 17.4 Maxi Sound 64 mixer playback control

to DAT and recording digital signals directly into Cubase VST.

The majority of Cubase VST users will want to use the card in its daughter board mode so the following steps explain how to do this:

- Launch Cubase VST and then launch the Maxi Sound 64 mixer application. It may be convenient to create a shortcut to the mixer application in the Windows Start menu. This is achieved in the Taskbar Properties dialogue of the Start menu settings. Alternatively, you could put the mixer application in your start-up folder so that the application is automatically loaded each time the computer is booted up.
- The mixer application first appears with the playback controls in main board mode. Open the Choose Inputs menu and select daughter board. This opens the mixer controls for the daughter board as in Figure 17.4. These consist of the Master Volume fader on the left and then three faders for the audio wave playback level, the MIDI output level and the input level of the daughter board's line inputs. As an initial setting leave all the faders unmuted. At this point you should be able to monitor audio and MIDI output from Cubase VST and if you apply a signal to the line inputs you should be able to hear that too (assuming that Analog In is selected on the input select panel).
- If you wish to record using the digital inputs then choose Digital In on the input select panel.
- Selecting Record in the properties sub menu of the Options menu opens the Record control mixer (Figure 17.5). The analog line in fader adjusts the recording level of the digital signal processor. If you view the input signal via VST's monitor mixer level meters you will see that it is this line in fader which regulates the recording level. Adjusting this for an optimum record level helps get the best results with the card and Cubase VST.
- To monitor via Cubase VST alone you must mute the daughter board In fader on the playback control panel. However, monitoring via VST gives an unavoidable delay (557ms). To monitor via the card do not mute the daughter board In fader and make sure that Global Disable is selected in the monitoring section of Cubase VST's audio system setup dialogue.

Testing

The Home Studio Pro64 card gave the following signal-to-noise ratio results:

- main board signal-to-noise ratio: 74dB (unweighted)
- daughter board signal-to-noise ratio: 87dB (unweighted)

In subjective tests of recordings made with Cubase VST, those made with the daughter board line inputs were perceived to contain excellent clarity and detail. Those made with the main board line inputs were less impressive, as would be expected. All indications were that this card is a rock-steady performer with Cubase VST. Full duplex operation provided full 16 bit playback while recording.

Overall impression

The Home Studio Pro64 card performs well with Cubase VST. At the time of publication there was no special ASIO driver available for this card. When used with the standard ASIO multimedia driver, it suffers from a latency of 557ms.

The downside with the card is that it does not support sample position sync and you must, therefore, choose DMA Block sync reference in the Global settings pop-up of the ASIO multimedia advanced settings dialogue. This is a less reliable method of synchronising MIDI and audio and can lead to timing drift. However, during the test period, no timing drift problems were encountered with the Home Studio Pro64. The documentation which accompanies the card is thorough but not always clear.

The sound quality of the main board is probably not sufficient for the majority of Cubase VST users but the quality of the daughter board is excellent. The daughter board provides gold plated RCA phono connectors and these help the card's quality performance and practicality when used in a studio environment. Note that the S/PDIF digital I/O supports 44.1 kHz alone; 48 kHz digital transfer is not supported.

Although the sounds in the wavetable synthesiser are not first class, it is extremely useful to have an on-board MIDI sound source as standard. Guillemot have also been kind enough to include a MIDI connector cable and basic microphone in the package and this, along with its many features, make this card outstanding value.

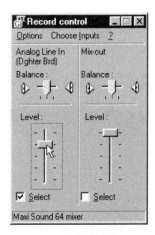

Figure 17.5 Maxi Sound 64 mixer record control

Turtle Beach Fiji pro series audio card

General specifications

The Turtle Beach Multisound Fiji is a high performance audio card aimed at the demanding audiophile and audio professional (Figure 17.6). The Fiji's general specifications are as follows:

Card type: ISA
Audio features:
    20 bit delta-sigma analog-to-digital (ADC) and digital-to-analog converters (DAC)
    sampling rate: 5.5125kHz to 48kHz
    signal-to-noise ratio: >= 97dB (A weighted)
    THD: better than 0.005% (A weighted)
    frequency response: 10Hz – 22kHz (+/– 1dB)
    full duplex operation
    on-board Motorola 56002 DSP, 20 million instructions per second (MIPS)
    Hurricane architecture (accelerated digital audio transfer)
    microphone input (supports low impedance dynamic or condenser microphones)
    CD audio input on card
    stereo line in
    stereo auxiliary input
    stereo line out
    (all external inputs/outputs on 1/8 inch mini-jacks)
    optional S/PDIF digital I/O interface
MIDI:
    MIDI in/out connectors (via 15 pin D connector, cable available as an option)
    optional Kurzweil HOMAC 32-voice synth module
    (synthesiser daughter board connector is WaveBlaster compatible)

Figure 17.6 The Fiji pro series
audio card

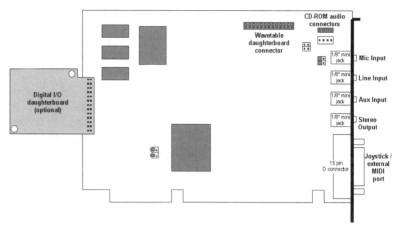

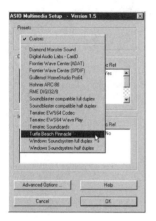

Figure 17.7 Basic ASIO
Multimedia Setup dialogue

Installation

The physical installation of the Fiji is straightforward, helped by the simple, clear instructions in the Getting Started Guide and the digital I/O connector is attached to the main part of the board with no difficulties. The Fiji is plug and play compatible and the installation of the card and its drivers is easily achieved. Version 4.0 drivers (or higher) should be used with Cubase VST.

Setting up for use with Cubase VST

- Select System from the Audio menu. In the Audio System Setup dialogue which appears click on the ASIO Control Panel button. This opens the basic ASIO Multimedia setup dialogue (see Figure 17.7).
- Open the presets dialogue and choose 'Turtle Beach Pinnacle' from the list. This is another Turtle Beach card and its settings are the same as for the Fiji. Once chosen, the card is ready to use with Cubase VST. At this point you should not need to make any further changes to the settings so, if you do not wish to explore further, move onto the next section about using the audio mixer.
- If you need to verify the settings, click on the advanced options button to open the Advanced Options dialogue.
- Ensure that 'TBS Pro Series Wave Out 1' in the output port device list and 'TBS Pro Series Wave In 1' in the input port device list are activated.
- Verify the following values in the appropriate columns:
  Audio Buffers: 5
  Buffer size: 5512
- Also verify the following parameters
  Sync reference: sample position - output
  Card options
  Activated: Full duplex, Open all devices before start
  De-activated: Start input first

Using the audio mixer

The Fiji audio card is supplied with a number of very good software applications of which the PC Audio mixer (Figure 17.8) is among the most immediately useful. The audio mixer is the most convenient location from which to control the audio signals passing through the card. It contains both the playback and the record faders. The playback channels may be muted using the right hand square button below the faders, and the record inputs are activated by clicking on the right hand square buttons below the record faders. The mixer layout also includes useful meters for monitoring incoming and outgoing signals. The left hand buttons for each fader strip provide advanced functions.

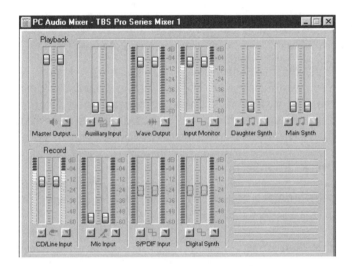

Figure 17.8 Voyetra Technologies PC audio mixer

To set up the mixer to record from the line input of the card in a Cubase VST session, proceed as follows:

- With Cubase VST already launched, open the PC audio mixer. This is achieved by double clicking on the blue speaker icon at the right of the Windows Taskbar. The standard Windows speaker icon is replaced by the Voyetra Technologies icon by running the program named 'Vtray.exe', which is found in the 'Tbspros' folder. This folder is available on your system if you have installed the applications on the CD.
- Select the CD/Line input. The line signal is only available if the source is actually connected to the line In mini-jack socket. Otherwise the input defaults to the audio from the CD-ROM drive. Clicking on the advanced button opens an input gain dialogue where the gain for the incoming signal can be adjusted in much the same way as the input gain on a conventional mixing console. With the source signal playing, adjust the input gain and the faders for the optimum level.
- To monitor via VST activate the mute button on the input monitor strip and de-activate the input monitor's advanced options record monitor. The signal should be available via Cubase VST upon selecting Record Enable for the current audio track. Ensure that Global disable is not selected in the monitoring section of the Audio System Setup dialogue.
- To monitor via the card de-activate the mute button on the input monitor strip and ensure that Global Disable is selected in the monitoring section of the Audio System Setup dialogue of Cubase VST.

Note that the S/PDIF digital input remains de-activated unless a digital-source has been connected to the digital in connector.

Note also that there are additional software applications supplied with the card including Audio Station 2 and Audio View. Audio Station 2 provides a similar mixer utility, a MIDI file player, a WAV player and a CD player in virtual rackmount form. These provide a more comfortable alternative to the standard Windows applications. Audio View is a simple WAV editor.

Testing

The Turtle Beach Fiji produced the following:

signal-to-noise ratio: 89dB (unweighted)

The audio quality of this card is particularly good and it performed perfectly with Cubase VST. The card provided normal full duplex operation with the program. At the time of publication there was no special ASIO driver available for this card. When used with the standard ASIO multimedia driver it suffers from a latency of 750ms.

Overall impression

Overall, the Fiji performed very smoothly with Cubase VST. The Getting Started guide is clear and concise but the installation of the software on the CD was sometimes confusing.

The Turtle Beach Fiji boasts a flat frequency response and ultra low distortion. In tests with recordings from different sources the subjective impression was certainly one of very high quality, crystal clear sound. The inclusion of input gain controls on the accompanying mixer allows the fine tuning of the line input to the incoming signal, which is particularly important in optimising the record level in any given recording scenario.

The card also features Turtle Beach's Hurricane architecture which helps handle simultaneous digital audio streams. This technology is up to eight times faster than the traditional DMA (direct memory access) which is used by many other cards.

The card would have been more attractive if it had included a basic on-board synthesiser as standard. However, this is a card which is aimed at the audio professional so the high quality Kurzweil synth module has had to remain an option. This card has the edge on many of its competitors for sheer sound quality and those interested should also check out its big brother, the Turtle Beach Pinnacle.

Creative Labs Soundblaster AWE64 Gold audio card

General Specifications

The AWE64 Gold is a high quality, value-priced audio card from the well-known Creative Labs Soundblaster range. It features a main board and a S/PDIF digital output on a separate bracket (see Figure 17.9).

The general specifications for the AWE64 Gold are as follows:

Card type: ISA
Audio features:
   16 bit analog-to-digital (ADC) and digital-to-analog converters (DAC)
   sampling rate: 5kHz to 44.1kHz
   signal-to-noise ratio: 90dB
   THD: 0.005%
   frequency response: 15Hz - 50kHz (+/- 1dB)
   full duplex operation
   microphone input (1/8 inch mini-jack)
   CD audio input on card
   stereo line in (1/8 inch mini jack)
   stereo line out (RCA phono connectors)
   S/PDIF digital output on separate metal bracket (20 bit)
Advanced WAV effects synthesizer featuring:
   32 note polyphony
   16 part multi-timbral
   GM/GS compatibility
   4Mb built-in DRAM
Stereo music synthesizer:
   4 operator 11 voice synth or
   2 operator 20 voice synth
MIDI:
   MIDI in/out connectors (via 15 pin D connector, cable supplied as standard).

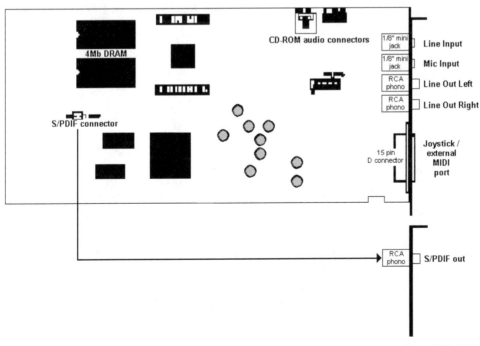

Figure 17.9 AWE64 Gold card
and digital output

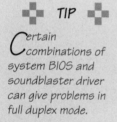

Installation

The AWE64 Gold's main card is a neat, well designed item which fits into the ISA slot with no physical difficulties. It is plug and play compatible and Windows recognised the card and installed the drivers with no problems.

Setting up for use with Cubase VST

To use the AWE64 Gold with Cubase VST you must de-activate the Wavesynth/WG MIDI output port in Steinberg's Setup MME program (supplied with Cubase VST). Launch Setup MME from the Windows program menu and select Creative Music Synth in the MME outputs list. Next, click on the Set inactive button.

To set up the ASIO Multimedia Control Panel proceed as follows:

- Select System from the Audio menu. In the Audio System Setup dialogue which appears click on the ASIO Control Panel button. This opens the basic ASIO Multimedia Setup dialogue (Figure 17.10).
- Open the presets dialogue and choose 'Soundblaster compatible full duplex' from the list. This is the optimum setting for the AWE64 Gold and, once chosen, the card is ready to use with Cubase VST. At this point you should not need to make any further changes to the settings so, if you do not wish to explore further, move onto the next section about using the audio mixer.
- If you need to verify the settings, click on the advanced options button to open the Advanced Options dialogue.
- Ensure that 'AWE64G Wave Out' in the output port device list and 'AWE64G Wave In' in the input port device list are activated.
- Verify the following values in the appropriate columns:
    Audio Buffers: 5
    Buffer size: 5512
- Also verify the following parameters:
    Sync reference: sample position - input
    Card options
    Activated: Full duplex, Start input first, Open all devices before start
    De-activated: none

Figure 17.10 Basic ASIO Multimedia Setup dialogue

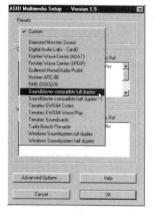

Using the AWE64 Gold mixer

The recording and playback controls of the AWE64 Gold are accessed via the standard Windows mixer applet, Sndvol32, which is normally installed as part of your Windows setup. It is opened by double clicking on the speaker icon on the Windows Taskbar (see Figure 17.11).

To record into Cubase VST using the line inputs proceed as follows:

- In order to optimise the recording quality it is recommended that you de-select all inputs except the line-in on the audio recording mixer.
- As a rough guide, try setting the level of the input signal moderately high on the external unit or mixer fader and set the AWE64 Gold line-in fader on the record mixer to moderately low. This should help keep the background noise to a minimum but,

depending on what you are recording, you may have to experiment to find the best settings.

- To monitor via VST, enable mute (ticked) on the line-in fader and disable the mute (unticked) on the wave fader of the AWE64 playback mixer. Set the desired level on the Wave fader. The signal should be available via Cubase VST upon selecting Record Enable for the current audio track. Ensure that Global disable is not selected in the monitoring section of the Audio System Setup dialogue.
- To monitor via the card, disable the mutes (unticked) on both the Wave fader and the line-in fader of the AWE64 playback mixer. Ensure that Global disable is selected in the monitoring section of the Audio System Setup dialogue.

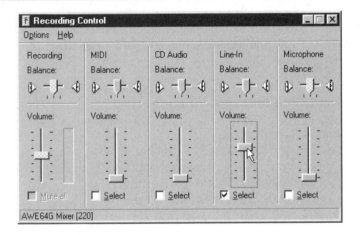

Figure 17.11 Standard Windows mixer applet for the AWE64 Gold

Testing

The AWE64 Gold produced the following:

signal-to-noise ratio: 81dB (unweighted)

Despite a poorer signal-to-noise ratio than the high-end cards on the market, the audio quality of this card is judged to be very good. However, it suffers from some difficulties with full duplex operation when used with Cubase VST.

Unfortunately, you cannot play back the audio in its full 16 bit glory while recording with Cubase VST. For as long as the inputs of the AWE64 Gold are activated in Cubase VST's audio inputs window (green light on), you can only play back any existing audio in 8 bit resolution. Playback in 16 bit resolution is possible only when the audio inputs are de-activated. This is disappointing since, in all other respects, the card performs very well.

The AWE64 Gold has no special ASIO driver. When used with the standard ASIO multimedia driver, it suffers from a latency of 750ms.

Overall impression

The AWE64 Gold has been included in this Chapter since it belongs to the popular Creative Labs Soundblaster family, is available at an attractive price and is already installed in many PC computers. The card was originally targeted at musicians, audio enthusiasts and high end game players and it may appeal to some Cubase VST users. If you don't mind monitoring in 8 bit whenever you are recording, then this card may be adequate for your needs.

Due to its various shortcomings, it is difficult to recommend the AWE64 Gold as a main audio card for use with Cubase VST but it works well as a second card for MIDI purposes, when installed in your computer alongside dedicated audio cards like the Event Gina.

The subjective impression of the AWE64 Gold's sound quality was one of clean, crisp, high quality audio. The inclusion of a S/PDIF output is an added bonus but it is a pity that it had to be supplied on a separate metal bracket. The gold plated RCA phono socket line-outs help maintain audio output quality and the inclusion of a microphone and MIDI cable as standard are welcome additions. The on-board synth sounds are useful for demos and MIDI files.

Event Gina multiple I/O audio card

General Specifications

The Event Gina is a professional multiple I/O audio card. It features 2 analogue inputs and 8 outputs on a separate breakout box and S/PDIF digital in/out connectors on the card (see Figure 17.12).

The Gina's general specifications are as follows:

Card type: PCI
Audio features:
  2 analog inputs with 20 bit 128x oversampling analog-to-digital converters
  8 analog outputs with 20 bit high performance digital-to-analog converters
  All analog inputs and outputs on breakout box with unbalanced 1/4 inch connectors
  sampling rate: 11kHz to 48kHz
  Dynamic range: 98dB
  THD: less than 0.003%, 20Hz-22kHz (A weighted)
  frequency response: 20Hz - 22kHz (+/- 0.25dB)
  full duplex operation (can simultaneously record 4 channels while playing back 10 channels)
  on-board 24 bit Motorola 56301 DSP, 66 million instructions per second (MIPS)
  S/PDIF digital I/O with up to 24 bit resolution
  24 bit data resolution maintained throughout internal signal path

The Gina requires a PCI 2.1 Pentium System running Windows 95 with at least 16Mb RAM

The Gina is an audio only card with no MIDI features. The breakout box is connected to the card via the supplied 1 metre shielded audio cable with standard 25-way D-type connectors.

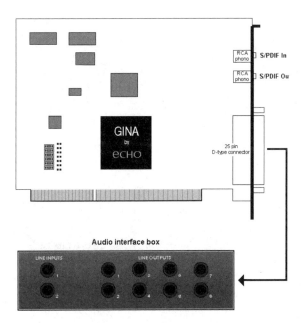

Figure 17.12 The Event Gina card and breakout box

Installation

Before proceeding with the installation, note that the Event Gina is supplied with a software application on the CD-ROM called the Echo Reporter. This tests the suitability of your computer for the card and for digital audio recording in general. It is strongly recommended that this program is run before the actual physical installation of the card. However, beware of using this software if you have a disk compression utility running in Windows as it can cause loss of data or system failure!!

The physical installation of the Gina card is very easy. If possible, it is advisable to choose a PCI slot which is not adjacent to the video card. The card is a short length PCI size which should fit into any PCI slot. The Gina is plug and play compatible and upon switching on the computer is detected automatically. The drivers are requested from the supplied CD-ROM and the overall installation process should present no problems to most users. The manual provides clear advice on every stage of the installation process and includes a QuickStart installation guide.

Figure 17.13 Basic ASIO Multimedia Setup dialogue

Setting up for use with Cubase VST

- Verify that your Gina card has been successfully installed by selecting Settings\Control Panel\System\Device Manager and look for the Event Gina in 'Sound, video and game controllers'. Select Properties and ensure that the device is working properly in the Device status area. Also select Settings\Control Panel\Multimedia\Audio and ensure that the Preferred Playback Device is set to one of the Gina's analogue playback channel pairs (normally 'Gina 1/2 Analog Playback'). If all is well, launch Cubase VST.
- Select System from the Audio menu. In the Audio System Setup dialogue which appears click on the ASIO Control Panel button. This opens the basic ASIO Multimedia setup dialogue (see Figure 17.13).

- The top of the dialogue features a pop-up menu of presets which, at the time of writing, did not feature the Event Gina. Therefore, you must set the parameters manually, as follows.
- Click on the advanced options button to open the Advanced Options dialogue.
- Activate all devices in the input and output port device lists by clicking on the small boxes to the left of the device names. (When the box contains a cross it is activated).
- Set the following values in the appropriate columns:
  Audio Buffers: 5
  Buffer size: 4096
- Adjust the Global settings sections as follows:
  Sync reference: Sample position – Output
  Card options
  Activated: Full duplex, Start input first, Open all devices before start
  De-activated: None
- Click on the store button and enter an appropriate name into the dialogue which appears. Click on OK to leave the Advanced Options dialogue. Your new preset should be selected in the basic ASIO Multimedia Setup dialogue and your card is now ready to use with Cubase VST at 44.1kHz.
- If you need to use Cubase VST at other sampling frequencies select a sample rate from the pop-up list near the top of the window and click on the Detect Buffer Size button for each frequency on both the input and output ports. This should find the correct buffer size for each sampling rate and the new information can all be saved as part of the same preset.
- To use the multiple outputs of the Gina open the Master faders by selecting Master in the Audio menu. A number of extra buses are present to the right of the standard Master fader bus. Click on the Active buttons to activate each of the extra buses (The buttons are illuminated in green). Rename each bus in the name button just below the Active button. The original Master faders are always named as 'Master' and would normally be assigned to the Gina's physical outputs 1 and 2. Name the next three buses as, for example, '3+4', '5+6' and '7+8'. This makes life easier when you come to route audio channels to different buses from the Monitor Mixer. Verify that the corresponding analog output pair (i.e. 3&4, 5&6 etc.) is present on the physical output assignment buttons of each of the extra buses (the assignment buttons are found at the foot of each dual fader strip).

Using the Event Gina audio mixer features

The recording, playback and monitoring controls of the Gina are accessed via the standard Windows mixer applet, Sndvol32, which is normally installed as part of your Windows setup. It is opened by double clicking on the speaker icon on the Windows Taskbar and when it is first opened it shows the Gina Output Levels panel (see Figure 17.14).

To set up the Gina to record into Cubase VST via the analog inputs proceed as follows:

- With Cubase VST already launched double click on the speaker icon on the Windows Taskbar to open the mixer applet.
- Select Properties in the Options menu and activate Recording in the Adjust Volume for section. This opens the Gina In Levels panel (Figure 17.15).

- Connect the input source to one of the analog inputs of the breakout box and commence input of the signal. If all is set up correctly you should be able to regulate the record level of the incoming signal using the Gina 1/2 fader and there should also be a corresponding signal visible in the level meter to the right of the fader.
- To monitor via the card, disable mute (unticked) on the chosen channel pair. Many users will do all their monitoring via a single channel pair (normally 1 and 2) but, depending on how you are using the Gina, you may choose to do otherwise. Ensure that Global disable is selected in the monitoring section of the Audio System Setup dialogue.
- To monitor via VST, enable all mutes in the input monitor panel. The signal should be available via Cubase VST upon selecting Record Enable for the current audio track. Ensure that Tape Type or Record Enable Type monitoring is selected in the monitoring section of the Audio System Setup dialogue.

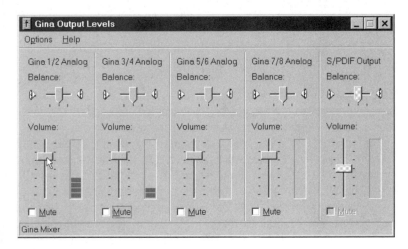

Figure 17.14 Gina output levels panel

Testing

The Event Gina produced the following:

signal-to-noise ratio: 90dB (unweighted)

Put simply, the audio quality of the Gina is beyond reproach. Its audio performance matches and often betters that of many DAT machines. The S/PDIF in/out was also exemplary. Full duplex operation was as expected and the Gina showed itself to be a rock-steady performer in all recording and playback functions with Cubase VST.

At the time of writing the Gina had no special ASIO driver, although one is promised in the near future. When used with the standard ASIO multimedia driver, it suffers from a latency of 557ms.

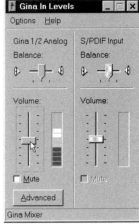

Figure 17.15 Gina input levels panel

Figure 17.16 Gina input
monitor panel

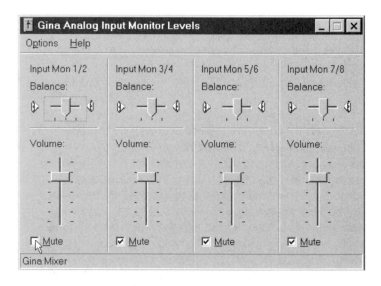

Overall impression

The Event Gina is the perfect choice if you need a mid-priced multiple I/O audio card for use with Cubase VST.

It has the advantage of being a PCI type card. The PCI bus handles data significantly faster than the ISA bus. The breakout box is ideal for the studio environment and the use of 1/4 inch jack sockets adds to the convenience. The connecting cable between the breakout box and the card is also exemplary, being a rugged, custom manufactured, multi-way, shielded audio cable which looks and feels indestructible.

The only downside with the Gina is that it does not include a MIDI interface. However, the card works perfectly alongside a standard soundcard installed into the same computer, and this can be used for any MIDI requirements. By concentrating on the audio aspects alone the designers have developed a product which has quickly become an industry standard.

If you require still more features of the same quality then check out the Event Layla, which features eight analogue inputs, 10 analogue outputs, S/PDIF digital in/out, word clock in/out and a MIDI in/out/thru interface all housed in an external rackmounting case.

✦ **INFO** ✦

The audio quality of the Gina is beyond reproach. Its audio performance matches and often betters that of many DAT machines. To ensure optimum results make sure you are using the latest driver for the card (available from the Event website).

Summary

The above descriptions should have helped readers understand the kind of factors involved when considering an audio card for use with Cubase VST. (See also the audio card section in Chapter 18). Your choice of card is crucially important to the performance of the program so it is a choice which should be very carefully considered.

No matter how fast your processor and no matter how much RAM you have, the actual sound quality is finally governed by the audio card. However, this is not to say that if you have a first class audio card you are guaranteed a high quality audio result – you also need to have a high quality microphone, (if you are recording vocals or live instruments), and, if the signal is passing through a mixing console, then this too must be of the highest quality possible. In addition, you must be monitoring the results through a good amplification and speaker system. In other words, all stages in the recording and playback path should be of optimum quality. The audio card might be viewed as a kind of cross-roads along this audio path – it is at the critical point in the recording and playback processes.

The main factors to bear in mind before choosing an audio card include: the signal-to-noise ratio, the bit resolution of the A-to-D and D-to-A converters, the THD and frequency response figures, the number of line inputs and outputs you need, whether you need a microphone input, whether the card has MIDI I/O, whether you need digital I/O, whether the card has on-board synthesizer features, whether you need to interface to an ADAT, whether the card has an ASIO driver (or is likely to have one in the future) etc. However, it should be noted that sound cards tend to fall into two groups; those which concentrate on high quality audio alone (these tend to be multiple I/O cards), and those which are good all-round cards providing acceptable audio performance along with good MIDI and synthesizer features (these tend to be stereo I/O cards).

Although there are still a wide range of ISA type cards available, most new cards appearing on the market are PCI. Good performance can be achieved from ISA type cards but the preferred option, if you have the choice, is the emerging PCI standard, since it is faster.

The performance of each product is also highly dependent on the setup in which it is being used and readers must make their own judgements as to their particular requirements and their final choice of soundcard. It is worth finding out the full specifications of any card being considered and comparing it to others in the same category. The internet is an excellent resource for this kind of information (see the internet section at the end of this book, which provides the website addresses for a number of soundcard manufacturers). In addition, to help readers in their search for what is available, the following table (overleaf) provides a brief guide to some of the main cards and devices which are suitable for use with Cubase VST:

Table 17.1 Soundcards for Cubase VST

Mfr	Model	Card type	ADC	DAC	Number of analogue IPs	Number of analogue OPs	Digital I/O	VST channels in/out	MIDI I/O	ASIO driver (available or expected)
Multiple										
Aardvark	20/20	PCI	20-bit	20-bit	8	8	S/PDIF, word clock	10/10	No	Yes
Event	Darla	PCI	20-bit	20-bit	2	8	No	2/8	No	Yes
Event	Gina	PCI	20-bit	20-bit	2	8	S/PDIF	4/10	No	Yes
Event	Layla	PCI	20-bit	20-bit	8	10	S/PDIF, word clock	10/12	1 in, 1 out	Yes
Korg	1212	PCI	20-bit	18-bit	2	2	ADAT, S/PDIF, word clock	12/12	No	Yes
Lexicon	Studio System	PCI	24-bit	24-bit	2 (expandable)	2 (expandable)	ADAT, S/PDIF, optical, word clock	up to 32/32	No	Yes
Midiman	Dman 2044	PCI	20-bit	20-bit	4	4	optional	4/4	No	Yes
Sonorus	StudI/O	PCI	–	18-bit	–	stereo monitoring	2 ADAT (switchable to S/PDIF)	16/18	No	Yes
SEK'D	Prodif Platinum	PCI	–	18-bit	–	stereo monitoring	2 ADAT (switchable to S/PDIF)	16/18	No	Yes
Stereo										
Creamware	MMPort	ISA	18-bit	18-bit	2	2	S/PDIF	2/2	1 in, 1 out	Yes
Digital Audio Labs	CardD Plus	ISA	16-bit	18-bit	2	2	optional	2/2	No	No
Guillemot	Home Studio Pro64	ISA	16-bit	18-bit	2	2	S/PDIF	2/2	1 in, 1 out	No
Terratec	EWS64 XL	ISA	18-bit	18-bit	2	2	1 S/PDIF coaxial in, 1 optical in, 2 S/PDIF out	2/4	2 in, 2 out	Yes
Turtle Beach	Fiji	ISA	20-bit	20-bit	2	2	optional	2/2	1 in, 1 out	No
Turtle Beach	Pinnacle	ISA	20-bit	20-bit	2	2	optional	2/2	1 in, 1 out	No

18

PC hardware requirements in detail

Please note that this chapter gets technical with a capital T. Those of you who do not really wish to know about the insides of a PC may find much of the information irrelevant. However, it is advised that all Cubase VST users read this chapter since it contains information which may save you time and may provide solutions to some of the problems faced when setting up a Cubase VST system. It is particularly relevant to those Cubase VST users who are considering upgrading their hardware.

General computer concerns

Into the 21st century

The first thing to understand about computers is that a standard model does not really exist ! We can be reasonably sure that a computer will have a monitor screen, a QWERTY keyboard and some kind of pointing device (mouse, trackball etc.) but thereafter there may be major differences from one machine to the next. The concerns of which computer to buy and exactly what hardware needs to be included to run Cubase VST can therefore be problematic to the uninitiated.

The reality is that at the time of the publication of this book advancements in the technology are progressing at such a rapid rate that it is extremely difficult to keep up with. However, as we move into the 21st century we are likely to see this rate of change slow down slightly and we mere mortals might finally get the chance to catch up (at least, let's hope so!).

However, those new to the domain of computer technology and those who even find it rather daunting and tiresome should not be afraid. Despite all the jargon, technicalities and speed of change, there is a way through the hardware jungle. The more you know about the hardware, the more you are likely to get out of Cubase VST.

The difference between computers and musical instruments

It is worth thinking about some of the general concerns of musicians and sound engineers in relation to computer technology. Many musicians struggle for years to gain the skills needed to play a musical instrument and, once these skills have been acquired, with a little regular practise they can be maintained at an acceptable level for a whole lifetime. These skills rely on the fact that the essential designs of the popular musical instruments do not change from year to year. We can be fairly sure that, for example, the essential design of a piano keyboard made next year will largely resemble that of the one we are playing today. At the very least, there will be white keys and black keys and pressing middle C or playing a sequence of notes on one keyboard will produce very similar results on another.

Computers, on the other hand, cannot be mastered like musical instruments. The skills gained in operating a computer system in one year may not be relevant the next. The software and hardware changes extremely quickly. New versions of the same program require more power from the hardware. This means you need a faster computer with more memory and more storage capacity. The new software presents new functions which must also be mastered. And then suddenly you need still more memory because they have just upgraded the software yet again. To make matters worse some of the hardware inside the computer is also constantly being upgraded and improved by the manufacturers. Many of you are already familiar with the story. However, there is one big plus point to all this constant change - prices have gone down continually for some years and the performance of the hardware has increased dramatically.

What skills and hardware can we hang onto?

So, both the software and the hardware keep changing but surely there are some skills and knowledge that can be carried over and some hardware that does not go out of date too quickly. Indeed there are, and it is these elements that we need to be aware of and we also need to appreciate exactly which components of a PC are particularly relevant to the use of Cubase VST.

As already mentioned, obvious hardware elements to the technology which remain fairly unchanging are the monitor screen, the humble QWERTY keyboard and the mouse (or other pointing device). These are easy to deal with since even those with the most basic of computer hardware knowledge are familiar with these items and their functions. Those Cubase VST users with good keyboard and mouse skills will benefit more from the software. As far as the choice of monitor is concerned, the higher the resolution and the larger the size, the better. This book recommends a minimum monitor size of 15 inches with the ability to run at a screen resolution of 800 x 600 pixels.

As for the software, knowledge and skills learnt on previous versions of Cubase are largely transferable to the more recent versions, including Cubase VST. The essential core operating environment of Cubase has not changed for many years and this is one aspect of the package which makes it attractive to musicians.

Of course, it is also important to have as much knowledge as possible about your chosen operating system. By operating system we mean a system like Windows 95/98 or Windows NT, which is automatically loaded when the computer boots up. The operating system provides the essential operating environment, (such as the desktop etc.), and communicates with the hardware. Like Cubase, much of the knowledge and skills learnt in previous versions of Windows are transferable to the more recent versions.

Background information before buying a PC

A general and rather obvious piece of advice is to buy the system with the fastest processor and the largest amount of RAM you can possibly afford and you should not invest in anything lesser than the system recommended in Chapter 2. However, the speed and capacity of the hard drive and the quality of the audio card are also major considerations when choosing a PC for multi-track digital audio recording.

Since the technology is changing so quickly it is unlikely that this part of the book will remain right up to date for very long so it is important that the prospective buyer obtains information from the latest magazines on the market. Flicking through the advertisements from the large mail order computer suppliers and reading some of the articles on the latest gear will give you an idea of what is available and the kind of price you should be paying.

There are essentially three ways of buying a PC:

1 As a complete system from a high street shop or computer superstore
2 As a complete system supplied partly assembled from one of the major computer suppliers
3 As separate components from one or several suppliers which you then use to build your own computer

Option 1 has the advantage of being less time consuming but you are not able to specify exactly which components are included and the price is likely to be more than the other two options. Option 2 is slightly more time consuming but you can choose the components that you want in your system and you have the added convenience of not having to spend the time and effort building the entire computer yourself. This option might be in the form of the company giving you the opportunity to get a pre-built machine for which you choose the components. The basic building block machine might contain a case of your choice with a built-in floppy drive and a Pentium motherboard. Your choice of processor, hard disk, sound card, and CD ROM etc. are then added, and the complete machine is delivered ready to use. Option 3 is both more time consuming and inconvenient than the other two options and is not certain to result in significant savings in the purchasing price. It does, however, have two advantages: you can choose exactly which components to include and you will learn a lot more about computer hardware. Assembling your own custom made computer from separate components is certainly worth considering but you should be aware that it is not always easy. Even those with experience can run into difficulties. If you do intend to build the computer yourself and you have never attempted anything like this before then you are advised to seek the help and advice of somebody who is already experienced.

In addition to the above options, there are also various musical equipment suppliers who specialise in supplying and building PC's which are specifically tuned to the needs of the high-tech musician and audio professional. Although sometimes rather expensive this option is also well worth checking out.

There now follows a break down of the essential components of a PC. The descriptions do not tell the whole story but give information which is specific to the needs of Cubase VST users.

Processor choice

The processor or CPU (Central Processing Unit) is effectively the brain of the computer where all the calculations and decisions are made. Processors are rated in terms of their clock speed. An Intel Pentium processor is described by the Pentium name followed by a number, as in: Pentium 166 or Pentium 200. Pentium 200, for example, simply means that it is a Pentium chip with a clock speed of 200MHz (200 million pulses per second). The clock speed could be likened to tempo in music and the instructions that the processor must perform could be likened to the notes in the piece. The faster the tempo, the shorter the performance time. Luckily we don't have to dance to music running at these speeds as 200 million pulses per second is extremely fast!

There has been a continual development in the types of processor available for the PC. In the not so distant past the 286 and 386 were the main contenders in the processor market, to be replaced soon afterwards with the 486. In 1996, the standard Intel Pentium processor was introduced and by the end of the year Intel introduced the MMX extension to the chip. 1997 has seen the introduction of the Pentium II processor which is taking over from its predecessors in 1998. In the future we are likely to see similar processors but with more features and greater speeds.

Before you get too confused with all these processor numbers remember that the 286, 386 and 486 are NOT suitable for Cubase VST (see Basic PC requirements in Chapter 2). So we are concerned with the Pentium chips and preferably those with clock speeds of 166MHz or more. The standard Pentium chip is available with typical clock speeds of 166, 200 and 233MHz and features a 16K 1st level cache. This is a temporary storage area used to speed up the performance of the system. The Pentium MMX processor is available with similar clock speeds but features a series of additional instructions designed specifically for multimedia. MMX stands for 'Multimedia Extensions'. More importantly, the Pentium MMX chip also features a 32K 1st level cache which improves average performance over the standard Pentium chip by about 10% - 15%. Typical clock speeds for the Pentium MMX processor are the same as those for the standard Pentium. The Pentium II processor runs at speeds of 233, 266, 300, 333, 350, 400 and 450MHz with higher speeds promised in the future. Note that for Pentium II processors of 400 MHz or more, you must have a motherboard with a BX chipset.

Other processors exist which are manufactured by companies other than Intel. These have names such as Cyrix and AMD. Although their existence promotes healthy competition they are unfortunately not recommended for use with Cubase VST. To be sure of the best performance ensure that the processor installed in your computer is a genuine Intel product. Cubase VST works with all of the following Intel processors: Pentium, Pentium MMX, Pentium Pro and Pentium II.

Motherboard concerns

The motherboard is the large circuit board found inside the case of the PC and is the centre of activity for all the I/O (input/output) and general data flow of the system. All the components of the system are connected in some way to the motherboard via its various slots and connecting sockets and it also contains the CPU, the RAM (Random Access Memory), 2nd level cache memory and the BIOS (Basic Input Output System).

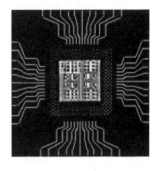

Each motherboard also has what is known as a chipset. Pentium motherboards are supplied with a number of different chipsets, with names such as VX, HX and TX. VX is optimised for multimedia processing and can support up to 64MB of SDRAM. HX is similar to VX but uses fewer chips and is optimised for multi-tasking. The TX chipset supports SDRAM and, more importantly, ultra DMA drives (see hard disk information below). If you are intending to use an ultra DMA hard drive with a Pentium or Pentium MMX processor for your Cubase VST setup then a motherboard with a TX chipset is your best option. Pentium II processors use LX or BX chipsets. The LX chipset supports Pentium II processors from 233 to 333 MHz and the BX chipset supports Pentium II processors from 233 to 450MHz. The motherboard for Pentium II processors must be an ATX type, which is a different size to the standard AT type used for Pentium and Pentium MMX processors.

1st level cache memory was mentioned in the previous section about processors but the motherboard also contains another level of cache memory known as 2nd level cache. Cache memory is essential to allow data to flow around the system with maximum efficiency. Pentium processors are faster than the systems which supply them with data so a cache supplies a temporary storage area into which data can be fed in advance of when it is actually needed. The processor can then access and process data from the cache at high speed. In effect, this prevents bottlenecks in the system and improves overall performance. 2nd level cache memory on Pentium motherboards will normally be of the variety known as 'pipeline burst' (or PB) cache which is the most efficient. It is typically supplied in 256K or 512K capacities. It is particularly recommended that you choose a motherboard with 512K 2nd level cache, as this can significantly improve the performance of Pentium processors of 166MHz and above.

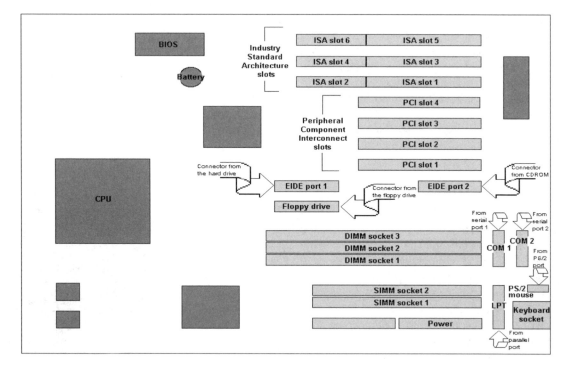

Figure 18.1 Typical layout of a Pentium motherboard

As can be seen in Figure 18.1 the motherboard contains the SIMM and DIMM slots for the RAM (explained below) and all the connectors for the installation of the peripheral components and devices which go to make up a PC. These include connector sockets for the serial and parallel ports and for the floppy drive, CD ROM drive and hard drive. The connectors require what is known as I/O controllers. These are built into most motherboards and, in the case of EIDE drives (Enhanced Intelligent Drive Electronics), the controller circuitry is built into the drive itself. Other connections provided are the ISA (Industry Standard Architecture) and PCI (Peripheral Component Interconnect) slots which are used to connect peripheral devices such as sound cards, graphic cards, SCSI cards etc.

RAM matters

RAM stands for Random Access Memory. This is the main area used for the manipulation of data, and anything that needs to be processed must first of all be put there. This includes the operating system, any applications running and any data currently being processed. The RAM can then be accessed at high speed by the CPU. RAM is volatile memory, which means that when the computer is switched off all its current contents are lost.

RAM is of great importance to the operation of Cubase VST. As has been mentioned in the description at the beginning of this book, the program utilises something called 'native audio processing' - this means that the program makes use of the actual processing power of the computer to deal with the audio data with no additional hardware. If there is insufficient RAM memory the hard disk will be used as a virtual memory expansion area. This will slow things down since access to data on the hard drive is slower than access to RAM. The Windows 95 and Windows NT operating systems are also rather memory hungry and although they will run on less than 16MB this would not be very practical when combined with the additional requirements of Cubase VST. It pays to have as much memory as possible and this book recommends a minimum of 32MB, and preferably 64MB or more for the best results. If you intend to use a large number of audio tracks, effects and plug-ins in Cubase VST, a large amount of RAM is particularly important.

RAM comes in several varieties with names such as DRAM, EDO RAM, and SDRAM and is usually supplied on a small 72 pin board known as a SIMM (Single Inline Memory Module) or a DIMM (Dual Inline Memory Module). DRAM (Dynamic Random Access Memory) was the most common type of memory but is now being replaced by EDO RAM and SDRAM. EDO RAM (Extended Data Out Ram) is cached to improve its performance and suits most Pentium systems. At the time of writing, SDRAM (Synchronous DRAM) is the fastest kind of memory available with a speed of around 10ns (nanoseconds) and featuring the simultaneous input and output of data. For Cubase VST, fast EDO RAM (60ns) or SDRAM is strongly recommended.

The hard disk

Along with the audio card, the hard disk is extremely important for recording audio with Cubase VST. Digital audio eats up hard disk space extremely quickly. Recording audio at the usual 44.1kHz sampling rate (CD quality) takes up 5MB of disk space per mono minute. This means that a CD in its final stereo format would need around 600MB of hard disk space. If you are recording multiple tracks, (most users of Cubase VST will want to do this), then your space requirements are likely to be much greater. Approximate hard disk capacity requirements for any number of tracks can be calculated using the following equation:

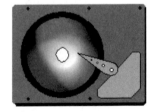

Capacity = 5MB x no. of tracks x 0.75

This equation assumes that each audio track has been filled to 75% of its capacity. It is rare that multi-track audio fills all the available space on each track so this provides a reasonable guideline for the amount of hard drive space needed to achieve the desired number of tracks in most recording situations. However, space is certainly not the only consideration when choosing a hard drive.

Multi-track digital audio also puts heavy demands on the speed of the drive and it is the speed which is often the limiting factor for the number of tracks possible on any given system. Large amounts of data must be transferred from the drive to the audio card in the fastest possible time. The data stream for each track is accessed in rotation and the data blocks may not always be found in convenient locations on the disk. For 16 track audio the read head of the drive is effectively attempting to be in 16 different places at the same time so that we can hear our audio with no delay and in perfect synchronisation. In reality, the data is stored in advance in a buffer which helps speed up the rate of data transfer. Add to this the fact that the hard disk may also be expected to simultaneously record during playback, then you can begin to appreciate why the hard drive needs to be particularly efficient.

The measurement of speed for a hard drive is not particularly easy since the manufacturers do not always give us the specifications we need. The main indicators of hard drive performance are the average access time and the sustained data transfer rate (DTR). The average access time is the average time it takes for a drive to find and retrieve a piece of data on the disk. The 'average' part of this is important since the read head travels various distances to retrieve data depending on its current position and the actual location of the data itself. The DTR is the amount of data which can be transferred within a given time frame and this is usually measured in MB per second.

Many manufacturers do not quote an average access time and sometimes use the drive's average seek time as a measure of performance. The average seek time should not be confused with the average access time since it only measures the time taken for the read/write head to move to the correct position.

Another key specification is the rotation speed of the disk. The faster the rotation the quicker a piece of data will arrive under the read head. The rotation speed is often quoted alongside something known as the rotation latency. This is the time it takes for the disk to go through half a rotation, which is a good indicator of average speed. For example, a hard drive specified as running at 7,200 rpm (revolutions per minute) has a rotation latency of 4.17ms. This time needs to be added to the average seek time to get an idea of the average access time of the hard drive.

The following specifications indicate typical hard disk requirements for handling 8 stereo tracks of digital audio at 44.1kHz with Cubase VST:

- An average access time of 20ms or less (if specified)
- An average seek time of 9ms or less
- A sustained data transfer rate of 5MB per second or more
- A rotation speed of 5,400 rpm or more (giving a rotation latency of 5.56ms)

Many of the modern drives are capable of better performance than these specifications, which should only be used as an approximate guide.

The other main concern is what type of drive is best for Cubase VST. Hard drives fall into two main categories, as follows:

- EIDE (Enhanced Integrated Drive Electronics) hard drives
- SCSI (Small Computer Systems Interface) hard drives

EIDE hard drives are the standard variety which invariably fit inside the computer case and are attached directly to the motherboard. SCSI hard drives either fit inside the computer case or are found as separate stand-alone units. These connect to the motherboard via a SCSI interface which may be SCSI 1, SCSI 2, wide SCSI etc. SCSI drives also often feature the additional option of removable media, (data is stored on large capacity removable disks which can be interchanged as required).

Until recently SCSI drives generally out-performed their EIDE counterparts but the gap is now closing. For this reason the choice of EIDE or SCSI is not always a clear-cut decision.

Many audio professionals use SCSI drives since they generally have better RPM speeds and superior buffer sizes. High-end users also recommend the use of two simultaneous SCSI drives, one for the system and program files and the other for audio and MIDI data. EIDE drives are not so suitable for this application since they do not support true simultaneous access. In addition, external SCSI devices are portable between different host computers, (as long as they are equipped with a SCSI interface). This means that the same drive could be attached to any one of a number of PC's and several SCSI devices may be attached in sequence to a single host computer. Although SCSI drives still have the edge over EIDE drives for hard disk recording applications, the disadvantage of SCSI for many users is one of price, since SCSI drives tend to be significantly more expensive.

Other options for the professional environment are extremely large capacity AV drives (Audio Visual). These tend to be in the order of 9Gb or more capacity with very fast average access times and impressive DTR's. Unfortunately, these are often outside the budget of many Cubase VST users, although, as always, prices are dropping all the time.

Another major concern for multi-track digital audio is recalibration time. As a hard drive warms up the read/write heads may go slightly out of alignment and so the drive must periodically recalibrate itself. This involves a momentary pause and the longer this lasts the more likely it is to interfere with any audio data which is currently being recorded or played back. For this reason you should choose a hard drive with a minimal recalibration time. As a guide, professional AV drives specify recalibration times of around 30ms or less.

Recent developments have meant that speed and high data transfer rates are within the grasp of all computer users. Many EIDE drives now feature ultra DMA (ultra Direct Memory Access). Direct memory access allows data to be transferred to and from the hard drive without using the CPU. This results in a more efficient use of the system's resources since the CPU can engage in other calculations while the hard drive transfers data to and from RAM. Standard DMA drives allow a data transfer rate of 16MB per second and the newer ultra DMA drives have increased this to 33MB per second. However, to have access to the ultra DMA features you must have a motherboard with a 430TX (or later) chipset. Ultra DMA drives are not particularly expensive, especially when compared to a similarly specified SCSI drive, yet they are capable of performing as efficiently as their SCSI counterparts in some respects. This is good news for Cubase VST users, especially those on a budget who nevertheless must have high quality performance from their hard drive.

Lastly, remember that whatever kind of hard drive you use for your Cubase VST setup, you should also organise a method of backing up the data. Hard drives can develop faults, and system crashes can result in damage to data on the disk. Popular back-up media include: SCSI drives with removeable cartridges, magneto-optical (MO) drives, zip or jaz drives, tape streamers and recordable CD (CD-R). Although hard disk failure is thankfully not a common occurrence, backing up your data is essential if you wish to avoid the potentially disastrous situation of losing all your files.

The audio card

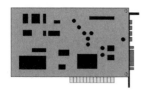

The audio card (also referred to as the sound card) is one of the most important items of hardware in a PC Cubase VST system intended for semi-professional or professional applications. By audio card we mean a sound card which can record and play back digital audio using the hard drive to store the data. The card plugs into one of the computer's ISA or PCI slots and standard models are stereo in/stereo out devices. Most modern sound cards are plug and play (PnP) compatible which means that when the card is first installed Windows will automatically assign IRQ (Interrupt Request) and memory address numbers to the new device.

Other card concerns include the following:

- the card may have a built-in digital interface or it may come with an optional digital daughter board (an additional card which fits separately onto the back plane of the computer and is attached to the main audio card via a ribbon cable).
- the card may also include a MIDI interface, usually on a dual joystick/MIDI port D type socket and, in addition to the audio recording features, it may also include MIDI synthesiser and/or sampling facilities.
- last, but not least, cards (and external devices) which allow multiple inputs and outputs are also available.

As you can see, the choice is already rather confusing but for use with Cubase VST we can narrow things down considerably. The following specifies the kind of audio card we need. The card should:

- be able to record and play back digital audio using the hard drive as the storage medium
- be full duplex (able to record and play back digital audio simultaneously)

- be a stereo or multiple input/output device with at least 16 bit resolution and 44.1 kHz sampling rate
- be Windows multimedia compatible or have a separate ASIO driver (Audio Stream Input Output)

The first thing to decide is whether you require a multiple I/O device or a standard stereo in/stereo out sound card. Most new cards arriving on the market are now of the PCI variety. The PCI bus is faster than the older ISA bus and is preferable for the handling of high quality digital audio, especially if you intend to use a multiple I/O card. The presence of digital in and out sockets is also important, especially if you intend to record from or mix down to DAT (Digital Audio Tape). Digital I/O improves the quality of both the record and playback path and is usually on S/PDIF (Sony Philips Digital InterFace) phono connectors. Next is whether the card features a MIDI interface and what kind of MIDI instrument, if any, is on board. Another thing to look out for is an on-board DSP chip (Digital Signal Processor). This is a special kind of processor which is optimised for the intense number crunching needed to convert analogue signals into digital data. The presence of a DSP can greatly enhance the card's performance. After checking the general specifications of the card it is then a matter of judging which choice of card gives you the best overall performance for your particular application.

For home studio use the more basic cards might be adequate but for professional applications it is advisable to get the highest specified card possible. This is not always an easy matter since the manufacturer's specifications can be rather misleading. They are best used as a guide. For example, the quoted signal-to-noise (S/N) ratio is likely to be an ideal figure based on a test carried out in perfect conditions, and the ratio may or may not be 'A weighted'. For the uninitiated, the signal-to-noise ratio is a measure of the noise floor of an audio system. The higher the S/N ratio, the less noisy and the better the perceived sound quality. An 'A weighted' figure improves the noise measurement over an unweighted figure so, if you are comparing the signal-to-noise ratio of two cards you must first make sure that they have both been measured in the same way. In reality, the signal-to-noise performance of the same model of card may vary slightly from card to card and from PC to PC. The position of the card in the PC and the other components near to it can also affect the noise level in a real world recording situation.

If you are considering a card with analogue ins and outs the bit resolution of the analogue-to-digital and digital-to-analogue converters should be taken into account. Although it is not always the case, a higher bit resolution usually means a better signal-to-noise ratio and better overall sound quality.

Before investing in any sound card, it is advisable to read all the latest reviews, search the internet (if available to you) and get the opinions of those who are already using the hardware. Chapter 17 of this book analyses a selection of audio cards with particular emphasis on their suitability for use with Cubase VST. This should help in the final choice of card.

As has already been emphasised, no matter how fast your processor and no matter how much RAM you have, the actual sound quality is finally governed by the audio card. However, this is not to say that if you have a first class audio card you are guaranteed a high quality audio result - you also need to have a high quality microphone, (if you are recording vocals or live instruments), and, if the signal is passing through a mixing console, then this too must be of the highest quality possible. In addition, you must be monitoring the results through a good amplification and speaker system. In other words, all stages in the recording and playback path should be of optimum quality. The audio card might be viewed as a kind of cross-roads along this audio path - it is at the critical point in the recording and playback processes.

The CD-ROM drive

A CD-ROM drive is essential for Windows and Cubase VST and is now a standard feature of any currently available PC. CD-ROM stands for Compact Disk Read Only Memory and describes a format which is similar to a normal audio CD except that the contents of the disk are computer data rather than audio data. The main advantage is that a CD-ROM can store up to 680MB of data - this is equivalent to 485 high density floppy disks, a considerable saving in media and space. The disadvantage is that a CD-ROM can normally only be read from and cannot be written to without a special CD-R drive (Compact Disk Recorder).

Compared to the hard drive, the CD-ROM drive does not have to be enormously fast for Cubase VST. CD-ROM's are supplied in a number of speeds usually referred to as 12 speed, 16 speed, 24 speed etc. and any of these are adequate for general purpose use. The speed refers to the number of times faster the data is read from the CD-ROM when compared to an ordinary audio CD drive. It is advisable to choose one of the faster CD-ROM drives since their prices are not much higher than the other speeds.

Other advantages of having a CD-ROM drive is that they can also play normal audio CD's. Most will feature an audio output which can be connected to your sound card and you can thus play audio CD's conveniently through the audio system you have connected to your sound card's audio outputs.

The floppy disk drive

Almost all PC's are supplied with a 3.5 inch floppy drive. The standard capacity of this drive is 1.44MB. This is extremely small considering the large capacities of data which often need to be saved onto removable media, but the standard was devised long before the large capacity storage requirements of current technology. Standard floppy disk drives are slowly being replaced by larger capacity versions which provide 100MB or more of removable storage with the additional convenience of still being able to read standard 1.44MB floppies.

Drivers and small applications are often supplied on floppy diskettes so a floppy drive is still a standard requirement for any PC. They are also handy for the saving of small files (such as text files or standard MIDI files) and Cubase VST Song and Arrangement files (without the audio data). However, due to the particularly large size of audio files, standard floppy disk drives are of little use for the saving of audio data.

The graphics card

Modern PC's require a graphics card in order to produce the image we see on the screen. These are available in 2D or 3D varieties and many of their specifications are aimed at the games market. Although you do not need a 3D card to run Cubase VST it is probably still a good idea to invest in one since the market is saturated with 3D graphics cards which are fine for general purpose use. A quality 3D graphics card is also essential if you intend to also use your computer for multimedia and games (although this book does not recommend mixing games and Cubase VST on the same computer).

The card usually contains a small amount of onboard RAM, often 2 or 4MB. No less that 2 MB, and preferably 4MB, is recommended for use with Cubase VST. The more RAM available, the greater the number of possible colours and the greater the potential resolution of the images produced. More importantly, more RAM means that graphics operations are less likely to interfere with audio operations. 4MB is recommended if you intend to run at resolutions greater than 800 x 600 pixels.

For Cubase VST, it is not essential to have an enormous number of colours and it is unlikely that many users will use a screen resolution of greater that 1024 x 768 pixels. As the resolution is increased, the image takes up less space and you can cram more onto the monitor screen but the windows also become smaller and the text more difficult to read. This is OK if you also have a large screen of 17 inches or more, but it is unworkable on 14 inch and 15 inch monitors. Most users who cannot afford a larger monitor will normally choose to work with a resolution of 800 x 600 pixels and this is recommended here as a minimum requirement for working comfortably with Cubase VST on a 15 inch screen. All modern graphics cards support this and higher resolutions.

A graphics card normally comes complete with supporting graphics tools and utilities for Windows and these will normally include a display configuration window where the user can experiment with the number of colours and the resolution.

It is worth checking the latest PC magazines to find out the best buys in graphics cards but you can be reasonably sure that the graphics cards found in most Pentium PC's will be adequate for Cubase VST. However, beware of some cards which cause problems like audio clicking, audio channel swapping and synchronisation faults. For more information check Steinberg's knowledge base website which, at the time of writing, was at http://metalguru.steinberg.de/sc/knowledge.nsf.

The monitor

You probably thought that the monitor would be the easiest part of a PC to judge. The choice of monitor is, however, deceptively difficult. Standard colour monitors come in 14, 15, 17, 19, 21 inch and greater sizes. Due to price considerations some are tempted to buy the smallest monitor (14 inches) but, for use with Cubase VST, this is a false economy. The smallest monitor this book recommends is 15 inches and, although this does not sound much bigger than 14 inches, that extra inch makes the difference between being impractical and workable. Cubase VST needs space to spread out and the use of multiple windows and their organisation on the screen demands a lot from the monitor. Without enough screen space you will always be struggling for more room. As has already been mentioned, to be comfortable you will need to work at a minimum resolution of 800 x 600 pixels and your graphics card and monitor should be capable of this. For resolutions greater than 800 x 600 pixels it is recommended that you use a monitor of 17 inches or more.

Remember that the monitor is one of the most important points of contact you will have with the program and you will probably spend an awful long time gazing into it. As well as size, it is important to have a monitor capable of giving a crisp, clear image. Some monitors have superior focus, brightness and colour. A flat image screen can cut down on image distortion and those monitors with an anti-glare coating will be easier to look at. These kinds of features are worth having since they can reduce eye strain and general fatigue when working with Cubase VST.

The keyboard and mouse

Of all the peripheral devices surrounding the computer, the keyboard and mouse are the most familiar. They provide points of tactile contact with the machine and methods by which we can give it instructions.

In many ways, the keyboard and mouse are archaic and bizarre methods of interacting with a computer and one of the main thrusts of research by the big corporations involves the search for alternatives. Natural language processing (NLP) is the most important and involves speech recognition, the long-time holy grail of computer science research. When computers can recognise normal speech efficiently (which may not be in the too distant future) we will all be talking to them instead of typing instructions or dragging things around a screen.

However, for now we must make do with the humble keyboard and mouse, so it pays to know how to use them and what to look for in the hardware sense. Some Cubase VST users may not think that learning to type has anything to do with creating music; they are probably right, but if you are the kind of user who must search for each letter and symbol before you type it, then you are going to be handicapped in your use of Cubase VST and, for that matter, most other computer software. Naming tracks, saving songs and using keyboard shortcuts all require some level of keyboard skill. So, if you are going to use the keyboard, you may as well choose one which is comfortable.

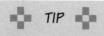

TIP

The basic advice here is try before you buy. Some of the cheaper keyboards are not very pleasant to use and for the faster typist may not be sensitive enough. The final choice is a personal matter.

As for the mouse, the most comfortable shape and size depends on the characteristics of your hand. Choice is once again a personal matter but it pays to make some comparisons between different models. Some users may prefer a trackball, where the cursor position is regulated by a rolling ball in the top part of the device. Whatever your choice, it is absolutely essential to master the use of the mouse.

The case

If you intend to update or expand your PC system in the future then the size of the case is important. Cases come in several varieties which can be broadly categorised as desktop, mini tower, midi tower and full tower.

Desktop will be familiar to the majority of users as the traditional horizontally rectangular case, as commonly seen on the desks of offices and reception areas. These have limited expandability. Mini towers are upright cases with reasonable expandability but, due to internal space considerations, may obscure access to the components if you need to update an item. Full towers are the largest of the upright cases. They give good access to the internal components and have the maximum potential for expandability. Midi towers come somewhere in between the mini tower and the full tower and make a good compromise.

Many cases comply with the European CE safety standard and, for the privilege, are priced slightly higher. A case like this will normally be marked as CE Approved, and this is desirable from a safety point of view. All cases are invariably supplied with a PSU (power supply unit), which should have a rating of 200W or more.

Cases are designed for two main types of motherboard, AT or ATX. Standard cases are designed for AT motherboards but if you intend to fit a Pentium II motherboard you must make sure that the case is ATX. Case design will be of most concern to those building their own computer or to those updating the motherboard.

PC system example

For reference purposes and to help users in the choice of their own PC system, the PC used for testing Cubase VST during the writing of this book had the following specifications:

Intel Pentium MMX 200MHz processor
Gigabyte GA-586 430TX chipset motherboard with 512K 2nd level PB cache
64MB EDO RAM (60ns)
Maxtor Diamond Max 3.2 Gb EIDE Ultra DMA hard drive (1750 series, model 83240D4)
Turtle Beach Fiji and other sound cards (as tested in Chapter 17)
Hercules Terminator 4MB 3D/DX graphics card (model T3314EDO)
16x EIDE CD ROM drive
1.44MB 3.5 inch floppy drive
CE approved midi tower case with 230w PSU
View Sonic Optiquest V655 15 inch colour monitor (0.28mm dot pitch, up to 1280 x 1024 pixel resolution)

Cubase VST ran perfectly on this system throughout the entire testing period. Although machines with similar specifications are more than adequate for running Cubase VST, if you have the choice, it is recommended that you invest in a Pentium II machine. The Event Gina audio card (and Layla) is also particularly recommended for multiple I/O systems, and the Korg 1212 for systems combining VST and ADAT.

19

Final comments and recommendations

After using Cubase VST for a short time it soon becomes apparent that there are an extremely wide range of features available. However, it is not essential to understand all of them in order to use the program and some readers are more interested in the audio aspects while others might mainly use the MIDI features. Whatever your interest, the program facilitates the making of music and the recording of sound with the minimum of fuss, in an adaptable and creative software environment.

Most of us quickly find our own particular way of working with Cubase VST. However, in the early stages of using the program it is easy to fall into bad habits and unwittingly indulge in repetitive tasks which are not really necessary. This can lead to confusion and may even make the program more difficult to use at a later stage. With a little initial effort, this can be avoided.

The following tips provide solid advice on a number of Cubase VST issues and may help you avoid some of the common pitfalls:

Customise Cubase VST

- Many users use Cubase VST with the windows sized and positioned in their default configurations. Remember that the Arrange window and editors can be sized and positioned according to your own needs and saved as part of the definition file (def.all).
- Some users also use the system with many other aspects of the program left in their default configurations. By customising the program for your own specific needs and in relation to the rest of the hardware in your system, you can enhance the smooth operation of the software. This might involve the use of special Parts containing MIDI data for the setting up of your MIDI instruments, it might involve specific settings in the Preferences or MIDI setup dialogues or it could mean the pre-loading of one or more modules. You should not shy away from taking some time to set up your own customised workspace and saving this as the def.all file. (see 'System preparation' Chapter 10).

Organise your song and audio files

- When you launch Cubase VST at the beginning of a session, it is good practice to immediately use the 'Save as' option in the File menu to re-save the song into a new folder and under a new name, onto the drive you are using for audio. Name the folder with the same name as the song you are about to record. You are then ready to start work. Subsequently, when you come to record any audio Tracks in the song, choose this same folder for the audio files. In this way, the song file and all the audio material associated with it are neatly packaged in the same folder. This makes it easier to keep track of the audio files on the hard disk. You may also wish to consider putting all your song folders into one overall folder called, for example, 'MySongs', to help keep things tidy.
- Always re-name audio Tracks before starting to record. Cubase VST uses the Track name for the name of the audio file which is written to the hard disk and, by using meaningful names, the files will be easier to recognise if you need to find them individually at a later stage. The audio file for each subsequent take on the same Track is given the same name with a new take number. For example, the audio files for a Track named 'vocals' are 'vocals.wav' for the first take, followed by 'vocals_tk 2.wav', 'vocals_tk 3.wav' etc. for subsequent takes. These files are easier to identify than if you use, for example, a default audio Track name like 'Audio 1'.
- If you need to change the name of an audio file after having recorded it, double click on the file name in the Audio pool and enter a new name into the pop-up name field.
- When you use the same audio file in more than one song, it is preferable to actually copy the file rather than work from a single original. This avoids accidents and confusion.
- Occasionally, you may be unfortunate enough to accidentally delete one or more important audio files. It is worth having a utility installed on your computer which can recover deleted files. For example, Norton Utilities includes an UnErase Wizard which works in conjunction with the Windows recycle bin to provide a convenient method of recovering recently deleted files.
- Although hard disk failure is not a common occurrence, backing up your data is essential if you wish to avoid the potentially disastrous situation of losing all your files. Popular back-up media include: SCSI drives with removable cartridges, magneto-optical drives, zip or jaz drives, tape streamers and recordable CD (CD-R). CD-R is fast becoming the most convenient and cost-effective method of backing up important material but has the disadvantage of slow writing times. Larger capacity removable solutions, like Iomega's jaz drive or one of the many tape streamers popularly available, might be a better option if you need to backup a large amount of data.

Keyboard shortcuts

Knowledge of the keyboard shortcuts can significantly increase your operational efficiency. Users finding themselves totally reliant on the mouse should perhaps review their technique. A good mix of both mouse and keyboard moves is the most efficient way of operating Cubase VST.

- If you find yourself disorientated when working in the editors, try the following: before opening an editor, press alt + ctrl + P (Mac: option + P) on the computer keyboard to position the left and right locators at the start and end points of the chosen Part. Also select cycle on the Transport bar. This helps you navigate around the chosen Part while in the editor and avoids the song position pointer disappearing from view.
- Ctrl + E (Mac: command + E) opens the default editor for the chosen Part but, in many circumstances, it might be easier to simply double click on the Part, which also opens the default editor.
- To leave an editor without keeping the edits, it is easier to use the escape key rather than search to close the window using the mouse. Similarly, to keep the edits, it is easier to use the return key. It soon becomes apparent that some tasks are faster using the mouse and others using a keyboard shortcut. Remember also that the escape and return keys have similar effects when leaving all windows and dialogues.
- While in the MIDI editors, you might be in the habit of always manipulating the notes using only the mouse. However, this can be clumsy when, for example, you are stepping through a sequence of notes in a melody. In this case, it is more efficient to use the left and right arrows of the computer keyboard. In addition, by selecting the loudspeaker icon in the Functions bar, you can monitor each note as it is selected.

Don't overdo the quantizing

A tendency to over use the quantize functions is a common pitfall among MIDI sequencer users, sometimes resulting in music which is robotic and lifeless. It is often better to try several takes to capture a good musical performance rather than to attempt the correction of a poor one. Using quantize as the magic cure for all musical evils should be avoided. If quantize really has to be used then try Iterative quantize first, as this will tighten up the feel of the performance without destroying the original inspiration. However, some styles of music actually rely on hard quantize and strictly regulated grooves, so deciding when and how to use the quantize functions must be judged separately for each musical situation.

Remember Logical edit

When you find yourself involved in MIDI editing tasks which seem laboriously repetitive and time consuming, remember Logical edit. This editor can often provide a solution which will save you a lot of time and energy.

Know your system

You may sometimes encounter operational problems owing to a lack of experience with your computer platform. You should try to be proficient in all aspects of your chosen platform and operating system as this can only help in your understanding of Cubase VST.

Knowledge of the hardware connected to Cubase VST, including the keyboards, modules, mixing console, sound card etc., is also very important. It is well worth learning all you can about the units in your system.

Know your theory

Some theoretical knowledge of audio recording and MIDI is strongly recommended. As has been stressed at various points throughout this book, the audio aspects of Cubase VST do not exist in isolation from the rest of the audio recording world. The principles of making a successful sound recording depend on more than just Cubase VST, so it pays to have some background knowledge of sound engineering and the larger recording process. Things are similar with MIDI; any background theoretical knowledge of MIDI can only help in your use of Cubase VST. Much of what you need can be found within this book but those readers who wish to know more are encouraged to consult other relevant texts and magazines, (see Recommended reading).

And finally

I hope readers have found this book useful in their quest for a better understanding of Cubase VST. Equipped with the essentials provided here you should feel confident to go on to explore other aspects of the program. And Cubase VST is a very big program! But remember that you do not need to know every aspect of it in order to be a competent user. Part of the secret to using Cubase VST is being able to identify exactly which aspects of the program you really need for your particular music making or sound recording purposes. As final words of advice, do not forget to use your most important piece of equipment, your ears!, and take plenty of breaks from being glued in front of that computer screen. Above all, enjoy it!

20

Recommended reading

Some readers may wish to enrich their knowledge of the subjects related to the use of Cubase VST. There are a wide range of books available on MIDI, sequencing, sound recording and digital audio and, depending on your needs, one or more of the following may be suitable:

Beat It! (MIDI drum programming). Joe and Pauly Ortiz (PC Publishing, 1997), 114pp.

Creative Recording 2 – Microphones and Recording Techniques. Paul White (Music Maker Books, 1995), 99pp.

Handbook of MIDI Sequencing. Dave Clackett (PC Publishing, 1996), 244pp.

Home Recording Made Easy. Paul White (Sanctuary Publishing,1997), 205pp.

Making Music with Digital Audio (Direct to disk recording on the PC). Ian Waugh (PC Publishing, 1997), 250pp

Microphones – Technology and Technique. John Borwick (Focal Press, 1990), 241pp.

MIDI – A Comprehensive Introduction. Joseph Rothstein (Oxford University Press, 1992), 226pp.

MIDI for Musicians. Craig Anderton (Amsco Publications, 1995), 120pp.

MIDI for the Technophobe. Paul White (Sanctuary Publishing, 1997), 184pp.

Modern Recording Techniques. Huber and Runstein (Focal Press, 1997), 496pp.

Music Technology Reference Book. Peter Buick and Vic Lennard (PC Publishing, 1995), 160pp.

Recording Techniques for Small Studios. David Mellor (PC Publishing, 1993), 208pp.

Recording the Guitar. John Harris (PC Publishing, 1997), 156pp.

Sound Recording Practice. ed. John Borwick (Oxford University Press, 1996), 616pp.

The Audio Workstation Handbook. Francis Rumsey (Focal Press, 1996), 286pp.

The MIDI Manual. David Miles Huber (Sams, 1991), 268pp.

Useful websites

The internet is a very good resource for the latest information about Cubase VST and related products. The following table lists some websites which may be of interest. For a continuously updated list of these URLs, and some new ones, take a look at

http://www.pc-pubs.demon.co.uk/fgcvstlinks.htm

Steinberg Cubase VST

Steinberg main website	http://www.steinberg.net
Steinberg download page	http://www.steinberg.net/service/download.html
Steinberg knowledge base	http://metalguru.steinberg.de/sc/knowledge.nsf
Steinberg UK website	http://dialspace.dial.pipex.com/steinberg-uk
Club Cubase UK	http://www.clubcubase.com
PC Cubase independent website	http://www.instanet.com/~thedusk/

Plug-ins

Arboretum	http://www.arboretum.com
Duy	http://www.duy.es
Prosoniq	http://www.prosoniq.com
Qsound	http://www.qsound.ca
Sonic Foundry	http://www.sfoundry.com
TC Works	http://www.tcworks.com
Waldorf	http://www.waldorf-gmbh.de
Waves	http://www.waves.com

Free plug-ins

Dave Brown	http://www.dbrown.force9.co.uk
Vellocet	http://www.cs.uwa.edu.au/~skot/vellocet/software.html
Vincent Burel	http://wwwperso.hol.fr/~vburel
Maxim	http://www.abel.co.uk/~maxim
Thomas Rehaag	http://www.netcologne.de/~nc-rehaagth/tr.htm

Soundcards

Creamware	http://www.creamware.com
Digital Audio Labs	http://www.digitalaudio.com
Event	http://www.event1.com
Guillemot	http://www.guillemot.com
Korg	http://www.korg.com
Lexicon	http://www.lexicon.com
Midiman	http://www.midiman.net
Terratec	http://www.terratec.co.uk
Turtle Beach	http://www.tbeach.com

General

Future Music magazine	http://www.musiciansnet.com
MIDI Farm	http://www.midifarm.com
Sound on Sound magazine	http://www.sospubs.co.uk
Textures for VST Part background	http://www.sci.fi/~contacts/vst_textures.html
The best of MIDI page	http://www.student.wau.nl/olivier/midi/
The Music Site	http://home3.swipnet.se/~w-31215/music/
Tom's hardware guide	http://www.tomshardware.com

Glossary

Active sensing A MIDI message sent by a master MIDI instrument to a slave to guard against MIDI errors such as notes which drone on endlessly because they have not received a Note Off message. If Active Sensing messages stop being sent, the slave assumes that there has been some kind of system error and immediately returns to its power up state, switching all droning notes off.

Active Sensing was designed primarily to mute MIDI modules if they lose contact with a remote keyboard. Most sequencers do not record or transmit this kind of data. It is not implemented by all manufacturers and is not an essential requirement for all MIDI devices.

ADC Analogue-to-digital converter. A device which converts analogue data into digital data. For example, to record audio onto DAT the analogue signal must first be converted into digital form before it is stored on the tape. This conversion process is carried out by the analogue-to-digital converter.

AES Audio Engineering Society. International organisation responsible for setting standards in the audio industry.

AES/EBU A digital signal interface standard agreed by the Audio Engineering Society and the European Broadcasting Union. AES/EBU digital interfaces are often found on professional audio products as they provide more reliability than the S/PDIF alternative.

Aftertouch The action of applying pressure to one or more keys of the musical keyboard after the onset of a note or chord. It is transmitted via MIDI as Aftertouch messages and is also referred to as 'Channel Aftertouch' or 'Channel Pressure' and affects all notes present on the same MIDI channel by the same amount. It can be used to produce various performance effects by changing, for example, the volume, vibrato or brightness of a sound. Aftertouch is not implemented on all instruments.

Analogue In audio, refers to an electronic signal whose waveform has a value at every point in time. There are no steps between each point and the waveform of a recorded analogue signal will closely resemble that of the original. All phenomena found in the natural world are analogue (see Digital).

ASIO Audio Stream Input Output. System for handling audio recording and playback in Cubase VST.

Balance MIDI Controller number 8. Used to adjust the balance in volume between two components of a sound.

Bank Select A combination of MIDI Controller numbers 0 and 32. A Bank Select message is usually immediately followed by a Program Change and allows switching to as many as 16384 different Banks.

BIOS Basic Input Output System. A program at the root level of a computer system for controlling its elementary operations. The BIOS configuration of a PC can usually be accessed by pressing the delete key during boot up. Editing the system's settings should not be attempted if you are not sure of what you are doing.

Bit Contraction of 'binary digit'. The smallest unit of information in a binary number, represented as a 1 or a 0.

Boot A term used to describe starting a computer. This can take the form of a 'cold start', when the computer is booted from its switched off state, and a 'warm start', when the computer is restarted in its switched on state. The latter can be initiated on a PC by pressing the reset button or the key combination 'ctrl alt delete'.

Breath Controller A breath operated device connected to a synthesizer used to change the volume or timbre of a sound. It is transmitted via MIDI as controller number 2.

Byte An 8 bit binary number (e.g. 0011 1010), creating the fundamental unit of measurement for computer media. A kilobyte (Kb) is 1,024 bytes, a megabyte (Mb) is 1,024 kilobytes and a gigabyte (Gb) is 1,024 megabytes.

Buffer Temporary storage area used to store data as it flows in, out and through a computer system.

Cache memory RAM memory area in which data resides temporarily ready to be used at high speed by the main processor. A larger cache memory usually results in a faster computer.

CD ROM Special kind of non-audio, read-only CD containing data which can be read by a computer rather than a normal audio CD player.

Control Change In MIDI based music, Control Change messages are used to control various parameters other than the notes themselves. Control Change messages are also known as MIDI Controllers or Continuous Controllers. They provide a more generalised kind of MIDI message which can be used to control a wide variety of functions. Control Change messages contain information about the Controller Number (0 - 127) and its value (0 - 127). Each Controller Number has a specific function and the more commonly used Controllers are as follows:

Controller 01 Modulation
Controller 02 Breath Controller
Controller 07 Main Volume
Controller 10 Pan
Controller 11 Expression
Controller 64 Sustain Pedal
Controllers 32 – 63 provide the LSB (Least Significant Bit) for Controllers 0 – 31. Control Change messages are also used to transmit 'Reset All Controllers' messages (Controller 121), 'Local On/Off' messages (Controller 122) and MIDI Mode changes to devices (Controllers 124 – 127).

CPU Central Processing Unit. The main processor or chip controlling the operations of a computer, usually found inside the computer case on the main circuit board.

DAC Digital-to-analogue converter. A device which converts digital data into analogue data. For example, the audio on a CD is in digital form. Before we hear the music this digital information must first be converted into analogue waveforms which can be sensed by the ear in the normal way. This conversion process is carried out by a digital-to-analogue converter.

DAT Digital Audio Tape. Digital audio recording format using 3.81mm wide tape in small cassettes. Began as a consumer format but now widely accepted in the audio industry for mastering and general purpose use. Features include 16bit recording and playback at 44.1kHz or 48kHz and various tape lengths up to 120mins.

Decibel (dB) A unit of relative measurement between audio signals on a logarithmic scale. For example, increasing the level of an input signal by 6dB results in an output which is double the amplitude (voltage) of the original. Attenuating the level by 6dB results in an output which is half the amplitude (voltage).

Digital Digital systems handle information as numerical data. A digital waveform is made up of discrete steps each of which is represented by a number. The quantity of these steps (samples) within a given time frame forms the sampling rate of a digital recording. The higher the sampling rate the better the quality. The audio on a CD is recorded at a sampling rate of 44.1kHz, i.e.: 44,100 samples per second.

DMA Direct Memory Access. Describes access to RAM without passing through the main processor.

Download The process of loading a file from another system, such as from the internet or other network, into one's own computer.

Driver Software which provides the communication protocol between an item of hardware and the operating system of the host computer. The hardware is usually set up and initialised via the driver software.

EBU European Broadcasting Union, an organisation responsible for setting audio and broadcasting standards in Europe.

EIDE Enhanced Integrated Drive Electronics. A standard for fast data transfer between the host computer and mass storage devices, such as hard drives and CD ROM drives.

Expression MIDI Controller number 11. Used to change the volume of a note while it is sustaining.

FAT File Allocation Table. A small area of a computer's hard drive containing an index which is used to keep track of all data stored on the disk.

Full duplex Describes the ability of an audio card to record and play back simultaneously. This is particularly important in multi-track hard disk audio recording when it is often necessary to monitor existing recorded tracks while recording a new one.

General MIDI (GM) An addition to the MIDI protocol, (not formally a part of the MIDI Specification), providing a standard set of rules for Patch Mapping, Drum and Percussion note mapping, multi-timbrality, polyphony and various other elements. MIDI devices supporting this standard are known as GM or GM compatible instruments. Theoretically, music recorded using one GM module should be compatible with the parameters and sounds of any other. The essential requirements for any GM instrument are as follows:

- It must provide a standard bank of 128 pre-defined sound types organised according to a standard Patch Map. For example, Programs 1–6 are specified as various kinds of piano, Program 7 is a harpsichord, 8 is a Clavinet and so on.
- It must support all 16 MIDI Channels and provide 16 part multi-timbrality if required.
- It must provide 24 note dynamically allocated polyphony or 16 note dynamically allocated polyphony with 8 voices reserved for drums and/or percussion.
- Drum and Percussion sounds must be on MIDI Channel 10 and mapped in accordance with standard GM positions.
- A GM Instrument must also provide the ability to respond to Pitch Bend, Modulation, Main Volume, Pan, Expression, Sustain, Reset All Controllers, All Notes Off, Aftertouch, Registered Parameters for Pitch Bend Sensitivity and Master Tuning and Universal System Exclusive messages for switching GM Mode On and Off.

The Roland Corporation have introduced an enhanced version of the GM standard known as GS (General Standard) and Yamaha have introduced similar enhancements known as XG (Extended General MIDI). Hence, some MIDI devices now appear with the statement GM/GS compatible or GM/XG compatible.

Headroom The difference between the current level of a recorded signal and the maximum output level of the recording medium.

Hertz (Hz) A unit for measuring frequency. It expresses the number of oscillations per second of a periodic soundwave. The greater the number of Hertz, the higher the perceived pitch of the sound.

Hexadecimal A base sixteen numbering system often used by computer programmers as an alternative to decimal or binary systems. The decimal numbers 0-9 are expressed as 0-9 in hexadecimal and decimal 10-15 are expressed as the letters A-F. Various symbols are used to denote that a number is hexadecimal including 'H' or '$' signs. The following lists some hexadecimal number examples:

```
09H (zero nine hexadecimal) = 9 (nine decimal)
0AH (zero A hexadecimal) = 10 (ten decimal)
0BH = 11
10H = 16
15H = 21
1AH = 26
FFH = 255
```

Hexadecimal numbers have much more in common with the way that computers actually work than decimal numbers and they are less cumbersome than binary numbers. Thus they have proved extremely efficient for the analysis and understanding of computer data.

HTML Hypertext mark-up language. A language used in the creation of web pages.

IDE See EIDE.

Internet Global network of computers all of which are interconnected via telephone lines. The internet is now the largest information resource in the world and provides a wide range of services and entertainment.

Interrupt A command which interrupts the central processing unit so that data from a system component can be processed.

IRQ Interrupt Request.

ISP Internet Service Provider. Internet users must subscribe to one of the ISP's which provide access to the internet.

ISA Industry Standard Architecture. An ISA bus is the standard type of PC slot for accepting cards and extension boards. An ISA bus enables data transmission at a rate of 8MHz.

Jumper A small clip for connecting pins on a circuit board to enable hardware re-configuration. Jumpers are found on motherboards and extension cards.

Main Volume See Volume.

Master Keyboard Strictly speaking, a Master Keyboard is a MIDI equipped keyboard with no sound generating circuitry used to control a MIDI network of sound generating modules and devices. However, the term is also commonly used to refer to any electronic keyboard instrument which is used as the main keyboard in a MIDI network, whether it has sound capabilities or not. The keyboard at the centre of a MIDI network is also sometimes referred to as the 'Mother Keyboard'.

MIDI Musical Instrument Digital Interface. A data communication standard, first established in 1983, for the exchange of musical information between electronic musical instruments and, subsequently, computers. This involves the serial transfer of digital information, (MIDI Messages), via 5 pin DIN connectors. Like any other language or code, these Messages are governed by a pre-defined set of rules and syntax. MIDI's set of rules is known as the MIDI Specification.

MIDI Channel MIDI devices send and receive data on 16 MIDI Channels through a single cable. Most MIDI Messages which make up this data are encoded with one of these Channel numbers. Each MIDI device can be set to be receptive to messages on one of these Channels or, in the case of a multi-timbral instrument, on several specified Channels at the same time. This allows the sending of data to specific instruments or sounds within the same MIDI network. Many instruments can also be set to receive on all MIDI Channels at the same time, (Omni On Mode).

MIDI Clock (MIDI Timing Clock) A timing related MIDI Message embedded in the MIDI data stream. MIDI Timing Clocks are sent 24 times per quarter note and along with 'Song Position Pointer', 'Start', 'Stop' and

'Continue' messages are used to synchronize MIDI based sequencers, drum machines and other MIDI devices. Unlike SMPTE/EBU Time Code, MIDI Timing Clock is tempo-dependent.

MIDI Controller A type of MIDI Message used to control various musical parameters other than the notes themselves, such as Modulation, Volume and Pan. Controllers are also referred to as 'Continuous Controllers' and 'Control Change Messages'. This kind of data is often manipulated using the wheels and other physical controls found on MIDI equipped keyboard instruments (see also Control Change).

MIDI Event Used to refer to any MIDI data once it has been recorded into a MIDI based sequencer. This is in contrast to 'MIDI Message' which refers to the same data as it is being sent down the MIDI cable.

MIDI File MIDI Files, also referred to as Standard MIDI Files, provide a way of transferring MIDI data between different software sequencers, hardware sequencers and computer platforms. There are three kinds of Standard MIDI File known as Type 0, Type 1 and Type 2. Type 0 stores the data as a single stream of events, Type 1 files contain multiple parallel tracks and Type 2 allows sets of independent sequences to be stored in a single file. Type 0 Files are the simplest and most portable but Type 1 Files tend to be the most popular and convenient format with computer based sequencers.

MIDI Interface A hardware interface which provides a link between a computer and external MIDI devices. A MIDI Interface normally provides at least one MIDI Input and one MIDI Output and more advanced units provide multiple MIDI sockets and synchronization facilities. MIDI Interfaces may plug into the serial or parallel ports of the host computer or, in the case of the PC, may be in the form of a card which is installed inside the computer. The Atari ST and Falcon computers feature a built in MIDI Interface.

MIDI In 5 pin DIN socket found on all MIDI equipped instruments used to receive MIDI data. The receiving instrument might receive data from a variety of sources including a Master Keyboard or a sequencer.

MIDI Out 5 pin DIN socket found on all MIDI equipped instruments used to send MIDI data. When played, a Master Keyboard would send out Note On and Note Off messages via its MIDI Out.

MIDI Thru 5 pin DIN socket found on most MIDI equipped instruments providing a copy of the MIDI data received at the MIDI In. In other words, the data passes *through* the unit on to a further destination, such as another Module. Some early MIDI instruments did not provide a MIDI Thru socket.

MIDI Machine Control (MMC) A more recent addition to the MIDI Specification to facilitate the control of tape transports and other devices. The code has a standard protocol which, when more devices adopt it, will facilitate the remote control of machines via MIDI.

MIDI Message The data transferred between MIDI equipped instruments contains MIDI Messages. MIDI Messages include such things as Note On, Note Off, Polyphonic Pressure, Control Change, Program Change, Aftertouch, and System Exclusive data.

For example, when a key is pressed on a MIDI keyboard this sends out a Note On message via MIDI. The first part of this message specifies its message type, known as the Status Byte, and the second part of the message contains two elements expressing the Pitch (or Note Number) and the Velocity (the strength or speed) of the event, known as the Data Bytes. When the key is released a Note Off MIDI Message is sent out via MIDI. This contains a different Status Byte followed, once again, by two Data Bytes describing the Pitch of the Note and the speed with which it was released. Any MIDI instrument set to receive this data would understand the messages and instruct the sound making part of its circuitry to play a note of the appropriate Duration, Pitch and Velocity.

MIDI Mode In addition to the rules governing the actual language of MIDI there are also four MIDI Modes which govern how a receiving device reacts to data on different MIDI Channels and whether it will perform polyphonically or monophonically. These modes are defined as follows:

Mode 1 Omni On/Poly. The receiver responds to data on all MIDI Channels and performs polyphonically.

Mode 2 Omni On/Mono. The receiver responds to data on all MIDI Channels and performs monophonically.

Mode 3 Omni Off/Poly. The receiver responds only to data sent on its chosen MIDI Channel(s) and performs polyphonically.

Mode 4 Omni Off/Mono. The receiver responds only to data sent on its chosen MIDI Channel(s) and performs monophonically.

Most electronic keyboard instruments and modules power up in Mode 3 which is appropriate for most applications. Mode 4 is an advantage for MIDI guitar users where six monophonic MIDI Channels can be selected to respond to the six strings of the guitar, each with its own separate note allocation and Pitch Bend. This mirrors more exactly the actual performance characteristics of a guitar. MIDI devices may not always include all the MIDI Modes in their specification.

MIDI Module A sound generating device with no integral keyboard. MIDI Modules are most often standard 19 inch rackmount units which can be neatly arranged in any rackmount system in the studio or at home.

MIDI Time Code (MTC) A type of time code which can be sent via MIDI, used to synchronize MIDI based sequencers and other MIDI devices. Similar to SMPTE/EBU time code, MTC is an absolute timing reference measured in hours, minutes, seconds and fractions of a second and so does not vary with tempo. MTC is often used to synchronize tape recorders to MIDI based sequencers via SMPTE-to-MTC converters.

MIDI Thru Box A device which splits the data it receives at its MIDI In to two or more MIDI Thru sockets. Thus a Master Instrument with one MIDI Out could simultaneously send its data to several slave instruments via a MIDI Thru box. This avoids daisy chaining instruments together, simplifies the MIDI network and cuts down on possible timing problems.

MMC See MIDI Machine Code

MMX Multimedia extensions. The extra multimedia instructions and 32Kb cache memory of the Pentium MMX processor.

Mode See MIDI Mode

Modulation In electronic musical instruments, 'modulation' refers to a vibrato effect which can be applied to the sound. The intensity of this modulation or vibrato is usually controlled by the modulation wheel found on the control panel. Modulation is transmitted via MIDI and is specified as MIDI Controller 1.

MROS MIDI Real Time Operating System. Operating system developed by Steinberg to manage complex MIDI software systems where timing considerations are a priority.

MTC See MIDI Time Code.

Multi-timbral The ability of a synthesizer or module to produce several different sounds at the same time controlled on different MIDI Channels. Rather like a collection of synthesizers in one box.

Note On In MIDI based music a Note On message describes the action of pressing a key on a musical keyboard. In other words it starts the sounding of a musical event. It contains information about the Pitch and the Velocity of the note. Note On messages with a velocity of zero turn the note off in exactly the same way as the Note Off message (see below).

Note Off In MIDI based music, a Note Off message describes the action of releasing a key on a musical keyboard. In other words, it terminates a musical event. It contains information about the Pitch of the note to be switched off and the Velocity with which the key was released.

Operating system An organised collection of software at the next level up from BIOS which enables the user to communicate with the computer. The operating system provides the interface between BIOS and the applications running on the computer.

Pan The panoramic position of a sound within the stereo image. Most MIDI devices with two or more audio outputs are able to place each sound in the mix according to a Pan control. The Pan information is also usually sent and received via MIDI as Controller 10 thus allowing, for example, the control of the stereo mix from an external sequencer.

Patch In electronic musical instruments a 'patch' describes the configuration of the synthesis part of the instrument which creates a specific sound. Also referred to as program, voice, sound or preset. Each patch can usually be stored in the instrument's memory. (See also Program Change).

PC Card Also known as PCMCIA. A standard allowing connection of peripheral equipment via small credit card-sized interfaces.

PCI Peripheral Component Interconnect. A PCI bus is a standard computer slot for accepting cards and extension boards and is faster than ISA. A PCI bus enables data transmission at a rate of 33MHz.

Pixel Picture element. The smallest dot on a monitor screen.

Pitch Bend The continuous variation of the pitch of a sounding note. It is similar to the action of bending a note on a guitar. It is transmitted via MIDI as Pitch Bend messages and on electronic keyboard instruments it is usually controlled by a pitch wheel to the left of the keyboard.

Plug and Play A standard developed by Microsoft and Intel to enable extension cards and peripheral hardware to be automatically recognised and installed in PC computer systems.

Program Change A type of MIDI message used to remotely change the Program Number or 'patch' in a MIDI device. It can select program numbers between 0 - 127 and is transmitted on any of the 16 MIDI Channels. Many MIDI devices do not follow a strictly logical arrangement for the location of sounds, which are often found in banks of 8, 32 or 64.

Quantize A term used in hardware and software sequencers to describe the action of automatically moving recorded notes onto the nearest fraction of a bar according to a Quantize Value. For example, using a Quantize Value of 16 (meaning 1/16 notes or semiquavers) will shift all inaccurately played notes onto the nearest 1/16 division of the bar. While this is useful for correcting inaccurate playing it can also produce undesirably robotic music. The more advanced sequencers provide several different methods of Quantizing material. These include the ability to move notes 'towards' a Quantize value according to a percentage value and moving notes according to a pre-recorded 'feel' template.

RAM Random Access Memory. Memory which is available for the temporary storage of data.

Real-Time Recording music into a sequencer in real-time simply means that the actual performance as it is played is what is recorded, much like recording onto a tape recorder (see Step-Time).

ROM Read Only Memory. Memory with fixed contents which cannot be overwritten.

Sampling rate Also referred to as sampling frequency. In the recording of digital audio the sampling rate is the number of times an analogue signal is measured per second during the process of analogue to digital conversion. For example, the audio on a CD is recorded at a sampling rate of 44.1kHz, i.e.: 44,100 samples per second.

SCSI Small Computer System Interface. A communication bus system available in several standards which allows very fast data transfer times and the connection of several devices on the same bus.

Signal-to-noise (S/N) ratio The ratio of the signal level to the noise level in a system, usually expressed in decibels (dB's). The larger the value of the S/N ratio the lower the level of the background noise.

SIMM Single Inline Memory Module. Small standard size circuit boards containing memory chips, which plug into the SIMM sockets of PC's.

SMPTE Society of Motion Picture and Television Engineers. An American organisation responsible for setting film and audio standards and recommended practices. For convenience, time code is often referred to as 'SMPTE' (pronounced 'simptee') but, in fact, this is only one type of time code (see Time Code).

Song Position Pointer A MIDI message often included when synchronizing MIDI devices using MIDI Timing Clocks. It enables the slaved instrument to synchronize to the same position in the music as the master instrument. The user may therefore fast forward and rewind to any position in the song and, going into play mode, restart all units from the same bar in perfect synchronization. Most MIDI sequencers provide the option of transmitting and receiving MIDI Clocks with Song Position Pointers, as do many drum machines.

'Song Position Pointer' is also a term used by Steinberg Cubase to refer to the vertical line in the Arrange Window and editors marking the Song position. This is also known as the Song Position Triangle or Indicator.

S/PDIF Sony Philips Digital InterFace. A digital signal interface standard often found on PC audio cards and DAT machines. S/PDIF sockets take the form of RCA phonos.

Step Time A method of entering notes into a sequencer one step at a time (also referred to as Step Input). The pitch, position and duration for each entry is pre-determined and after input is complete the music can be played back at any tempo. Step Time provides a useful method of entering notes into a sequencer when the passage to be played is either too fast or too complicated (see Real-Time).

Sustain Pedal MIDI Controller number 64 also known as the Damper Pedal. Used to produce the same effect as the sustain pedal on a piano and is either On or Off.

SVGA See VGA.

SysEx See System Exclusive.

System Exclusive A type of MIDI Message allowing non-standardised communication between MIDI devices. Used for the transfer of Manufacturer Specific System Exclusive and also Universal System Exclusive data. Manufacturer Specific System Exclusive includes a unique ID for each manufacturing company and might be used to change or control almost any parameter in the receiving device as deemed appropriate by the manufacturer. Universal System Exclusive encompasses a number of more recent additions to the MIDI Specification including MIDI Machine Control, MIDI Show Control, Sample Dump Standard, MIDI File Dump, General MIDI On, General MIDI Off and other data.

Time Code A time encoded signal recorded onto audio or video tape for time and point location and synchronization purposes. Sometimes referred to as 'SMPTE' (pronounced 'simptee') but, in fact, SMPTE is only one standard, as used in the USA The other is EBU Time Code as used in Europe. Time code is measured in the following format:

hours : minutes : seconds : frames : subframes

There are three essential types:

Longitudinal Time Code (LTC)commonly used for audio work.
Vertical Interval Time Code (VITC) popular for video editing.
MIDI Time Code (MTC) a special kind of time code transmitted via MIDI.

Time code may vary in the number of frames per second for the encoded signal. This is known as the frame rate and could be one of the following:

24 fps	traditional 35mm film rate (SMPTE Film Sync).
25 fps	European standard for audio and video (EBU).
30 fps	USA standard for audio only work (30 Non-Drop).
30 dfps	rarely used format.
29.97 fps	USA television and video non-drop frame format (29.97 Non-Drop).
29.97 dfps	USA television and video drop frame format (29.97 Drop).

When greater accuracy is required, as in audio work, the frame is divided into 80 subframes. For audio work it is normal practice to use 25 fps in Europe and 30 fps in the USA

Velocity The speed (or force) with which a key is pressed or released on an electronic keyboard instrument. In order to transmit Velocity information via MIDI the keyboard must be 'Velocity sensitive'. In other words, it must have been manufactured to detect changes in the speed with which its keys are struck. Normally, the harder a key is struck the louder it will become and the higher will be the Velocity value sent out via MIDI. However, Velocity might also be used to affect the brightness, vibrato, sustain or some other expressive element within the sound. These effects might be used individually or in any combination.

Velocity forms part of the actual MIDI note data, (the third byte of Note On and Note Off messages), and does not assume a separate MIDI data category like many other parameters. However, due to the importance of Velocity in musical expression for accent, dynamics and effects, MIDI sequencers provide easy access to this element of the data (see Note On and Note Off).

VGA Video Graphics Array A type of display for a computer monitor. VGA has a resolution of 640 x 480 pixels and can display 16 colours. SuperVGA (SVGA) can display resolutions up to 1,024 x 768 pixels and up to 16.4 million colours. SVGA is now the standard for computer monitors.

Volume The volume of sounds can be regulated via MIDI using Control Change 7. This is usually referred to as Main Volume and is implemented on most MIDI devices.

Windows 95 (Windows 98) 32 bit operating system for PC computers supplied by Microsoft.

World Wide Web A system allowing the jumping from one Internet site to another, (often referred to as 'surfing the net'). Although the World Wide Web and the Internet are, strictly speaking, different things, the two terms tend to have the same meaning in common usage.

Appendix 1

Active Sensing

FEH – Active Sensing message. This single unchanging message is normally transmitted once every 300 ms and is the master instrument's way of saying 'I am still here'.

Aftertouch (Channel Pressure)

DnH, vvH – Aftertouch message.
DnH = Aftertouch Status Byte and MIDI Channel number (n).
vvH = the amount of pressure applied (0 – 127).

Balance

BnH, 08H, vvH – Balance Controller message.
BnH = Control Change Status Byte and MIDI Channel number (n).
08H = Balance Controller number (8).
vvH = Control Value (0 – 127).

Bank Select

2 consecutive messages.
Message 1 – BnH, 00H, vvH – Bank Select Message MSB (Most Significant Bit).
Message 2 – BnH, 20H, vvH – Bank Select Message LSB (Least Significant Bit).
BnH = Control Change Status Byte and MIDI Channel number (n).
00H = indicates the first part of the Bank Select message (MSB).
20H = indicates the second part of the Bank Select message (LSB).
vvH = the Control Change value (0 – 127).

Breath Controller

BnH, 02H, vvH – Breath Controller Control Change message.
BnH = Control Change Status Byte and MIDI Channel number (n).
02H = Breath Controller number (2).
vvH = Control Value (0 – 127).

Control Change

BnH, ccH, vvH – Control Change message.
BnH = the Control Change Status Byte and MIDI Channel number (n).
ccH = the Controller number (0 – 127).
vvH = the Controller's value (0 – 127).

Expression

BnH, 0BH, vvH – Expression Control Change message.
BnH = Control Change Status Byte and MIDI Channel number (n).
0BH = Expression Controller number (11).
vvH = Control Value (0 – 127).

INFO

For those readers needing more technical details, the following outlines the actual message contents for the most popular types of MIDI data, as outlined in the Glossary. This list is by no means exhaustive, but provides most of the essentials. All messages are shown in hexadecimal notation.

INFO

In all these messages n is a value between 0 and 15. This corresponds to the 16 MIDI channels.

*The control change
message is the
generic message
structure for all the
Control Change
messages outlined
here i.e. Bank Select,
Breath Controller,
Expression,
Modulation, Pan,
Sustain Pedal and
Volume.*

Modulation

BnH, 01H, vvH – Modulation message.
BnH = Control Change Status Byte with MIDI Channel number (n).
01H = the Modulation Controller number (1).
vvH = the Control value.

Note On

9nH, kkH, vvH – Note On message.
9nH = the Note On Status Byte and MIDI Channel number (n).
kkH = the key or note number (0 – 127).
vvH = the Velocity with which the note was struck (0 – 127).

Note Off

8nH, kkH, vvH – Note Off message.
8nH = the Note Off Status Byte and MIDI Channel number (n).
kkH = the note number to be terminated (0 – 127).
vvH = the Velocity with which the note was released (0 – 127).

Pan

BnH, 0AH, vvH – Pan message.
BnH = the Control Change Status Byte and MIDI Channel Number (n).
0AH = the Pan Controller number (10).
vvH = the Control value (0 – 127).

Pitch Bend

EnH, ffH, ccH – Pitch Bend message.
EnH = the Pitch Bend Status Byte and MIDI Channel number (n).
ffH = a number between 0 – 127 for fine changes in pitch.
ccH = a number between 0 – 127 for coarse changes.

Program Change

CnH, ppH – Program Change message.
CnH = the Program Change Status Byte and MIDI Channel number (n).
ppH = the Program Number (0 – 127).

Sustain Pedal

BnH, 40H, vvH – Sustain Pedal Control Change message.
BnH = Control Change Status Byte and MIDI Channel number (n).
40H = Sustain Pedal Controller number (64).
vvH = Control Value (0 – 63 = Off, 64 – 127 = On).

System Exclusive

F0H, iiH, nnH – nnH, F7H – System Exlusive message.
F0H = System Exclusive Status Byte.
iiH = Manufacturer ID number (0 – 127).
nnH – nnH = Almost any sequence of data dependent on the function of
the message.
F7H = The end of the SysEx message, referred to as EOX (End of System
Exclusive).

Volume

BnH, 07H, vvH – Main Volume message.
BnH = the Control Change Status Byte and MIDI Channel number (n).
07H = the Controller number for Main Volume (7).
vvH = the value for the volume level (0 – 127).

Appendix 2

General MIDI

For the convenience of those using General MIDI (GM) synths and modules and in order to avoid some of the confusion which can arise on the subject, this appendix outlines the essentials of the General MIDI protocol. There are three main types of General MIDI devices:

- GM – General MIDI. The first GM standard devised by Roland.
- GS – General Standard. The same as General MIDI but with additional features devised by Roland.
- XG – Extended General MIDI. The same as General MIDI but with additional features devised by Yamaha.

The essential idea of GM/GS/XG MIDI synths and sound modules is that they all share a common language. A MIDI sequence played back using one GM module will sound much the same on any other GM module. Cubase VST provides the GM/GS/XG editor to allow the editing of the parameters of any GM/GS/XG synthesizer or module via MIDI. The controls are laid out in an easy-to-use arrangement similar to a mixing console, and give access to volume, pan, reverb, chorus and program change for each of the 16 MIDI channels. Changing the parameters on the computer screen is normally more practical and convenient than using the controls of the GM instrument itself.

The following outlines the basic practical protocol for all GM/GS/XG devices, (note that the full GM protocol encompasses many more parameters than those described here):

- A minimum of 24 voice polyphony.
- Multi-timbrality on 16 MIDI channels where each channel can play a variable number of voices from the available polyphony.
- Drum sounds are always on MIDI channel 10, and each drum sound is allocated to a specific MIDI note number.
- The sounds available comply with the program numbers and 128 presets of the standard bank of 'GM' sounds, as in the following table:

Standard bank of GM sounds

No.	Name	No.	Name	No.	Name	No.	Name
1	Piano 1	9	Celesta	17	Organ 1	25	Nylon-str. Gt.
2	Piano 2	10	Glockenspiel	18	Organ 2	26	Steel-str. Gt.
3	Piano 3	11	Music box	19	Organ 3	27	Jazz Gt.
4	Honky-tonk P.	12	Vibraphone	20	Church organ	28	Clean Gt.
5	E. Piano 1	13	Marimba	21	Reed Organ	29	Muted Gt.
6	E. Piano 2	14	Xylophone	22	Accordion Fr	30	Overdrive Gt.
7	Harpsichord	15	Tubular bell	23	Harmonica	31	Distortion Gt.
8	Clav	16	Santur	24	Bandneon	32	Gt. harmonics
33	Acoustic Bass	41	Violin	49	Strings	57	Trumpet
34	Fingered Bass	42	Viola	50	Slow Strings	58	Trombone
35	Picked Bass	43	Cello	51	Syn. Strings 1	59	Tuba
36	Fretless Bass	44	Contrabass	52	Syn. Strings 2	60	Muted Trumpet
37	Slap Bass 1	45	Tremelo Str.	53	Choir Aahs	61	French Horn
38	Slap Bass 2	46	Pizzicato Str.	54	Voice Oohs	62	Brass 1
39	Synth Bass 1	47	Harp	55	SynVox	63	Synth Brass 1
40	Synth Bass 2	48	Timpani	56	Orchestral Hit	64	Synth Brass 2
65	Soprano Sax	73	Piccolo	81	Square Wave	89	Fantasia
66	Alto Sax	74	Flute	82	Saw Wave	90	Warm Pad
67	Tenor Sax	75	Recorder	83	Syn. Calliope	91	Polysynth
68	Baritone Sax	76	Pan Flute	84	Chiffer lead	92	Space Voice
69	Oboe	77	Bottle Blow	85	Charang	93	Bowed Glass
70	English Horn	78	Shakuhachi	86	Solo Vox	94	Metal Pad
71	Bassoon	79	Whistle	87	5th Saw Wave	95	Halo Pad
72	Clarinet	80	Ocarina	88	Bass & Lead	96	Sweep Pad
97	Ice Rain	105	Sitar	113	Tinkle Bell	121	Gt. Fret Noise
98	Soundtrack	106	Banjo	114	Agogo	122	Breath Noise
99	Crystal	107	Shamisen	115	Steel Drums	123	Seashore
100	Atmosphere	108	Koto	116	Wood Block	124	Bird
101	Brightness	109	Kalimba	117	Taiko	125	Telephone 1
102	Goblin	110	Bagpipe	118	Melo Tom 1	126	Helicopter
103	Echo Drops	111	Fiddle	119	Synth Drum	127	Applause
104	Star Theme	112	Shannai	120	Reverse Cymb.	128	Gun Shot

Do you 'Read Me' yet?

• Read Me?

As a Cubase user, when you opened the box of your new **Steinberg** program you probably had only one thing in mind – let's load it, and get going! Like most users you are now probably getting along just fine and you will already know a few 'quick' ways to do things and may even have read the 'read me' files or dipped into the manual (only when you got really stuck)!

• Get the most...

If you want to work even faster and get more from your program then there is one publication we think you really should read – **Basique**, the bi-monthly magazine of **Club Cubase UK**. Basique covers all aspects of Steinberg programs plus other related news and reviews. We keep you up to date with what is happening in the world of **Steinberg** and provide articles and advice for the complete beginner right up to the power user. We also cover areas such as production – how do you set up a studio for **VST**? What's the best computer to buy? How do I optimise my computer for **Cubase VST**? Basique covers all these and many related topics which you won't find anywhere else in one magazine, from MIDI to Hard Disk recording. In every issue we have some of the music industry's leading writers working for us. Getting the most from your **Steinberg** program also means you will be more productive and creative. If you want to get ahead start reading **Basique** to get all those vital **Steinberg** hints and tips which you won't find in the manuals (honest). If you are on the Internet and have an email address you can enjoy our 'in between issue news' which we will send to you direct. You can also visit our home web pages at: http://www.clubcubase.com

• So what is CCUK?

Established in 1993, **CCUK** produces Basique magazine which covers all aspects of **Steinberg** products on all three computer platforms (Atari, Mac and PC). We also offer members special prices on many unique products through **Club Cubase Direct** which is a mail order service allowing members up to 15% discount on many products including all **Steinberg** Upgrades – you'll get them cheaper, faster and first directly from us! Offers include both software and hardware items. Many readers recoup more than the cost of membership with their first order from Club Cubase Direct!

• The cost?

Membership is only **£18.00** per year (UK Postcode) and £25.00 Sterling overseas, this includes Basique magazine and full access to Club Cubase Direct. If you would like to join right now just send your name and address together with payment, we accept Access, Visa or cheques made payable to 'Club Cubase UK' (sterling only)

• Win a VST plug-in

All new CCUK members are automatically entered in our 'win a **VST plug-in**' competition – one winner per issue – just join today to be entered!

For full details of CCUK write, phone, fax, or e-mail us:

Club Cubase UK
PO Box 6053
Nairn
IV12 4YA

Tel/Fax: 01667 451115
E-mail: m2m@dircon.co.uk

or download a PDF form from our web page:
http://www.clubcubase.com

• Club Cubase UK •

Index